Property of:
Ms Marie Kenote

More Precious

Than Silver

Books by Joni Eareckson Tada

All God's Children: Ministry with Disabled Persons
(with Gene Newman)

Barrier-Free Friendships:
Bridging the Distance Between You and Friends with Disabilities
(with Steve Jensen)

Diamonds in the Dust: 366 Sparkling Devotions

The God I Love: A Lifetime of Walking with Jesus

Heaven: Your Real Home

Heaven: Devotional Edition

How to Be a Christian in a Brave New World
(with Nigel M. de S. Cameron)

Joni: An Unforgettable Story

The Life and Death Dilemma:
Families Facing Health Care Choices

A Lifetime of Wisdom: Embracing the Way God Heals You

More Precious Than Silver:
366 Daily Devotional Readings

Pearls of Great Price:
366 Daily Devotional Readings

A Step Further:
Growing Closer to God through Hurt and Hardship
(with Steven Estes)

When God Weeps:
Why Our Sufferings Matter to the Almighty
(with Steven Estes)

More Precious Than Silver

366 Daily Devotional Readings

Joni Eareckson Tada

ZONDERVAN®

ZONDERVAN.com/
AUTHORTRACKER
follow your favorite authors

ZONDERVAN

More Precious Than Silver
Copyright © 1998 by Joni Eareckson Tada

Requests for information should be addressed to:
Zondervan, *Grand Rapids, Michigan* 49530

Library of Congress Cataloging-in-Publication Data

Tada, Joni Eareckson.
    More precious than silver : 366 daily devotional readings /
Joni Eareckson Tada.
       p. cm.
    Includes bibliographical references.
    ISBN 978-0-310-21627-8 (hardcover)
    1. Devotional calendars. I. Title.
BV4811.T35 1998
    242.2—dc21   98-28366

This edition meets the American National Standards Institute Z39.48 standard.

Published in association with the literary agency of Wolgemuth & Associates, Inc.

Interior design: Sherri Hoffman
Editorial assistance: Janet Kobobel Grant and Steve Jensen
Interior illustrations: Joni Eareckson Tada

Printed in the United States of America

13 14 • 37 36 35 34 33 32 31 30 29 28 27 26 25 24 23

To Kathy Eareckson,

Kath-Kath . . .

a little something to read

before you take that daily power walk

To Those Who Are Meeting
Joni for the First Time

These days it's not uncommon to encounter disabled people who are successfully imprinting their gifts and abilities on society. But when the disabled person has authored more than twenty-two books, many of them best-sellers, when that individual is an internationally known advocate and artist, we do a double take.

Joni Eareckson Tada, as a result of a diving accident, has lived in a wheelchair, paralyzed from the shoulders down, for over thirty years. In a quest to better understand the goodness of God in the midst of suffering, she has invested most of these years in a probing and personal study of God's Word. What has resulted from her latest studies is *More Precious Than Silver.*

Of this book she writes, "Nothing beats the rigorous yet simple discipline of spending a little formal time with God and his Word every day. And nothing kick-starts a daily quiet time better than a devotional book that reads easily and runs deep. That's why I've pulled together these devotionals. These pieces of silver include insights that, over three decades in a wheelchair, have made me rich in faith and wealthy in hope."

Joni has been presented scores of awards and honors, including two honorary doctorate degrees from Gordon College and Columbia International University. When asked about her involvements, Joni most often refers to her work at JAF Ministries, including Wheels for the World—a program through which used wheelchairs are collected, refurbished, and hand-delivered, along with Bibles, to needy disabled people in developing nations. Chuck Colson has stated, "My friend Joni Eareckson Tada is one of God's choice servants of today." Philip Yancey has added, "Through her public example, Joni has done more to straighten out warped views of suffering than all the theologians put together. Her life is a triumph of healing—a healing of the spirit, the most difficult kind." You can read more about this remarkable woman in the twentieth-anniversary edition of her autobiography, titled *Joni,* published by Zondervan.

Before You Begin

To the right of my bedroom mirror, hanging from a brass hook, is a necklace that holds a delicate little cross. It's one of my most precious pieces of jewelry. It's the only cross I own and it's made of silver.

I prefer things silver. That's unusual, for silver often takes a backseat to its richer brother, gold. We think of gold as warm, but silver, cool. Gold seems soft, but silver, hard. First-place medals are made of gold, not its second cousin, silver. Most people seem to prefer things golden. We even speak "words that are golden."

But when God speaks, it's *silver*. Psalm 12:6 says, "The words of the LORD are flawless, like silver refined in a furnace . . . purified seven times." Purity and silver go together best when it comes to describing God's Word. Why does God choose this precious metal? Perhaps it's because gold requires impurities so it can bond. But not silver. God is less interested in attractiveness and more interested in purity.

Dentists understand this—one unusual quality of silver that accentuates its purity is its ability to kill bacteria that comes in contact with it. So too the Word of God is not only pure, it has the ability, when applied by faith, to cleanse the reader of his or her sin. God is not as concerned about people finding his words "golden," all beautiful and attractive, as he is about people's lives being touched by the "silver" of his Word—becoming changed, holy, and pure.

I thought of this as I wrote *More Precious Than Silver*. It's a silver mine, and I'm grateful to a few good friends who have helped me select, polish, and present some exceptional and precious pieces. I thank Steve Jensen, who dug into his personal treasure trove and handcrafted thirty devotionals for me to use. I'm indebted to Steve Estes, whose ideas I occasionally borrowed from his chapters in the book we wrote together, *When God Weeps*. Ted Neale, our interim pastor at Church in the Canyon, also scattered silver my way in several of his sermons. Finally, I'm thankful to several key writers and thinkers whose ideas served as the springboard for my own—I have credited these contributors in parentheses at the close of certain paragraphs.

Having mined the ideas, I am grateful to dear friends who helped "set" the silver in this book, showcasing it like custom-designed jewelry. To Scott

Bolinder, John Sloan, and Bob Hudson at Zondervan. To Robert Wolgemuth at *Wolgemuth & Associates*. To Angela Hoogland, who gave me her Saturdays, and Francie Lorey and Judy Butler, who gave me their weekdays. I'm especially thankful to Janet Grant, who, in lending me her writing skills, helped to craft a large portion of my manuscript. My deepest appreciation goes to my husband, Ken, who cheers me on from the sidelines.

You hold in your hands a book that reads like silver, cool and fast. And like the shiny metal, you'll find the reading pure and deep. From the start of each day's vignette, you'll be brought into as close a contact as possible with the awesome truth of the Word of God. You'll have a chance to feel the smooth surface of each Scripture verse and discover the firm, solid reality beneath it. Have fun "wearing" a new piece of silver each day. And remember, when you come in touch with silver, refined and pure, your heart can't help but be changed.

—JONI EARECKSON TADA
SUMMER 1998

JANUARY

The Lord Out Ahead

By day the LORD went ahead of them.

—Exodus 13:21

I like the idea of a new year. It's a turning point where you say good-bye to the past and get charged up about the future.

True, I could be weighed down thinking of last year's trip-ups, those embarrassing things that still nag. I had a bad disagreement with Ken a couple of months ago; I disappointed a dear friend earlier in the summer; I spoke at an event back east and my message fell flat. No prayer behind it, no real preparation, I realized later. And there was that tough business decision that caused a lot of tension between Ken, me, and a family in our church. If I had to do it all over again, I'd change a lot.

You probably have your own list of things you wish you could change. If we thought about it long enough, we could become so heavyhearted that we wouldn't want to face the future. But thankfully, God is the God of all those past months. He was as much in control then as he is now.

What a relief! Because you'd better believe that the coming months will have the same sort of blunders, mistakes, and embarrassing *faux pas.* But wait . . .

God has gone before you! He's already there, up front, out ahead. And he will guard you with his grace and help you learn from past mistakes. For certain this year I'll be more careful in my relationship with my husband. I'll give business decisions more thought. And needless to say, I'm fully committed to being prepared and prayed up for every speaking engagement.

Before this year gets going, reflect upon last year. Page through your calendar and pray over those places, people, and decisions from which you can learn. Take inventory, then roll up your sleeves and get started. Hurray, the Lord has gone before you!

What comfort, Lord, to know that as I turn the corner into this new year, you have gone before me. You have carved out a path for me and covered it in your protection.

January 2

Repentance and the Rose Bowl

Save me from bloodguilt, O God, the God who saves me,
and my tongue will sing of your righteousness.
—Psalm 51:14

One New Year's Day while Ken and I and a friend of ours were watching a football game on television, we heard a horrible crash outside, followed by the sound of a car zooming away. As we rushed out the door, we found part of our lawn torn up by tire tracks, our mailbox smashed, and our friend's Mustang mangled.

A few minutes later we heard a gentle rap on our front door. Two boys about twelve years old were standing there. Red-faced and quivering, they were too frightened to speak. I asked, "Did one of you drive the vehicle that crashed into my friend's car?"

"Yes, ma'am," the slightly taller boy answered.

As the boys told us their story, I was grateful for guilt, that heavy weight on our consciences when we've done something wrong. The more we respond to guilt, the more sensitive we become to wrongdoing. For the two boys, confessing was important in keeping their consciences sensitive. A clear conscience, according to Bill Gothard, "is that inner freedom of spirit and assurance from knowing that you have a transparency toward everyone; and that no one is able to accuse you of wrongs that you have never made 'right.'"[1]

Turns out that while the "driver's" parents were attending a game at the Rose Bowl—the game we were watching on TV—the boy invited his friend for a joyride in his dad's Mercedes. Ultimately the insurance company paid for repairs, the boys were grounded, and we had a chance to witness to a neighbor. Best of all, the consciences of those two boys had become softened. That's how that story ended.

If guilt is crushing your conscience, how will your story end? Will you speed away? Or will you go back to confess to God? Acts 24:16 describes the Christian: "I strive always to keep my conscience clear before God and man."

Thank you, Father, that you have equipped us with a warning device in our hearts that alerts us when we need to confess a deed or word.

January 3

God's Autobiography

In the beginning was the Word, and the Word was with God, and the Word was God.

—John 1:1

Novelist Robertson Davies once wrote, "To ask an author . . . if his work is autobiographical is like asking a spider where he buys his thread."[2] No author ever weaves words from someone else's being. They are always his words, reflecting his soul.

The Bible reveals God's soul to us in a way that no other book is able to do. It is history, wisdom, and poetry. It is unparalleled as a compendium of theology, philosophy, and ethics. It is a gospel tract, distilling the essence of our relationship to the Lord, but it is also an epic, introducing us to the immensity of an eternal God.

Though the Bible contains all these things, it is at its heart an autobiography. The Bible is all about God. Through even the most twisted and unlikely narratives, some even tawdry, we see God's soul reflected to us. God is revealed as Jacob wrestles with him. God is showcased through the complaint of Job, the anguish of Jeremiah, and the courage of Hannah. God is the voice behind the people's shouting and singing over the new temple of Solomon; he is the echo behind the weeping over the rebuilt temple of Ezra. God is the silence of the four centuries before Christ, and the exultant glory in the night sky of Bethlehem.

Every word speaks something to us of his soul. It is not just from the prophets' mouths that we hear his lament over Israel. We hear it in the very telling of the captivity itself. It is not just from John's apocalyptic pen that we learn of God's coming judgment. We can see God's wrath reflected in the agony of his Son on the cross. It is not just from Jesus' mouth that we learn of God's love. We know from Jesus' daily walk with sinners like you and me.

Treasure God's Word today. In everything you read, you will come to know the soul of God, he who is the lover of your soul.

Father, write your words on my heart today, that I might be your story written to a lost and dying world.

Pointing to Jesus

Jesus answered, "I am the way and the truth and the life.
No one comes to the Father except through me."
—John 14:6

By my office telephone I keep a list of people to call. People who are in chronic conditions, often living alone and in need of encouragement. I used to post the list for "something to do" when I had a free moment between appointments or dictating. But after a few calls my reasons changed. I keep the list for my *own* encouragement. When I find myself rushing ahead, operating on automatic energy rather than the grace of God, I know it's time to stop, move to the phone, take a deep breath, and dial the number of a friend in need. Somehow, some way, when I hear that voice on the other end, when Scriptures are shared or hymns are sung over the lines, my office priorities straighten and my speed slows down.

It happened the other day when I called Bruce. He's new to his wheelchair. Lost his job. His wife just filed for divorce. Bruce's voice sounded tired from the hurt; my voice sounded tired from the hurry. We talked slowly, leaving lots of quiet spaces between our sentences. As his heart quickened, my heart, thankfully, slowed—soon our heartbeats matched each other's as we discussed, mused over, reflected on, and sang about our Lord Jesus. His hurt was eased; my hurry was quieted. All because we focused ourselves on and centered our thoughts around and sang our songs to . . . Jesus.

Often, gently pointing people to Jesus is the only thing that helps. Those who are hurting are like the crying child who looks up into his daddy's face and asks why. But the child doesn't really want answers; he wants Daddy to pick him up, reassure him, and comfort him. People in pain don't want a lot of words, they want the Word, the Word of flesh who felt the pang of death, too. He is the one, as I said to Bruce that day, who holds all the answers in his hands.

Lord Jesus, when I encounter those who hurt, enable me to point them to you, the only one who can satisfy their longings, who can comfort them and soothe their fears. In so doing, I am blessed.

January 5

A Near Miss

Show me, O LORD, my life's end and the number of my
days; let me know how fleeting is my life. You have made
my days a mere handbreadth; the span of my years is as
nothing before you. Each man's life is but a breath.
—Psalm 39:4–5

I still get goose bumps thinking about a certain Friday night back in 1966.
I had returned home early from a date to a dark and empty house, so
before I went upstairs to bed, I grabbed a snack out of the fridge, sat at my
baby grand piano and played a few favorites. Later as I was about to jump
into bed, I heard a horrible crash from downstairs. With no one yet home
and all the house still dark, I dived under the bed. I was convinced a bur-
glar was in the house.

Thirty minutes ticked silently by with not a stirring anywhere. Cau-
tiously I crept downstairs, flicking on lights as I went. When I switched
on the living room lamp, I gasped. There, covering the piano bench, were
huge, heavy elk horns. They had fallen from the high vaulted rafter above
the baby grand. I looked closer and collapsed on the steps when I saw two
of the horns piercing the thick wooden bench—the bench where I had sat
only an hour earlier.

God only knows the times your life is threatened by near misses and
almost accidents. Only heaven will reveal how the delays or detours
we call frustrating have deflected deadly tragedy. Every once in a while
God pulls back the invisible veil to show us "what could have been,"
as in my elk horn story. I was saved for a purpose! And so are you. As
Job tells us, "Man's days are determined; you have decreed the number of his months and have set limits he cannot exceed" (Job 14:5).

*Teach us to number our days aright, that we may gain a heart of wisdom.
That's Psalm 90 and it's also my prayer, O Lord.*

Epiphany

After Jesus was born in Bethlehem in Judea, during the time
of King Herod, Magi from the east came to Jerusalem and
asked, "Where is the one who has been born king of the Jews?
We saw his star in the east and have come to worship him."
—Matthew 2:1–2

Seem odd to still be talking about Christmas? It shouldn't. Today marks
the venerated twelfth day of Christmas. The holiday did not end on
December 25; it began. You'd never know it. On the twenty-sixth, people
immediately ceased singing "Joy to the World" and talking about
Immanuel, God with us. It seemed unseasonable to talk about Jesus' birth
even twenty-four hours after his birthday. Christmas cards and greetings
looked "out of place." Yet in ancient church times, people sang carols for
a full twelve days after Christmas, at which time, on Epiphany Sunday, the
celebration culminated with the appearance of the wise men from the east.

A friend of mine shows this in his living room manger scene. To his
children's delight, he has the Magi appear somewhere on the other side of
the room on the day after Christmas. With each passing day the threesome
are moved closer to the manger scene, traveling past coffee tables and along
the fireplace mantle until they reach the Christ child on Epiphany Sunday. The family continues to sing carols throughout the twelve days of
Christmas, celebrating the fact that Jesus has come and is with us.

The new year looks bright because of Immanuel, God with us. Don't
be timid about spreading a little Christmas joy, even this late in the
holiday season. "You who bring good tidings to Jerusalem, lift up
your voice with a shout, lift it up, do not be afraid; say to the towns
of Judah, 'Here is your God!'" (Isa. 40:9). In your quiet time today,
pick your favorite Christmas carol and sing it to God with a heart
full of holiday joy.

So bring Him incense, gold and myrrh,
Come, peasant, king to own Him;
The King of kings salvation brings,
Let loving hearts enthrone Him.

Lord, any season is the right season to spread the good news of "God with
us." Help me to do this today.

The Gift of the Magi

On coming to the house, they saw the child with his
mother Mary, and they bowed down and worshiped him.
Then they opened their treasures and presented him with
gifts of gold and of incense and of myrrh.

—Matthew 2:11

The number of wise men is never given in Scripture. The traditional
notion that there were three wise men stems from the number of gifts
they brought. These were not kings but Magi, or astrologers from the east.
Some say they came from the area of Persia. Why would Persian astrologers
be interested in the birth of a Jewish Messiah? How would they even know
about him? Their knowledge of the Hebrew Scriptures could be traced
back to the time of Daniel. Listen to what the Persians said about Daniel:
"There is a man in your kingdom who has the spirit of the holy gods in
him. . . . He was found to have insight and intelligence and wisdom like
that of the gods. King Nebuchadnezzar . . . appointed him chief of the
magicians, enchanters, astrologers and diviners" (Dan. 5:11). Where else
or from who else would Magi from the east learn about the Messiah except
from Daniel?

By the time the wise men arrived, Mary and Joseph were living in a
house, not a stable—possibly two years had passed since Jesus' birth, given
that Herod, in an attempt to kill Jesus, had ordered the death of "all the
boys in Bethlehem and its vicinity who were two years old and under"
(Matt. 2:16). The Magi found the holy family and presented gold, frank-
incense, and myrrh, gifts suitable for a king. After Herod's decree, Mary
and Joseph escaped with Jesus to Egypt, where during the next two years
they perhaps lived off the income from their expensive gifts.

Why give myrrh to a child? It's a sticky, gum resin from a shrubby
tree and is used as a painkiller or an embalming fluid. Little did the
Magi or Mary know that myrrh would figure into the last days of
the Messiah's life on earth: first, Jesus refused myrrh when it was
offered him on the cross to deaden his pain (Mark 15:23), and then,
after Jesus' body was taken down from the cross, Nicodemus
wrapped it in seventy-five pounds of myrrh and aloe (John 19:39).

Thank you for this lesson from your Word, Lord. Everything . . . fits!

January 8

Out of Season

> Preach the Word; be prepared in season and out of season;
> correct, rebuke and encourage—with great patience and
> careful instruction.
>
> —2 Timothy 4:2

It's easy to witness when it's easy. You wake up to a bright day brimming with possibilities, spiritual energy surging as you breeze out the door, giving your smile and a "God bless you" to everyone you encounter. You're stouthearted, you feel good, and God has never seemed so gracious. You're happy that neither headache, heartache, or backache distract you from freely offering words of witness. You are, as they say, witnessing "in season."

Then there are "out of season" days. Your shoulders sag, your heart feels dry, and you wonder if God has abandoned you for some more happy-spirited Christian. Before the day hardly begins, you write it off, promising God you'll be back in action tomorrow or at least by Sunday. You slump into retreat, hoping no one passes your car and "honks because they know Jesus." You're just not up for encouraging others in Christ.

But God is. He wants you to encourage and instruct in season and out of season, whether you're up for it or not. In fact, he may use those unseasonable moments more powerfully than the easy ones. God always honors gutsy faith, sacrificial service, and tough love. He is glorified when you push through the doldrums, shake off the fog, and shine his love. Sharing Christ out of season shows a real, lived-out human act of preference for him.

Are you out of season today, intending to take a break and some time off from encouraging others in Christ? Don't allow your emotions or the day's events to deter you from sharing the Word. The season may not seem opportune, but with Christ it always is. Encourage and instruct!

Lord, will you please be my energy today? Will you be my strength? Lend me your words, your attitude, and your desire. Help me to be your witness, no matter what the circumstances. I may be out of season, but I take you at your Word. I'm ready.

January 9

Acts of God

Is it not from the mouth of the Most High that both
calamities and good things come?

—Lamentations 3:38

As I write, a fierce winter ice storm has hit the Northeast and parts of
Canada. Televised reports show a winter wonderland, but a closer look
reveals power lines sagging under heavy ice. Tree limbs have snapped, wires
are down, and the entire city of Montreal has been plunged into darkness.
Some say parts of Canada will be without power for a week. "Mother
Nature has pulled a fast one," reporters are saying.

The Bible says otherwise. When it comes to the physical world, God's
working is so discreet, so regular, that normally we cannot tell he's involved.
In fact, the so-called laws of nature are merely people's descriptions of his
usual dealings. When an ice storm strikes, it's not irreligious for the
Weather Channel to give a scientific explanation. Yet at the same time,
today's verse indicates that God has his hands on everything from the
upper-atmospheric jet stream to the low pressure systems that are creating
havoc across Canada today.

Is it Mother Nature? An act of God? The Lord answers in Isaiah 45:7:
"I form the light and create darkness, I bring prosperity and create disaster; I, the LORD, do all these things." When the death toll rises from a dev-
astating tornado or a hurricane, people call such tragedies "acts of God."
The term is even used in insurance contracts for house damage caused by
floods or fires. If we are quick to attribute weather calamities to God, let's
be fair and also credit him for beautiful breezes and balmy days. Remember, God forms not only darkness and disaster but light and prosperity.

Weather calamities make us feel out of control. This isn't bad. Larger-
than-life insecurities force people to wonder: "My life is so fragile. I'm confused when props are kicked out from under me. Maybe God is bigger and
more awesome than I realized!"

What's the weather like outside your window today? Use the weather
report to jump-start a prayer to God about his awesome power over
nature.

*When I feel the cold—or the warmth—today, may I praise you, Lord,
for all your acts in nature.*

Humble Yourself . . . How?

In his distress he sought the favor of the LORD his God and
humbled himself greatly before the God of his fathers.
—2 Chronicles 33:12

Manasseh was one evil dude. Although he was a leader in Israel, he
threw infants on the sacrificial fire to appease pagan gods. After he
was captured by the Assyrians, bound in shackles, and led away to Babylon by a hook in his nose, he "humbled himself greatly before the God of
his fathers."

We wouldn't want Manasseh's experience, but we do want to be humble. So we uproot all the "pagan gods" in our life, such as petty resentments
and an overstuffed ego. Yet when we drive ourselves to our knees for sin's
sake or our sake or the sake of our marriages or churches, friendships or
family, we fail. If we're looking for humility, we don't look at ourselves or
how greatly we miss the mark; we gaze at God. We seek his favor. We humble ourselves *before the Lord.*

To humble yourself before the Lord is to meditate on, brood over,
muse upon, and consider the Lord and his greatness. An old Puritan, in
The Valley of Vision, wrote, "Let me never forget that the heinousness of sin
lies not so much in the nature of the sin committed, as in the greatness of
the person sinned against."[3]

By the way, Manasseh was not only forgiven but reinstated as king of
Israel. What an incredible example of the enormous extent to which God
will go to forgive. But remember that Manasseh humbled himself *greatly.*

Ponder the greatness of God today. You'll find yourself becoming
slow to speak and quick to listen, thanking busboys at restaurants,
praying more fervently, pinch-hitting for the Toddler Praise lady who
usually does diaper duty, and sacrificing an extra hour of sleep in the
morning for a more earnest quiet time.

*Keep me from growing self-sufficient today, Lord. Help me to focus not
on my pride but on you, not so much on my sin as on the greatness of you
whom I have sinned against. Please give me the spirit of humility.*

Humble Yourself before the Cross

They will look on me, the one they have pierced, and they
will mourn for him as one mourns for an only child, and
grieve bitterly for him as one grieves for a firstborn son.
—Zechariah 12:10

Yesterday we learned that if we're looking for humility, we gaze at God.
More specifically, we focus on Christ. No, even more humbling, we
drag ourselves to the cross. It is there that pride is suffocated . . . self withers . . . and humility results. Why the cross? Because the spirit of humility
is lavished not on the deserving but on the undeserving. Nowhere do we
recognize ourselves as more undeserving than in the shadow of the cross.

How do you humble yourself before the cross? Just take a look up into
the night sky. Jesus, who set suns and stars spinning in motion, who
dreamed up not just our galaxy, which is one hundred thousand light-years
across, but a billion other galaxies the Hubble telescope will never photograph; this Jesus who "determines the number of the stars" and "gives to
all of them their names" (Ps. 147:4 RSV), looking at the distinctiveness of
each star and then dreaming up a name that fits; this same Jesus who on
the cross did not suspend his commands for squirrels to hibernate or birds
to fly south; Jesus who held together by his word the very sinews and joints
in the hands that hammered spikes into his wrists; this same Jesus bore his
Father's wrath against you and your sin when he hung on the cross.

Amazing love! How can it be that God should plunge the knife in his
own chest for me and you—for us who yawn and make a mental note to
get a manicure when we lift the Communion cup to our mouth? Humility is just another word for the little-last-lost-least position we hold when
gazing at Christ.

Tackle a word study of *redemption* and *reconciliation, atonement* and
propitiation. When you meditate on exactly what occurred at the
cross, you'll be inviting the spirit of humility.

*Lord, if you could make yourself "of no reputation," as it says in your
Word, so can I. I humble myself before you, Lord Jesus.*

Little Foxes

Catch us the foxes, the little foxes that spoil the vines, for
our vines have tender grapes.
—Song of Songs 2:15 NKJV

For a time I lived with my sister Jay in a beautiful farmhouse out in the
rolling hills of Maryland. Part of the house was a log cabin whose wood
dated back to the last century. With such old timbers, we had to watch out
for termites.

The first year or two we didn't pay much attention to termites. We
spotted just a few. We considered calling an exterminator but then decided
to compromise and use a can of bug spray. We paid for it the following
year. The termites came back and brought all their second cousins.

Compromise in little things leads to a greater downfall. Today's verse
tells us to be wary of "*little* foxes." We are usually on guard against the
"foxes," the big sins in our lives, but it's the little foxes, the minor, incidental sins that we tend to trivialize. God's Word warns us that it's the little foxes, the small sins, that spoil tender grapes. Small sinful habits stifle
small good beginnings. Little sins kill good intentions—intentions that
are tender and young, like the new, little grapes on the vine that haven't had
a chance to mature. This is the fruit most susceptible to ruin.

Andrew Bonar says, "It is not the importance of the thing, but the
majesty of the Lawgiver that is to be the standard of obedience. Some
people might reckon such minute rules as trifling. But the principle is simply this—is the Lord to be obeyed in all things?"

Today you may be sweeping some so-called little sins under the carpet: hedging on the truth, claiming more deductions than you deserve
on your income tax forms, or fantasizing yourself into a real soap
opera of a daydream. Wake up. Compromise on little issues can lead
to big spiritual problems. Don't let any little foxes spoil God's vine.

*Lord Jesus, I don't want small sins to spoil whatever new things you want
to begin in my life. Help me to obey you in all things.*

January 13

Ordained Differences

The LORD thy God in the midst of thee is mighty; he will
save, he will rejoice over thee with joy; he will rest in his
love, he will joy over thee with singing.
—Zephaniah 3:17 KJV

When I spoke at a pastors' conference a couple of years ago, I wheeled
out onto the platform and got the jolt of my life. Somehow it escaped
me that I would be among so many men—eighteen hundred, to be exact.
The song leader had them stand up, and when they broke into a rousing
chorus, a jet blast of sound hit me head-on. I tried to sing along but my
voice sounded so wispy and thin. I was surrounded by a sound so pure and
powerful that it seemed to resonate in my bones and shake my wheelchair.
It was a thunderous waterfall of perfect bass and baritone, so passionate
that it made my heart break.

I enjoyed something else: I felt very female. Looking into the faces of
the happy men, I relished in them being so . . . male. Virile and vigorous,
direct and to the point, punctuating each note with importance. I
delighted in the God-blessed differences between those men and me, a
woman.

That evening reminded me that our differences are ordained so men
and women can be a better blessing to each other. In the same way melody
and harmony complement each other, the role of men and women in ministry is complementary. Thank God for men. I'm glad the Son of Man was
so *male.* A man of flesh-and-blood reality. Who knows? Maybe he sang
baritone.

It would be hard to trust God if he were only Prime Mover or First
Cause, with no respect to gender. It would be impossible to love a
Lord who was only a vague, theological concept. Our verse today
tells us that God sings! Could a genderless Source of All chip in with
a tenor harmony? I doubt it. Sing to God your favorite Scripture
chorus and ask him to hum along!

*Thank you, Lord, for the differences between men and women, harmony
and melody. And thank you that you sing!*

Loaves and Fish

Here is a boy with five small barley loaves and two small
fish, but how far will they go among so many?

—John 6:9

Remember the heartwarming story of how Jesus took the loaves, broke
them, multiplied the fish, and gave everybody lots to eat with lots left
over? Jesus even said, "Let nothing be wasted." They gathered baskets full
of bread so nothing would be thrown away.

I think about that story when I watch a Christian go through tough
times yet hang on to God's grace. Maybe you're such a person. Day-to-day
heartache is your routine, and problems seem to have a permanent place
in God's plan for you. Yet you're faithful—or should I say, you hold on to
God's faithfulness. What God is doing with you is like what he did with
the barley loaves and fish. Jesus broke the bread. And out of the brokenness, he multiplied the blessing so thousands would be nourished.

Yes, it hurts to be broken. But sometimes that's part of God's plan,
especially if he wants to use you to feed others. It's a way your faithfulness
can be multiplied. Out of your brokenness, the blessing can be bestowed
on more people than you ever dreamed possible. And here's the thing: If
you've been broken by the hand of God, you can be certain nothing will
be wasted. God will gather up and use all the hurt; not a bit of it will be
discarded or cast aside.

That little boy with the small loaves and fish must have been amazed
to watch Jesus do such marvelous things through his little lunch. Be
sure that God knows what little you have to offer. Is it a bit of obedience? God will multiply it. Is it a weak prayer? A small word of testimony? A feeble effort to encourage others in their pain? I promise
you (no, God promises you) that he will expand your offering. It will
not be wasted.

Brokenness is something you know all about, Jesus, for your body was
broken for me. Today remind me of how close you are to me in my bro-
kenness, and soothe my heart with your nearness. Multiply the blessing
to many through me.

January 15

If I Had a Dream

When the LORD brought back the captives to Zion, we were
like men who dreamed. Our mouths were filled with laughter, our tongues with songs of joy. Then it was said among
the nations, "The LORD has done great things for them."
—Psalm 126:1–2

M artin Luther King Jr. was born on this day in 1929. As leader of the
civil rights movement, he inspired hope for millions of Americans of
all colors. He was both revered and reviled, but no matter on which side
of the battle line you stood, there is no denying that Martin Luther King
Jr. had a dream. In one of the most stirring and memorable speeches made
in this century, called "I Have a Dream," he took us to the heights and
depths of human experience.

We all need to dream. Though skeptics will argue that racial equality
or sanctity of life are unattainable, I believe it is those who dream who will
one day enter the gates with joy. Only those who dream will harvest the
best in all of us. Only those who dream will set our sights on that which
lies ahead. Only those who dream will make each day's hardship bearable.

People like Moses, Abraham, Sarah, and Rahab all dreamed. They
moved on blessed impulse to see what others could not—or would not—
see. Peter, James, and John, seeing the promise of Jesus' return fulfilled one
day, dreamed aloud on the streets of Jerusalem for all humanity. They
dreamed boldly and loudly, that we might enter into the gates of Zion like
those captives returning from Babylon.

Do you dream? Does someone, somewhere, know there's a glorious
and attainable future in heaven, because you dare to dream aloud?
Dream, friend, dream. Don't let the skeptics and the sinners scoff.
Don't let that which you have seen of tomorrow die today.

*Dear Lord Jesus, I live in a troubled time. There's not a day goes by that
the world is not in turmoil. Lift me out of turmoil's grip and let me
dream the dreams of my forefathers. Give me courage to share that dream
with others.*

A Faith Test

"Do not lay a hand on the boy," he said. "Do not do anything to him. Now I know that you fear God, because you
have not withheld from me your son, your only son."
—Genesis 22:12

Abraham, with his heart and hands trembling, was prepared to offer up
his son. "Stop!" came the voice from heaven. But why would God say,
"Now I know that you fear me"? God already knew what was in Abraham's
heart; he alone knows the hearts of all men (1 Kings 8:39). If God knew
the patriarch would pass the test long before Abraham reached for the
knife, why put the old man through the ordeal? Simple: God didn't lack
information about Abraham, but Abraham may have lacked information
about himself.

This is why God tests our faith. Not that he might know what's in us
but that *we* might know. We say that we love God, that he is first in our
lives, that our marriages are centered around him, that we trust and obey
him. But we easily deceive ourselves unless that love for God is frequently
put to the test. God wants us to know the actual, lived-out reality of our
preference and inclination for him. Not merely through words (it's easy to
say words) but through gritty obedience. A faith test forces us to ask ourselves, "Do I love God? Do I prefer him?" A faith test reveals the stuff inside
our souls.

One of the dangers of the Christian life is that we too often imagine
it. We imagine we are people of prayer and disciples that obey, but are
we in fact? What we believe must be lived out in reality. You will face
many choices today, many opportunities to show God through your
obedience that you prefer him. Trials are the best way, the only way,
of putting our love for God to the test. Our faith then becomes real.

*I love you, God, and I welcome whatever test may come today so you will
see ... and I will know ... the depth of that love.*

Among the Nations

Give thanks to the LORD, call on his name; make known
among the nations what he has done.

—Psalm 105:1

Christians everywhere seem to be stepping up efforts to evangelize, looking for new ways to share the gospel with people far and wide. For myself, the Lord has put a burden on my heart for a different kind of foreign mission. I'm talking about the Armenian gentleman who runs a shoe repair shop, and three Iranians who run a nearby gas station. These people are intrigued by the smile I offer them from this wheelchair.

Despite their limited English, I try my best to share Christ with them. In fact, an Armenian friend hunted up some tracts and books I gave to the shoe repairman. The other day I stopped by the Texaco station and gave the elder Iranian serviceman a copy of the Bible in Persian. He flipped through it and jabbered something in Farsi about reading a portion of the Bible sixteen or seventeen years ago. I could tell he was glad to receive his own copy. As I drove away, I thought how wonderful it was that this man, who probably was raised a Muslim, had received the Word of God so warmly.

These are just a few people God has placed in my life, folks in my community I see all the time. I could tell you more stories—about the Japanese gardener in our neighborhood, the Chinese owners of the Lotus Inn, the Mexican guys who clean our office, and the Nicaraguan girl at the supermarket checkout stand. All these receive either Bibles in their own languages or tracts (Campus Crusade has a ton of foreign-language tracts!). Sometimes I give them a *Joni* book if I have one in their language.

God has brought the nations to your doorstep. Gas station attendants, waiters, repairmen, dry cleaners, maître d's, and waitresses. Find a way to share with these thirsty people a drink of living water. Do it today.

Ruler of all nations, how amazing that you have given humans—not angels—the privilege of being messengers of your most important news: the gospel. Give me the courage to spread that news today.

Hand-Tailored Hardships

No test or temptation that comes your way is beyond the course of what others have had to face. All you need to remember is that God will never let you down; he'll never let you be pushed past your limit; he'll always be there to help you come through it.

—1 Corinthians 10:13 THE MESSAGE

Have you ever looked at someone going through a tough time and thought, *Boy, I'm glad that's not me. I could never handle that situation.* Sure you have. I have, too. And I'll tell you someone else who thinks that: my friend Charlene. She was recently in the hospital, having temporarily lost control of her muscles. She had to be fed and had to wear an indwelling catheter. That meant no trips to the bathroom (she carried her bathroom with her) and lots of discomfort.

Charlene later told me, "Joni, I don't know how you do it. I'm glad you're the quadriplegic rather than me. I love my independence."

I couldn't believe my ears. Charlene is blind and deaf. She was saying, "Hey, I can do the deaf-blind thing. But that's it; no quadriplegic stuff for me."

Which just goes to show that God will never push you past your limit. He hand-tailors your trials. Don't think you can do the deaf-blind thing? The quadriplegic thing? Well, if you're neither deaf, blind, nor paralyzed, chances are you're right. And if by some quirk you lose your hearing or the ability to walk, God will then give you immediate grace to match your need. As Romans 11:33 says, "Oh, the depth of the riches of the wisdom and knowledge of God! How unsearchable his judgments, and his paths beyond tracing out!" God knows—and he is the only one who knows—what you can bear.

No, God probably hasn't called you to be a quadriplegic, and you probably will never be blind and deaf. But he has called you to bear up under the burden he has placed on your shoulders. He thinks you can do it. Fact is, you *can*. And if you think you can't, take heart: that's when his grace shows up best.

Father God, enable me to bear up under my burden by your grace. Help me to remember that you have handpicked my circumstances to accomplish your purposes for my life. May I humbly submit to your choice for me.

The Noble Spork

In a large house there are articles not only of gold and silver,
but also of wood and clay; some are for noble purposes and
some for ignoble. If a man cleanses himself from the latter,
he will be an instrument for noble purposes, made holy, useful to the Master and prepared to do any good work.

—2 Timothy 2:20–21

I was having lunch at a friend's home recently, a wise Christian woman with discerning eyes. Before we ate, I had to borrow one of her spoons and have her bend and twist it in a contorted angle. She then inserted the spoon in my hand-splint, and I was able to feed myself.

As we ate and casually talked, I noticed she kept glancing at the bent spoon. When lunch was over, I offered to have my husband straighten it out—to return it to its original shape. She protested. "I want to keep this spoon just the way it is. You can only use a spoon that's been bent. A straight one won't do. A twisted tool in your hand can better accomplish a task. What a great illustration of the kinds of people God enjoys using!"

She's right. God can better accomplish his unique plan when he bends us to suit his will. This makes us different from most people (just like my spoon doesn't look like the rest of the utensils in the kitchen drawer). But in the hand of God we serve an express purpose. The metal of our souls may be hard to bend, but when we allow God the privilege of shaping our lives, we discover new purpose. Isn't it great to realize you are a chosen vessel for God—perfectly suited for his use?

The dictionary says that *noble* means "grand, splendid, magnificent; having greatness of character and excellent qualities."[4] Wouldn't you like to be one of God's chosen vessels for noble use? You can be, you know. Read again 2 Timothy 2:21, paying special attention to the last part of the verse. What kind of work could be considered noble? How can you prepare yourself to be used for noble purposes?

I may be different from others, but I look perfect in your hands. Reach for me today, Lord, and use me.

January 20

A Cross Too Heavy?

If anyone would come after me, he must deny himself and
take up his cross and follow me.

—Mark 8:34

Several times a year Mike, a pilot with Mission Aviation Fellowship
(MAF), approaches a jungle airstrip in Ecuador. He circles the field and
looks down to see a young man carrying his father on his back. Close
behind, someone else is pushing an empty wheelchair.

The man being carried on his son's back is Humberto. A tree fell on
him years ago and paralyzed his legs. Now he must push himself in a wheelchair through the snaking paths of the jungle. If the trail gets too rough,
his son carries him on his back.

Humberto never complains. Somehow I don't think his son does,
either. Humberto has a mission. He's helping to translate the Old Testament into his native language so his people can read God's Word. This
means that every few months Mike flies Humberto to the village of
Makuma, forty-two miles away, where MAF has a base of operations.
There Humberto sits next to a missionary, and together they painstakingly
feed Humberto's revisions into a computer.

Some would think, *Humberto is carrying too heavy a cross. His is a noble,
divine mission—shouldn't God then lighten the load?* Humberto would say
no. As a writer put it, "The cross God sends is a cross that He understood
with His divine mind, tested with His wise justice, and weighed with His
own hands to see that it be not one inch too large and not one ounce too
heavy for the person to whom He has given it."

Second Thessalonians 1:5 was written for people like Humberto: "All
this is evidence that God's judgment is right, and as a result you will be
counted worthy of the kingdom of God, for which you are suffering."

What about your cross? In what ways has it contributed to those
around you? How has God used it to advance his kingdom through
you?

*God, as I make my way through today, bring to my mind the weighty
cross you bore for me. It will make mine lighter.*

On My Feet Walking

We ourselves, who have the firstfruits of the Spirit, groan inwardly as we wait eagerly for our adoption as sons, the redemption of our bodies. For in this hope we were saved.
—Romans 8:23–24

Recently, when Ken and I were back in Maryland, my family showed 8 mm home movies. There, larger-than-life on the living room wall, I saw me at the age of sixteen. I had the same basic hairstyle and hair color, but my head was attached to a walking body—my body! I watched my hands hold the reins of my horse and pat his neck. I watched how I put one foot in front of the other. It gave me goose bumps.

Later on Ken asked me how I felt as I watched myself walk. "There was a time I would have sighed and said, 'Aww, that's the way it used to be. I wish I could go back to that,'" I said. "But now, thirty years later and having spent almost as many years sinking my heart and head in the Word of God, I can say, 'Oh, wow, this is the way it soon will be. I can look forward to having a body that works. And I'll do so much more than walk!'"

I am closer to this side of gaining my heavenly body than to the other side of losing my earthly body. Philippians 3:12 says, "I press on to take hold of that for which Christ Jesus took hold of me." The past is the past. The future is *much* more interesting to think about. Watching home movies doesn't make me sad; it makes me happy to think of all I will gain back—and more!

What are you dwelling on today? The loss of something or someone in your past? Let your groanings be not for what once was but for what will soon be! Colossians 3:2 says, "Set your minds on things above, not on earthly things." Count the years. You just might be closer to the future than you think.

Lord, help me to set my heart and mind on things above!

Like Father, Like Son

> The Son is the radiance of God's glory and the exact representation of his being, sustaining all things by his powerful word.
>
> —Hebrews 1:3

God sits above the space-time continuum, scattering galaxies and exploding supernovas. He sets stars and suns spinning in motion, ladles out rivers, and puckers up mountain ranges. He needs no one and does nothing to seek anyone's favor. He is lofty, magnanimously absorbed in matters of the universe. He is happy up there.

But we're down here drowning in misery. How do we know he even thinks about us? We know he does, because we know his Son. The Son "is the image of the invisible God" (Col. 1:15). What did God look like when he walked in our sandals? He was likable. People enjoyed the kid who worked with his dad at the carpenter's shop in Nazareth (Luke 4:22 says, "All spoke well of him"). After God "grew up," he had the undying affection of blind beggars, spine-twisted women, and people who ran out of wine at weddings. It's the everyday people who took to him—fishermen, spinsters, tax rakers, widows, guys out on parole, half-breeds, bakers, and bag ladies. (Estes)

Does the Father care? Is he so invisible, omnipresent, and omniscient that he cannot or will not consider you in your pain? Is there too much "lightning and thunder on Mount Sinai" in the Father? Listen to the words of Jesus where it concerns the Father: "I tell you the truth, the Son can do nothing by himself; *he can do only what he sees his Father doing*, because whatever the Father does the Son also does" (John 5:19, emphasis added).

The Father, for all his grandeur and loftiness, loves the beggars and the bag ladies just as much as does the Son. "The LORD is compassionate and gracious, slow to anger, abounding in love" (Ps. 103:8). His love that covers the universe . . . covers you.

God, you are tender beyond description. Thank you for showing us who you are through the Lord Jesus.

Propitiation

All have sinned and fall short of the glory of God, being justified freely by His grace through the redemption that is in Christ Jesus, whom God set forth as a propitiation by His blood.

—Romans 3:23–25 NKJV

The word we are focusing on today is *propitiation*. It's a word rarely found in newer translations of the Bible. Unfortunately, it's out of fashion, even in Christian circles. Propitiation carries the idea of appeasement or satisfaction—in this case Christ's violent death satisfied the offended holiness and wrath of God against those for whom Christ died. Blood spilled to quench the wrath of an angry God? It almost makes the cross sound like a pagan sacrificial rite. Little wonder many Christians are uncomfortable with the idea of sinners in the hands of an angry God.

But wait! In pagan religions it is the worshiper, not the god, who is responsible to appease the wrath of the offended deity. But in reality man is incapable of satisfying God's justice apart from Christ, except by spending eternity in hell. *In Christianity it is God, not the worshiper, who took the responsibility of satisfying his own wrath.*

Herein lies the amazing love of God—the Father's wrath was appeased through the willing sacrifice offered by his own Son. "It was the LORD's will to crush him and cause him to suffer. . . . After the suffering of his soul, he will see the light of life and be satisfied; by his knowledge my righteous servant will justify many, and he will bear their iniquities" (Isa. 53:10–11).

This is what makes the Good News so *great*. "God did not appoint us to suffer wrath but to receive salvation through our Lord Jesus Christ" (1 Thess. 5:9). God has no more anger left for us, only mercy, pardon, forgiveness, compassion, and grace upon grace.

Lord Jesus, thank you for being the propitiation for my sins. I don't deserve that; I deserve God's wrath, but you've given me heaven. Thanks be to God for his indescribable gift!

January 24

Loved Ones in Glory

> The time came when the beggar died and the angels carried him to Abraham's side. The rich man also died and was buried. In hell, where he was in torment, he looked up and saw Abraham far away, with Lazarus by his side. . . . "I beg you, father, send Lazarus to my father's house, for I have five brothers. Let him warn them, so that they will not also come to this place of torment."
>
> —Luke 16:22–23, 27–28

Jesus relays here not a parable but an amazing real-life occurrence. The rich man was very conscious of his hellish surroundings, as well as the condition of his brothers who were still on earth, and he wanted desperately to warn his family. The rich man saw and recognized his family, remembered them, was concerned for them, and pleaded on their behalf. Here's the lesson: *if lost souls can feel and care, how much more can those who have died in the faith!*

Our Christian loved ones who have graduated into glory presently reside with the great I AM, the Lord of love. How deeply they must feel, pray, and see. How fervent and ongoing must be their love; after all, "love never fails" (1 Cor. 13:8). Love does not die; it cannot die, because it cannot fail. Love is a part of a departed saint's being, not his body but his person. Our loved ones may very well love us presently with a purer, holier, and more intense love than they ever did on earth.

Can our departed loved ones observe our mistakes and blunders? Even if they can, they have the benefit of an end-time view. They see the bigger, better picture. When we die, we are not in some soul-sleep of a stupor, not in purgatory, and we're certainly not unconscious; we are "away from the body and at home with the Lord" (2 Cor. 5:8). The departed are full of the joy of having come home!

How wonderful, Lord, to think that I am one with my brothers and sisters in Christ who are now with you.

January 25

Never Alone

Therefore, since we are surrounded by such a great cloud of
witnesses, let us throw off everything that hinders and the
sin that so easily entangles, and let us run with perseverance the race marked out for us.

—Hebrews 12:1

We behave differently when we know people are watching. We bite our
tongues, hold our tempers, help meet a need, say the encouraging
word, and even pray more circumspectly. This is why today's verse is a great
follow-up to yesterday's lesson—if the departed saints are able to observe
our actions, our talk quickly becomes our walk.

I know the Lord Jesus is always watching (and that fact alone is
enough to keep me on the straight and narrow), but a different slant is
added when I consider that my earthly father, who is now in heaven, may
also be watching. It's something I remember when I'm alone. When I'm
tempted to blurt out malicious remarks or do something over which I'd
be embarrassed if I were found out, I stop. I'm surrounded by a great cloud
of witnesses. A host of departed Old and New Testament saints, as well as
Christian friends and family, are watching (and cheering me toward obedience). They are my witnesses, and this fact inoculates me against the
temptation of foolish, private sins.

When you're driving by yourself, how do you respond when someone cuts you off? What do you do when you're in a hotel room with
an array of cable channels at your fingertips? Perhaps no fact better
deters us from sins done in secret than Hebrews 12:1. "Let us put
aside the deeds of darkness and put on the armor of light. Let us
behave decently, as in the daytime" (Rom. 13:12–13).

*When I honor you in public today, Lord, help me to also remember to
honor you in private. More than a great cloud of witnesses, I have you
one day to answer to!*

Be Late for Something

While Jesus was still speaking, some men came from the
house of Jairus, the synagogue ruler. "Your daughter is
dead," they said. "Why bother the teacher any more?"
Ignoring what they said, Jesus told the synagogue ruler,
"Don't be afraid; just believe."
—Mark 5:35–36

The Procrastination Club of America has proclaimed a certain day each
year as "Be Late for Something" Day. If you're like me, you don't have
to join; you're already a charter member.

Even though I try hard to be on time, sometimes I'm just late. But the
most interesting things can happen when you're late. Sometimes actual
miracles. Have you ever noticed how many wonderful things took place
while Jesus was on the way to somewhere? He was walking down the streets
near Jericho, and a blind man grabbed his attention and distracted him. He
was on the way to see Lazarus (who had just breathed his last), when he got
delayed—not just for a couple of hours but for a couple of days. Jairus
asked Jesus to please come heal his sick daughter, but when the Lord started
out, he was interrupted by a woman with a hemorrhage.

Each delay brought good things: a blind man was healed; a woman
with a hemorrhage was cured; Jairus's daughter and Lazarus were raised
from the dead. Sometimes God's best plans are hidden in that inconve-
nient phone call that interferes with your routine, or in a conversation
someone engages you in that makes you late for an appointment. Who
knows—it could even be a miracle.

Try to stay on schedule today, but if something happens and you end
up being late, just remember the Lord. Jesus took delays in stride and
used them for everyone's benefit. Amazing things can happen when
you're late.

*Time is in your hands, Lord. Help me to remember that when the line
in the grocery store is long, the phone won't stop ringing, or a friend indicates she needs to talk. Remind me to relax so I can be part of anything
amazing you might want to do through me or for me.*

January 27

Unreasonable Requests

> When he had finished speaking, he said to Simon, "Put out into deep water, and let down the nets for a catch." Simon answered, "Master, we've worked hard all night and haven't caught anything. But because you say so, I will let down the nets." When they had done so, they caught such a large number of fish that their nets began to break.
>
> —Luke 5:4–6

Think of the most unpleasant routine task you have to face. Attending one more meeting? Washing dishes? Whatever it is, it's probably made more unpleasant by the thought that you have to do it every day. Now think of your most humiliating moment. An important check bouncing? A wet sneeze and no Kleenex? Finally, think of the most unreasonable request ever made of you. Your boss asking you to work overtime on your anniversary? Now pull all these moments together—the unpleasant routine done in humiliation fueled by the resentment of an unreasonable demand. You'd want to throw in the towel, right?

It happened to the apostle Peter. Every morning, after fishing all night, Peter and his partners faced the boring job of cleaning their nets of weeds and disgusting, unkosher shellfish. On this particular morning the net profit was zero. Then a landlubber carpenter tries to tell Peter a thing or two about fishing. Peter wants to balk but sighs and says, "Because you say so, I'll do it." No sooner does the net burst with fish than Peter forgets the unreasonableness of the demand.

The Lord can ask you to do something at the worst times—days when routines slump your shoulders and you're tired or resentful. God seems to be presuming far too much upon you. Today stand in Peter's shoes. Shelve the humiliation and resentment and reply, "Because *you* say so, Lord, I'll do it." You'll discover that the Lord's request was more, much more, than reasonable . . . and your nets will burst.

I don't want to balk at your demands on my time and attention, Lord. Just tell me what you want, and I'll do it.

January 28

When Gifts Aren't Good

> They all alike began to make excuses.... "I have just
> bought a field, and I must go and see it." ... "I have just
> bought five yoke of oxen, and I'm on my way to try them
> out." ... "I just got married, so I can't come." The servant
> came back and reported this to his master. Then the owner
> of the house became angry.
>
> —Luke 14:18–21

Anything can stand in the way of true intimacy with the Lord Jesus. Even oxen and fields. Sometimes even a special person.

Dr. John Piper says, "It is not the banquet of the wicked that dulls our appetite for heaven, but endless nibbling at the table of the world. It's not the X-rated video, but the prime-time dribble of triviality we drink in every night. The greatest adversary of love to God is not his enemies but his gifts. And the most deadly appetites are not for the poison of evil, but for the simple pleasures of earth. For when these replace an appetite for God himself, the idolatry is scarcely recognizable, and almost incurable."[5]

Jesus said that a desire is awakened in some people's hearts, but then "as they go on their way, they are choked with worries and riches and *pleasures of this life*" (Luke 8:14 NASB, emphasis added). In another place he said, "The *desires for other things* come in and choke the word" (Mark 4:19, emphasis added). The desires for other things may not be evil in themselves. Only when they dull our appetite for God.

Gardening and reading, decorating and shopping, cooking and vacationing, investing and TV watching and Internet surfing, exercising and Saturday afternoon at the ball game. Heartily enjoy all these things as gifts from God's hand—but don't allow them to become deadly substitutes for God.

Jesus, your gifts are wonderful. Help me to keep your gifts in perspective—I don't want them to have a deadening effect on my love for you. I want to preserve my wholehearted devotion to you, the Gift-giver.

January 29

Door Openers

Woe to you, teachers of the law and Pharisees, you hypocrites! You shut the kingdom of heaven in men's faces. You
yourselves do not enter, nor will you let those enter who
are trying to.

—Matthew 23:13

One of the nicest courtesies someone can afford me is to hold open a
door. When I approach a door, let's say at a mall, I adjust my speed to
reach it at the same time I see another person approaching. I ask, "Pardon
me, mind holding that door open? Thanks." Frankly, I think the person
who helps me feels good to have lent a little assistance.

I have yet to encounter a person who has said, "Forget it." Wouldn't
it be ridiculous if someone said, "Look, I'm not very good at opening
doors. Let me find someone else."

In the same way, you and I are door openers. Each opportunity we
have to share the gospel with an unbeliever is a chance to hold open the
door to the kingdom of heaven. But some decline to open doors. Some
think they're not very good at it. They feel that a more experienced, more
gifted person ought to do the door opening. Others, through the kind of
self-righteousness described in today's verse, slam the door in another's face.
They make the gospel sound like a twisted labyrinth or a series of difficult
hoops one must jump through. They insist that unbelievers must clean up
their act and "be like me" before entering. Jesus talks about them in
Matthew 23:13.

Jesus likens witnessing to something that ought to be as natural as
opening a door for another. You can be a kingdom door opener. You
don't have to be an expert, just available, sensitive, and courteous.

*As I face many doors today, help me, Lord, to remember that you've asked
me to usher people into your kingdom. Enable me to be gracious, courteous, and thoughtful as I offer to do so.*

January 30

Giving Grace

Let no unwholesome word proceed from your mouth, but
only such a word as is good for edification according to the
need of the moment, that it may give grace to those who
hear.

—Ephesians 4:29 NASB

Before this day is done, an occasion will arise in your life that today's
verse calls "the need of the moment." It will happen this way: God has
someone in mind he wants to touch today. He has grace available for this
person. At the same time, God is looking for another person to serve as
his conduit. What does he do next? He crosses your paths. He puts the
two of you together in a grocery checkout line, on a golf course, at choir
rehearsal, in chemistry class, in the parking lot, or at the ATM booth.

What happens after that is up to you. You have before you a need of
the moment. You also have God, who desires to give divine help. You can
choose to sidestep the moment and thus miss the opportunity, or you can
give "such a word as is good for edification . . . that it may give grace to
those who hear."

Every day you and I have a chance—many chances—to nudge people
closer to the Lord. To be one more stepping-stone in the many it will take
to bring that person to Christ. You have a chance to extend the magnific-
cent grace of God through what you say and do. You are a pipeline, an
aqueduct through which he keeps meeting needs of the moment in the
lives of others.

We can be in partnership with the Lord to reach those he has special
designs on. Ephesians 4:29 says so. Your encouragement becomes grace
that is strengthening, enabling, and empowering for others. This is the
ministry God will call you to today.

Don't miss it. Sometime before you lay your head on the pillow,
someone will be positioned to directly benefit from your words.
When the opportunity arises, don't forget to speak that word of
grace.

*Put me on alert, Lord. Thank you for using me as a conduit of your love
and care to someone else.*

God's Timing

Do not interfere with the work on this temple of God. . . .
The expenses of these men are to be fully paid out of the
royal treasury.

—Ezra 6:7–8

God can turn things around in amazing ways. Take the time the Israelites
had been exiled for seventy-some years. Then, out of nowhere, the
Lord stirred up Cyrus, the king of Persia, to send this scruffy bunch of
exiles back to Jerusalem to rebuild their temple. Who would have dreamed
it would happen that way? But the best was yet to come.

Rebuilding the temple wasn't easy. The Jewish refugees had enemies . . .
threats were made . . . there was vandalism . . . the people became discouraged. Soon work on the temple ground to a halt.

Imagine how frustrating that was. God had seemingly opened the
door for the Jews to rebuild the temple, yet everything was against them.
The Israelites encountered nothing but opposition. Why would the Lord
prevent that which he wanted?

Then came the turnaround. God sent two prophets, Haggai and
Zechariah, to inspire the people to begin building again. Of course, the
enemies were still hanging around. Those enemies, in an attempt to demoralize the people, wrote a letter to Darius, the new king of Persia, asking
him to stop once and for all the building of the temple. But the letter backfired. Darius found the original decree from Cyrus, and the result was stunning: Darius wrote back that the enemies were to leave the work on God's
house alone, and what's more, they were to pay the full cost of rebuilding
out of their tax money.

Now you see why God had planned the setbacks. He did so to insure
that the temple would be not only built but paid for!

Are you in the middle of some setback? Maybe God has opened a
door only to slam it shut. Remember these words from an old hymn:
"Judge not the Lord by what you sense, but trust Him for His
grace. . . . Behind His frowning providence, He hides a smiling face."

*Help me to believe, God, that behind your seeming frown is your smile
of blessing.*

FEBRUARY

February 1

The Gospel's Scandal

> They received the message with great eagerness and examined the Scriptures every day.
>
> —Acts 17:11

Our country is in the midst of a White House scandal as I write today. Newspapers are devoting numerous pages to the story, and television manages to create hour-long documentaries within less than a day. Conversations around the dinner table abound, with people acting like professional reporters and commentators.

One group of friends engaged in such talk for quite a while, recounting precise details of what had been reported. Then one person noted, "You know, folks, none of us here could explain the war in Bosnia. But we sure seem to have learned a lot of the facts and nuances of this scandal. Says something about us, doesn't it?"

Yes, it does. Oh, how quickly we engage in an in-depth study of that which tickles the flesh. We are fascinated by evil and by evil reports. Whether it's White House scandals or Nazi atrocities, we are drawn to these messages like moths to a candle. How unlike our interest in, and conversations about, the message of God. The people who enthusiastically argue or share about what they've learned in Scripture that day are a minority.

A scandal is news that causes a stumbling block and violates a community's sense of morality. The Bereans poured over Paul's message with "scandalous intensity" because what he purported was indeed scandalous. If the gospel was true, after all, it would be a stumbling block to the Jews and an offense to the world's self-righteous morality.

God was pleased with the Bereans. Their character is said to have been noble because of their eagerness about the message. We too can be noteworthy in our attitude toward the gospel, by frequently and enthusiastically discussing what happened in God's kingdom today and what he promises for tomorrow.

Capture my mind, dear Lord, to seek with scandalous intensity your word for today.

February 2

Fan the Flame

For this reason I remind you to fan into flame the gift of
God, which is in you through the laying on of my hands.
For God did not give us a spirit of timidity, but a spirit of
power, of love and of self-discipline.

—2 Timothy 1:6–7

Nothing dampens the fires of enthusiasm more than discouragement.
When you're discouraged, the glow of excitement for the Lord dims,
like embers of a dying fire. That's the time to "fan into flame the gift of
God, which is in you."

For years Mrs. Hanover prayed for her husband's salvation. Then one
day he was killed in an automobile accident. She lost her husband—not
only to this earth but for all eternity. Discouraged, she stopped living for
the Lord.

Five years later she met Roger Sims, who told her an amazing story.
Roger said he had been hitchhiking when Mr. Hanover picked him up.
During the course of their ride, Roger witnessed to Mr. Hanover. Well,
Mr. Hanover was so convicted that he pulled his car over on the side of the
road and prayed. Roger explained that eventually Mr. Hanover dropped
him off. Mrs. Hanover was wide-eyed. It was later on that very day that the
fateful accident happened.

While Mrs. Hanover felt immense surprise and joy, she also cried tears
of regret for having given up in discouragement. From that point on she
fanned the dying embers of her faith until her confidence in God was
restored.

We Christians often give over to discouragement with hardly a fight.
We let doubts gain a toehold, and before you know it they have a foothold,
then a handhold. Then we chuck it all.

Each of us faces disheartening circumstances. But no matter what
happens, keep trusting, keep obeying. Discouragement is like a dark
tunnel. The only thing that will brighten your path is to fan the
flames of your faith until it's a fire. Obedience then will light your
way out the other side.

*Our Father, give me perseverance in the face of disappointment. Enable
me to keep on keeping on.*

Jesus the Promise Keeper

You know with all your heart and soul that not one of all
the good promises the LORD your God gave you has failed.
Every promise has been fulfilled; not one has failed.

—Joshua 23:14

He stood out in a crowd—a tall, handsome, black man from Jamaica
with a big smile. I saw him shaking people's hands and heard each person tell him how encouraging his testimony was. As the crowd thinned, I
wheeled up to him, leaned forward, and lifted my arm, a hint to let him
know I wanted to shake hands. He smiled and leaned forward to extend
his hand. Then a surprising thing happened: I realized he had no hands.
This joyful Christian wore black fiberglass hands. We commented that
even though we couldn't feel it, our "handshake" sure looked good!

He smiled broadly and said, "Sister, aren't you glad we have Jesus? We
have his promises!" Jesus and his promises. They are virtually one and the
same.

This disabled man from a poor country has staked his life on God's
promises. His promise to lead. To sustain. To protect and provide. To meet
every need. How can I be so sure this Jamaican thrives on God's promises?
Because he loves Jesus, and as 2 Corinthians 1:20 says, "no matter how
many promises God has made, they are 'Yes' in Christ." To believe in
Christ is to believe in God's promises.

What promises anchor your faith? Can you say that not one of them
has failed? You can if your anchor is Jesus. He and his promises have
been there all along—consistent, faithful, tested, and true. If you ever
bump into a tall, black Jamaican guy with no hands, just ask him.

*Father, help me to sink my anchor deep in your promises. As life's waves
broadside my boat, enable me to remember that every promise has its
beginning and ending in Jesus.*

February 4

God's Icy Breath

The breath of God produces ice, and the broad waters become frozen.... He brings the clouds to punish men, or to water his earth and show his love.

—Job 37:10, 13

Midwest winters between mid-January and early March are notorious for their lack of romance. God's cold breath is felt daily. The deepest lakes thicken their icy crust, and the wind's biting fury finds the tiniest crack in your down-filled armor, blowing snow into every nook and cranny of your coat. It's no wonder millions of birds—and people—move to Florida and other more habitable places! For those left behind, it can sometimes feel like getting God's cold shoulder, a sort of punishment for living.

As creatures of comfort, we easily interpret the harshness of such winters, or any kind of circumstance, as God's punishment. And pleasant skies—or pleasant living—are seen as God's favor. Elihu, Job's friend, rightly observed that God's breath and hands, as well as his purposes, are varied. He does not order the events of the universe to fulfill the desires or deservedness of a single soul without considering a world of souls. He will care for his planet as he sees fit. What seems like hardship for one is blessing for another—the same snow that extends the morning commute by an hour keeps the earth insulated and moist for next year's planting.

Have no doubt that your circumstances are ordered by God. But whether they become for you a celebration or crisis depends upon your humble relationship with him. After all, every hearty Midwesterner knows that harsh winters come with the territory. It's at the moments when we accept, endure, and even embrace the seeming frigidness of God's breath that we see his larger purposes, his broader love. He has not turned his back on creation at all. He's simply loving it as only a creator could.

It's yours, Lord—the earth and all that it contains. Remind me of my place in it. Not at the center of it all but simply as a part of your loving creation.

The Blessed God

... the glorious gospel of the blessed God ...
—1 Timothy 1:11

... God, the blessed and only Ruler, the King of kings and
Lord of lords, who alone is immortal and who lives in
unapproachable light ...
—1 Timothy 6:15–16

To be blessed is to be happy. Actually, scholars use the word *blissful* for
blessed. Exultant and joyous, radiant and rapturous. God is not a
threatened, pacing deity starving for attention. He is not easily angered,
touchy, or out of sorts on bad days. He is not biting his nails or blowing
his stack when the world goes awry. Rather he is the exultant and raptur-
ously happy God.

This is why the Good News sounds so great. If we're in trouble, God
had better not be. If we're miserable, it would do us no good to go to Someone who's miserable. People in deep distress need to reach out and find a
strong, secure, and happy anchor. God is just that: a joyful foundation, a
blissful rock, a happy fortress. When we fall and stumble into sin, or when
we willfully transgress in stubborn disobedience, it does not throw God's
nose out of joint. We never need to worry about whether he got up on the
wrong side of the bed only to face us with an angry growl. Nothing we do
can disturb the blessedness of God—we will always find him full of compassion and tender mercies. (Estes)

Jesus had in mind joy and happiness when he said, "Blessed are the
poor ... the meek ... the peacemakers" (Matt. 5:3, 5, 9). He meant
that such people are divinely favored; they are smiled upon; they are
truly the delightfully contented ones. We are most like God when
we are full of joy—godly joy that overflows from meekness, humility, and spiritual poverty—that is, a deep awareness of our desperate
need of him.

*May I feel the overflow of your joy today, Lord. May I see myself as
blessed, happy, and delightfully contented in you.*

Different Yet the Same

There is no fear in love. But perfect love drives out fear,
because fear has to do with punishment. The one who fears
is not made perfect in love.

—1 John 4:18

Sometimes you do read good things in the newspaper, like this story that was in the newspaper recently. As I recall the details, the writer began,

> It was one of those rainy days that threatens to go on forever. The kids whined; the house closed in on us. So we escaped to the video store. While my husband stood in line with the movie that promised to lift us out of the doldrums, my children and I waited near the front of the store.
>
> Our three-year-old son, Joe, commented on everyone. Why was that man smoking? Why did that other boy have an umbrella—when he did not? Why did other people get to check out more than one video? What was that little girl's name?
>
> Suddenly Joe saw a person who left him speechless. A boy, a few years older than he, was being pushed into the store in a wheelchair. Joe took in every detail of the child—the boy's braced legs, slumped posture, tilted head, crooked smile. As the boy got closer, I held my breath, hoping that Joe would stay quiet.
>
> Just as the boy got within hearing distance, Joe looked at him and then glanced at me, opened his mouth, and smiled. "Mommy," he said, "that boy has an Orioles baseball cap just like mine!"

Somewhere along the line, little Joe had learned to look for the things he had in common with people. When we look at people through Jesus' eyes, the fear of being different disappears. The Bible says that perfect love casts out fear.

No matter what race you are, what age, what your abilities or disabilities, whether you are homeless or sitting secure in suburbia, good attitudes begin when you realize you have more in common with people than you thought.

Lord Jesus, enable me to put on a compassionate heart that concentrates on matching ball caps rather than obvious differences.

February 7

The Nation's Conscience

Rather, we have renounced secret and shameful ways; we do
not use deception, nor do we distort the word of God. On
the contrary, by setting forth the truth plainly we commend
ourselves to every man's conscience in the sight of God.
—2 Corinthians 4:2

Conscience operates by applying God's Word to situations. It's true for
Christians and nonbelievers alike. This is because God has written his
moral law in the hearts of all people, and when society ignores either the
written or the unwritten Word of God, its collective conscience becomes
dead or indifferent. In short, good ethics—whether medical, legal, business, or personal—cannot be achieved except through the Word of God.
A moral understanding of right and wrong is a reflection of the working
of the Spirit.

When the Spirit begins working on the conscience of a nation, that
nation begins to call things by their biblical names. Society learns that sex
outside of marriage is adultery, not recreation. Abortion is killing, not the
extraction of fetal tissue. Lying is sin, not fudging the truth. People are
very much like King David, who, even though he was a believer, could not
discern adultery from simple self-gratification for want of a sensitive conscience. For him, the light only dawned after Nathan the prophet plainly
set before him the truth.

If you believe it is time for our country to wake up to the facts about
materialism or racism, it's time to "set forth the truth plainly," as
today's verse suggests. You, like Nathan, are a prophet. You are the
point person for the Spirit's influence. The only hope for our country's dulled conscience is *you*, through your prayers and Christlike
living. This is what the Bible means when it says, "If my people, who
are called by my name, will humble themselves and pray and seek
my face . . . *then* will I . . . heal their land" (2 Chron. 7:14, emphasis
added). Let's pray for our country—then let's live for it, too.

*Quicken the minds and enlighten the hearts of the people in my com-
munity as I shine your light, Lord, and shake the salt of your gospel.*

February 8

Thinking the Best

Love does not delight in evil but rejoices with the truth.
—1 Corinthians 13:6

The scene of the crime was a disability rights conference. Actually, the real crime scene was the handicap stall in the ladies' rest room. I was rambling on to my friend as she emptied my leg bag, but I should have kept my opinions to myself. After all, we were in a public rest room. And—yikes!—one of the ladies beyond the closed door was the individual with whom I had a difference of opinion.

When my friend and I exited the stall, I came face-to-face with that lady. Thankfully, her face was lit up with laughter. "Gotcha!" she said good-naturedly. "I'm assuming you were about to come back to the table to tell me your opinion, right?"

I was as red as a watermelon. "Right," I said, relieved.

This woman demonstrated grace. I deserved a good scolding, but instead she believed the best of me. Don't you love it when people think the best of you? You say something stupid but your friend discounts it. She doesn't hold anything against you, and she even chooses to think the best. Now, that's grace.

God expresses that kind of grace, too. He doesn't hold anything against you; he thinks the best. As 1 Corinthians 13 says, love "thinketh no evil" (KJV). If ten different interpretations could be made of a thing, with nine of them bad and one good, God's grace will take the good one and leave the other nine.

If that's how God chooses to deal with us, shouldn't we treat each other the same way? Someone may have wronged you, and you feel that person deserves a good scolding. But why not choose to think the best? Discount any unkind or thoughtless words spoken about you. After all, it's the graceful thing to do.

Lord, sometimes I forget how graciously you overlook my shortcomings and outright wrongdoings. Bring to my mind now anyone against whom I've harbored resentments. Teach me to extend grace to that person in your name.

Selling Everything

The kingdom of heaven is like treasure hidden in a field.
When a man found it, he hid it again, and then in his joy
went and sold all he had and bought that field.

—Matthew 13:44

I wouldn't trade it for the world. I'm talking about God's will for my life—including this wheelchair. When we embrace God's will, everything changes.

It's very much like the parable of the hidden treasure. The key word in today's verse is *bought*. We must buy the field. When we think of the field God wants us to buy, we assume it's attractive, something we would love to purchase anyway, a sun-drenched meadow dappled with wildflowers. It rarely is. The field—that thing God wants us to embrace—is usually bleak (like a sandlot with broken bottles and old tires scattered here and there). Of course, once we know that the scrubby field contains a treasure, the whole picture changes. The empty scrap of land suddenly brims with possibilities. Now we're ready to sell everything to buy it. (Elisabeth Elliot)

In my case, selling everything meant giving up self-pity and resentment over a body that no longer worked. Selling everything meant tossing aside the questions and investing the hours I sit in this wheelchair. It meant using that time in God's Word and in prayer (the pick and shovel needed to unearth the hidden treasure).

On the surface my field still looks bleak—the paralyzed legs, the hands that don't work. Probably nobody else would want to buy this field. But to me, it's beautiful because underneath the surface is the treasure, the priceless treasure of knowing Jesus better. I agree with Matthew 13:44: it's the kingdom of heaven.

What does your field look like? What treasures have you found thus far? What investments do you need to make to uncover other finds?

Lord Jesus, as I survey the land I've bought at such a great price (I've given up my will, my preferences, and my pride), help me to see the treasures it contains. Help me to remember that more treasure lies buried, ready to be dug up.

February 10

Better and Better

Do you want more and more of God's kindness and peace? Then learn to know Him better and better. For as you know Him better, He will give you, through His great power, everything you need for living a truly good life: He even shares His own glory and His own goodness with us! And by that same mighty power He has given us all the other rich and wonderful blessings He promised. . . . But to obtain these gifts, you need more than faith; you must also work hard to be good, and even that is not enough. For then you must learn to know God better and discover what He wants you to do.

—2 Peter 1:2–5 LB

If you're like me, you're looking for ways to love God more. Not just to obey him (although that's what proves we love him) but to love God with a passion. With spirited affection. Intense desire. I'm talking about longing to know God better and better, with fire in your eyes and a furnace in your heart. The passage for today explains exactly how.

If you want to increase your desire for God, get to *know* him in a deeper way. And there is no better way to know him than through his Word. Get into God's Word, and you will get a heart for Jesus. Get passionate about Scripture, and your passion for him will increase. Feelings follow faith . . . and faith comes by hearing, and hearing by the Word of God.

Take a look back over the past week. How much time did you spend in the Word? What does that say about the direction your relationship with God is going? Mark down specific times in your calendar to be in the Word this upcoming week. Be realistic but stretch yourself a bit. After all, you want to know God better, don't you?

Lord God, help me to remember how amazing it is that you have revealed yourself through the Word. Teach me to treasure Scripture more and to love you more through it.

February 11

My Father's Crutches

How beautiful on the mountains are the feet of those who bring good news, who proclaim peace, who bring good tidings, who proclaim salvation, who say to Zion, "Your God reigns!"

—Isaiah 52:7

Once while Ken was cleaning out our garage, he came through the kitchen door holding up a pair of Canadian crutches. "Do you want to dump these?" he asked. I stared at the dusty crutches and my throat tightened. "They're Daddy's," I said with wet eyes. The aluminum was scraped and the rubber tips were scuffed, but the crutches brought into focus a flood of memories.

All through his seventies and eighties, my father hobbled around on crutches due to arthritis. He had used them to shove around chairs or boxes or even ring a doorbell. On a good day he could hit a ball tossed to him by a grandkid. Around the farm we could always tell when Dad was off on a horseback ride—his crutches would be leaning against the hitching post.

When I was in the hospital, I could always tell when my father was coming for a visit. "Click-click" his crutches would echo on the hallway tile. *Oh boy, Daddy's here!* I would think, grinning to myself. I felt that he, more than anyone else in the family, understood my situation. This is why for me that clicking sound was so welcome. Today's verse talks about the beauty of feet that bring good news—that includes crutches!

Think today about all the friends and family members you know who bring you good tidings and the words of peace. The sandaled feet of your daughter, home from college. The tennis-shoed feet of your neighbor with whom you walk every morning. What do people think of when they hear *your* feet coming? Do they say, "Oh boy, here comes . . . !"

Make my feet beautiful, Lord. May I be mindful to carry the good news of your glad tidings to others today.

Altogether Lovely

His mouth is sweetness itself; he is altogether lovely. This is
my lover, this my friend.

—Song of Songs 5:16

The moon is full tonight. And romantic that I am, I will sit outside in my
backyard ogling up at the sky. Full moons make me think of love, and
there's nothing like being in love.

Even if you're not really in love right now, you can recall what it felt
like. Your heart grows faint and your breathing short just picturing the soft
eyes and tender smile of the one you adore. Being in a room with him is a
thrill. You ply him with questions just to hear the sound of his voice. And
the thought of a kiss? An embrace? You all but melt. When you're in love,
one thing is for certain: you can't keep it to yourself. You just have to tell
that person who grips your affection. I often say to Ken, "I love you. . . .
You are one great, handsome guy." I don't say this stuff to compliment or
flatter him. I just have to . . . say it.

Likewise, we are happier and more complete when we express our love
for God in praise. C. S. Lewis said, "It's not out of a compliment that lovers
keep on telling one another how beautiful they are. The delight is incomplete until it is expressed. In the same way, we delight to praise God because
our praise of him not merely expresses, but it completes our enjoyment."[1]

Express your love for God in a way you seldom choose: sing a (solo!)
praise song to him, write him a love letter, put some balloons on your
porch as a symbol of your love. Grab a hymnal and go outside when
the moon is full this month—flip to the hymn "Jesus, Lover of My
Soul" and happily praise him. Let your heart direct you to an idea
that delights you. It will delight God too.

*Lord Jesus, lover of my soul, so fill me with effusive love for you that I
have to find some way to express it.*

February 13

Love Displayed

Who shall separate us from the love of Christ? Shall trouble or hardship or persecution or famine or nakedness or danger or sword? . . . No, in all these things we are more than conquerors through him who loved us. For I am convinced that neither death nor life, neither angels nor demons, neither the present nor the future, nor any powers, neither height nor depth, nor anything else in all creation, will be able to separate us from the love of God that is in Christ Jesus our Lord.

—Romans 8:35, 37–39

This is a verse I'm *supposed* to believe," we say with a sigh, full of doubts. It sounds more like theological doctrine than practical reality, especially when we are the ones facing trouble, hardship, danger, or sword. But the apostle—who, incidentally, suffered a lot more than persecution or famine—wrote this sweeping statement specifically for those who would doubt the love of God in the midst of hardships.

Look at the last eleven words: "the love of God that is in Christ Jesus our Lord." If ever we are tempted to doubt God's good intentions, if ever he seems to be an uncaring deity sequestered in an ivory tower untouched by pain, we must remember the love of God *that is in Christ*. Christ who bore the weight of sin, the sting of spit, the bite of the whip, the accusations of ignorance, and the sufferings of the world. This is love poured out like wine, as strong as fire. This is love never to be doubted or betrayed.

Thomas Merton said, "In order to suffer without dwelling on our own affliction, we must think about a greater affliction and turn to the cross."[2] If you are questioning the love of God because of a disappointment or trial, turn your eyes upon Jesus. He is the love of the Father in the flesh displayed. When Jesus hung on the cross, God was saying, "I love you," and nothing can separate you from that.

If I'm tempted to doubt your love today, Lord, place before me the cross.

The Lover of Your Soul

We love because he first loved us.

—1 John 4:19

When my husband, Ken, and I were dating, one word marked the expression of his love for me: *excessive*. I received more candies, stuffed animals, sweetheart cards, and vases of fresh yellow roses than I care to remember. I pleaded with him to lighten up, but I learned that not only is love blind; it's deaf. The next day I would receive pink roses instead of yellow ones. There were more solid evidences of Ken's love I could point to, but it was the excesses that delighted me.

We never need doubt the love of Christ. We have plenty of solid evidence. But there may be times when we might wonder just how much Jesus delights himself in us. It is true that bearing the Father's wrath on the cross was the ultimate test of how immense Christ's love is, but our soul wants to know more. I want to know how passionately, how intensely, he *feels* about me. Did Jesus desire to come to earth? Or was it a matter of fulfilling divine duty?

The question is answered in blood. There is a word that marks the love of Christ, and that is *excessive*. His love for you overflows all reason, all expectations, all your hopes and dreams. For Christ to lay down his life for you tells you that his covenant is no schoolboy pledge or head-of-state agreement or legal contract. Christ's love is riddled with powerful emotion. For him to die for you is for him to be delighted in you.

Let Christ's passion for you stir the depths of your yearnings for him. Let yourself be drawn to him today, not only because of his sacrifice for your sin but because of his desire for your soul.

Lord Jesus, I am moved deeply by the extravagant, excessive display of your love for me. I am gripped by the intensity of your desire and emotion for my soul. You take delight in me ... and my heart rises to take delight in you.

February 15

Fighting Fair

[Love] is not rude, it is not self-seeking, it is not easily
angered, it keeps no record of wrongs.
—1 Corinthians 13:5

My husband is a pretty fair fighter. For the most part he can get angry
without getting destructive.

But not so the other night. We were arguing in the living room, and
his temper got a little hot. So he stomped out of the room and shut the
door. I put a lid on my own temper and reminded him that shutting doors
was a low blow. With that the door cracked open. I was able to wheel into
the kitchen, where, I am happy to tell you, our silly argument was resolved.

Fighting fair is essential if Ken and I are going to air our differences
and effectively deal with them. We have four fair-fighting rules: First, stick
to one topic. The issue becomes clouded if you start to drag in past
offenses. State your complaint in one sentence, such as "It bothers me that
you always speed up when the light at an intersection turns yellow." Second, allow the other person to respond. Don't use the door-slamming technique as a punctuation mark. Third, don't keep a list of wrongdoings. Like
it says in 1 Corinthians 13:5, love "keeps no record of wrongs." Fourth,
take the initiative in forgiving. God didn't wait around until he had an
apology from you and me before he sent his Son. If God can take the initiative like that, so can we.

Conflicts come up in any relationship. But with patience and some
good fair-fighting rules, they can be resolved. Besides, making up is *much*
better than fighting.

Read over the list of rules again, this time asking yourself if in one of
your relationships there's a conflict that needs resolution. Do one
thing to take the initiative to settle your differences. And then follow
the rest of those fair-fighting principles.

*Father, thank you that you took the initiative when my sin separated us.
You have given me this example to follow in my relationships with others. Give me the courage to settle differences.*

February 16

The Yoke

Come to me, all you who are weary and burdened, and I will give you rest. Take my yoke upon you and learn from me, for I am gentle and humble in heart, and you will find rest for your souls.

—Matthew 11:28–29

Over the living room fireplace, Ken and I have hung a family treasure. It's an old-fashioned oxen yoke hand-hewn out of wood. It's been in the family forever. As a little boy, my father would yoke his dad's oxen to haul coal. That yoke doesn't quite go with the decor in our living room, but that doesn't matter. It's a treasure. And it's an object lesson.

Have you ever wondered why Jesus called his yoke easy and light? A yoke appears to be a weighty burden, but it makes the workload light for the animal. A plow or a coal drag would be intolerable if it were attached to the oxen in any other way (before yokes were devised, farmers of old used leather straps around the animal's neck—but it hampered the animal's breathing). But when you work an animal by means of a yoke, the weight the animal has to pull doesn't harm it. The load becomes light.

A yoke is not a contrivance to make work hard. It's a gentle device to make hard labor light. A yoke is meant not to give pain but to save pain. Think of that as you read Jesus' words for today.

Work is a fact of life. Burdens are inevitable. But you have a choice: either drag your workload under your own strength or put on the yoke of Christ.

Jesus says, "Come." If you're weary and burdened, let him give you rest. You'll find a deep, sweet, peaceable rest even in the midst of your labors when you put on Christ's yoke.

Lord, as I feel the burdens of this day, remind me that you have provided a yoke that eases the stress and keeps me from straining needlessly. Show me how to experience your rest for my weary soul.

The Lord Is Good

Give thanks to the LORD, for he is good; his love endures
forever. Let the redeemed of the LORD say this.

—Psalm 107:1–2

It was a dull Saturday. My spirits were drooping, and it was all I could do
to fight off depression. A corset riding high was digging into my ribs,
forcing me to draw deep breaths now and then. And when I did, I would
say, "The Lord is good." Somewhere after the fifth "Lord is good," my
friend turned and gave a good-natured dig, asking, "What are you doing?
Trying to convince yourself?"

"You've got it," I replied. It's not that I doubted God's goodness; I
simply wanted to remind my dry, cracked soul of the truth. David, the
psalmist, often grabbed his innermost being by the scruff of the neck,
demanding, "Why are you downcast, O my soul? Why so disturbed within
me? Put your hope in God, for I will yet praise him, my Savior and my
God" (Ps. 42:5–6). It's easy to announce God's goodness when your spirits are soaring; it's another thing—a more God-glorifying thing—to proclaim the goodness of God out loud when you're under the weather.

Voicing the goodness of God is a testimony not only to your downcast soul but to others listening in. And not just people but powers
and principalities who stand on tiptoe to see what you have to say
about your Savior when times are tough. "Let the redeemed of the
LORD say this," our verse today advises. Find moments today to speak
aloud of the goodness of God, no matter what your emotions insist.

*Prone to wander, Lord, I feel it; prone to leave the God I love. This
describes me to a tee. But not today. Today I insist that my soul listen. The
Lord is good.*

Open My Eyes

When he was at the table with them, he took bread, gave thanks, broke it and began to give it to them. Then their eyes were opened and they recognized him, and he disappeared from their sight.... They found the Eleven and those with them, assembled together and saying, "It is true! The Lord has risen and has appeared to Simon." Then the two told what had happened on the way, and how Jesus was recognized by them when he broke the bread.

—Luke 24:30–31, 33–35

How difficult is it to recognize Jesus? What are the distinguishing characteristics that reveal him as Savior? We know *who* opened the eyes of the two disciples as they ate bread with Jesus, but *how?* What brought that "Aha!" moment?

"Jesus was recognized by them when he broke the bread." Their eyes saw the plate, the loaf, and the hands reach for the bread, then tear it apart. Something seemed familiar. Was this the same man who, just days earlier in the Upper Room, broke bread in similar fashion? They looked closer, watching him as he handled the loaf. Suddenly they knew. The disciples surely spied the scars in his hands. How could they miss it as he passed them chunks of bread? This had to be Jesus. What other living man could walk around, bearing the marks of crucifixion?

When we talk about God to others, we must always point to Christ. And when we talk about Christ, we must always point to the cross. "The cross ... is the power of God" (1 Cor. 1:18). The Father will open the eyes of seekers when they contemplate the cross. It is what makes the Christian faith utterly unique. When we point people to Calvary, they cannot miss the exclusivity of Christianity. What other man died from crucifixion yet still lives?

Open my eyes that I may see, Lord. Show me more of what the passion of Christ means. Help me to know Jesus better by contemplating today all that he suffered for my salvation.

Keeping the Sabbath

To [those] who keep my Sabbaths, who choose what pleases
me and hold fast to my covenant . . . these I will bring to my
holy mountain and give them joy in my house of prayer.
—Isaiah 56:4, 7

L ast week when my friend Mary Jean came to town to visit, I took her
to the mall for coffee after church. I started to tell her about my friend
Bonnie who is living in a nursing home. "Bonnie's neuromuscular disease
has advanced to the point where she lies in bed all day," I told Mary Jean.
"It would be good if we could spend some time praying for her today. I
heard that she's been very depressed."

A silent moment passed. Then we both said at the same time, "So
what are we doing here?" We gathered our things, headed up the freeway,
and hurried down the nursing home's hallways to Bonnie's room.

Her eyes lit up when she saw us. She couldn't communicate much
through her stiffened smile, but that didn't daunt Mary Jean and me. We
sang to Bonnie. We occasionally sat quietly, enjoying birds chirping outside the window. At the close of our visit, I asked Bonnie if she would like
to slowly repeat with us the Lord's Prayer. She nodded.

While a bedpan clattered on the floor down the hallway and someone kept babbling by the nurses' station, we prayed. Mary Jean did many
things during her visit, including a jaunt to the beach and an evening out
at a fancy restaurant. But the highlight was that marvelous chance to keep
the Sabbath with a friend in need.

We say we don't have time to follow spiritual disciplines or to visit
"the widow and the orphan" as the Bible tells us to, but the best time
for Christian ministry or spiritual disciplines (like prayer, fasting, or
Bible memorization) is the time that is already God's—the Sabbath.
Make it a day set apart for holy gifts to God and others.

*Father God, what would you like to have me do this Sunday that would
bring your light and encouragement to someone, that would make the
Sabbath a holy day I can offer back to you?*

February 20

Kingdom Play

> Let the little children come to me . . . for the kingdom of
> heaven belongs to such as these.
>
> —Matthew 19:14

I'll never forget the first time someone showed me in the Bible that I
would one day have a new, glorified body. "You're kidding!" I said in wonder. We cross-referenced other passages, and sure enough, it was there as
plain as day. "You mean, I'll be able to walk and run? Not be a spacey spirit-
being with no legs or arms?" My joy was so great that my friend pushed me
outside in my wheelchair (it was near midnight) and we hooted and
howled at the full moon. He circled my chair around and around, and we
"danced" with glee over the kingdom promises we'd just read.

I call it kingdom play. It happens when you experience an "Aha!"
moment of delight in God. It bursts beyond happiness and calls for rejoicing out of sheer generosity. Like a child, you just *have* to go outside, beyond
the four walls of normal human experience, and play!

Peter Kreeft writes,

> This state of mind is like light: traveling faster than matter, yet mak-
> ing no sound, no perturbation. Pleasure is the restless mind moving
> along a line, never reaching the end. Happiness is the mind resting
> at the end. Joy is the mind eternally moving *at* the end, motion at a
> point: the cosmic dance. Pleasure is moving; happiness is still; joy is
> moving while still. Pleasure is like work, happiness is like sleep, joy
> is like play. Pleasure is like action, happiness is like rest, joy is like
> contemplation. Pleasure is a river running to the sea; happiness is the
> full, calm sea; joy is a great and glorious storm on the sea.[3]

When was the last time you did something childlike out of sheer joy?
Said something childlike? If today's thoughts energize you, express
your delight in God in the way a child would: finger-paint a wild
and colorful poster, sing at the top of your lungs a song you learned
in Sunday school, buy a Tootsie-Pop and lick it for fun. Most of all
do a little kingdom play, telling God in song, word, or deed how
delighted you are in him.

Hip, hip, hurray! I love you, Lord!

February 21

Grace Unadorned

I know what it is to be in need, and I know what it is to
have plenty. I have learned the secret of being content in
any and every situation, whether well fed or hungry,
whether living in plenty or in want.

—Philippians 4:12

"The winter of our discontent" is a line from Shakespeare, but it's also a
line people tend to mumble this time of year. In February many grow
discontent; people are restless with the long winter. We are tired of trees
that look stark. The landscape is barren, the ground hard like iron.

But look deeper into February. There's beauty in the barren landscape.
Earth is stripped of its foliage, and we see the uncluttered foundation of
ground and sky. It's as though nature wears no makeup. Earth's face is
unadorned and plain, like the scrubbed face of a woman whose wrinkles
add to her elegance. February is not pretty; it is handsome in an unem-
bellished manner. For those who take time to look, they will discover a
deeper beauty.

Something else is hidden from view, and there's no better time than
this month to uncover it. Now is the time to learn the secret of contentment Paul talks about in Philippians. To live "hungry" or "in want," as
Paul puts it, is a little like looking for beauty in a stark landscape. Life,
stripped of its trappings and reduced to its bare essentials, shows us how
lean and in need of God we really are. Embrace spiritual poverty as you
would embrace the strange beauty of February. When you do, you'll find
the grace of God.

If your life feels as cold and barren as the hard ground in winter, take
this month to learn the secret. God's grace will furrow the ground of
your cold heart and turn its sod to the sunshine of hope. His grace
will warm and revive you, like the early breezes of spring reviving the
earth.

*Father God, I confess a restless spirit and a roving eye. Teach me to sit
contentedly in the warm embrace of your grace this cold day.*

February 22

Sufferings Showcase

His intent was that now, through the church, the manifold
wisdom of God should be made known to the rulers and
authorities in the heavenly realms.

—Ephesians 3:10

The powers and principalities, all the heavenly hosts and the dark rulers
of the universe, millions of unseen beings, are intensely interested to
see just how able God is to sustain the weak and the weary.

Ephesians 3:10 tells us that God teaches the unseen world all about
himself, and he does it using you and me as his audiovisual aids. We are
used of the Lord to show the universe how great, awesome, and wonderful God and his grace are. Let's say some demon dares waltz up to heaven's
throne and sneers, "God, people only trust you because you bless them
with health and strength. But let me put a kink in the lower back of some
missionary. Then allow me to take away his financial support. I'd just bet
that missionary would end up denying you."

But God would answer, "Oh no, you're wrong. That exact scenario happened to Mr. Brown and he trusted me. I worked through his obedience,
and because of his testimony many more people heard of the Son's love."

At that point the demon would shrink away, and the glory surrounding God would glow even brighter. Mr. Brown's sufferings not only helped
him to grow in Christ, but they demonstrated to that demon and millions
like him how powerful God's sustaining grace is. The result? Greater glory
to God. One day it will be shown to all that God was able to rescue sinners, redeem suffering, crush the rebellious, restore all things, vindicate his
holy name, provide restitution . . . and come out all the more glorious for
it! What an honor to share in that.

When you feel surrounded by tough circumstances, remember: you
have the chance to be a Mr. Brown. God will use that situation to
build you up spiritually and to highlight his glory.

*Lord, I can't see so much of what is going on in this world. But I sure can
have an effect on what's happening! May I do so to your glory.*

February 23

Poor and Needy

Hear, O LORD, and answer me, for I am poor and needy. Guard my life, for I am devoted to you. You are my God; save your servant who trusts in you. Have mercy on me, O Lord, for I call to you all day long. Bring joy to your servant, for to you, O Lord, I lift up my soul.

—Psalm 86:1–4

Several years ago I traveled to Ghana, west Africa, to give wheelchairs and Bibles to homeless disabled people who lived in the filthy slums. A disabled boy who lived in a box by a trash heap said, "God has blessed people in your country so much; why are so many unhappy?" Another said, "Welcome to our country, where our God is bigger than your God." I heard it time and again in Ghana: "We have to trust God. We have no other hope."

Don't think I'm glorifying the poor and needy of Africa. This isn't a snobby one-upmanship over whose Purple Heart medals shine the brightest. They are more like us than we realize. They too want what they do not have, and have what they do not want. The difference is in the way they look at God.

God always seems bigger to those who need him the most. Spiritual and physical poverty is the tool God uses to help us need him more. Hardships press us up against him. It's a universal truth we all learned in the old Sunday school song: "We are weak and he is strong."

Who are the poor and needy? People in Africa? The homeless? The disabled? It is you if you see yourself as empty and impoverished. That's not a bad position in which to be. When you cry, "Have mercy on me, O Lord!" you are in a *great* position. God seems bigger when we, in our eyes, seem poor.

I lift up my soul to you today, Lord. I am poor and needy, empty and destitute, without you. As I make myself small in my eyes today, please help me to see how big you are.

February 24

A Restful Peace

> May God himself, the God of peace, sanctify you through
> and through.
>
> —1 Thessalonians 5:23

Winter is a siege of darkness and cold for many. Sun-short days, harsh winds, and gray scenery hold sway. We fly to warmer climates or dream of May skies. But then it snows and everything changes. We awaken to a stillness that is winter at its best. The cold, gray siege has crept away in the night, yielding to the quiet army of white. Sounds are muffled in the cushion. Shapes that were once jagged soften their attitude under the blanket of snow. The sense of beauty and contentment is breathtaking. It is heart-resting.

When I choose to commit some major or minor sin, I find it ends up holding a tight siege of darkness over me. Though I try to ignore it for a while, eventually my spirit blackens and I hide. Like a hibernating creature, I curl up in myself and just wish it would all be over in the morning.

God will not let me hibernate long in such a state. I'm soon pressured by his Holy Spirit to confess what he already knows. But get this: he doesn't merely send a blanket of grace to cover my sin. His forgiveness goes deeper than a covering over or hiding of my sin, as when snow blankets the ground. The Bible says it is God himself, "the God of peace," who sanctifies me *through and through.* God's peace is not a dispensation of medicine for the soul but his powerful presence. When he sanctifies me, no part of my soul is left untouched by the white of his mercy. My sin is whited out completely! At such times I enjoy the sweetest part of my walk with him—the peace of a completely cleansed heart.

Have you had the peace of knowing you are cleansed through and through? Come out of hibernation. Confess, be cleansed, then mark this page for today. It can serve as a reminder of God's provision of himself in a hectic and troubling world.

Lord, I want your rest and peace. Enable me to believe you will sanctify me through and through as I confess to you.

Who's the Judge?

Do not judge, or you too will be judged. For in the same way you judge others, you will be judged, and with the measure you use, it will be measured to you.

—Matthew 7:1–2

While my husband and I were sitting in a fast-food restaurant discussing gardening plans for the afternoon, we overheard a couple having a heated argument. The place was rather empty, so Ken and I couldn't help but get an earful. At one point the woman hissed, "You jerk, why don't you ever listen to me?" She said it with such venom that I immediately condemned her as the guilty party.

The Bible has advice not only for that woman but also for people like me who are sometimes quick to judge. Only Jesus has the right to judge, for only God knows all the facts and the heart's motives. Scripture also says that whatever sentence we render to others may turn around to condemn us.

That very afternoon when Ken and I were in the backyard with clippers and fertilizer, I found myself steamed up with him about a gardening technique. Hardly a word came out of my mouth before God brought to mind the woman in the restaurant. I felt the gavel come down on me. We must not judge rashly, assuming the worst in people. We must not judge unmercifully. Finally, we must not judge the hearts of others. Of course, we ought to weigh between right and wrong and hold believers to scriptural standards, but judging goes a giant step beyond discernment.

Judgment carries with it an attitude of condemnation. One day Jesus will come "to judge the living and the dead" (1 Peter 4:5). I, for one, am relieved to leave the gavel in his hand. After all, no one knows what is in a heart but him. Let's pray for people rather than render judgments. In fact, I think I'll pray for that woman in the restaurant right now.

God, remind me how sensitively and precisely you have balanced your scales of justice. Keep me from rushing to conclusions about others. Enable me to turn any insights I do have into prayers.

February 26

Take No Prisoners

Now therefore I tell you that I will not drive them out before you; they will be thorns in your sides and their gods will be a snare to you.

—Judges 2:3

Containing an enemy is expedient but deadly. History has shown time and again that such a policy simply gives opportunity for the enemy to regroup and train itself for more deadly assaults. The fatal blow must be struck or there will be no peace.

It seemed wise at the time to the Israelites. Nations either struck peace accords with them or pledged to be their servants. Not a bad deal when you've wandered for forty years in the desert and then had to fight to stake your claim. Most of us would have applauded our leaders for such diplomacy. But the Israelites practiced containment with deadly results. Not only were they perpetually harassed by enemies; they lost the battle for their souls to idols and immorality.

I'm quick to practice containment in my own life—I corral those sins I think I can tame, fencing in small transgressions, putting borders around my disobedience. "This far and no further," I will say to certain bad habits. Once my disobedience settles down to a manageable level, like a low-grade fever, I easily move to other, more pressing needs at work or with family. But sin is never contained for long.

If God does not get his way with your sin, his mortal enemy, it will rear its ugly head at another time and in uglier ways. Our contained sins can limit our effectiveness, kill our joy, and fool us into thinking we are gods that are able to manage our sin life quite nicely on our own.

God won't have it. His enemy must be defeated. He loves you too much.

Lord God, enemy of sin, reign victorious in the battle that has already been won. Kill your enemy that I might know the peace you've secured for me.

Did You Know What
You Were Getting Into?

Dear friends, do not be surprised at the painful trial you are suffering, as though something strange were happening to you.

—1 Peter 4:12

When you first became a Christian, did you realize what you were getting into? Did you read the fine print in the contract? God plainly spelled it out: "If anyone would come after me, he must deny himself and take up his cross and follow me" (Mark 8:34); "It has been granted to you on behalf of Christ not only to believe on him, but also to suffer for him" (Phil. 1:29).

God made it clear that following him would mean real hardship. Life is supposed to be difficult. More than that, it has been *granted* to us to suffer. Granted? Like a gift or a privilege? And what does "for him" mean? Problems are built into the Christian life for a privileged purpose. If we're to follow Jesus, we have to follow him to Calvary. That's something God wants us to understand the moment we come to Christ. God also wants us to realize it's a privilege to follow his Son this way. To follow Christ to the cross is to suffer for him.

When I first came to Christ, I sort of knew it meant suffering, but I had no idea it would involve paralysis. I was surprised at the painful trial at first, thinking something strange had happened to me. But now I praise God for this wheelchair. It has taken me down Calvary's path. It's the path to deep-down joy and peace.

Did you know what you were getting into when you became a believer? The question isn't all that important now that you've signed up. What's important is that you not be surprised at the fiery trial—it comes so that through it you might take up your cross and follow Jesus. It comes so you might find your life after you lose it. Fine print or no, it's the deal.

Lord Jesus, help me to remember that following you means taking up my cross. Keep me pliable rather than resistant when fiery trials greet me.

February 28

What a Pain

Jabez was more honorable than his brothers. His mother
had named him Jabez, saying, "I gave birth to him in pain."
—1 Chronicles 4:9

Can you imagine someone whose name is Pain? He's mentioned in
today's Scripture. Why would a mother give her son the name Jabez,
which in Hebrew means "pain"? Just think of the razzing little Jabez got
from his playmates.

Yet Jabez didn't let his name get him down. In fact, Scripture says he
was more honorable than his brothers. It even says that when he cried out
to God, the Lord blessed him and granted his request to be kept from
harm. As a wheelchair user, I can understand a little of the stigma that
Jabez must have faced. It's not fun to be looked on as different, even to the
point of being nicknamed after your handicap, as when someone says,
"Hey, Crip." (That happened a lot in the hospital, when older teenagers
who were paraplegics teased us younger quadriplegics.)

But I believe that being different—even having a stigma—can drive
us closer to God.

Have you felt the sting of social stigma? Of negative stereotype? You
may never have felt the pain of being called names like Metal Mouth (that's
what Rocky, my classmate, called me when I wore braces in ninth grade),
but there may be something about your abilities or appearance that you
wish you hadn't been saddled with.

Can you, like Jabez, turn it around for good and not let it get you
down? Can you let it push you into the arms of Christ? God has a
special love for you, so look to him in your pain. Whether it be physical or emotional, you may find that you'll be as blessed as Jabez.

God, when life is a real pain, teach me to come to you with my hurts.
And help me to be like Jabez and concentrate not on the negatives but
on how to live honorably.

February 29

Competition

I have no one else like him, who takes a genuine interest in your welfare.

—Philippians 2:20

I am a competitor, even though I can't move much. But I'm not the only one. There's Thad Mandsager. When his parents invited me to their home, I watched Thad and his brother, Nathan, play Nerf basketball in the hallway.

Thad was twelve years old at the time, and because he is paralyzed from the neck down, he operates his power wheelchair with a chin control. This kid balanced the Nerf basketball on his mouth stick and flicked the ball up against the backboard to make his basket. He asked, "Hey, Joni, want to give it a try?" I replied, "Okay, but fair warning: I just might beat you." Wishful thinking! Me, the famous mouth artist, could barely balance the Nerf ball on the mouth stick. As far as flicking it for a layup, forget it. I couldn't even hit the backboard.

Another time the Mandsager family came over for a barbecue. Thad brought his Nerf baseball bat. Clenching the bat between his teeth, he sent the ball sailing over the backyard fence. "Hey, Joni," said he, spitting out the bat, "want to give it a try?" Three strikes later I was out.

Needless to say, Thad is doing okay. He is such an inspiration!

You don't have to overcome the kinds of obstacles Thad has to inspire other people. The Scripture today reminds us that taking a genuine interest in the welfare of others—taking part in their activities, contributing to their efforts, cheering them on from the sidelines—will place you in a league like "no one else," as the apostle Paul puts it.

In what ways do you encourage others? How do you strive to use all the gifts God has given you? How are you working to quit complaining? Thad reminds me of all these sterling qualities whenever the paths of our wheels happen to cross.

Heavenly Father, sometimes I feel I have no special gifts to give. Help me to remember that it takes no extraordinary talent to say an encouraging word or to live a life of faith that encourages others. It just takes trust—and genuine interest in someone else.

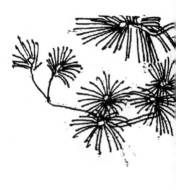

MARCH

Helping the Blind

God, who said, "Let light shine out of darkness," made his light shine in our hearts to give us the light of the knowledge of the glory of God in the face of Christ.

—2 Corinthians 4:6

If you saw a blind person stumble and fall, how would you feel? What would you do? Your heart would go out to that person. Compassion would move you to do something. You wouldn't stop to consider whether or not you were strong enough to help.

In 2 Corinthians 4:4 the Bible talks about a different kind of blindness. "The god of this age has blinded the minds of unbelievers, so that they cannot see the light of the gospel of the glory of Christ." Some people are physically blind; many more people are spiritually blind.

Don't you think it's curious that on one hand we would rush to the aid of a physically blind person who stumbles, but when we see unbelievers walk into a wall of sin, stumble over a transgression, or head for a cliff completely unawares, we keep our distance? What's more, few of us would scold a blind person for tripping over something he or she couldn't see. But many of us are quick to berate unbelievers who bad-mouth the gospel or refuse to go to church. What do they know? They are spiritually blind!

Compassion is what's needed, the godly compassion Jesus showed to people with blind eyes and blind hearts. If God made his light shine in our spiritually dark hearts, if someone once lifted us up out of darkness with a compassionate hand, isn't it our turn to perform that same good deed for another person?

The "blind" need help. They need a hand. Today run to the aid of someone who cannot see through his or her sin. Don't worry about whether you are able; trust God to provide you with the resources.

Father of light, help me to remember the pain and disorientation of living in darkness. Move me to show compassion to those who haven't seen your light.

March 2

Godly Losing

> Whoever finds his life will lose it, and whoever loses his life
> for my sake will find it.
>
> —Matthew 10:39

It's tough to lose. Ask any competitor. Ask any human. Yet God makes the supreme request of us: lose yourself. Ah, but not for our sakes and certainly not for nothing. To lose your life for Jesus' sake is to not only find him but find the "you" you are supposed to be. The you God has in mind. Let me explain. . . .

No matter how connected we are with our loved ones, we are always left aching for more, for someone to comprehend our world and enter our struggle—to embrace us with a passion that seizes and melts us into a union that will never be broken. God answers this ancient longing. We melt into him when we let go of pride, when we let go of the itchiness to have things our own way, when we let go of desires and dreams and feast on him. But in losing ourselves for his sake, we discover our true identity; we step into the person we've been predestined to be.

You can't lose when you lose like this. After all, it's the godly thing to do. Even the Son pleases the Father, not himself. The Spirit reveals the Son, never himself. The Son reveals the Father and never points to himself. The Father begets the Son, the Son honors the Father, and the Spirit reveres them both. It's a divine "dying to self."

The offer to lose yourself for Christ's sake is incredibly enticing: to catch God's good mood, to delight in the cascade of his joy, and to feel him embracing you with a passion, seizing and melting you into a union with him that can never be broken. As the Spirit defers to the rest of the Trinity, as the Son divests himself for the sake of the Father, so Jesus asks the same of you. Fusion with him means finding who you are.

I step by faith closer to you today, Lord. I leave behind my wants and wishes. Show me who I am in you and I shall be ecstatic.

March 3

Divine Distastes

> I have indeed seen the misery of my people in Egypt. I have heard them crying out because of their slave drivers, and I am concerned about their suffering.
>
> —Exodus 3:7

There are a lot of things God doesn't like. We can tick off a few—like, well ... sin, spiritual snobbery, rebellion, fudging the truth, stepping on people's toes to get ahead, and so on, ad infinitum.

But besides sin, God has a strong distaste for suffering. This is movingly pictured in Judges 10:16. God has been watching the Ammonites oppress Israel. The Jews cry out in prayer and toss out their idols. Finally—here's the line—God "could bear Israel's misery no longer." His tenderness was roused by human anguish. Years earlier he said to Moses the words in today's Scripture passage. To God, suffering is distasteful, to say the least. God is truly grieved at how we've ruined the world and abused each other. This grief is partly why he gave the Ten Commandments: Don't murder, he says—I hate unjust killing. Don't commit adultery—I despise seeing families ripped apart.

Your tears touch God. He aches to show his compassion. If Adam had never fallen, if God could rewrite the story, I'm convinced he never would have let suffering out of the cage, much less allowed sin to pollute his planet. "He does not willingly bring affliction or grief to the children of men" (Lam. 3:33).

Habakkuk spoke accurately of God when he said, "Your eyes are too pure to look on evil; you cannot tolerate wrong" (Hab. 1:13). And God won't. One day very soon—much sooner than we think—God will close the curtain on sin, sweeping suffering and all its pain and tears away forever. Until that time he permits what he hates, to accomplish something mysterious and wonderful that he loves: Christ in us.

I realize, Lord, that you permit all sorts of things you don't approve of. It's a mystery to me. I'm just grateful you understand my pain. Help me to hold on to you, dear God. I want Christ to come forth in my life through my suffering.

March 4

Who Hurts the Most?

If we walk in the light, as he is in the light, we have fellowship with one another, and the blood of Jesus, his Son, purifies us from all sin.

—1 John 1:7

A father warns his child time and again to stay away from those containers underneath the sink. But one day Dad walks into the kitchen and sees his little boy pale and unconscious on the floor. Somehow the boy managed to pry the lid off that old bottle of insecticide. The paramedics, after a few anxious minutes, revive the child. Yet in the coming days the tragedy continues to unfold. Doctors report that the boy will be permanently impaired. Although the child has no concept of what life could have been had he not disobeyed, his father will carry the pain of his son's disobedience for the rest of his life.

Let's apply this story to our relationship with God. Just who felt the deepest hurt back in the Garden of Eden? It's true Adam and Eve suffered dreadfully for their disobedience, and it's true their children suffered the consequences—they couldn't begin to understand what might have been. We can't understand, either. Blinded by our fallen nature, we have only the vaguest notion of what consequences our disobedience causes in our lives.

But God has complete understanding. He sees not only what is and will be but also what might have been. Scripture indicates that he feels anguish deeper than you and I can understand. He is the Father who carries the pain of our disobedience.

Fortunately, a miracle drug has been applied. Christ's blood on the cross is an antidote for the awful impairment of sin. That's what 1 John 1:7 tells us. We who have brought such pain to God can also bring joy, delight, and companionship as we accept his cure and walk with his Son.

Father God, strengthen me and enable me to walk with you, that I might delight your heart.

The Understatement of God

God saw that it was good.

—Genesis 1:18

Isn't it great to step back from a project well completed and just enjoy the joy? You've seen the happiness in a child's face whose crayon masterpiece gets taped to the fridge. It's the same contentment and joy you feel after serving the applauded turkey dinner or receiving the "Great job!" red-inked on the top of your history exam. Plus, the pleasure doesn't stop with one glance. We keep returning to admire the wooden bench we shellacked and finished, the row of pansies we planted along the wall, or the counted cross-stitch that took 150 hours to complete.

Now imagine the pleasure God derives from everything he has made. What do you think surged through him the minute after a billion galaxies burst into being? With typical understatement, the Bible tells us, "God saw that it was good." After standing back to take in the panorama, God rested—not to catch his breath from exhaustion but to savor the moment and relish in the pleasure of what he created.

Think of what surges through God's heart when you—his epitome of creation—make it your ambition to be pleasing to him, aspiring to fulfill all his greatest desires for you. God may say of his inanimate creation, "It is good," but what he is creating in you—"Christ in you, the hope of glory" (Col. 1:27)—is *great!*

God excels in the art of understatement. To say of his incredible work in creating the universe, "It is good" employs a style that is restrained, to say the least. This means we can be assured that when we please him, we *really* please him, with a joy that is humanly indescribable. "So," 2 Corinthians 5:9 says with more understatement, "we make it our goal to please him."

I am awestruck to think that I can do something—anything—that brings you enormous pleasure and joy. What a privilege to play a part in giving you, the Lord of the universe, great pleasure.

March 6

Seize Today!

Be careful how you walk, not as unwise men, but as wise,
making the most of your time, because the days are evil.
—Ephesians 5:15–16 NASB

Don't grasp for the future, Joni," my dad used to say. "Pay attention to the present." That's the way Daddy lived; that's the way he worked. Whenever my dad would build stone walls on the farm, he wouldn't rush. He would pick up a rock, brush off the dirt, turn it over in his hands, and line it up this way and that, trying to place it just right. He paid attention to what he was doing at that moment. As a result, forty years later the walls haven't crumbled.

My stone-laying father would say it's the only way to live. We make the mistake of thinking God is always preparing us for future ministry. We rush through the present moment to quickly reach the next one. As a result, we don't pay sufficient attention to the immediate. Oswald Chambers has said, "Grace is for 'right now.' It is not the process toward some future goal, but an end in and of itself. If we would only realize this, then each moment would become rich with meaning and purpose."[1]

This is what today's verse means. Some translations say, "Walk circumspectly" and "Redeem the time." Modern translations say, "Make the most of each moment." God is very interested in the situation we find ourselves in this instant. It's incidental that he may use our circumstances to prepare us for the future.

Right now it's easy to look at the month of March and start grasping for April. Then it's tempting to hurry ahead and red-ink the pages of May and June without giving today a thought. But that's no way to build a season, just as it's no way to build a wall. Take it slowly. Look at today and, as my father would say, pay attention to what you do with it.

God, I turn today over in my hands and ask you to help me to pay attention to what you have for me in it, not for the future but for right now.

March 7

Contentment in Christ

In [him] are hidden all the treasures of wisdom and knowledge.

—Colossians 2:3

Christ is not a magic wand that can be waved over our problems to make them disappear. Wisdom and knowledge—including knowing how to be content—are *hidden* in him, like a treasure that needs to be searched for. To search for something concealed requires work: "You will seek me and find me when you seek me with all your heart" (Jer. 29:13).

God doesn't leave us to search on our own. "I have learned the secret of being content. . . . I can do everything *through him who gives me strength*" (Phil. 4:12–13, emphasis added). The apostle Paul not only wrote this but had to master it. It meant making tough choices—deciding this, not that; going in this direction, not that one. Why does it involve such hard work? Because it's not our natural bent. Seeking the hidden treasure of contentment in Christ doesn't come automatically. Just look at a few of Paul's well-chosen words: "press on . . . strive . . . stand firm."

As we wrap our hands around a problem and in faith press on, strive, and stand firm, divine energy surges through us. You make the choices; God gives you the strength. He gives you the strength to hold your tongue when you feel you have cause for complaining. He imparts the strength to look out for another's interest before your own. He infuses the strength to choose a bright attitude when you wake up in the morning. The problems don't go away, but you have quietness of heart and a settled soul.

Is there a problem needling you? An irritation? Something festering discontentment? See it as a chance to search for hidden treasure: contentment in Christ. Present to God today one thing you'd like to be contented in. Reread today's devotional and underline the steps to begin your search. You have the secret: as you press on, he will give strength.

As the apostle says, I want to learn to be content. I want internal quietness of heart, supernaturally given, that gladly submits to you, God, in all circumstances. Today I begin seeking this treasure in you.

March 8

Fasting's Purpose

When you fast, do not look somber as the hypocrites do,
for they disfigure their faces to show men they are fasting.
—Matthew 6:16

You've heard Bible teachers say it before: Jesus doesn't say *if* you fast but *when* you fast. For the Christian, fasting is not an option. It is a spiritual discipline our Lord expects us to practice. It seems Jesus is always getting us to do physical things to make a spiritual point.

Fasting reveals the stuff inside us. It shows us what we are made of, what we prize and prefer. When we abstain from food (or observe some other "fast" in which we refuse ourselves physical fulfillment), the stuff of which we're made will show itself. You will see it, be confronted by it, and have to deal with it. When midafternoon comes and you want a Burger King Whopper so bad you can taste it, you'll have to stop and think, *Am I going to cave in, or am I going to let these urges drive me to the Lord in prayer?*

It's irritating. It's stressful. Often the Whopper wins. God notes, "Your fasting ends in quarreling and strife. . . . You cannot fast as you do today and expect your voice to be heard on high" (Isa. 58:4). Food is basic to our existence (little wonder we get irritated), and when we remove ourselves from food, it's a way of getting down to the real basics of our existence—God himself.

Fasting is a way of reminding ourselves just how essential God is. It's a way of putting our love for God to the test, not so much to show God we love him but to prove to ourselves the extent of our love. Carve out a day this week and say no to food and yes to more soulful, powerful praying and deeper intimacy with your Savior.

Lord, when I fast this month (not if), please reveal yourself to me in a fresh way. Thank you that I live not by bread alone but by the Bread of Life.

Bridge of Honor

Each of you should learn to control his own body in a way
that is holy and honorable.

—1 Thessalonians 4:4

Route 1 along the California coast is dotted with bridges that traverse deep canyons, towering some two thousand feet above sea level. The integrity of these bridges has enabled us to enjoy the spectacular scenery along the ocean for years.

Steve Jensen is a middle-aged man with a wife and three kids. He's one of those bridges of the kingdom, living in a world of enormous pressures and temptations. He wrote this concerning his role:

On my bridge of honor rides the faith of my wife, to whom I have been called to be faithful. She dares to trust God for sustenance on the journey because her hands touch the strength of my honesty. Her doubts are lessened, her peace is found, her joy is made more complete as she lives for today on my bridge of honor.

On my bridge of honor journeys the hopes of children seeking life's way. They dare to dream beyond the cliffs because their feet feel the security of my integrity. Their fears are allayed, their yearnings are fanned, and their expectations are raised as they move from yesterday to tomorrow on my bridge of honor.

On my bridge of honor travels the love of the brethren in Christ. They dare to follow Jesus because they see the pillars of my love sunk deep into the heart of Jesus. Their hearts are encouraged, their hands are made strong, and their passion is ignited as they see one of their own maintain his bridge of honor.

My bridge of honor cannot bear the weight of sin's traffic. Honor is ever at risk because it is a living, breathing structure of faith made incarnate. It is fragile, prone to warp and crack under the pressures of life. It is vulnerable, exposed to elements of a sea of emotions and desires beneath it. Only God can uphold this bridge of honor over the chasm of time that is mine.

How is your bridge of honor? Protect its fragile nature by faith in Christ. It will secure a lifetime of peace for those you love.

Build and hold my bridge, O Lord, till all those whom I love have passed and my span of time has ended.

All I Care For

All I care for is to know Christ, to experience the power of
his resurrection, and to share in his sufferings, in growing
conformity with his death.
——Philippians 3:10 NEB

Paul writes, "All I care for is to know Christ." Yes, we agree with the apostle. We'd like to know Jesus better, to be on good terms with him. "All I care for is . . . to experience the power of his resurrection." Absolutely! Who wouldn't want the Lord's power in his or her life? "All I care for is . . . to share in his sufferings." Uh, sure. I guess tough times in moderate doses isn't all that bad; we all need a good soul-scrubbing now and then. "All I care for is . . . growing conformity with his death." Wait a minute; not so fast. Like, martyrdom? Chronic pain? Rejection and abuse? I really don't care to know Christ *that* badly, we silently admit to ourselves.

Most of us would love to experience the sort of closeness the apostle Paul enjoyed with Jesus. We would love to have his faith and strength of character. We yearn to live that nobly, speak that boldly, fight our vices that manfully. And who wouldn't want to have prayers answered as Paul did? But to know Christ is always a personal invitation to suffer with Christ. No one enters the Lord's intimate fellowship without first entering his fellowship of suffering. Paul knew this, but it did not deter him. The sweetness of communion with Christ far, far outweighs the sufferings.

Don't be deterred from your desire to know Christ. In your quest, the Lord promises he will never give you trials that, without his enabling, you cannot handle. He wants you to have a deep knowledge of himself, and he knows just how much—and no more—it takes to press you to his side.

I want to know you, Christ. I realize that will mean hardships and headaches, but knowing you—really knowing you—is worth it.

It's Better Together

Praise the LORD from the earth ... young men and maidens, old men and children.

—Psalm 148:7, 12

"Would you look at this? Isn't it wonderful!" My coworker Angela always beckons me away from my desk at the end of the day whenever a beautiful sunset emblazons the coastal hills by our office. She simply must share her joy with others. That's the nature of praise, isn't it?

When we consider some aspect of life praiseworthy, we simply must have others join in. Whether it's a sunset, a baby's smile, a beautiful new painting we just hung in the living room, our delight is multiplied when others enjoy that special something with us.

That's why, according to C. S. Lewis, the writers of the psalms keep encouraging us to join them in praising the Lord. They are saying, "Look, I just have to show you. . . . God is so great, you just have to praise him with me." Lewis also said, "I used to think of praise in terms of giving a compliment or approval or the giving of honor. But it's more than that. We praise the things we value, the things we enjoy. It's a spontaneous overflow. We can't help but praise what we value."[2]

I love Jesus. I enjoy and value the Lord Jesus. And yes, my delight in praising him is an expression of what I feel. But when I praise him, the joy is more complete if others join in. It's the nature of praise.

Find some aspect of nature—the texture of the tree trunk in the backyard, or a blue jay's brilliant feathers—and then rejoice in it with someone else. Consider together some glorious aspect of God. Maybe his mighty work in creation will come to mind. Or his attention to details. Or his infinite array of colors in creation. The point is to praise him with someone else.

Father God, I will come upon many reasons to praise you today. Give me the ability to see them, to take time to enjoy them, and to find someone to share them with.

His Light and Glory

The moon will be abashed, the sun ashamed; for the LORD
Almighty will reign on Mount Zion and in Jerusalem, and
before its elders, gloriously.

—Isaiah 24:23

The gray skies of winter are finally breaking apart, and the bright sunshine of spring is bursting through, touching our cheeks and caressing our shoulders. The long season of winter is almost over and, oh, how grateful we are for warmer days. It's in our nature to love light. Well . . . not in all of us. Many people love "darkness instead of light because their deeds [are] evil" (John 3:19). I've traveled around the world and am always amazed at how dark they make hotel bars in the daytime (and how many people frequent them). When you pass by lounges or adult bookstores, you can't help but notice: no windows.

It is the nature of light to expose and to show things for what they are. It is the nature of light to heal and nurture, to warm and soothe. It is the nature of light to push back the darkness (have you ever noticed how a room can be illumined by just one candle?). Darkness does not overtake light; light invades darkness. Light is always on the offensive. Light is a little like God. No, it is very much like God!

Heaven will shine by the Lamb who is the Lamp. Light will so much *be* in heaven that the sun will be ashamed. The Lord Almighty will reign gloriously. God's glory and his light go hand in hand. Heaven is a place full of glory and light.

If today is one of those bright days of spring that excite you, take it as a hint of the soon-and-coming day when the Lamb shall be the Lamp. In heaven we will, like diamonds, give off prismlike praise as every facet of our being reflects and refracts his light and glory.

On the next beautiful spring day, I will walk outside, turn my face to the sun, lift my hands, and praise you, the Light of the World, the glory of the Father.

March Winds

The wind blows wherever it pleases. You hear its sound, but you cannot tell where it comes from or where it is going. So it is with everyone born of the Spirit.

—John 3:8

I love the winds of March. The smell of the wind, bearing the fragrance of early spring blossoms. The feel of the wind, blustering and straining against the string of a kite. The sound of the wind, whispering through the pines or snapping damp sheets on a line. Jesus must have loved the wind. I can picture him feeling a cool breeze touch his face and then hearing the murmur of leaves, gesturing toward a nearby tree, and commenting, "The wind blows. You hear its sound. You can't tell where it comes from. So it is with the Spirit."

Little wonder Jesus likened the wind to the Spirit. Wind *moves*. So does the Spirit. It—or I should say, he—never stays still. He is always moving and making his presence known. And if this Holy One lives at the center of our lives, we will see, feel, and at times almost smell and hear the effects. The Spirit is constantly doing something in us. Just as we can see the effects of the wind in the trees (although we cannot see the wind itself), others will observe and appreciate the effects of the Spirit in our lives.

It's absurd to suppose you can have the Spirit of Christ within you and not see, feel, and experience his presence. The Holy Spirit will produce holy living. Paul says in Galatians 5:22–23 that "the fruit [or evidence] of the Spirit is love, joy, peace, patience, kindness, goodness, faithfulness, gentleness and self-control."

Step outside on a breezy March morning and notice that the wind marks its movement by what it touches. In its wake it leaves freshness and cleansing. As you allow the Spirit to touch your life, others will mark his presence and breathe deeply of his fragrance. They will give thanks to God . . . and thanks to you.

I sense your stirrings in my life, Lord. Move powerfully in me. Blow a fresh breeze through my soul and sweep away anything that displeases you. May I be different for it, and may others see and notice your touch.

The Stump and the Sapling

He condemned sin in sinful man, in order that the righteous requirements of the law might be fully met in us, who do not live according to the sinful nature but according to the Spirit.

—Romans 8:3–4

An ax was once laid to the root of an old crab apple tree, barely leaving the vestige of a stump above ground. The old tree was not only felled but mortally wounded, never to produce another crab apple. The owner of the orchard then grafted into the dry stump a sprig bearing the flower of Golden Delicious apples. In time a sturdy sapling had grown from the base of the stump and bore . . . what? Crab apples? No way. The fruit took on the identity and distinctiveness of the living graft, not the old stump. It was new fruit from a new tree. This delighted the owner of the orchard. But his work wasn't over. He still had to snip off crab apple sucker shoots that would sprout from the stump. As long as he did, the Golden Delicious sapling flourished.

This analogy from my pastor serves as a marvelous word picture of how, as new creatures in Christ, we are dead to sin yet alive to God. This is a difficult concept to grasp, for although the Bible says we are dead to sin, sometimes it doesn't feel like it! The story of the stump and the sapling clears it up. "Therefore, brothers, we have an obligation—but it is not to the sinful nature, to live according to it. . . . If by the Spirit you put to death the misdeeds of the body, you will live" (Rom. 8:12–13). And therefore we, who have taken on the identity and distinctiveness of Christ, have an obligation to put to death those sucker shoots of sin that, if we're not careful, will rob us of fruit that pleases God.

You are one Golden Delicious apple in the Father's eye! "You have been born again, not of perishable seed, but of imperishable, through the living and enduring word of God" (1 Peter 1:23). You have every right, every reason, and every resource today to grow and produce fruit in your life that pleases the Owner of the orchard.

Help me to recognize those shoots of sin in my life today, Lord. And then give me strength to put to death those sinful things that threaten to control.

Darkness and Light

Clouds and thick darkness surround him; righteousness
and justice are the foundation of his throne.
—Psalm 97:2

... who alone is immortal and who lives in unapproachable light, whom no one has seen or can see.
—1 Timothy 6:16

Notice a discrepancy there? Well, not really. More of a paradox. On one
hand, God is pictured as being cloaked in thick darkness; on the other,
he lives in unapproachable light. So which is it? It's both. And there's a reason why.

God wants it that way. He knows there is an inherent danger in allowing us to think we can understand him or explain him in naturalistic terms.
"Left to ourselves we tend immediately to reduce God to manageable terms.
We want to get him where we can use him, or at least know where he is when
we need him. We want a God we can in some measure control. We need the
feeling of security that comes from knowing what God is like," observes A.
W. Tozer.[3] So what does God do? He tells us he is surrounded by utter darkness and unapproachable light. *That's impossible,* we think. Exactly.

Psalm 145:3 says, "Great is the LORD and most worthy of praise; his
greatness no one can fathom." Romans 11:33 underscores, "Oh, the depth
of the riches of the wisdom and knowledge of God! How unsearchable his
judgments, and his paths beyond tracing out!" Our minds are helpless
before the great, incomprehensible God. And although we yearn to know
what can't be known and to touch and taste the unapproachable, we can
reach for the Lord Jesus. Yet even the apostle Paul said in Ephesians 3:8,
"... the *unsearchable* riches of Christ" (emphasis added).

In what ways do you think you have God figured out? Do you expect
him to act or be a certain way? He is "the Alpha and the Omega, the
Beginning and the End" (Rev. 21:6). That's impossible, you say.
Exactly. But Christ helps us break through the darkness and the light
a little. "In him and through faith in him we may approach God with
freedom and confidence" (Eph. 3:12).

*I praise you that you have disclosed not so much yourself, God, as things
about yourself in Christ. How awesome you and the Son!*

Broken Cups

This precious treasure—this light and power that now
shine within us—is held in a perishable container, that is,
in our weak bodies. Everyone can see that the glorious
power within must be from God and is not our own.

—2 Corinthians 4:7 LB

I was spring-cleaning with a friend the other day. While reaching into the
recesses of the cupboard, she accidentally dropped a cup. It didn't shatter, but the fall to the counter was enough to cause a crack. I wondered
whether to save it but in the end decided to trash it.

God, on the other hand, saves broken cups. In fact, broken vessels are
often his most useful tools. The verse for today reads like his fix-it manual.
It tells us God pours his treasure into fragile vessels that are prone to shatter. That way everyone will know God is doing the living in us.

A broken neck has taught me this. But so has a broken heart. At times,
whether in my paralysis pain or emotional pain, I have gone to God, sighing and saying, "I give up. I can't do anything right. I have no idea how to
pull myself out of this mess." The world would say, "Yep, you're useless."
The Devil would say, "Told you so." But God says, "I've been waiting for
you to come to me in your brokenness. Here, let me heal you. You need
my help, for without me you can do nothing."

What's more, Psalm 51:17 tells us God will only use a life that is broken: "The sacrifices of God are a broken spirit; a broken and contrite heart,
O God, you will not despise."

Don't be ashamed of being shattered. God is looking for broken vessels like you through whom he can showcase his splendor. Remember, when it comes to God's grace, even broken cups can be filled to
overflowing.

*Thank you, God, for not throwing away my broken life but treasuring
it and redeeming it. Use my brokenness to help others.*

Dust

He poured water into a basin and began to wash his disciples' feet, drying them with the towel that was wrapped around him.

—John 13:5

I'm a little self-conscious about my wheelchair. Don't get me wrong; I've adjusted to it. But I have this thing about dressing up in nice slacks, a pretty blouse, and earrings—and then sitting in a wheelchair that has dust on the motor casing, greasy dirt on the drive belt, or grimy fingerprints on the power box. And believe me, my wheelchair collects dust. In fact, before I enter somebody's house, I don't wipe my feet; I wipe my wheels.

It's good to keep dust from accumulating. Jesus made a point of this when he washed the dust off the disciples' feet. If you'll recall, the disciples protested at first. But Jesus reminded them that unless he washed their feet, they could have no part with him. The Lord went on to explain that a person who has had a bath needs only to wash his feet, since the rest of him is clean.

As Christians, you and I have been made clean by our salvation. Yet we can't help but gather dust from walking around in a world dirtied by sin. It's a fact: your soul gets dusty. If we don't watch it, the dust builds up into a layer of dirt. I'm reminded of this when Ken has to clean some of my wheelchair "dust" with a scouring pad and Formula 409. In the same way, I need to keep after my soul.

What about you? Stop and make a quick inspection. Do the bottoms of your shoes look as if you have tracked through a quarry? Well, you wouldn't think twice about wiping your feet before entering someone's home. Please show as much concern today about the dust on your soul.

Lord Jesus, wash me clean as I confess my lazy attitude. Show me the places in my life that have accumulated dust, places that you are eager to polish up.

He Cares for You

Cast all your anxiety on him because he cares for you.
—1 Peter 5:7

Some Christians attest that God cares so much for us, he would never want any hurt or heartache to touch us. "Why, if we really trusted in him," they reason, "God would go to any length to release us from our pain." But is this so?

While no one is saying God enjoys watching us struggle, Scripture indicates he has no qualms about allowing suffering to wound us. But it never means he no longer cares. God certainly cared for Timothy, who struggled with frequent illness. He cared for James, run through with Herod's sword because of his testimony. He cared for John, exiled on a lonely island. He cared for Stephen, even though he was dragged away from the synagogue and stoned.

God cared about Paul. He told him in his prison cell, "Take courage! As you have testified about me in Jerusalem, so you must also testify in Rome" (Acts 23:11). With that I'm sure Paul cast all his anxiety on the Lord. Yet he remained in custody for at least two years after the Lord appeared to him. Did God stop caring in those two years? Of course not. God answered his servant's prayer by giving him the kind of peace that allowed him to write, "I have learned the secret of being content in any and every situation, whether well fed or hungry, whether living in plenty or in want" (Phil. 4:12).

God's care for you goes deeper than your comfort zones. The focus of God's care is your soul. And the expression of his care will be peace and contentment. It's a beautiful promise that reminds you of God's intimate concern whether you're ill for weeks, bedridden for months, or struggling within your marriage for years. Grab hold of that truth and hang on. No matter what.

In the middle of my cares, Lord, remind me you care for me. Give me the ability to picture myself casting those concerns onto your shoulders, one anxiety at a time.

First-Line Defense

O LORD, God of our fathers, are you not the God who is in heaven? You rule over all the kingdoms of the nations. Power and might are in your hand, and no one can withstand you. . . . We have no power to face this vast army that is attacking us. We do not know what to do, but our eyes are upon you.

—2 Chronicles 20:6, 12

By all rights it was a battle God's people should never have won. The odds against King Jehoshaphat and his outnumbered troops were astronomical. The frightened king had no strategy, no chariots, no allies, no time, and no army worth writing home about.

But he had a secret weapon. He gathered the people and poured his heart out before God. He didn't rattle his saber or make a patriotic speech. He just prayed as though his life depended on it—and it did. God answered, "Do not be afraid or discouraged because of this vast army. For the battle is not yours, but God's" (2 Chron. 20:15). Within days the enemy was completely routed. The secret weapon? Praise!

When it comes to a frontline defense against the Devil's attacks, we often bypass praise and scramble to *do* something—anything—to remedy, rectify, or resolve the problem. Make lists, set goals, get counseling, go shopping, raid the fridge, read a book on the subject, or talk about it with others. But praise? Yet we learn from Jehoshaphat that praise must always be our first line of defense.

Try memorizing, if you haven't already, the doxology:

Praise God from whom all blessings flow;
Praise Him all creatures here below;
Praise Him above, ye heavenly host;
Praise Father, Son, and Holy Ghost.

Now say it! Sing it in the shower as you start your day. Think about it while you're waiting in line . . . at the fast-food drive-in, the bank window, or the grocery store checkout. Say it at the dinner table to replace your usual blessing for the food. Finally, whisper it as you feel yourself drifting off to sleep at night.

Today, Lord, may praise be my first line of defense against the Enemy.

A Humiliating Word from God

> How can you say, "I am not defiled; I have not run after the Baals"? See how you behaved in the valley; consider what you have done. You are a swift she-camel running here and there, a wild donkey accustomed to the desert, sniffing the wind in her craving—in her heat who can restrain her? Any males that pursue her need not tire themselves; at mating time they will find her.
>
> —Jeremiah 2:23–24

Every time I find pride raising its ugly head or when I feel a bit too complacent, I read the book of Jeremiah. All fifty-two chapters. I say, "So I think I have it all together? Not sullied with sin's stain?" Then I launch into the first chapter. Somewhere around Jeremiah 2:23–24 my pride deflates. God's Word hits hard: my pride sniffs out trouble like an ass in heat sniffing the wind. How humiliating!

Yes, God's Word can produce humiliation in our hearts. That's because a passage like Jeremiah 2:23–24 reveals the core of who we are. If pride has its way, evil in us will fizz to the surface and spread poison. Pride will make us hateful, and in order to avoid the scrutiny of the Spirit, we will inflict pain on ourselves and flail out at others. But who wants to live like that? I'd rather let God's Word humiliate me. Yes, it hurts to be sandblasted to the core. To be told by the Spirit that we are not as wise or winsome, loving or patient, as we thought. But when the mask of pride is ripped away, there's something refreshing about knowing ourselves at the core.

When we admit to the Lord the stain of sin in us, he gives a spirit of humility. We rise, renewed. When we begin to get a tad self-sufficient, the Spirit presses in. So we seek the humiliation of God's Word again, destroying the self-display. The transaction then is able to continue. God offers the spirit of humility as we hold fast to God's Word. Stray away from a passage like today's, and . . . humility dissipates.

Humble me by your Word today, Lord.

March 21

Grab On to Grace

See to it that no one misses the grace of God and that no
bitter root grows up to cause trouble and defile many.
—Hebrews 12:15

I love it when the gang rolls up its sleeves to help a neighbor. That happened recently when a new family moved into our church community. Friends from the congregation set aside a Saturday, donned their grubbies, and brought brushes, ladders, and paint to spiff up the place. Ken and I arrived early, he with his white painting pants on and me with a bucket of paint on my lap. But as I wheeled through the front door, I realized my wheelchair presented an obstacle to people on ladders and stools.

I had a choice. Was I going to feel sorry for myself because I couldn't take part? Or was I going to listen to Hebrews 12:15 and let no bitterness take root?

Sighing, I grabbed hold of God's grace and tried to figure out a way I could participate. I glanced out the living room window and noticed a planter with nothing in it. *It looks pretty drab,* I thought. *I'll bet my friends would appreciate a couple of geraniums.* I drove to a nursery, got one of the clerks to help, and then came back with a bag of soil and a few plants. It wasn't hard to find someone looking for an excuse to escape the paint fumes inside and eager to do some planting. Soon the red geraniums were potted to welcome the new tenants.

We make little choices for grace every day. Because every day, stuff happens. Your friend shows up late for the car pool. The bag boy drops your eggs. A friend forgets to say thank you for the gift you gave him. Your neighbor's dog leaves his calling card on your front lawn. How do you respond?

Perhaps today you are pressed up against one of those choices. Take hold of Hebrews 12:15. Choose grace. It's always the better way.

Help me, Father God, to release bitterness. Then enable me to grab on to grace—for my sake and for those around me.

No Gift Too Small

He also saw a poor widow put in two very small copper coins. "I tell you the truth," he said, "this poor widow has put in more than all the others. All these people gave their gifts out of their wealth; but she out of her poverty put in all she had to live on."

—Luke 21:2–4

Recently our ministry delivered wheelchairs to people in homes and institutions in Africa, including the Ghana Society for Crippled Boys. These African boys, for the most part, are disabled from polio. Without wheelchairs they have to drag themselves through the dirt, using their hands.

They wear shoes or thongs on their hands. They spend their weekends begging on the streets. Then, during the weekdays, they come to the Society and learn how to use sewing machines so they can develop a job skill. The Society is just a couple of cinder block huts with rusty, corrugated tin roofs . . . no running water . . . a few bare lightbulbs. But you should have seen the boys' smiles when we gave three wheelchairs (they were all we had at that point). They stopped in the middle of their work at the sewing machines to sing and clap for us with that wonderful African harmony.

I looked at the few chairs we had presented. They barely scratched the surface of need. Were we really making a difference? Was the gift meaningful? Maybe it was a gesture that only frustrated them. Perhaps it was so small that it was a mockery.

But then I remembered the words of an African pastor I met earlier that day. "No gift given to the Lord is ever too small," he said. That's the lesson I learned in Ghana, and it's a lesson we would do well to learn here. Nothing is unworthy of the Lord when it is given in his name—especially when it's all we have to give, such as the two copper coins given by the widow in today's passage. No action is unimportant, no effort too tiny.

Today you can give some gift of encouragement, some action, some small prayer. Remember, no gift is too small.

God of the widow with the mite, show me what small contribution I can make to others today—a word, a prayer, a kindness. Keep me from withholding it because of its size.

March 23

Highs and Lows

After six days Jesus took Peter, James and John with him and led them up a high mountain, where they were all alone. There he was transfigured before them.

—Mark 9:2

Then he returned to his disciples and found them sleeping.

—Mark 14:37

Does it mystify you that one day you can be on top of the world, in love with the Lord, soaring in his Spirit, having faith to see far into eternity, and the next day you go splat? You find yourself at rock bottom, your faith dried up, your spirit as dull as dishwater.

It happens to you and it happens to me. And it happened to the Lord's three best friends, Peter, James, and John. In Mark 9 they were on the Mount of Transfiguration. They got an up-close-and-personal, snow-blinded look at the dazzling glory of the Lord as he revealed himself in a way he never had before. They dropped to their knees, jaws agape, dumbstruck with wonder. What ecstasy!

Now, you would think that experience would carry the disciples for years to come. But a short time later in the Garden of Gethsemane, Jesus revealed another part of himself. He showed them how deeply distressed and troubled he was. You know what happened next: Peter, James, and John yawned, then hit rock bottom. All that spiritual get-up-and-go got up and went.

We are no better than they. We rise to some new level of spirituality and commit ourselves to a fresh allegiance to the Savior. Then we are bewildered at the depths to which we fall almost the next day.

Your spiritual life must not hinge on your commitment to Christ. That only sets you up for defeat. Rather glory in his commitment to you. Daily come to him in spiritual want and leanness. Acknowledge moment by moment that he is the one whose arms are underneath you as you rise to the mountaintop and he is the one who preserves you as you descend the other side.

Lord Jesus, thank you for your sustaining power and everlasting arms that I can lean on.

Notice the Me's

> To keep me from becoming conceited because of these sur-
> passingly great revelations, there was given me a thorn in
> my flesh, a messenger of Satan, to torment me.
> —2 Corinthians 12:7

Suffering deflates self. At least, it's supposed to. The apostle Paul inferred in this verse that affliction was given so his focus might be not on self but on the Savior. Paul said that when he was weak, God was strong. He added that his sufferings helped him to know God better. We would say the same.

So why do we squirm when we feel the thorn in our flesh? Why do we keep asking why? The clue is hidden in the questions we ask when we suffer: "Will I ever be happy again?" and "How is this fitting together for my good?" The questions themselves are technical and me-focused. Even when we hit upon good reasons why, those reasons can be centered around self:

"Suffering sure has helped me get my spiritual act together."
"I see how this trial is improving my character and prayer life."
"This tribulation has really strengthened my relationships."

Notice all the me's. God notices, too. The main point in suffering is to know God better. The subpoints are all the benefits. We must never distance God's benefits in suffering from God.

Most of us grant that hard times in moderate doses can be a good tonic for the soul. *Suffering is an important part of Christian living that we all should know more about. Just keep the heat down to a manageable level,* we think. We come unglued, however, if suffering has us at the end of our rope. But that's not a bad place to be. At that point we are forced to think about a greater suffering and turn to Christ on the cross. Don't ponder "me" if you're hurting today . . . ponder the Messiah.

Teach me through hard times about you, Lord. Not me but you.

The Annunciation

> In the sixth month, God sent the angel Gabriel to
> Nazareth, a town in Galilee, to a virgin pledged to be married
> to a man named Joseph, a descendant of David. The
> virgin's name was Mary.
>
> —Luke 1:26–27

Today marks exactly nine months until Christmas. It was around this time the angel announced to Mary she would give birth to the Lord. Mary was at first afraid of this "birth announcement," but then she rejoiced at the thought of being the mother of the Messiah. She went straight to her cousin, Elizabeth, with the fantastic news.

Elizabeth had good news of her own. Although she was old and childless, she was also expecting. Mary and Elizabeth had plenty to hobnob about. For three months these two moms-to-be delighted in their miracles. They probably did all the first-century versions of things expectant mothers do today: knitted baby clothes, collected blankets, diapers, bibs, toys, rattles, and pacifiers (a small piece of chamois, maybe?). I picture them as two birds on a perch, chattering and chirping about their impending families. Expectant mothers deserve this kind of luxury, right?

But just at the time Mary was due, there came a big switch in plans. Uprooted from her house, Mary embarked on the long, dusty journey to Bethlehem. She may have thought, *Nobody who's nine months pregnant should be riding a donkey over these rough roads. . . . Here we are in Bethlehem, and the place is a zoo. People shoving, shouting. Everywhere we look, all we see are "no vacancy" signs. . . . Surely God has things backward. None of this makes sense.*

Perhaps Mary wrestled with those thoughts. But then she submitted, as she always had, to the lordship of God in her life.

Is your situation askew? Do you wonder what God is up to? If plans in your life are going haywire right now, join Mary in submitting. The outcome might just be miraculous.

When the puzzles of life have me stymied, Lord, help me to lean on you and trust your choices for me.

March 26

Follow the Leader

When the princes in Israel take the lead, when the people
willingly offer themselves—praise the LORD!

—Judges 5:2

Deborah and Barak had just broken twenty years of oppression under
Jabin. They erupted in a song of victory, a victory that had been
assured by God. Their song opened with a simple statement of the obvious: The leaders led. And the people volunteered.

Their song captures a world of management theories, military policies, and parenting techniques. But most importantly it describes a victorious church. Churches whose leaders lead and whose people offer
themselves willingly cannot be stopped. There is not one inch of Satan's
gates that can withstand the cooperative venture of people leading and following according to the will of God.

And there's the rub—God's will. Many a leader and follower have
fought battles of their own making. Deborah and Barak would not have
had a chance against Jabin's nine hundred chariots if God had not wanted
Canaan to be defeated. Likewise there is not one venture in our churches
that can have any effect for God's kingdom if it is not decreed by him.

Our task is to search the Scriptures and see how plain and direct
God's commands are for the church: make disciples, love one
another, be salt and light, show compassion, and more. To claim
these victories, we need you to lead or follow. Are you a leader? Lead.
Lead courageously. Are you a follower? Follow. Follow willingly.

Enjoy the parade!

*Lead on, O King eternal, in our church and in my life. Help us to see
your will. Bring leaders and followers together. Make me to know my
place in such a victorious quest.*

What If?

> If the dead are not raised, then Christ has not been raised either. And if Christ has not been raised, your faith is futile; you are still in your sins. Then those also who have fallen asleep in Christ are lost. If only for this life we have hope in Christ, we are to be pitied more than all men.
>
> —1 Corinthians 15:16–19

I once heard a Christian on a religious television program say with glee, "The Christian life is so great, I'd believe it even if it weren't true." Her cohost agreed and added, "Even if in the end we found out that the whole thing is not true, I'd still be glad for all the spiritual disciplines that have helped us live better lives." Something about their words did not sit well. Would we honestly say, "It was a good life anyway" if we ultimately discovered that Scientology was the real answer?

The apostle Paul had an answer: "If only for this life we have hope in Christ, *we are to be pitied more than all men*" (emphasis added). This is how critical the resurrection of Christ is. If Christ is not raised from the dead, our faith is not only futile but a mockery. Our pain has no purpose. If no resurrection, the universe is ruled by the roll of the dice. Unlike the hosts of the religious program, I wouldn't weakly smile and say, "Well, it was worth the try." I would collapse in horror.

"But Christ has indeed been raised from the dead, the firstfruits of those who have fallen asleep" (1 Cor. 15:20). Take a moment and consider all that Christ's resurrection means. The cross satisfied God's justice and holiness. A way was opened up by which to know the Father. Not just our souls but our bodies will one day be redeemed. Our suffering is not in vain, and our hardships fit into a plan for our good and God's glory. We have escaped hell. Heaven is our inheritance. Alleluia, Christ is risen! He is risen indeed!

I'm relieved Good Friday didn't have the last say . . . Sunday did! Thank you, Lord, for all that your resurrection means.

March 28

Silence Was Golden

> "Where do you come from?" he asked Jesus, but Jesus gave
> him no answer.
>
> —John 19:9

The cold chamber is dimly lit. It's two o'clock in the morning. Jesus is shoved, stumbling, up the rich, red carpet to stand in front of Pontius Pilate, who has been rudely awakened to hear the case of this King of the Jews. But Pilate hadn't been sleeping anyway. The night before, he had drunk too much, partied too long, and smoked too many cigarettes. (When I think of Pilate, I can't help but picture him with a cigarette hanging out of his mouth, even though I know cigarettes didn't exist back then.)

I imagine Pilate rubbing his chin and asking a few questions, to the first of which Jesus replies, "Everyone on the side of truth listens to me." Jesus' answer is thought-provoking. *What does this uneducated peasant know about truth?* I can imagine Pilate thinking. So he reaches for a pack of cigarettes, lights up, and squints through the haze of smoke. "Tell me," he sneers as he takes a drag, "what is truth?"

A long moment passes as the smoke clears. Jesus is silent. He says . . . nothing. The suspense mounts. Finally, in disgust, Pilate flicks an ash on the floor. The suspense drains.

Why was the Lord silent? He could have defended himself. Maybe that's the key. How can you say in twenty-five words or less that you are the Lord of the universe? Maybe Jesus' lack of words was the best way to answer. Perhaps more meaning was crammed into that moment of silence than we can imagine. Heaven may have been whispering, "Be still and know that the Lord is God." (The idea for this story came from Robert Farrar Capon.)

How do you respond when God is silent? With fear? Doubt? Impatience? Maybe the Lord is being silent so you might know in a new way that he is the Lord of the universe.

Teach me, Jesus, to sit and wait for word from you, as long as it might take. And give me the ability to hear your answer in the stillness.

A Costly Offering

The king replied to Araunah, "No, I insist on paying you for it. I will not sacrifice to the LORD my God burnt offerings that cost me nothing." So David bought the threshing floor and the oxen and paid fifty shekels of silver for them.
—2 Samuel 24:24

Araunah the Jebusite was just being polite. When he found out that David wanted to purchase his threshing floor to build an altar, he bent over backward and offered his oxen for the sacrificial offering, as well as the wood on which to burn it. David wouldn't hear of it. If it was going to be a true sacrifice, David knew that he himself would have to sacrifice something. Like his hard-earned cash.

With us, it doesn't have to be our cash. It could be our time or our prayers, our gifts and talents. I'm thinking right now of Carolyn, a seamstress friend of mine who barely makes ends meet by sewing and tailoring. Carolyn lives alone in her small apartment with her cat and works late into the night, stitching up a storm. Last Christmas she wasn't able to buy the gifts she would have liked, so she went one better—she stayed up extra late, making presents of skirts and vests. Her friends were going to receive the best she could offer, even if it meant missing a deadline on a commission, even if it meant early hours and sore fingers. Those skirts and vests are, to us blessed folks who received them, more valuable than anything you'd purchase at Saks Fifth Avenue.

Oswald Chambers has said, "Our notion of sacrifice is the wringing out of us something we don't want to give up, full of pain and agony and distress. The Bible idea of sacrifice is that I give as a love-gift the very best thing I have."[4]

What is your best thing? No doubt it is something that has cost you. When we offer our best, it always takes a bite out of something we hold dear—whether it's our billfold, time, friendships, sleep, food, pride, or our clothes closet. Always offer to God your best.

If I offer you something today, may it be my best. If it's not, Lord, stop me from thinking of it as an offering!

March 30

You're an Example

You will receive power when the Holy Spirit comes on you;
and you will be my witnesses in Jerusalem, and in all Judea
and Samaria, and to the ends of the earth.

—Acts 1:8

People are watching you. If they know you're a Christian, they are *really* watching. And sometimes they're watching when you least expect it.

The other day I purchased a new computer (my old one had crashed). Instead of making life simpler, the new computer had me lost in a sea of special commands and option keys. I flipped open my owner's manual and rang up the 800-number. A machine answered and presented me with layers of messages to work my way through. That only added to my frustration. Finally I spoke to a real person. "Hi, I'm Michelle, and I'm here to help you. First, what's your name?"

I growled, "Joni—spelled J-o-n-i but pronounced 'Johnny.' I hope you can help me."

After a silence on the other end, Michelle said, "Are you *the* Joni Eareckson Tada?"

I'd been caught. Here I was about to chew out this lady and her computer company, but she knew who I was. She said with a laugh, "I know who you are, so you can't get too frustrated with me!" At that point we both laughed; she was right.

Should you, as a Christian, weigh every word? Never tell a lie? Always keep your temper under control? Say only what you mean and mean what you say? Of course. When you name the name of Christ, people expect you to act like him. Is that a bad thing? Not at all; for the Christian, it's reasonable.

Now, you can do your part well and build up other Christians as well as make unbelievers thirsty for God, or you can act out your frustrations and defame Christ's name. You have received a high calling—even when your computer isn't working.

Lord Jesus, enable me to live in a way that honors you. When others aren't looking or when I think I'm anonymous, remind me that you see me and know just who I am.

March 31

Good Friday

They put a purple robe on him, then twisted together a crown of thorns and set it on him.... Again and again they struck him on the head with a staff and spit on him.... And when they had mocked him ... they led him out to crucify him.

—Mark 15:17, 19–20

Some things are bitter and sweet at the same time. Certain kinds of fruit can be sour yet sweet. How about when a woman gives birth? She's in pain yet she feels joy. Yes, a person can experience two different things at the same moment. Good Friday is both bitter and sweet.

That's why, as a kid, I was so moved when I attended the Good Friday services at our little Reformed Episcopal church. The service was somber. Sometimes a black cloth was draped over the Communion table. Sad hymns were sung like "O Sacred Head Now Wounded":

O sacred Head, now wounded,
With grief and shame weighed down,
Now scornfully surrounded
With thorns, Thine only crown;
O sacred Head, what glory,
What bliss till now was Thine!
Yet, though despised and gory,
I joy to call Thee mine.

Most of all I recall leaving the church in silence. No one casually chatted out in the narthex. It was the one day of the church year that our congregation would come together in a somber mood. As a child, the seriousness of the occasion was branded in my memory. I'm glad. Happy Scripture choruses were appropriate for Resurrection Sunday, but Friday night was for pondering the incredible weight of our sins on our Savior.

At some point today, even if just for ten minutes, meditate on Calvary. Think about the cross. Contemplate the pain our Savior went through to secure our right to sing lighthearted Scripture choruses. Good Friday is a day to taste something sweet and something sour.

Lord Jesus, bring to my mind during the bustle of everyday life that Good Friday was the day you died. Thank you for that unspeakably enormous sacrifice.

APRIL

April 1

The Easter Spirit

Grieve, mourn and wail. Change your laughter to mourning and your joy to gloom. Humble yourselves before the
Lord, and he will lift you up.

—James 4:9–10

Remember a few months ago when you were in the Christmas spirit?
The laughter, the joy, and all the good feelings? Now that we're
approaching Easter, the obvious question is, "Are you in the Easter spirit?"
Does that strike you as odd? It should. You hardly ever hear people talking about getting into the spirit of Easter. And there's a good reason why.

Never in the history of the church have Christians associated happiness and good feelings with the time leading up to Good Friday. You cannot sentimentalize the gruesome carnage that happened at Calvary. The
cross is nothing to laugh about (it's probably why we don't have parties
during the Easter season as we do at Christmastime). These weeks leading
up to Good Friday place us in the middle of the Lenten season. This is a
time of self-examination and somber reflection on the pain our sins gave
Christ.

If the Easter season is to have a spirit about it, it's the spirit of repentance. Only when we contemplate the full weight of our transgressions can
we genuinely celebrate all that happened on Resurrection Sunday. When
we consider the depth of our depravity, we are able to fully enjoy the height
of our happiness over Christ's victory from the grave. Our joy is only as
real, deep, and sincere as our grief over our sin—otherwise we have no
idea what he's saved us from.

The Easter spirit can't be mustered up with baskets of eggs, chocolate
rabbits, hot cross buns, or honey-baked hams. This stuff has about as
much connection to the real meaning of Lent as Santa Claus has to
Christmas. To get into the spirit of this season, ask yourself, "What
thing, habit, person, or fantasy—what is it I can bring to the cross?"

*I humbly ask for the spirit of repentance, O Lord. Help me to truly
lament my sins . . . so I can indeed celebrate your resurrection.*

April 2

Sentimentality and Jesus

God raised him from the dead, freeing him from the agony
of death, because it was impossible for death to keep its
hold on him.

—Acts 2:24

Have you ever noticed that we treat a person or an object sentimentally
because of emotion, not reason? That's certainly true when it comes to
the sentimental pictures we have of Jesus: Jesus with his hair parted down
the middle, surrounded by cherublike children and bluebirds. Everywhere
this Jesus walks, strains of organ music sound.

We even have sentimental hymns about the Lord. "He speaks and the
sound of his voice is so sweet, the birds hush their singing." That's a line
from one of my father's favorite hymns, and I know those thoughts can
comfort us. But they are more reinforcement of a romanticized image. We
have gilded the real Jesus with so much "dew on the roses" that many
people have lost touch with him.

Why do we prefer a sentimental picture? It requires nothing from us,
neither conviction nor commitment. Because it lacks truth, it lacks power.
We have to change that picture. And one way to do it is to think about
the Resurrection. Sure, romanticists try to color the Resurrection with lilies
and birds, but lay aside the emotions and think of the facts for a moment:
a man, stone-cold dead, rose from his slab and walked out of his grave.

That's almost frightening. But that's what Jesus did. That reality has
power; it's truth that grips you. Some people believe Jesus came to do nice,
sweet things like turn bad people into good people. Not so. Our Lord and
Savior came to turn dead people into living people—and there's nothing
sentimental about that.

Erase images of syrupy sweetness. Replace them with mental pictures
of a powerful God who overcame the harshest foe—death itself.
Then you will begin to grasp how amazing God really is.

*Lord of all, refocus my softened view of you onto aspects of yourself that
demand much more of me. And help me to respond to what I see.*

April 3

Brooke Schrader

> Out of the same mouth come praise and cursing. My brothers, this should not be. Can both fresh water and salt water flow from the same spring?
>
> —James 3:10–11

Brooke Schrader walked into my office last week, an eleven-year-old girl with soft blond hair, a smattering of freckles, pixielike eyes, and a full mouth that easily broke into a grin. She was joined by her mother and pastor. They thought it would be good for her to meet another person who is facing tough limitations. Brooke has juvenile arthritis. I would never have guessed except that her mother pointed out Brooke's fused ankle. After that I noticed how Brooke kept squeezing her hands and rubbing her knuckles. I also noticed her stiff gait. She was in a lot of pain. But her smile never showed it.

I asked if Brooke and I could spend some time alone in my art studio. We sat and talked about her friends at school, her hobbies, and her interest in art. Our discussion turned to spiritual things. I asked what her favorite verse was, thinking it might be the typical "John 3:16" or "Romans 8:28" most kids would choose. I was not prepared for her answer. Brooke proudly quoted our verse for today.

This eleven-year-old girl with the ready smile explained, "I could do a lot of complaining about my arthritis, but I've learned that's not right. I want to trust God." Brooke's eyes held mine, revealing a wisdom far beyond her years. Her gaze burned right through me. I squirmed and privately confessed my disobedience in grumbling over a backache earlier in the day.

When Brooke left, a trail of some fresh scent remained. She had cleared the stuffy air in my office, reminding me I have nothing to complain about. God used a little child to lead me. "'Do you hear what these children are saying?' they asked him. 'Yes,' replied Jesus, 'have you never read, "From the lips of children and infants you have ordained praise"?'" (Matt. 21:16).

Lord, show me your wisdom through a child this week.

April 4

A True Disciple

A little later someone else saw him and said, "You also are
one of them." "Man, I am not!" Peter replied.

—Luke 22:58

Peter's denial is a well-known story. It heightens the drama of the Crucifixion. It underscores the forsaken nature of Christ's death. And more
importantly it serves as a vivid reminder of the ability in all of us to deny
our Savior. Dr. Craig Barnes, in his book *Yearning*, points out, however,
that Peter's denial was not a lie but rather the truth.

> Why does Peter fail? Is he a coward? Apparently not. Earlier that
> same night Peter went charging with a sword into the crowd that
> arrested Jesus. It's doubtful that Peter denies Jesus because he is afraid
> of dying. I think Peter denies he is a disciple because it is the truth.
> He knows now that Jesus is going to a cross. From the start Jesus
> has been determined to go there. Peter has tried hard to save him from
> the cross, to talk him out of it, even raising his sword in an act of hero-
> ism. But Jesus has turned his face toward the cross, and there is no
> turning him back. Peter simply cannot follow Jesus to the cross. So he
> takes his place by the fire with those who have taken Jesus captive.
> The questions just keep coming: "Are you a disciple?" The truth is
> finally out: "No. No. No." This isn't Peter's moment of denial. It is
> his moment of confession. He is not a disciple. He never has been.
> What he has been following is not Jesus, but his expectations of Jesus.[1]

The day we recognize the difference between our expectations of
Jesus and the real Jesus is the first day of our journey as a true disci-
ple. Tell the truth. Have you been a disciple of eternal security or of
Jesus the King of Heaven? Have you been a disciple of civility or of
Jesus the Holy One? Have you been a disciple of warmth and fel-
lowship or of Jesus the True Love?

Don't be afraid of the truth. Jesus firmly and tenderly restored
Peter to the status of a true disciple and then commissioned him to
shepherd other disciples.

*Lord Jesus, crucify every false expectation of who you are. Make me a
disciple who confesses the truth and then confesses you, without fear.*

April 5

The Puzzle Fits

Concerning this salvation, the prophets, who spoke of the
grace that was to come to you, searched intently and with
the greatest care, trying to find out the time and circumstances to which the Spirit of Christ in them was pointing. . . . It was revealed to them that they were not serving
themselves but you.

—1 Peter 1:10–12

The Spirit of Christ moved the prophets to write the books of the Bible
and then, after they penned the Word of God, they searched intently
and with the greatest care to understand what in the world they had written! It was a little like trying to solve a puzzle.

Consider the book of Genesis. Chapter after chapter unfolds into a
neatly organized story, from Abraham to Isaac, Jacob to Joseph. In fact,
just as Joseph's story is getting really interesting—bam!—chapter 38 takes
a weird turn with an odd and sordid story of incest between Judah and
Tamar. The chapter ends with Tamar giving birth to Perez. And then the
story of Joseph picks right up where it left off, as if that thing between
Tamar and Judah had never happened.

But it did. And it must have driven Moses, the prophet who penned
Genesis, crazy. He had a real puzzle on his hands! Why had God inspired
him to write such a thing? As many times as Moses must have searched
intently with the greatest care to understand how it fit, he came up empty-
handed. The puzzle couldn't be solved.

But as today's verse says, Moses was not serving himself but you. The
puzzle pieces fit for us. When Matthew 1:3 records the genealogy of
Jesus, guess who shows up? Tamar, the mother of Perez, the fore-
runner of Boaz, the great-grandfather of King David, whose descen-
dant was the Messiah, Jesus Christ. Thousands of years before the
birth of Christ, God inspired Moses to take a detour and write about
Tamar. Moses had no idea that this story of incest needed to be
recorded so we might understand the generosity of the Father in placing Tamar in the family tree!

*Lord, when I see these puzzle pieces of your Word fit together, it proves
how divinely inspired the Bible really is.*

God's Word at Work

My God, my God, why have you forsaken me?

—Psalm 22:1

You're already aware that Jesus quoted this verse when he hung on the cross. Aside from it being a prophetic utterance, it was still an agonizing and honest question voiced from the gut of the Son of Man as he died. What amazes me is that our Lord, even in the time of his deepest agony, was showing us the way.

The way in suffering is to keep voicing the Word of God. Something suffering-shaking happens when we handpick a psalm or some other portion of Scripture to give expression to our heart-wrenching questions. "For the word of God is living and active" (Heb. 4:12). Our words become alive and active because they are God's words. We are speaking God's language, echoing his own vocabulary back to him. When we wrap our heartache around a biblical psalm, it's a way of searching for him. And when we seek, we will find (Matt. 7:7–8).

Gut-wrenching questions honor God. Despair directed at God is a way of encountering him, opening ourselves up to the one and only Someone who can do something about our plight. And when, with our questions, we either collide with the Almighty or merely bump up against him, we can never be the same. We never are when we experience God.

If you have something to voice to God today, borrow your words from a passage of Scripture. God delights in his children when we speak his language. "'Is not my word like fire,' declares the LORD, 'and like a hammer that breaks a rock in pieces?'" (Jer. 23:29). God's Word is *powerful*. Even the angels are moved into action at the mention of his Word (Ps. 103:20). Encounter the Lord today through his Word!

If I'm to speak your language, Lord, I need to know your Word. Direct me today to those passages through which I can voice my questions, gratitude, petitions, and praise to you. I'm looking forward to encountering you in your Word.

Palm Sunday

> The righteous will flourish like a palm tree, they will grow like a cedar of Lebanon; planted in the house of the LORD, they will flourish in the courts of our God. They will still bear fruit in old age, they will stay fresh and green, proclaiming, "The LORD is upright; he is my Rock, and there is no wickedness in him."
>
> —Psalm 92:12–15

What a day Palm Sunday must have been! People spreading their garments on the dirt road, frantically waving branches of palm and shouting at the top of their lungs, "Blessed is he who comes in the name of the Lord!" Expectations were at a feverish pitch: *Jesus will throw out the Romans! He'll release us from the terrible burden of these taxes! Jesus will feed us, provide for us, and protect us. We're ready to crown him our king!*

As the week wore on, everyone's mood shifted. People couldn't understand why Jesus wasn't making his move. Although he continued to heal and teach, he remained strangely aloof—a real recluse. He kept retreating to a nearby village every night, far removed from the power brokers and political hotshots in the city. Why wasn't he getting on with the agenda? Why wasn't he taking control? Little wonder they began to think, *Maybe this man's not all he's cracked up to be. Perhaps he's been pulling the wool over our eyes all this time. It was all just a fluke.* The rest is history. Not more than a week passed and they were clamoring for his crucifixion.

I wonder . . . are we all that different? When our expectations are running high, when we think we've got God's plan neatly figured, when we've even convinced ourselves that the King's job is to make our lives easier, relieve our burdens, and lighten our pressures, do we cave in to doubts if God doesn't come through?

The King's agenda is to make you fit for service in the kingdom. He may not relieve your burdens or lighten pressures, but you can be sure he'll do all he can to conform you to his image. As Easter week approaches, do a double check on your praises. Let's be certain we give Jesus praise for who he is rather than what we think he ought to be.

Blessed are you, Lord Jesus. My heart is a palm branch of praise. Hosanna in the highest. You are King!

April 8

The Passover Lamb

> They are to take some of the blood and put it on the sides and tops of the doorframes of the houses where they eat the lambs. . . . On that same night I will pass through Egypt and strike down every firstborn. . . . The blood will be a sign for you on the houses where you are; and when I see the blood, I will pass over you. No destructive plague will touch you when I strike Egypt.
>
> —Exodus 12:7, 12–13

We usually think of the Day of Atonement as a time of sin sacrifice. It was during Atonement Day—sometime in the month equivalent to our August—that the nation of Israel sought reconciliation for its sins. After sacrificing a bullock, the high priest chose a goat for a sin offering and sacrificed it. After that a scapegoat bearing the sins of the people was sent into the wilderness—this scapegoat symbolized the pardon for sin brought through the sacrifice. With all this emphasis on sin and sacrifice, ever wonder why Jesus didn't go to the cross on the Day of Atonement?

God chose Passover rather than the Day of Atonement as the time his Son would go to the cross. Jesus is not symbolized as a bullock or a goat but a lamb. At the first Passover in Egypt, it was the blood of a lamb that was smeared on the sides and tops of the doorframes, ensuring that the firstborn of the family would not be killed. God provided a way for his people to escape judgment. He provided deliverance. He provided a means of rescue.

This is what God provided through Christ's death and resurrection. A way of escape. A deliverance. The Day of Atonement was an opportunity for the people to do something for God; Passover symbolizes a time when God did something for his people. So also it is true of the cross—we have done nothing for it, but it has done everything for us.

Notice that the blood of the lamb was not smeared on the threshold of the doors of the Israelites' homes. The blood was not to be trampled underfoot. The lesson is for us today: Christ has rescued us through his precious blood. May we never tread on his gift nor crush underfoot his favor.

Praise you, Lord Jesus, for rescuing and delivering me just as you delivered the Israelites from judgment. Thank you, Lamb of God.

April 9

A Really Big Inheritance

> I pray also that the eyes of your heart may be enlightened
> in order that you may know the hope to which he has called
> you, the riches of his glorious inheritance in the saints.
> —Ephesians 1:18

You could use up a month of Sundays thinking about all Jesus secured for us. That's what the Scripture for today talks about—our inheritance.

It all began in the garden with Adam and Eve and their decision to disobey. We lost innocence and our right to rule—everything, really. However, God had a plan, a plan that involved the cross.

But wait. . . . Jesus did a lot more at the cross than buy back our innocence. He didn't purchase our redemption just so we could get back to the garden and be reinstated alongside Adam. Thank heavens, God had much more in mind than that. The Father's marvelous plan was that we would end up as co-heirs not with Adam but with Christ. We don't gain Adam's innocence; we gain Christ's righteousness! For "the gift is not like the trespass. For if the many died by the trespass of the one man, how much more did God's grace and the gift that came by the grace of the one man, Jesus Christ, overflow to the many!" (Rom. 5:15).

If God had in mind merely to restore us to our state in the Garden of Eden, we would, like Adam, be children of God and subdue the earth. But as believers in the Lord Jesus, we are a brand-new creation. Our inheritance with our elder brother, Jesus, means that we will rule over not only a new earth but also the new heavens. All the treasures of the heavens that belong to the Lord will one day belong to us as well.

Adam and Eve could never have hoped for that. Theirs was a state of bliss and innocence. But secured for us is a state of joy and righteousness. We are much more than co-heirs with Adam. There are so many things that happened at the cross to thank God for. Take a few minutes to do just that.

Father, touch my heart so my gratitude would abound for all you have done.

April 10

Exponential Blessings

"Well done, my good servant!" his master replied. "Because you have been trustworthy in a very small matter, take charge of ten cities."

—Luke 19:17

I love serving God. And if we've been faithful in earthly service, our responsibility in heaven will increase proportionately. No, I take that back. It won't be increased in proportion. God is too generous for that. Our service will increase completely out of proportion. It doesn't take a rocket scientist to read the formula Jesus gives in his heaven parable in Luke 19:17.

In fact, read it again. Ten cities? In exchange for faithfulness in a very small matter? Not just small but *very* small? Whoa! When it comes to blessing us, Jesus goes beyond basic math and blows the lid off calculus. Those who are faithful on this earth in a few minor things will have the pleasure and privilege of being put in charge over multitudinous matters. Are you faithful in your marriage or mission? Even if only in a small way? God is already thinking exponentially, as in his "ten cities" equation. He will generously raise your capacity for service (and thus joy) to the nth degree. The more faithful you are in this life, the more responsibility you will be given in the life to come.

If such large responsibility frightens you, don't panic. He will fit you for your heavenly task. And are you worried about getting tired? Would you rather heaven be a place of rest? It will! "There remains . . . a Sabbath-rest for the people of God; for anyone who enters God's rest also rests from his own work" (Heb. 4:9–10). In heaven your service will be utterly serene. You will be busier than ever yet completely at peace. Perfectly active yet eternally at rest.

Help me, Lord, to be faithful in the small but important matters you've entrusted to me. And thank you in advance for recognizing my humble service on earth.

April 11

Your Destiny

If anyone obeys his word, God's love is truly made complete in him.

—1 John 2:5

I made a tough decision the other day. My desires were pulling me one way, my conscience the other. What made it tougher was that it was a watershed decision for me, a crossing of the Rubicon, an "I never can turn back" for me. By God's grace I rose to the occasion and chose the right course. At once I felt an incredible sense of freedom, as though invisible chains had fallen off me.

Why is it that when we obey, we feel so *free?* Peter Kreeft suggests, "Since our highest freedom means freedom to be ourselves, we are most free when we are most obedient to God's will, which expresses his idea of us. Thus freedom and obedience coincide. To obey God is to be free in the most radical sense: free from false *being*."[2]

At the moment of the most-free choice, it feels most like destiny, and at the moment when you feel destined to make a certain choice, it feels so free. You've experienced this when you chose to accept Christ as your Savior, or you may have sensed this when you said, "I do" at the altar. C. S. Lewis's explanation of this principle is that it is all of us that chooses, with nothing left over.

When you obey God in wholehearted devotion, you step closer toward his idea of who he has determined you to be: the real you, the you he predetermined before the foundation of the world. This means that when you obey God, in the process you discover who you are. You know yourself better than before. You become the more excellent you, and therefore you step into your destiny. What freedom! And it can happen to you today as you obey.

Empower me to obey you today, Lord. It brings glory to you, and it brings me closer to my true self.

April 12

Mother Memories

Her children arise and call her blessed.

—Proverbs 31:28

Today is my mother's birthday, and for her I have a message: Mother, I love the crazy, wonderful way you raised my sisters and me. I remember the time you turned off the oven, untied your apron, and called us to walk with you to watch the sunset. The brilliant splash of pink and purple will stick in my mind forever. I love the way you made us night people. I'm sure it stemmed from the evenings on the back porch when we would watch the moonrise with you and Daddy as you both sang songs from the forties.

How I loved going beach camping and remember your strapping me into that bulky life preserver and tossing me into the waves. I didn't want to tell you how frightened I was of the gigantic swells. You hung on to my straps, and that was enough to chase the fear. Thank you for helping me to face fright head-on. Mother, do you recall watching Daddy hoist me into my new saddle on Thunder, that big Appaloosa? I cantered into the pasture, whooping and hollering. But I knew you were biting your nails, wondering if I could hang on. I love you for letting me be brave.

And thanks, Mom, for playing hopscotch with me. It seemed embarrassing that you, a grown woman, would toss an oak bark chip and jump around. But on the inside I was proud of you. Thank you for teaching me to appreciate older people. Thank you for teaching me about God. And table manners. For visiting me in the hospital nearly every day for more than a year after I broke my neck. What a mother.

Who taught you the important lessons of life? Write a letter listing a few of the memories you treasure and the lessons you learned. If that person is still alive, send the letter. If not, keep it for yourself as a reminder of how blessed you were.

Lord, thank you for placing in my life people who taught me how to live. Help me to pass on the lessons.

April 13

A Promised Peace

Do not let your hearts be troubled. Trust in God; trust also in me.

—John 14:1

Spring fulfills a promise given before winter that life will return. "Wait and you'll see," the tangled, bare branches seem to say in late autumn. "Life will return in full green." The assurance that spring will come back helps us make it through the drearier days of winter.

The same promise of return is often spoken between loved ones. Every little girl has heard it from her mom at the nursery door. Every beloved has heard it from her husband at the airport. Every mother has heard it from her soldier son.

During such partings, promises of soon returns are spoken because the one leaving seeks peace for the one being left. "I'll be back" must be said or no peace will be found.

The words are not enough, however. Only when the hearer truly believes does the promise become effectual. Assurance of a reunion has a calming influence. Such was the peace that calmed the disciples when Jesus left them. He told them that their hearts should not be troubled. That they should wait. That he would come back to get them. Just as he would come back for you and me.

His resurrection must have had a profound effect on the disciples' ability to believe. After Jesus went up into the clouds, they recalled that he not only promised his resurrection but delivered on that promise. The immense peace that settled on them was evident as they obeyed his command to wait for the Holy Spirit and then to declare the gospel.

How does Jesus' assurance that he will be back affect you? Which of his words could you concentrate on that would help you to believe? What signs of spring has God tucked into your winter?

Creator of all seasons, open my eyes to promises of new life slipped into even the dreariest of situations. Give me the ability to believe they are harbingers of the good things you have in store for me.

April 14

Big and Small Miracles

So that we may not offend them, go to the lake and throw
out your line. Take the first fish you catch; open its mouth
and you will find a four-drachma coin.

—Matthew 17:27

If you made a list of all the big creation miracles Jesus did before he came
to earth, what would be on it? My list contains galaxies, black holes, solar
systems, the law of gravity, the law of thermodynamics, the atmosphere, the
asteroid belt, constellations, and photosynthesis. All of them are God-sized
wonders.

When this same Lord lived in Palestine, he performed smaller-scale
miracles: withering a fig tree; finding a coin in the fish's mouth; healing
Peter's mother-in-law of a fever; restoring a man's shriveled hand. He performed powerful miracles but at a different speed and on a smaller scale
than when he created the cosmos.

C. S. Lewis said the Lord's earthly miracles are a retelling in small letters of the very same story that is written across the whole universe in letters too large for some to see. How exciting to look up into the heavens and
realize that a personal God created in a personal way all that we see. Stars,
suns, and galaxies are the very stamp of his power and personality. And
this same Lord of creation loves you and me.

But I think the most epic of all miracles will be raising us up and transforming our lowly bodies into glorious bodies like our Lord's. Talk about
power that's personal! The law of gravity will be turned upside down, and
the resurrection of the dead will be written across the whole universe in
letters large enough for everyone to see.

Make a point of looking up into the heavens tonight. Even if it's
overcast, there's a magnificence to it all. Contemplate how marvelous
God's creation is, including you.

*Just as David prayed, thanking you for being mindful of him despite
how infinitesimally small he was in light of your creation, I join him in
that thought, Lord. Thank you that I am significant to you.*

April 15

A Story of Friendship

Mephibosheth lived in Jerusalem, because he always ate at
the king's table, and he was crippled in both feet.

—2 Samuel 9:13

I relish stories about love, not just the romantic kind between a man and woman but love between any two people. One of the most beautiful love stories in the Bible is the story of Jonathan and David.

Their souls were knit together, the Bible says (1 Sam. 18:1 KJV). Like-hearted, like-minded, standing shoulder to shoulder, looking face-forward together, theirs is a unique story. Even though their friendship ended in tragedy, David's love for Jonathan, his extraordinary friend, lived on through David's relationship with Jonathan's disabled son, Mephibosheth. David's love for Jonathan went beyond the grave: "Set me as a seal upon thine heart, as a seal upon thine arm: for love is strong as death" (Song 8:6 KJV).

Mephibosheth should have been hunted down and killed by David, because Jonathan's son could have posed a threat to the throne. But remember, love is stronger than death. So Mephibosheth enjoyed a place prepared just for him at the king's table.

Perhaps King David saw in the young man's face the features of his beloved friend. Maybe when Mephibosheth smiled, David could see a vestige of Jonathan's grin. The young man could have had his father's eyes. His inflections. Plus, the two shared memories of the loved one they had in common.

It's a love story, all right. And maybe, like Mephibosheth, we might cry out to God, "What is your servant, that you should notice a dead dog like me?" (2 Sam. 9:8). We should know the answer. It lies in this story of love and friendship.

God the Father invites us to his table to commune with him, because he sees in our countenance the remembrance of his dearly beloved Son. There is something about us, those of us who are hid with Christ, that shows a trace of Jesus. Little wonder that God delights to welcome us to his table.

It is for Jesus' sake that he raises us from poverty to nobility. Now that's a love story.

God, our Father, thank you for looking on me and seeing Jesus in me. Thank you for your loving grace and for allowing me to be a part of the greatest love story ever.

April 16

"I Need You"

He said to them, "My soul is overwhelmed with sorrow to
the point of death. Stay here and keep watch with me."
—Matthew 26:38

Jesus and his disciples had slipped out of the Upper Room and into the
darkness, through a city gate, down the steep ravine, and up into the hill
of olive trees. He trembled with a deep sense of foreboding. Would his
three closest friends mind coming just a little further to pray a stone's throw
away? His soul was overwhelmed with sorrow, so for the only time in his
life Jesus asked for something for himself: *Be with me . . . stay beside me . . .
stay awake with me. . . . Please, would you?*

Jesus had often asked his disciples to do things *for* him. Organize the
people on the hill in groups. Pass out baskets of loaves and fish. Find a
boat in which to cross a lake. Go two by two and preach the message in the
towns of Judea. Always and always he had others in mind. Even on the
night he was betrayed, he dispensed instructions for others, and in his own
prayers that same night he interceded for others (John 14–17).

But on this night, in this lonely olive grove, he asked his disciples for
something *from* them. He wanted human comfort. Instead Jesus' need was
answered with a yawn, and in no time everyone's prayers had degenerated
into dreams. Eleven men—some accustomed to working all night on their
fishing boats—could not keep awake to lend moral support to the Son of
Man.

"Then he returned to his disciples and found them sleeping. 'Could
you men not keep watch with me for one hour?' he asked Peter"
(Matt. 26:40). In his moment of greatest need, Jesus asked his disciples to watch with him for just one hour. He asks the same of you.
Can you say with David Brainerd, "Oh! One hour with God infinitely exceeds all the pleasures and delights of this lower world."[3]
Spend an hour alone with God this week.

*Yes, Lord, I will stay with you. . . . I will be with you, remaining beside
you in prayer.*

Completed, Paid For, and Nailed

Comfort my people, says your God. Speak tenderly to Jerusalem, and proclaim to her that her hard service has been completed, that her sin has been paid for, that she has received from the LORD's hand double for all her sins.

—Isaiah 40:1–2

Let's do an inventory of our life in Christ, using Isaiah's announcement. Our slavery to sin has ended. Check. Jesus paid for our sins. Check. God has given us double for all our sins. Che—Hey? What's going on here? Are you saying, Lord, that you're gonna get us back double for all the sins we've committed? Whatever happened to forgive and forget?

No, it's not some scheme of God to get back at us with twice the punishment. Rather Isaiah is describing a business transaction common in those days that illustrates just how wonderful our Lord is. Whenever a person mortgaged his property, a stake was driven into the ground upon which the papers describing the terms of the loan were tacked for all the world to see. When the terms of the agreement were fulfilled, the lender took the bottom part of the note and folded it up to the top, where it was then nailed closed. Any passerby could see that the owner had paid off his debt—the agreement was "doubled over."

Do Isaiah's words ring a bell? Our debt for sin was paid for by Jesus, who was placed on the wooden cross and nailed there. It was a public declaration to the world that whoever looked upon Jesus and believed in him would be saved and have eternal life restored to him. Though you and I would never have been able to repay the debt of original sin, let alone the compounding interest of our daily sin, Jesus did. Praise God!

It's incredible to imagine that my debt is paid. But I can't argue with the records, Lord. You've doubled over my sin. Forever. Thank you. I am forever grateful.

April 18

High Stakes

When words are many, sin is not absent, but he who holds his tongue is wise. The tongue of the righteous is choice silver, but the heart of the wicked is of little value.

—Proverbs 10:19–20

To the apostle Paul, it must have seemed as though his life were spinning out of control at times. How could he avoid shipwrecks? He had no control over the phony apostles who were jealous of him and slandered his reputation. He never asked to be dumped over the city wall in a basket. He couldn't help it when that demon-possessed girl followed him around Philippi, shouting obscenities.

Yet for all his lack of control over his wild and crazy circumstances, there was one thing Paul *could* control. His attitude. He realized his response could either greatly advance Christ's gospel or seriously set it back. In other words, there was much more at stake than simply Paul's life. Other lives would be influenced by his godly response to trials. The reputation of the gospel was on the line. Angels were watching. God was taking notice.

Now, I'm not in prison like Paul. There are no chains biting into my ankles. But I do have a wheelchair, and like Paul, I can't claim direct responsibility for this particular circumstance. But I am responsible. I will be held accountable for my attitude.

You may not be responsible for that irritating phone call from your neighbor or for the fact that your wife can't balance the checkbook—but you are responsible for your response, and you will be held accountable by God for the choices you make. There's much more at stake here than simply your comfort zones. Others can be influenced to make eternal decisions. Angels are observing. So is God.

Sometimes we demonstrate better responsibility for our attitude when we enlist the help of others. Ask a trusted friend to hold you accountable, to help you make the right choices. Ask your friend to nail you when he or she observes you handling a certain tough time with a complaining or grumbling spirit.

Feel uneasy with the idea? If so, remember this—Someone far greater than your friend is watching.

Before a word comes off my tongue, may I first check it out with you, Lord.

April 19

Am I Glad to See You!

We do not want you to become lazy, but to imitate those who through faith and patience inherit what has been promised.

—Hebrews 6:12

Today marks the anniversary of the Oklahoma City bombing that gutted a U.S. federal office building, leaving 168 people dead. That day a pastor friend in the city invited me to hurry and come visit families who were anxiously waiting for news of their loved ones.

When I wheeled into the Red Cross center to be cleared and credentialed, an official from across the room exclaimed, "My God, are we glad to see you!" I looked over my shoulder. Did the woman in the white lab coat mean me? Later I learned she was in charge of counseling services. I asked why she gave me such an effusive welcome. "Honey, when victims come in here for help and see someone like you, handling your own crisis with grace, it gives them hope. You are a powerful example, a promise that they too will survive their tragedy."

Oklahoma City is surviving its crisis. But so many in our culture are not. Slump-shouldered and near defeat, they need the power of an example. They need to see someone experiencing greater conflict than they are *make it*. If people are floundering in the mire of their problems, or if they are (God forbid) lazy like the battle-weary believers mentioned in Hebrews, they need to be reminded that God's power works—really works, not in theory but in reality—in someone else's life.

Oh, if we only knew how influential our lives really are.

The woman in the white lab coat was right. People in the midst of crisis need to see other people handle their problems with grace. They need to see flesh and blood wrapped around the Word of God in a convincing, believable way. Why don't you share your smile at a nursing home? Or show someone in a hospital or at a rescue mission that God is at work in your life? Volunteer your hands and your heart.

Lord God, keep me from being so self-absorbed that I miss a chance to be to others an example of your grace.

April 20

A Spiritual Prayer

> This is what we speak, not in words taught us by human
> wisdom but in words taught by the Spirit, expressing spir-
> itual truths in spiritual words.
>
> —1 Corinthians 2:13

Corrie ten Boom survived the Nazi concentration camps and went on to travel the world to share Christ with millions. A series of strokes severely incapacitated her, after which she retreated to the sanctuary of her small home in southern California. But Corrie's ministry did not stop. Her house became a sanctuary of prayer.

Shortly before Jesus took her home, I went to visit her. I wheeled into Tante Corrie's house—the air was fragrant with the aroma of European coffee. A clock ticked and a kettle whistled. I sat in her parlor, enjoying old photographs of the ten Boom family while I waited for Pam, her helper, to wheel Corrie out of her bedroom. When she arrived, we talked—actually, I did most of the talking, since the strokes limited her speech. I also sang to her several favorite hymns. What a grand visit!

Before I left, Corrie grasped her paralyzed hand with her good hand and then with great effort entwined her fingers. Pam, understanding this gesture, kneeled by Corrie's wheelchair and looked up into that determined face. "Tante Corrie, may we pray with you, too?" We bowed our heads and Corrie began. Her words were indistinct—half Dutch, half English, and a lot of gibberish—but her voice was strong as she prayed earnestly in the Spirit. The Spirit was in fact the only one who could understand her.

Sometimes it's hard to pray. We can't find the words. When we do, they don't seem to make sense. Take heart: Romans 8:26–27 says, "In the same way, the Spirit helps us in our weakness. We do not know what we ought to pray for, but the Spirit himself intercedes for us with groans that words cannot express. And he who searches our hearts knows the mind of the Spirit, because the Spirit intercedes for the saints in accordance with God's will." When you pray in the Spirit, God always hears, understands, and is moved mightily.

Move in my heart, Spirit, and help me to pray in heartfelt honesty.

April 21

Follow the Wrangler

I will lead them beside streams of water on a level path
where they will not stumble, because I am Israel's father.
—Jeremiah 31:9

The Patapsco River runs white water between Marriottsville and Woodstock, Maryland. I ought to know, because as a child I rode horses there. Over the course of a half mile, the river drops several meters, tumbling over jagged rocks. A sharp ledge of granite and slate rises up on the left bank. On the right bank lies a flat, grassy meadow.

Now, you could travel either riverbank, for the trail splits there. One path leads up the dangerous, slippery slope; the other meanders through the meadow. As a child riding a horse, the unspoken rule was that I had to stick close behind Dad, who rode the lead horse. He was the trail boss and had the final say as to which trail we would take. But every time we came to that fork in the path, I would look longingly to the left side of the river.

I had seen boys race their horses up and down that ledge like wild cowboys, and while it looked dangerous, it also looked exciting. But my dad refused to let me do such a reckless thing.

Even now, every once in a while, I find myself wanting to take the path with the crazy risks. But my heavenly Father is the boss. He has the final say, and to move off the path he chooses is foolish.

Jeremiah 31:9 reminds us of that truth. God says he will do the safest and wisest thing for his children because, simply put, he's our Father. I, for one, am glad that God holds his ground with me. I also like the fact that God chooses the level path, the one where we will be less prone to stumble.

How about you? Are you willing to follow the path chosen for you?
Or do you veer toward the slippery slope?

Heavenly Father, the rocky ledge may look inviting, but help me to want to just view it from the meadow.

April 22

We *Will* Have Trouble

In this world you will have trouble. But take heart! I have
overcome the world.

—John 16:33

It was a long, tiring flight, and we were glad to be back. We waited curbside at LAX Airport for the handicap Super Shuttle. It never did turn up.
Judy hailed a cab and enlisted the reluctant cab driver's help to throw me
into the front seat. We chugged away from the curb and—clunk!—the
engine died. After the police jump-started us, we proceeded up the freeway,
crawling at twenty-five miles per hour. Rush hour. I eyed the ticker chalk-
ing up miles and money.

We pulled up to my driveway. Judy realized to her horror that we
didn't have enough cash for the enormous cab fare. She marched to the
front door, turned the key, and—brrrring!—the house alarm went off. She
fumbled with the alarm buttons and let me in. I told her I'd be okay while
she and the cab driver went to Ralph's Market to cash a check. After they
left—brrrring!—I tripped the motion sensor! My head was pounding but,
no, it was the front door and the Calabasas cops. I screamed, "I can't open
the door!" I couldn't hear their reply: the phone was now ringing. What a
mess! But, ah, we slept well that night.

I shouldn't be surprised at trials like these, especially on the heels of a
ministry trip. I'd like to describe no-show shuttles, kaput engines, and
tripped alarms as malfunctioning things possessed by the Devil, but in fact
they are simply a dead engine and a perfectly working house alarm. It's
part of the territory that comes with serving Jesus.

If we're going to stand up to make a difference for Christ, we will
encounter more hardship—more obstacles, dead batteries, nuisances,
administrative hassles, broken copy machines, and inconveniences—
much more than the average couch potato. We shouldn't be surprised. Such difficulty while serving Christ is not necessarily suffering. It's leadership.

Help me not to be surprised by trials. Rather help me to expect them.

The Touch of the Master's Hand

Sing to the LORD with thanksgiving; make music to our
God on the harp.

—Psalm 147:7

My favorite classical guitar piece is called "Recuerdos del Alhambra."
And nobody plays it like Christopher Parkening, probably the greatest classical guitarist in the world. My husband, Ken, is friends with Christopher. They both like to fish, so whenever we're together, the subject is trout and tuna.

Recently the three of us were at our home, and Ken left the room to get a fishing rod to show Christopher. I said, "Chris, I'm sorry to sound like such a fan, but one day I would love it if you would play for me 'Recuerdos del Alhambra.'" Then Ken was back in the room, and the subject turned to fish.

Later that night as Christopher was about to leave, Ken said, "Hey, I want to show you my high school guitar and see what you think of it." Ken brought out that old, beat-up clunker that had never played much more than "Michael, Row Your Boat Ashore." It was cracked, its strings fossilized.

I watched Christopher turn the guitar over in his hands and tighten the ancient strings. Eventually he was able to get the guitar on key. Then he kneeled by my chair and played "Recuerdos del Alhambra." Our living room became a symphony hall, the guitar a wellspring of soft, melodic, yet powerful music.

Afterward as Ken walked Christopher to his car, I stared at the guitar on the couch. I started to laugh. That old guitar never knew it had it in it. I had just seen and heard what the touch of a master's hand could do.

The same is true for you and me. On our own we can't do much more than "Michael, Row Your Boat Ashore." But then along comes the Lord Jesus. Suddenly we're capable of much more than we ever dreamed. We never knew we had it in us, and really we didn't. It's just the touch of the Master's hand.

Lord Jesus, so much power rests in your hands—to heal, to enlighten, to enable. Touch me. Thank you.

April 24

A List of Tears

> Record my lament; list my tears on your scroll—are they
> not in your record?
>
> —Psalm 56:8

Think of all the tears you've ever cried. That time at recess when you weren't picked for dodgeball. The Saturday night of the prom when you sat home alone. The job interview that went sour. The time your neighbor down the street told you to "quit talking about religion." The day your father died. The day your spouse left.

You may have thought no one noticed your red eyes. Not so. God saw. What's more, he has every intention of rewarding your endurance through that pain. Why else would he meticulously chronicle every one of your tears?

Every tear you've cried—think of it—will be redeemed. God will give you indescribable glory for your grief. Not with a general wave of the hand but in a considered and specific way. Each tear has been listed; each will be recompensed. We know how valuable our tears are in his sight—when the woman anointed Jesus with the valuable perfume, it was the tears with which she washed his feet that moved him most powerfully (Luke 7:44). The worth of our weeping is underscored again in Revelation 21:4, which says, "He will wipe every tear from their eyes." It won't be the duty of angels or others. It'll be God's.

I've cried a few times over not having use of my hands (though nowhere near like I used to). I think it's ironic that on the day in heaven when I finally get back use of my hands so I can dry my own tears . . . I won't have to.

Make a list of the times you've cried from hurt, disappointment, or physical pain in the last few years. How might God recompense you? Did you cry tears in the midst of praise or prayer? These tears have special power with God, as we saw from Luke 7:44.

Thank you, Lord, for numbering my tears and recording in your book the pain I have experienced. Nothing—not even my crying—will be wasted. Bless you for that.

April 25

For the Beauty of the Earth

Can you bind the beautiful Pleiades? Can you loose the cords of Orion? Can you bring forth the constellations in their seasons or lead out the Bear with its cubs?

—Job 38:31–32

For the wonder of each hour of the day and of the night,
Hill and vale and tree and flower, sun and moon and stars of light.
Lord of All, to Thee we raise this our hymn of grateful praise.[4]

I was thinking about this hymn recently when I showed up early at church for a prayer meeting. The front door was locked, so I sat outside and enjoyed the stars. Within a minute or two Chris, a college student, drove up.

As we waited together, I pointed out to Chris the various constellations. I could tell he thought I was a little strange to know so much about the stars, as though I were into astrology or something. I said, "Chris, did you know Orion is mentioned in the Bible?" He really looked at me funny then. I told him we would look it up when we went inside.

Later I showed him Job 38:31. To put it mildly, he was pleasantly surprised. All the beauty of the earth, the glories of the night sky, the fields, the birds, all this magnificent beauty is God's. It's not the property of astrologers, naturalists, Greenpeace, or New Agers. It's all owned by the Lord. And it's another reason to praise him.

Go outside and look around you. Find five things in nature to praise God for. And if that's too easy, look for ten. He has surrounded us with bounteous beauty—and a myriad of reasons to sing his praise.

Lord of all, I praise you for the beauty you spread out before me to enjoy any hour of the day or night. When I try to take it in, I realize it's too wonderful to fully comprehend, just as you are. I am grateful for all this.

April 26

Justification

Consequently, just as the result of one trespass was condemnation for all men, so also the result of one act of righteousness was justification that brings life for all men.

—Romans 5:18

Someone once said that Jesus, when he hung on the cross, bore the
weight of the sins of more than 40 billion people in the space of nine
hours. We haven't a clue to that horror, let alone the love. We can only
drop to our grateful knees that Jesus *justifies*. Amazing love! How can it be
that "he forgave us all our sins, having canceled the written code, with its
regulations, that was against us and that stood opposed to us; he took it
away, nailing it to the cross" (Col. 2:13–14)?

Your justification happened at the cross. It means God has acquitted
you of your sins, vindicated you and pronounced you righteous in his eyes.
You are as much justified the hour you first came to Christ by faith as you
will be for all eternity. It's a finished and complete work—a special reference
to your *person,* to your position before God. When the Father looks at you,
he looks through rose-colored glasses, stained red because of the blood of
Christ. Jesus is "our righteousness, holiness and redemption. Therefore, as
it is written: 'Let him who boasts boast in the Lord'" (1 Cor. 1:30–31).

Pause today and boast in Jesus. Boast in his love. Boast in his mercy.
Boast that he has given you a title to heaven and boldness to enter in.
When it comes to your justification, he's it!

Not the labors of my hands
Can fulfill Thy law's demands;
Could my zeal no respite know,
Could my tears forever flow,
All for sin could not atone;
Thou must save and Thou alone.[5]

You, Christ, are my justification. Thank you.

April 27

Sanctification

Finally, brothers, we instructed you how to live in order to please God, as in fact you are living. Now we ask you and urge you in the Lord Jesus to do this more and more. . . . It is God's will that you should be sanctified.

—1 Thessalonians 4:1, 3

As they would say in King James's times, "Be ye sanctified." We are to stomp on that natural love of sin and set apart ourselves unto God. Whether it's willful rebellion or the tiny transgressions you sweep under the carpet of your conscience, from these things . . . separate yourself. No doubt about it; it's a tall order. But a doable one.

That's because you have help from out of this world. The Lord Jesus has undertaken everything that your soul requires, delivering you not only from the guilt of sin, through justification, but from the dominion of sin in your life, through sanctification. How? Through placing in your heart both the Holy Spirit and a new principle, a "bent for good." You have power to follow through on life choices that please God, and that power is Christ: "[He] gave himself for us to redeem us from all wickedness and to purify for himself a people that are his very own, eager to do what is good" (Titus 2:14).

Listen to this little Bible lesson from Bishop J. C. Ryle:

Justification is the *reckoning* and counting a man to be righteous for the sake of another, even Jesus Christ the Lord. Sanctification is the actual *making* a man inwardly righteous, though it may be in a very feeble degree. The righteousness we have by our justification is *not our own,* but the everlasting perfect righteousness of our great Mediator Christ, imputed to us, and made our own by faith. The righteousness we have by sanctification *is our own* righteousness, imparted, inherent, and wrought in us by the Holy Spirit, but mingled with much infirmity and imperfection.[6]

Lord Jesus, I realize that my own works have no place at all in justification—your work on the cross did it all. But my works are of vast importance when it comes to my sanctification. May I fight, watch, pray, strive, and take great, great pains to be holy!

April 28

Justified and Sanctified

We maintain that a man is justified by faith apart from observing the law.

—Romans 3:28

What good is it, my brothers, if a man claims to have faith but has no deeds? Can such faith save him? Suppose a brother or sister is without clothes and daily food. If one of you says to him, "Go, I wish you well; keep warm and well fed," but does nothing about his physical needs, what good is it? In the same way, faith by itself, if it is not accompanied by action, is dead.

—James 2:14–17

Justification is a finished and complete work, and we are perfectly justified the moment we believe; sanctification is an incomplete work and will never be perfected until we reach heaven. Justification admits to no growth (we are as much justified the hour we first come to Christ by faith as we will be for all eternity); sanctification is a progressive work as we keep changing and enlarging our hearts for Christ.

Justification has special reference to our person, our standing in God's sight. Sanctification has special reference to our character and the moral renewal of our hearts. Justification is the act of God about us and is not easily discerned by others; sanctification is the work of God within us and cannot be hidden from others. Justification gives us our title to heaven; sanctification prepares us for heaven.

In heaven it will be useless to plead that we believed in Christ unless our life supports it. When our graves are opened, when we stand before God, evidence will be crucial. The issue will not be how we talked and what we professed but how we lived and what we did. Jesus justified you. Today is your chance . . . your privilege to sanctify yourself.

Lord, may my life be evidence of what I believe. It can't be any other way. Holy Spirit, grant me strength to set myself apart to God.

April 29

Food and Drink

Come, all you who are thirsty, come to the waters; and you who have no money, come, buy and eat! Come, buy wine and milk without money and without cost. Why spend money on what is not bread, and your labor on what does not satisfy? Listen, listen to me, and eat what is good, and your soul will delight in the richest of fare.

—Isaiah 55:1–2

Today's verse speaks to those who are spiritually thirsty and hungry but have nothing in their spiritual pockets. They've spent it all, charging up their credit cards on things that simply don't satisfy. I'm not talking about splurging on Viva paper towels over generic brands; I'm talking about people's sustenance, their food and drink, their life focus: living in front of your computer screen, living on compliments, or living from one Friday night to the next at every cinema in town, quenching your thirst for excitement and feeding your appetite to fit in.

When it's all been spent, when you're bankrupt, have no resources, and still feel the hunger pains, this is when you recognize God's wine, milk, and bread—the richest of fare. "The bread of God is he who comes down from heaven and gives life to the world" (John 6:33). The spiritually hungry feed on any old bread; the spiritually starved know where the *real* bread's at.

In John 6:35 Jesus declared, "I am the bread of life. He who comes to me will never go hungry, and he who believes in me will never be thirsty." Jesus is the only one who satisfies. His redemptive work ensures that his benefits are free. You need not spend anything but yourself. The cost of feeding on the Bread of Life and the Living Water is simply the price of your soul.

May I feed on you today by faith, Lord. May my deepest longings be satisfied in you. May I not settle for tap water when I have you, a living spring. May I forgo day-old rolls when I have you, the bread from heaven. May I not be satisfied with hamburger when I have you, the choicest of meats. May I turn down the world's Kool-Aid when I have you, the fruit of the Father's vineyard.

April 30

Crisis Intervention

If I had cherished sin in my heart, the Lord would not have listened; but God has surely listened and heard my voice in prayer.

—Psalm 66:18–19

I travel often, so I see lots of families with small kids in airport waiting areas. Such places, it seems, are most convenient for a kid to throw a tantrum or two. Tired from the trip, the child soon finds an excuse for a crisis. The crowd rolls its eyes as the parents hasten to control the child. The effort seems futile, however. It's as if the child is trapped in a frenzied orbit of self-pity and can't come down.

I've thrown a few tantrums in my life—tantrums in which I've become self-absorbed and ignorant of God's presence in the midst of a crisis. I'm able to muster up my stubborn German-Swede pride, with a dose of fleshly Joni, and lock on to an emotional and spiritual frenzy equal to that of a two-year-old. I hear or feel little of God at such times. But it is precisely at those times when I need to remember this principle: stop whining and dining.

Stop whining. God's voice can't be heard above my complaints. No matter that his voice shook the mountains; it's no match for a whining, negative spirit. I won't hear his comfort or his solution to my problem above the din of my self-pity.

Stop dining. Our solutions to crises sometimes come in the form of indulgences. I might indulge in food or fantasy. I'll work feverishly or play dangerously—anything to stop the pain. But the pain will not stop and the crisis will not pass until I stop trying to consume everything I desire. God's hand will not be felt while I grasp at pleasure.

What are you whining and dining on? When you end it, that's when God intervenes in quietness and strength. The crisis will pass. All things will work together for good. He will have his way. See it for yourself today.

Still my voice, Lord; quench my hungers. I'm listening.

MAY

May 1

The Reality of Heaven

He that hath an ear, let him hear what the Spirit saith unto
the churches; To him that overcometh will I give to eat of
the hidden manna.

—Revelation 2:17 KJV

At present, abstract things like truth and goodness have no substance.
Oh, we see these qualities manifested in others, but they are not concrete in themselves. In heaven, though, purity and goodness, righteousness
and joy will have more substance than anything we ever touched, tasted,
or smelled on earth. We are wrong in thinking heaven is wispy and
vaporous. It is earth that is like withering grass, not heaven. In C. S. Lewis's
The Great Divorce, the rock-solid reality of heaven is described this way:

> The earth shook under [the solid people's] tread as their strong feet
> sank into the wet turf. A tiny haze and a sweet smell went up where
> they had crushed the grass and scattered the dew.... Walking, for
> me, proved difficult. The grass, hard as diamonds to my unsubstantial feet, made me feel as if I were walking on wrinkled rock.... A
> bird ran across in front of me and I envied it. It belonged to that
> country and was as real as the grass. It could bend the stalks and spatter itself with the dew.[1]

As today's verse assures us, one day we will *eat* of the hidden manna.
We will *wear* righteousness like light. We will *shine* like the stars in
the universe. We shall *eat* from the Tree of Life. *Hold* the Morning
Star like a scepter. *Enter* into the joy of the Lord. There is nothing
vague or wispy about these verbs. Everything in heaven will have
more substance than we ever dreamed. Today get ready for the real
reality!

*You, Lord, are the hidden manna that one day I shall eat. I experience
this now, in a symbolic way, through Communion. But one day the symbol will become reality. One day I shall be completely in you, and you in
me.*

May 2

A Lesson from Corrie

When I came to you, brothers, I did not come with eloquence or superior wisdom as I proclaimed to you the testimony about God. For I resolved to know nothing while I was with you except Jesus Christ and him crucified.

—1 Corinthians 2:1–2

A number of years ago Ken and I attended Corrie ten Boom's funeral. It was a simple service, brief, not many flowers, very European. But, oh, how challenged we were when we left the church that day.

Several pastors spoke about Corrie's life, reading excerpts from her books or recounting incidents from her ministry. They all talked about her love of Jesus. One pastor said Corrie had instructed him to speak at her funeral about Jesus' love—not about Corrie ten Boom.

That was so like Corrie! Jesus was always at the center of her thoughts and words. She rarely spoke of "the Christian walk" or "the Christian experience." She didn't speak of Christ as though he were some creed, doctrine, or lifestyle. What's more, she didn't just say, "The Lord," as in "I love the Lord" or "The Lord told me this." She always named him. She said, "The Lord Jesus." She spoke about a Person—a Person she loved more than anyone else—and she was careful to always name him with confidence and pride. Pride, you say? It's okay to boast in the Lord: "As it is written: 'Let him who boasts boast in the Lord'" (1 Cor. 1:31).

As Ken and I left the graveside, he said, "How is it we get so caught up in explaining our walk in Christ or some spiritual experience instead of simply talking about him?"

Do you find yourself in the same situation? God forbid we should reduce our Savior to a fine-print doctrine squeezed between the pages of a theology textbook. May the Lord wake us out of spiritual slumber if we catch ourselves making a big deal of our "life in Christ" rather than the simple testimony of Jesus.

Jesus, I want you to be my message, my joy, and my hope. Today I want to share who you are and tell people about my love . . . just for you.

Flawless Word

The words of the LORD are flawless, like silver refined in a
furnace of clay, purified seven times.

—Psalm 12:6

Young Steven looked up from watching the Olympics on TV. "I'd rather
have a silver metal, I think."

"Why?"

"'Cause it looks better, shinier. Gold looks like it's got all kinds of junk
in it."

Silver often takes a backseat to its richer brother, gold. But in the mind
of the boy, silver had a greater attraction. It was shinier than gold. It looked
faster, cooler, purer. It didn't look as if anyone had added any "junk" to it.

According to today's verse, God seems to agree with Steven's views on
metallurgy. When describing his Word, God says that it is more refined
than silver. Gold can't "hang together" if it's entirely free of impurities. So
God chooses to liken his Word to silver. That's because God is less interested in attractiveness and more interested in purity. God's Word, because
it reflects a pure and holy God, must likewise be associated with that which
is refined and pure.

One unusual quality of silver that accentuates its purity is the ability
it has to kill bacteria when it comes into contact with it. It's as if bad things
can't survive in silver or around it! So too the Word of God is not only pure
in and of itself; it has the ability, when applied by faith, to cleanse the
reader of his or her sin. God is not as concerned about people finding his
words golden, all beautiful and attractive, as he is about people's lives being
touched by the silver of his Word—becoming changed, holy, and pure.

The purity of God's Word should make us treasure it highly. More
importantly for God, it should make a change for the better in our
lives. He wants us to apply his commands in order to refine and
change our hearts. And to those who are willing to allow the pure
words to effect that change, he grants an invaluable gift: the security
of knowing that his promises are as pure as his commands and truths.

*Jesus, I lay claim to the purity of your Word as the only hope for my life.
I want to know its cleansing power and its pure rewards.*

May 4

God's Main Thing

Surely the nations are like a drop in a bucket; they are regarded as dust on the scales; he weighs the islands as though they were fine dust.... Before him all the nations are as nothing; they are regarded by him as worthless and less than nothing. To whom, then, will you compare God? What image will you compare him to?

—Isaiah 40:15, 17–18

The *Voyager II* spacecraft recently sent back to Earth photos that were taken from four billion miles away. At that distance Earth appeared as a tiny dot on the photo, less than one seventy-secondth of an inch wide. And that's only from four billion miles away, just slightly beyond the orbit of the planets in our solar system. The prophet Isaiah didn't have photos from space, but in today's passage he gave a clear picture of God's greatness in comparison with Earth. God regards the nations on Earth as less than nothing. He weighs the Hawaiian Islands like fine dust and regards the United States as a drop in the bucket.

Yet here's the wonder. In this same chapter God bends over backward to remind us of his care for individuals: "He gives strength to the weary and increases the power of the weak" (Isa. 40:29). God's main thing is this: he so loved the people on this tiny blue ball that he sent his Son to bring individuals, such as you and me, to himself. He didn't die for nations . . . he died for people who live in those nations.

When you read *Time* magazine or watch *CNN Headline News,* when you hear about powerful countries in the Middle East on the brink of war, when you see the secretary of state shake hands with prime ministers, and watch the president wave and walk off Air Force One, you could feel extremely insignificant. But Isaiah 40:23 has something to say about this: "He brings princes to naught and reduces the rulers of this world to nothing."

God's main thing is *individuals.* Doesn't matter if you hold office or live in the most influential country in the world. He cares for the person behind the government desk . . . the individual living in whatever country. He died for people so people might live for him. Think about this as you watch the evening news tonight.

Little ol' insignificant me? You care about me? Thank you, Lord, that I count with you on this tiny blue ball of a planet.

May 5

No Scars in Heaven?

In a loud voice they sang, "Worthy is the Lamb, who was slain, to receive power and wealth and wisdom and strength and honor and glory and praise!"

—Revelation 5:12

He said to Thomas, "Put your finger here; see my hands. Reach out your hand and put it into my side. Stop doubting and believe."

—John 20:27

One of the most dramatic scenes in Scripture is when the Lord Jesus, after his resurrection, stretches out his hands to Thomas and challenges him to touch his wounds—and thus believe. Jesus could have left Thomas to stew in his doubts, but the Lord never breaks the bruised reed. Instead he bears the infirmities of the weak. He accommodates himself to help us through our doubts. He did it for Thomas and he's still doing it today. God goes to great extent to confirm our faith, just as he did when he invited Thomas to thrust a hand into his side.

That's what makes those nail prints so precious. And that's why I'm not surprised the nail prints still showed on the Lord, even after his resurrection. His wounds are not only an evidence of love but an encouragement to our faith. It is the wounds that help us believe.

Will Jesus bear his scars in heaven? Revelation 5:6 describes the scene: "I saw a Lamb, *looking as if it had been slain,* standing in the center of the throne . . ." (emphasis added). I have an inkling he will be the *only* one who will retain the painful reminders of his earthly journey. We, on the other hand, will bear no scars. All our tears will be wiped away. The scars of Jesus will not be painful for us to see but will be an eternal reason to rejoice.

Why wait for heaven to rejoice? Today the Lord accommodates himself to help you through your doubts. He'll go to great lengths to help confirm your faith. He invites you to place your hand in his and feel what it cost to purchase your salvation.

Lord Jesus, help me to have faith through the crisis I'm in right now. Remind me of all the evidence you have provided that I might believe.

May 6

Hidden with Christ

Set your minds on things above, not on earthly things. For you died, and your life is now hidden with Christ in God. When Christ, who is your life, appears, then you also will appear with him in glory.

—Colossians 3:2–4

When I was in Russia, my husband, Ken, purchased one of those wooden, hand-painted peasant dolls that twist open at the middle to reveal another doll inside. You take the smaller doll out, open it, and another, even smaller one is inside. Open that one and you discover a tinier doll! The fun is in discovering all that's hidden inside each doll.

To me, it was an excellent picture of being hidden with Christ in God. We are in him and he is hidden in the Father. The fun is in discovering all that this means. As the passage says, we have died and our true life lies in the other world, the spiritual world. The perfection of all that we shall one day be is reserved for us in heaven. It is hidden with Christ—not only from us (like a secret) but for us (like a safety deposit box). At the present time even Christ is hidden—but we take comfort that even though we cannot see him, our life is hidden in him and laid up safely with him. In the same way, we can rest, knowing that although our ultimate happiness is presently out of sight, it is nevertheless reserved in heaven for us.

What a picture of safety and protection. Nothing can touch us, nothing can harm us, for we are hidden in Christ and he is hidden in the Father. And one day, when Christ is revealed, when he appears, who we are—our true identity—will no longer be concealed.

As we follow the advice of Colossians 3:2 and set our minds on things above, we enjoy discovering "what's inside." Today ponder what you might be like, sound like, act like when you appear with Christ in glory. As you muse on things above, what is hidden becomes clear.

Lord, I want to understand this mystery, so I set my heart and mind on things above, where you are seated at the right hand of the Father. One day I will be the person you've intended me to be all along. Thank you for hiding me in your heart.

May 7

Preparing for Revival

Then we will not turn away from you; revive us, and we
will call on your name.

—Psalm 80:18

Who's the person in whom God is ready to work? Who's prepared for
revival? My friend Nancy Leigh DeMoss once described what such
an individual looks like. Are you ready for the Lord to do a marvelous work
in your life? Maybe you'll see yourself in this mirror. . . .

The person God is working in is overwhelmed by a sense of spiritual
need—he or she looks for the best in others. But proud people focus
on others' failures and are quick to find fault. The person God
chooses surrenders control and isn't itching to always be right, but
proud people demand to have things their own way; they have to
prove they are right.

Believers in whom God is moving desire to make others successful. Then there are those who do things to be a success, who are
wounded when others are promoted instead of them. Revival comes
to people who know they have nothing to offer God, to those who
are humbled by how much they have to learn. Revival is slow to come
to those who try to think of what they can do for God, to those who
feel confident in how much they know.

God looks for people who are not concerned with themselves,
who risk getting close to others, who receive criticism with a humble heart. God is not quick to use people who are self-centered, who
keep others at arm's length, who are defensive when criticized.

Broken people specifically confess sin. They are grieved over the
root causes of their sins. Then there are those who confess in gener-
alities. They're mainly concerned with the consequences of their sins
and with keeping up appearances.

Take a minute to pick out one or two character traits about which
God whispered to you, "That's you. Give this to me." If we're looking for revival to start, we need look no further than ourselves.

*Lord, change me. Make me one of your broken people who is willing to
let revival begin with me.*

May 8

He Sustains *Everything*

> In these last days he has spoken to us by his Son, whom he
> appointed heir of all things, and through whom he made
> the universe. The Son is the radiance of God's glory . . . sus-
> taining all things by his powerful word.
>
> —Hebrews 1:2–3

Behind Jesus' rough cloak and beard, behind his simple conversations
with neighbors, behind the humble circumstances surrounding his life,
powerful things were going on. Things of universal importance. Even as
Jesus plodded the dirt paths of Judea—preaching, debating, healing, and
listening—the entire universe leaned every hour on his divinity.

Even as Jesus walked the hills of Galilee, the North American brown
bear took his Creator's cue to begin hibernation. As Jesus told his disciples
to leave their nets and follow him, the Arctic tern awaited signal to leave
its breeding grounds eight degrees south of the North Pole and go winter
in the Antarctic. While Jesus took time to bless little children and listen to
the chatter of Jewish mothers, a female water spider listened to his echoes
in her brain tell her how to trap air bubbles and house her eggs in silk at
the pond's bottom. When Jesus woke up early to go to the mountains to
pray, the nocturnal owls listened for his command to leave their hunting
and return to their nests for rest. Even when Jesus looked up at the stars,
he was not only enjoying their splendor—the splendor he created—he
was sustaining all celestial orbits by his powerful word.

If Jesus could hold together, by his silent command, the muscles and
tendons of the soldiers who whipped him, breathing into them the
very energy required to flail him, if Jesus could bless his accusers in
this way—and he did—then, oh, think of the energy God can give
you to bless all those around you. What a powerful Savior we have!

You not only sustain everything else by your word, Lord, you uphold me.
Thank you that in you I live and move and have my very being.

May 9

Acceptable Praise

Sing joyfully to the LORD, you righteous; it is fitting for the upright to praise him.

—Psalm 33:1

Have you ever watched an infant caress his mother? He "goos" and "gaahs," slobbering his affection all over her cheek. He laughs in her arms, breaks into a squeal, and spits a "brrrrh!" of curdled milk into her face. In a bumbling attempt to reach for his mother's chin, he might even slap her neck and break her string of pearls.

You *could* turn that infant's face to yours and say, "Now see here, you're doing a pretty poor job of expressing affection toward your mother. Why, you have no idea of her fine character. If this is your idea of telling her how wonderful she is, forget it. All this blubbering is not impressing your mother one bit. So stop it right now."

If you chided that infant like this, you might get a sock in the jaw from his mother. That infant is doing exactly what he is supposed to be doing, and it is his mother's joy to accept her baby's love, no matter how awkward it may come across.

God is the same way. Some of us are babes in the Lord, but praise is becoming, even from a baby. Some believers start off well praising God but get sidetracked into listing petitions rather than lauding praise. Others seem to run out of words to say (or perhaps are fearful they're saying the wrong or unacceptable things). They give up, thinking, *Good grief, I can't even do a simple thing like praise God!*

Don't get down on yourself if your praises don't seem to measure up. Quote to God Psalm 104:34: "May my meditation be pleasing to him, as I rejoice in the LORD." Then get going with your praises, knowing that, like an infant's affections to his parent, they *will* be pleasing to the Lord.

Sometimes my praise is a tumble of words all mishmashed together, but I'm grateful, Father, that it is your joy to accept this babe in Christ.

May 10

Faces Unveiled

And we, who with unveiled faces all reflect the Lord's glory,
are being transformed into his likeness with ever-increasing glory, which comes from the Lord, who is the Spirit.
—2 Corinthians 3:18

Several years ago when they were reprinting the *Joni* book in Arabic, I
wrote to Johan, a missionary in the Middle East, asking whether he
thought I should change the photo of myself on the cover. I sought his
advice because in the Arab world, a woman looking directly at the camera
and pictured without a veil is offensive. Here's the story he told me. . . .

"Joni, I was in the Sinai Desert with a pile of books and Bibles to dis-
tribute to the Bedouins, when an Egyptian came up to me. It turned out
he was a policeman. He took me to the station, where the captain was very
nasty to me. But before he locked me in a cell that night, he took *Joni* from
my book pile.

"The next morning the captain brought me breakfast! He said, 'Last
night I took that book because I saw this beautiful girl with these beautiful eyes looking at me. I thought, *This is a great book about girls.*' Then he
found out the book was about God. The book changed his life. The captain then set me free from the jail. He would never have read *Joni* were it
not for the photo of the unveiled face of a woman on the cover. When I
got back to Israel, your letter asking about changing the book's cover was
waiting for me."

Needless to say, Johan advised me not to change the photo on the
cover. It means more Arabic men will be drawn to read the story!

My unveiled face on that Arabic *Joni* book serves as a fascinating
symbol. Our verse for today describes you as having an unveiled face
that reflects the Lord's glory. What are you communicating with your
eyes today? How ready are you to give your smile? When people look
at you, will they see Jesus?

*Lord God, I need to realize how much I communicate with my face. I
want others to see you in my smile; I want them to see your light in my
eyes today.*

The Written Code

He forgave us all our sins, having canceled the written code, with its regulations, that was against us and that stood opposed to us; he took it away, nailing it to the cross.
—Colossians 2:13–14

Sir," the maître d' whispered as he pulled my friend Gary aside, "you cannot enter here without the proper attire. Coat and tie are required." Unbeknownst to my shirtsleeved friend, the upscale New York restaurant had strict rules. He sighed, glanced wantonly at the mahogany walls, the crystal, the menu, and then turned to leave.

"Wait," the maître d' said, gesturing toward the coat check window. "We cannot violate our code, but we can help you meet it. May we provide this for you?" he said, holding up a medium-sized jacket and tie. Gary confided to me later that at first the restaurant's rules miffed him. His attitude changed when he saw how the management bent over backward to make provisions for those who could not meet their requirements. As Gary slipped into his borrowed clothes, he was profusely thankful. The thoughtful gesture not only ennobled the maître d' and his staff but made my friend respect the restaurant code all the more.

Revelation 19:9 announces, "Blessed are those who are invited to the wedding supper of the Lamb!" But the banquet has an important requirement: we must be clothed in righteousness. It's the written code, reflecting the highest of standards. Trouble is, it's impossible for flesh and blood to attain (1 Cor. 15:50). Yet rather than bend the standard to accommodate us (another impossibility), God takes an even higher, more glorious road. He ennobles himself by providing the righteousness of Jesus Christ as a covering for sinful humanity. God is magnified in our eyes when we read Revelation 19:8: "'Fine linen, bright and clean, was given her to wear.' (Fine linen stands for the righteous acts of the saints.)"

In darker moments, our flesh may resent the requirements of the Law. It's understandable for the flesh to feel that way, but our generous God has taken it upon himself to provide for us without compromising the written code. Today celebrate the fact that you wear the righteousness of Christ.

I don't deserve a place at the banquet, Lord, but thank you for generously providing your clothes of righteousness. I'm permitted to have a seat ... and I'm grateful!

May 12

Rumpelstiltskin

Our light affliction, which is but for a moment, worketh
for us a far more exceeding and eternal weight of glory.
—2 Corinthians 4:17 KJV

As a child, I was fascinated by the fairy tale about Rumpelstiltskin. The details are hazy, but I recall that he was an elfin sort of figure who was able to weave straw into gold. The color plate alongside the story in my old red fairy-tale book showed a little man hunched over a spinning wheel, mounds of straw on one side, gold coins on the other. I thought it would be wonderful to be able to do such a thing.

The fact is, you can. Your earthly problems are your pile of straw. On the other side of eternity in heaven is the treasure you are laying up. Problems on one side, gold on the other. In the middle is a kind of spinning wheel. That's where you sit. If the problem side seems overwhelming, focus your eyes on the glory side. When you do, you're a Rumpelstiltskin weaving straw into gold; like a divine spinning wheel, your affliction "worketh . . . a far more exceeding and eternal weight of glory." It's as J. B. Phillips, in *The New Testament in Modern English,* paraphrases today's verse: "These little troubles (which are really so transitory) are winning for us a permanent, glorious and solid reward out of all proportion to our pain."

It's not merely that heaven will be wonderful *in spite* of our anguish; it will be wonderful *because* of it. Suffering serves us. A faithful response to affliction accrues a weight of glory. A bounteous reward. The more faithful to God we are in the midst of our pain, the more our reward and joy.

Whatever suffering you are going through this minute, your reaction to it affects the eternity you will enjoy. Heaven will be more heavenly to the degree that you have followed Christ on earth. "I consider that our present sufferings are not worth comparing with the glory that will be revealed in us" (Rom. 8:18).

Today help me to take my trials, like straw, and weave in the midst of them a godly response. It will be golden in your sight, Lord.

"If Only" Living

Abraham said to God, "If only Ishmael might live under
your blessing!"

—Genesis 17:18

I admit it. I would be the first to line up with Abraham as one of those
guilty of buying things from the Do-It-Yourself Depot of life. Something's broke? Here, I'll fix that. Someone's hurting? I can solve that problem. Someone's mad? No worry, I'll talk to them. It seems I have an
unflagging spirit to make right that which seems wrong. My friends have
to warn me from time to time, "Now, don't try to fix this. I'm just sharing
it with you so you can pray."

It's too bad Abraham didn't listen to his friend, the Lord. Though he
had been promised a son, Abraham sought a solution apart from God. And
Abraham knew he had made a mistake in his haste to please God. You can
hear his regret in those words *if only:* "If only my solution were pleasing to
you. If only my way had been the right way. If only my idea were good
enough."

God would not abide by Abraham's solution. It was to be done God's
way, as he had promised—Abraham and Sarah would have a son. He ultimately fulfilled that promise, but not without Abraham's regret seeding
the ground of strife between Isaac and Ishmael. Abraham's do-it-yourself
solution has repercussions even in our day. The Middle East might be a
safer place had Abraham trusted fully.

What has God promised you? Are you attempting to fulfill that
promise with a do-it-yourself life? No matter how tempting a solution appears, always, always stop to ask God. Compare it with his
Word, his character, his Spirit. Anything short of complete trust in
God's instructions will ultimately lead to regrets. "If only" living is no
living at all.

*What does it take for me to remember, Lord, that I don't have to fix your
Word or "hurry it up" to make everything turn out right? You don't need
a helping hand. So please bind my heart to believe your promises and
obey your commands. I can't live any other way.*

May 14

The New Earth

The creation was subjected to frustration, not by its own choice, but by the will of the one who subjected it, in hope that the creation itself will be liberated from its bondage to decay and brought into the glorious freedom of the children of God.

—Romans 8:20–21

One day the earth will be liberated. The whole creation, like us, is "groaning as in the pains of childbirth right up to the present time" (Rom. 8:22). I sense this whenever I see smog, a junkyard, or dead raccoons in the road. When I drive the coastal mountains just a stone's throw from my home and marvel at the jutted, jagged rocks and canyons, I'm vividly aware I'm in the middle of earthquake country. Mud slides and aftershocks happen all the time around here. These hills are restless.

Even though this little jewel of a blue planet has been scarred and denuded, abused and polluted, it will not be abandoned. God doesn't waste things; he redeems them. And today's passage reveals the Lord's intentions for this blue marble of his. The earth upon which we trod is the earth that Christ will bring into his glorious freedom. You can hear it in the sighing of the wind. You can feel it in the heavy silence in the mountains. You can see it in the woeful eyes of an animal. Something's coming . . . something better.

If you want to know what this something is, study Revelation and Isaiah. "The wolf will live with the lamb" (Isa. 11:6), and "the burning sand will become a pool" (Isa. 35:7). We will have a part in liberating the new earth—perhaps uplifting the poor of Kurdistan, reforesting the hills of Lebanon, or planting trees along the Amazon. We may clear the slums of Rio de Janeiro, get rid of nuclear waste, and teach the nations how to worship God and how to beat their swords into plowshares.

God won't abandon earth. He will redeem it.

Thank you, God, that eternal life with you is rock-solid real. Heaven is not a never-never land of thin, ghostly shapes that I poke my finger through only to discover that my loved ones are spacey spirit-beings I can't really hug or hold. The new earth will be peopled with people and animals, mountains and valleys. It will be real and concrete and . . . liberated!

May 15

The Name of the Lord

Everyone who calls on the name of the Lord will be saved.

—Romans 10:13

I taught the junior high Sunday school lesson this week. I wondered, *How can I inspire these kids to pray for their friends at school who don't know Christ?* We made a list. On one side of the blackboard we wrote the name of a classmate, with a short description: Charlie—stuck on himself; Christie—parents divorced; Stephanie—fooling with drugs. The blackboard filled up quickly. On the other side we listed the names of Christ: Friend of Sinners, Healer of Broken Hearts, Prince of Peace, Bread of Life, and many more.

We prayed with eyes open, each junior higher linking the need of a classmate with a particular and suitable name of Christ. Their small voices became large with confidence as they began praying, "Prince of Peace, I pray that Christie comes to have peace in her heart" and "Friend of Sinners, Stephanie is in real trouble with drugs. . . . She needs to see her sin and see you as her friend" and "Bread of Life, Charlie doesn't know it, but he's hungry for you. . . . Let him feed on you." Thirty minutes passed quickly. Each young person was energized by this fresh way of weaving the name of the Lord throughout their prayers.

As the song goes,

> There is strength in the Name of the Lord;
> There is power in the Name of the Lord;
> There is hope in the Name of the Lord.

Become familiar with the many and varied names of Christ in Scripture, then employ those names in your prayers. The names of Christ give color and texture, meaning and depth to our prayer language. Plus, it's a way of becoming more familiar and intimate with your Savior. Finally, there is *power* in the name of the Lord—that's good news for your unsaved friend who needs prayer.

Lead me to pray for someone today, Lord, and show me in Scripture a new way to express your name in prayer. In fact, I want to do this right now. . . .

May 16

God Can't

> . . . a faith and knowledge resting on the hope of eternal
> life, which God, who does not lie, promised before the
> beginning of time.
>
> —Titus 1:2

It's been said that a child doesn't know the difference between a broken promise and a lie. To the parent, a promise is something we strive to fulfill but "Hey, one never knows what tomorrow might bring." But to the child, a promise is a statement of fact about future events. Period.

Before there was time, God made a promise that the people whom he chose, by their faith, would live forever. But then no sooner did time begin than the first rebellion broke out in the Garden of Eden. It was the first in a long line of reasons for God to back out of his promise. Who could blame him for backing out? I would renege, especially since the promise was made without a witness. And I would definitely suspend the promise if the provisions of the relationship were frequently and maliciously broken, as indeed they were.

But our verse for today says that God does not lie and that his inability to lie is related to the fact that he made a promise. The Greek uses the adjective form, saying the "not-lying God." To God, breaking a promise and lying are one and the same, and he can do neither. He does not have the propensity to alter his character or his intention toward us. What he started must be completed. He will not, and cannot, alter what was a part of his being even before we ever came into existence.

There is a great sense of security in knowing God's omnipotence. Likewise his inability to lie gives security. Worries about God changing his mind vanish when we realize that unlike us, God cannot lie or break a promise. And in his mind, truth and promises are the same. Think for a moment what you believe about promises. What promises have you made that you can follow through on today?

Father, I take great comfort in knowing that my sins have no bearing on your decision to grant me eternal life. Your inability to do otherwise binds my heart to yours. I love you.

May 17

The Perfect Response

The law appoints as high priests men who are weak; but the oath, which came after the law, appointed the Son, who has been made perfect forever.

—Hebrews 7:28

Jesus is the perfect priest who can completely empathize with our weaknesses. His response to our plight—especially our grief and pain—is utterly perfect. This is good news for the hurting widow, the rejected wife, the abandoned young person, and the stroke survivor dealing with loss of his ability to think clearly and walk steadily. It's good news because sometimes we think that God is far removed from our heartache. Yet Jesus—God in the flesh—is never, ever far removed from our grief.

Consider the grief shown by Jesus in the Gospels. See him with Mary, the sister of Lazarus, at the tomb of her brother. John 11:35 poignantly observes that "Jesus wept." Did only his human nature weep and not his divine? No, for Jesus explained, "The Son can do nothing by himself; he can do only what he sees his Father doing" (John 5:19). The grief Jesus showed on earth reflects not only the Father's heart but also the Holy Spirit's—for we learn in Isaiah 63:10 of the Spirit's reaction to a straying Israel: "They rebelled and grieved his Holy Spirit." The entire Trinity is able to grieve.

"As with his contentment, joy, and anger," says Steve Estes, "God's grief is a worthy emotion—without weakness, without impurity, without anything uncomely. It never paralyzes him, and it did not lead him sentimentally to ignore justice."[2] In other words, when God grieves, he does it perfectly. He does it without reservations or insecurities. He always knows the right thing to feel, do, and say. Others may stumble to offer the right response, but not God. When it is right to grieve, when grieving is the perfect response—this is what God does, because he is perfect.

If you know someone who is grieving, gently point that person to Christ. The Lord grieves better, more wisely, and more wonderfully than anyone can imagine.

Lord, thank you for always having the perfect response to whatever it is I am going through, whether grief, joy, pain, or contentment.

May 18

Elizabeth and Me

If the foot should say, "Because I am not a hand, I do not belong to the body," it would not for that reason cease to be part of the body.

—1 Corinthians 12:15

When I was in Germany a few years ago to speak at a church, I was linked up with a blind woman named Elizabeth, who served as my interpreter. For five sessions we were at the microphone, me with my wheelchair and Elizabeth with her white cane.

During a break, someone placed on my lap a magazine printed in English. It looked like good reading, but I couldn't hold it or turn the pages.

Elizabeth asked me a few questions about the cover, so I said, "Look, how about if you hold it up and turn the pages. That way I can read it aloud so we can both enjoy it." We did just that. After a few minutes Elizabeth and I attracted the attention of her pastor, who, upon watching us, decided to use us as an illustration for his sermon on 1 Corinthians 12. In short, we all have need of each other. Imagine, just imagine, a church in which each member used his or her strength to make up for another's weakness. Eyes see, ears hear, hands hold, and feet move the body forward. When everyone fulfills their function, the whole body benefits. When someone's not doing his or her thing, everybody suffers. My blind friend in Germany would agree: in the church body there's no such thing as a nobody.

What strengths do you bring to the body? Are you using them for the Lord? If not, give your pastor a call and offer to do your part.

Father God, sometimes it's hard to step forward and volunteer to help out. Strengthen my resolve to contribute to the church body the abilities you have given me, even if they seem not spectacular but quite ordinary. They are still the gifts you have given me, and I want to give them back as an offering to you.

May 19

Limited Resources

"How many loaves do you have?" he asked. "Go and see."
When they found out, they said, "Five—and two fish."
—Mark 6:38

Do you ever feel as if you're only one person who can only do so much, especially in the face of some pressing need? We can all find excuses to sidestep a problem. We can say that we're the wrong person for the job, that we can't do it alone, that we have other priorities, that God hasn't called us to meet the need, or we can use the ever-ready excuse "I only have limited resources."

That's the excuse the disciples reached for in Mark 6 when Jesus told them to give a huge crowd something to eat. They said to him, "Look, Lord, we only have five loaves and two fish." Well, you know what Jesus did with that excuse. He turned it into a miracle of multiplication, and before they knew it, the disciples ended up helping to feed five thousand.

God laughs in the face of limited resources. In fact, he often uses limitations on our resources to strengthen and test our faith as we step out and believe he will supply the need.

That's something to remember if today you are faced with a need, a project, a problem with which you feel bound and gagged because of your lack of resources. Remember: when you roll up your sleeves and dig into the task God has put before you, your resources will expand. Out of nowhere you will find you have the strength, you will see you have the time, and if money is the problem, watch to see how God will supply what's needed.

God of limitlessness, I confess that I'm often caught up in seeing the limits rather than the possibilities. Open my eyes, but more importantly open my heart, that I might see and believe.

The Shepherd

... our Lord Jesus, that great Shepherd of the sheep ...
—Hebrews 13:20

Phillip Keller, a shepherd (and also an author), once wrote,

The day I bought my first thirty ewes, my neighbor and I sat on the dusty corral rails that enclosed the sheep pens and admired the choice, strong, well-bred ewes that had become mine. Turning to me he handed me a large, sharp, killing knife and remarked tersely, "Well, Phillip, they're yours. Now you'll have to put your mark on them."

I knew exactly what he meant. Each sheep-man has his own distinctive earmark which he cuts into one or the other of the ears of his sheep. In this way, even at a distance, it is easy to determine to whom the sheep belongs. It was not the most pleasant procedure to catch each ewe in turn and lay her ear on a wooden block then notch it deeply with the razor-sharp edge of the knife. There was pain for both of us. But from our mutual suffering an indelible lifelong mark of ownership was made that could never be erased. And from then on every sheep that came into my possession would bear my mark.[3]

As a sheep of the Good Shepherd, you bear his mark, a cross. It may be painful, but it's your mark of identification with your Shepherd. Ask yourself, "Do I recognize his right and claim over me? Do I respond to his authority? Bear the mark he's given me?" If you do, you can exalt with the psalmist and say, "The Lord *is* my Shepherd!"

If his mark seems difficult to bear, remember: "He tends his flock like a shepherd: He gathers the lambs in his arms and carries them close to his heart; he gently leads those that have young" (Isa. 40:11).

Lord, I remember how you came to earth to give your life for us—all we are like sheep who have gone astray. Thank you for being our Shepherd. And thank you for laying your life down for your sheep—you, the Lamb of God.

May 21

When Goodness Comes Home

We are looking forward to God's promise of new heavens and
a new earth afterwards, where there will be only goodness.
—2 Peter 3:13 LB

O dear God, *"Where there will be only goodness."*
After centuries of war, greed, and lust.
After indulgences shamelessly practiced
After hatred, hostility, jealousy and abuse.
Murder and martyrdom, crime and cruelty, curses and rebellion.
After whimpering cries from starving children
After tragedy and catastrophe
Loneliness and despair
At last . . . at long last
"There will be only goodness."
O dear Lord
Your promise is Your guarantee
But please hurry a little!

Ruth Harms Calkin[4]

I love today's verse. In the NIV it says, "we are looking forward to . . .
the home of righteousness." Think of all that home, in its best sense,
means: warmth and acceptance, a place of love and welcome. Home, in
the truest sense, should mean a place where we fit like nowhere else. Right
now our souls have no real home on earth. There's so much loneliness and
despair, hate and violence. True, every once in a while, such as in our own
homes with our own families, we are refreshed by long moments of tran-
quillity, when everyone and everything around us is peaceful—wouldn't it
be wonderful if it were always that way? In our own homes and beyond?
In our communities and around the world? One day it will be so. Goodness will have come home to stay.

What can you do to make your surroundings more like "home"?
Hurry God's promise a little by spreading his righteousness today.

I am so thankful, Lord, that I have a home of goodness to look forward to.
May I feel at home in your righteousness today, sharing you with others.

Unusual Kindness

*The islanders showed us unusual kindness. They built a fire
and welcomed us all because it was raining and cold.*

—Acts 28:2

Imagine that scene. Two hundred and seventy-six people—prisoners, soldiers, and crew—all standing helpless on the shore. Each one was drenched, frigid to the bone. They had nothing with them except the clothes on their back. No trunks with goods to trade. No potential for spending lots of money to boost the island's economy. Just themselves.

Luke records that the islanders welcomed them with unusual kindness, unusual because the people responded to the need of the moment and not to the reputation of the castaways. Only later, after Paul avoided a venomous death and later healed the sick, was it noted that "they honored us in many ways and when we were ready to sail, they furnished us with the supplies we needed" (Acts 28:10).

What hospitable people! Given the strategic location of the island, I have no doubt that Luke and his companions were not the first to be shipwrecked there. Nevertheless, they received the castaways without reservation. And when the party was leaving, they gave them all they needed. We later learn in history that the entire island of Malta was converted to Christianity. Somehow we're not surprised. They welcomed the good news of God as readily as they welcomed the dying strangers.

What is the nature of our hospitality? Is it based on what we perceive the stature of the person to be? Fortunately, the Maltese didn't think that way. Their unusual kindness enabled Paul to advance the gospel in the West. Imagine what the face of Europe and the West would be like if the castaways had perished there on Malta.

Lord, I'm living on the beautiful island of Malta because I'm in your family. Help me to show their hospitality today. To everyone.

May 23

Vision

Your kingdom come, your will be done on earth as it is in heaven.

—Matthew 6:10

When I paint close to the canvas, I wear heavy-duty, industrial-strength prescription glasses. Those thick lenses help me see things as they should be seen. It's called vision—seeing things clearly. Vision is also what happens when we see the world as it should be seen, as God sees it. If we don't envision the world as God sees it, others won't get the picture. God's picture. The picture of his kingdom come. Christians see this. We are the ones who have "prescription glasses," as it were.

Communicating a kingdom vision to the world is a little like snapping a Polaroid and then holding it up so others can get the picture. We present God's snapshot of what the world should look like, so people might know what is possible. It's a little like paraphrasing today's verse: "Thy kingdom come, thy will be done. . . . May we see it happen on earth just as it is happening in heaven, where we can't see it."

Oswald Chambers said, "A man with the vision of God is not devoted simply to a cause or a particular issue . . . he is devoted to God himself."[5] If the Lord Jesus is the one to whom you are devoted, you can't help but be a person of vision. You can't help but see what he sees regarding the world around you. And you will see the kingdom picture come more into focus, become clearer, the more time you spend with him.

Would you say you are a visionary? If you love Christ, if you desire to see things as he sees them, you definitely are a person of vision. So pray his vision into being. Work to see it happen. Tell others about it. Watch the kingdom develop right before your eyes. And the world—your world—will never be the same.

Without a vision, the people perish. And Lord, without a vision, I would perish. Let me see my world through your eyes. May I pray today's verse with new insight. Strengthen my eyes. . . . Make clear the vision.

May 24

Following Hard

My soul followeth hard after thee: thy right hand uphold-
eth me.

—Psalm 63:8 KJV

You follow Christ, but do you follow hard after him? Another transla-
tion, *The Living Bible,* says, "My soul follows close behind you." The
soul that follows hard on the heels of God is childlike. I know that from
experience. My parents were hikers who took us often on backpacking
trips. As the youngest, I learned that if I didn't keep up, if I didn't stick on
the heels of my older sisters, I'd get lost in the woods (or so I thought).

We need to be the sort of followers who are constantly bumping into
God's back. We need a healthy dose of fear that without him we'd be lost
(and we would!). Don't fall behind. Don't think you can find your way.
Don't run ahead and don't detour around. Just stay close behind the Lord
where the trail is fresh. Psalm 16:11 says, "You have made known to me
the path of life; you will fill me with joy in your presence, with eternal
pleasures at your right hand."

And how does our heavenly Father feel about us tagging along so
closely? *Delighted.* Nothing could please him more than when we, his children, desire to stay close. Psalm 139:3 in *The Living Bible* says, "You chart
the path ahead of me, and tell me where to stop and rest. Every moment,
you know where I am."

What do you think it means to "step on God's heels"? To pump your
thinking, read Proverbs 3:5–6. Did you catch that phrase "In all your ways
acknowledge him"? To acknowledge means to follow hard after God: being
instant in obedience, absolute in your trust, immediate in your prayers,
and quick in your response to the Spirit's proddings.

Would to God that we all would keep stepping on the heels of the
Lord Jesus. Make it your goal today to follow hard after him. "The
steps of a man are established by the Lord. . . . When he falls, he shall
not be hurled headlong; because the Lord is the One who holds his
hand" (Ps. 37:23–24 NASB).

*I desire to follow you, Lord. But today I want to quicken my step and
follow hard after you. Show me the path. Tell me where to stop and rest.
Fill me with joy in your presence.*

May 25

A Good Kind of Anger

"In your anger do not sin": Do not let the sun go down
while you are still angry.

—Ephesians 4:26

My friend Robert exploded at God the other day when Joshua, his little boy with multiple disabilities, suffered yet another seizure. "God, I don't get it," Robert protested. "How can you allow Joshua to have a seizure that causes him to fall and bang his head?" Strong words. We're usually scared to talk to God that way. Too often we choose the polite route, bottling up our unspeakable feelings toward God. But all we've done is shove the problem to the back burner.

Anger at least keeps the problem on the front burner, propelling us into action. And that may not be all bad. When Ephesians 4:26 states, "In your anger do not sin," it's clear not all anger is wrong. Strong emotions open the door to ask the hard questions: Does life make sense? Is God good? More to the point, our deep emotions reveal the spiritual direction in which we are moving. Are we moving toward God with our heated questions, or are we moving away from him?

The thing I love about Robert is that he is taking his concerns to God. He is moving toward the Lord. He is not sowing seeds of discord, spreading slander or inciting rebellion against God among others. He's not talking about God behind God's back; he's engaging him head-on.

This makes Robert's anger good. When I listen to him, I can almost hear embedded between the lines an honest hunger, a desire to stay connected. After all, the people you really get angry with are sometimes the ones you trust the most.

Sometimes the anger we express toward God can be an upside-down way of trusting him. It's the dark side of trust but trust nonetheless. If your soul is in turmoil, all God is looking for is a thin thread of trust. Then God is able to work in your life. But only if you take your anger to—not away from—him.

Lord God, help me to remember that you are big enough to handle my honest feelings. If I'm angry or hurt, help me to express it to you without showing disrespect.

May 26

Ram Fat

Samuel replied: "Does the LORD delight in burnt offerings
and sacrifices as much as in obeying the voice of the LORD?
To obey is better than sacrifice, and to heed is better than
the fat of rams."

—1 Samuel 15:22

Elisabeth Elliot tells the story of a little girl who, instead of doing her
chores, decided she should spend that hour practicing on the piano.
She sat proudly plunking away "Jesus Loves Me." Her mother called from
the other room, reminding the child of her duties, but the girl continued
to fill the house with the melody of praise. Was her piano playing
rewarded? Not at all. Songs of praise lose their meaning when offered out
of disobedience.

We are not unlike the child at the piano. Like Saul, who disobeyed
God, keeping the best of the Amalekites' oxen and sheep to enhance his
sacrifices to the Lord, we try to justify our disobedience with a show of
religion. We remain in an evil trade, thinking that we can then earn more
to give to the Lord. We hold on to a small but corrupt habit with the excuse
that we balance it out with faithful attendance at prayer meeting and choir
rehearsal. But it's all ram fat.

The truth is, the Amalekites' sheep and cattle *were* a better breed.
Those animals would have made for a "better" sacrifice. For that matter,
the child's rendition of "Jesus Loves Me" at any other time would have
been sweet music to her mother's ears. In the same way, giving more to the
Lord is a wonderful thing, and faithful attendance at prayer meeting is to
be admired—but all of it is ram fat when offered through disobedience.

To heed is better than the fat of rams. Be quiet for a moment and let
the Spirit scrutinize your offerings of late to the Lord. What is he
whispering to you right now? Is there any ram fat you are presenting
to God?

*Lord, obedience is much more of a holy thing to offer you than anything
else, no matter how pleasing it appears or how much sacrifice was
involved. Help me to remember this.*

Life Would Be Great If Only . . .

In Christ all the fullness of the Deity lives in bodily form,
and you have been given fullness in Christ, who is the head
over every power and authority.

—Colossians 2:9–10

What do quadriplegics (people whose hands and legs are paralyzed) day-dream about? Running a marathon? Ballroom dancing? Climbing a mountain? Many of us have scaled down our fantasies. In my weaker moments I'm tempted to think life would be great if only I were a paraplegic—then I could use my hands. I see paraplegics transfer themselves out of their wheelchairs into their own beds, reach for items in the refrigerator, wash dishes at a sink, and quickly sort through the mail. Then old feelings of disappointment start to slink back into my heart.

Even able-bodied people look at others who seem more attractive, smarter, richer, healthier, and who get all the breaks in life. In comparison, minor defects begin to look like deformities. Thankfully, the Bible has good advice for people prone to compare. Paul tells us we have been given fullness in Christ. In other words, we are complete in him. We have everything. We lack nothing. There's no need to compare. Once we comprehend this truth, our so-called defects become reminders of how full we are—because we have fullness in Christ. The inferiority complex releases its grip. We become content.

I wouldn't be happier if I were a paraplegic rather than a quadriplegic. The fullness of Christ dwells in me, even with my infirmities. Therefore I will gladly boast as a quadriplegic. After all, you can't improve on complete.

In what ways do you feel incomplete, inadequate, or less than you had hoped? Rather than seeing these as insufficiencies, realize you are lacking in nothing. Why? Because Christ dwells in you. Bask in that knowledge for a few quiet moments, and feel yourself relax into contentedness.

Lord, help me to keep from drumming up "if only" scenarios in my mind. Fill my thoughts with satisfaction in you and in whom you have fashioned me to be.

May 28

Shortcuts

The way of a fool seems right to him, but a wise man listens to advise.

—Proverbs 12:15

Who would be dumb enough to take a shortcut through a narrow train tunnel? Well, I was, and I did it more than once. As a kid, when I rode my horse as far as Marriottsville, I would have to take the trail up and around a small mountain—or I could ride my horse through the tunnel.

Shortcuts. Our Scripture for today tells us about such craziness. And I lived it out. It seemed right to me to look for a shortcut, and I failed to listen to the advice of the big yellow sign at the head of the tunnel. Although I never came face-to-face with the B & O Express, I do think that reckless spirit caught up with me when I dove into shallow water and broke my neck.

Yes, the way of a fool often seems right, and a shortcut makes such good sense to that same fool. But sooner or later it has a way of catching up with us. We may take shortcuts in our Bible study, responding to the questions with the first thing that comes to mind. We may take shortcuts in our prayers, skipping over the words of a daily devotional rather than pressing them into our hearts. Or we may even take shortcuts in serving others, lest that service require sacrifice. We believe we can arrive at righteousness through a series of convenient shortcuts.

The way of a shortcut seems right in the eyes of those who foolishly think they can get away with it. And get away with it they will—for a short while. But whom are they fooling? Is it God? Is it others? Perhaps only themselves. If you would be smart enough not to walk through a train tunnel, take Scripture's advice. There's no quick way to reach spiritual maturity.

Lord, when I'm tempted to take spiritual shortcuts, please remind me that the Israelites wandered in the wilderness because they needed to take the long way home.

A "Kidney" Christian

> On the contrary, those parts of the body that seem to be weaker are indispensable, and the parts that we think are less honorable we treat with special honor. And the parts that are unpresentable are treated with special modesty, while our presentable parts need no special treatment. But God has combined the members of the body and has given greater honor to the parts that lacked it.
>
> —1 Corinthians 12:22–24

Some time ago I forced myself to watch *The Operation* on the Learning Channel. They show real operations, with real blood and real sutures. I made myself watch because they were showing a kidney transplant, and I wanted to see what a good friend of mine, Mike Yuen, had to go through when he gave a kidney to his brother, Geoff. Mike made this big sacrifice because people can't survive without a kidney.

You can live without your eyes, your ears, or use of your hands or legs. I know thousands of people who do. But here's the irony: while most of us are convinced we could never survive without these up-front, kind-of-showy body parts ("Oh, Lord, I could *never* survive without my eyesight!"), we never consider the pancreas, kidney, or liver. Because we don't see these hidden body parts, we quickly forget how critical they are to life.

There's a parallel here to the body of Christ. As 1 Corinthians 12 says, a church can't make it—the church can't survive as the functioning body of Christ—without that weaker person, that needy family, that man or woman who isn't up front. Without them, the church can't be what it's supposed to be. Hurting people give the rest of the body of Christ an opportunity to serve. And sacrificial service means there's no time for division, factions, or rivalry.

You need your kidney. And your church needs a kidney kind of guy who may be homeless, helpless, handicapped, or hurting.

Do you have needs you should express to the church? Or should you meet the need of another member? Maybe you need to do both!

Sometimes, Father God, I get so caught up in the part I think I should play in the church that I don't stop long enough to ask if I understand correctly. I'm listening to you now.

May 30

Take Care of the Temple

What is your life? You are a mist that appears for a little
while and then vanishes.

—James 4:14

Remember yesterday I told you about my friend Mike Yuen, who
donated his kidney to his brother, Geoff? As I write this, two years have
passed since the surgery. And the news is not good. It's been the typical
transplant rejection, coupled with complications from diabetes. Geoff is
aware that he is dying. And it's hard.

It's hard for Mike too. He was asked, "Would you give your kidney
again, knowing now the outcome?" His answer gripped me: "I would do
it again without hesitation because I'm grateful that Geoff has had two
strong years, with more time to come. Most of all I'm grateful that in the
year following the surgery, Geoff came to Christ."

Mike had something else to say: "I've learned we're not in control of
life, and it's arrogance we think we are. Each day is a precious gift from
God we shouldn't waste. We have a purpose in this life, so let's not neglect
it. Secondly, we can't take health for granted. While we do not have control over whether or not we contract cancer or have a disabling accident,
there's much we can do to take care of what we have—we owe it to those
who love us and depend on us, and we owe it to God who created us."

"Don't you know that you yourselves are God's temple and that God's
Spirit lives in you?" (1 Cor. 3:16). Too many of us take better care of our
cars than we do our bodies. We can affix a dollar figure to a luxury automobile, but who can put a price on the ability to see, hear, think, walk,
and talk?

What can you do today to better maintain your physical health?
Have you been putting off a checkup? Ignoring your body's warning
signals? As a Spanish proverb says, "From the bitterness of disease
man learns the sweetness of health."[6]

*Lord, you've given me so much, when I think of all the things my body
can do. I bless you for the gift of good health—I commit myself to taking better care of the temple you have given me.*

May 31

I Was Just Wondering

When the queen of Sheba heard of the fame of Solomon, she came to prove Solomon with hard questions at Jerusalem, with a very great company, and camels that bare spices, and gold in abundance, and precious stones: and when she was come to Solomon, she communed with him of all that was in her heart.

—2 Chronicles 9:1 KJV

Our questions haven't changed much since the queen of Sheba's time. Or have they? I recall reading an article not long ago that listed a few questions. I can't remember the author, but here are a few queries the queen may have missed. . . .

Why do people show great interest in "near-death experiences" but no interest in heaven? What makes God happy? Why do sinners so often feel attracted to Jesus but repulsed by the church? Why do so few Christians get around to reading Aleksandr Solzhenitsyn, a writer who sounds like a modern Amos or Isaiah?

Why are there so many kinds of animals? Couldn't the world get along with, say, three hundred thousand species of beetles instead of five hundred thousand? Why is it that the most beautiful animals on earth are hidden away from all humans (except those wearing elaborate scuba equipment)? Who are they beautiful for? Why is almost all religious art realistic, whereas much of God's creation—zebras, the swallowtail butterfly, and crystalline structures—excels at abstract design? When chimpanzees laugh and play with one another, are they happy like humans? Why did Solomon, who showed such wisdom in writing Proverbs, spend the last years of his life breaking a lot of those proverbs?

Here's a question for you. Why, when the gospel is replete with stories of grace, acceptance, and forgiveness, do you often feel more guilty than forgiven? Pause today and go to God, saying, "Lord, I was just wondering . . ." and then open your heart to him, as the queen of Sheba did with Solomon. You may be surprised at the answer.

I have many questions, God. Yet the closer I get to you, the more I see how you are all wisdom. I leave all things with you.

JUNE

Life Is So Daily

Your strength will equal your days.
—Deuteronomy 33:25

Have you ever thought of your days as being so ... daily? The minute you open your eyes in the morning, you can feel yourself shifting into routine. Turn off alarm. Fling back covers. Put feet in slippers. Turn on shower. Squeeze toothpaste on brush while shower heats up. Like I said: it's so daily.

That's especially true for me. I wake up every morning to the exact same series of events. A friend comes into the bedroom, turns on the tap to warm the water, heads for the kitchen and pours coffee, comes back and puts the coffee straw in my mouth, and begins to put my legs through their range-of-motion exercise routine. After that it's a bath, get dressed, and be lifted into my wheelchair. Some days I wish the routine could vary, but like you, I must accept the dailyness.

My friend Shirley Locker, who is also disabled, once reminded me that our daily challenges have rewards for those who trust God for hour-by-hour (sometimes minute-by-minute) strength. God promises, "Your strength will equal your days."

No matter how deep the rut of our daily routine, satisfaction in the Lord Jesus can be deeper still. In fact, God invites us to know his satisfaction on a more profound level as we remind ourselves to go to him for grace, especially during those so-called boring hours when we feel our life is on automatic. He knows that's when we need him most.

No matter how much the same your day appears, God's grace will make it different because his grace is fresh every morning. Lamentations 3:22–23 tells us his love and compassion are new every morning. What a relief. What parts of your day are routine? Why not infuse them with life by inviting God to be a part of them? Memorize Scripture during your bathroom routines, and pray while you're dressing.

Thank you, Lord, that your strength and grace are daily—not that they're routine but that they're consistently available. Every day. Every hour. Every moment. Help me to draw on them today.

June 2

God's Clean Slate

I, even I, am he who blots out your transgressions, for my
own sake, and remembers your sins no more.
—Isaiah 43:25

Every parent knows that sinking feeling when their kid blows it. They do
what you told them not to do, they lie to you, or they get in trouble at
school. You hope it was all a passing nightmare, but the deed's been done
and it won't go away.

At least, that's how it feels at the time. But have you ever noticed what
happens when grandparents get together with the family and reminisce
about what life was like? An amazing transformation takes place. The children who once were described as little devils are now angels. The brothers
and sisters who fought like cats and dogs are remembered as puppies and
kittens. They never talked back to Mom and they always obeyed Dad. Such
romanticizing by the grandparents elicits from their grown children either
guffaws or a silent rolling of the eyes. *How could they forget?* they wonder
about their parents.

Is it senility? Or were the transgressions not worth remembering? Neither. I think parents forget because their love can't retain those sins for very
long. Our love hasn't enough strength to hold on to that which is grievous.

God's paternal love has a weak memory as well. He tells us that he
blots out our transgressions and forgets them on purpose. Why? "For my
own sake," he says. Rather than our sin being an impersonal infraction of
his cosmic order, it is deeply personal. It strikes at the core of his relationship with his creation, his image bearers. It is grievous.

So grievous was our sin that God sought an effective and eternal erad-
ication. No sentimental, romantic senility would do. No divine
dementia. Only his Son could blot out the trespass forever. Only
Jesus could serve as the "forsaken one" so we might be embraced as
the "sins-forgotten ones." For God's sake.

*Lord, grant me as bad a memory about my sin as you have. Cleanse me
today of the sins I confess, and then help me to reminisce with your same
joy.*

Stir the Gift of the Spirit

*For this reason I remind you to fan into flame the gift of
God, which is in you through the laying on of my hands.*
—2 Timothy 1:6

One of my favorite summertime activities is to tent camp. There's nothing like a campfire in the morning when you get up. And the smell of
those sizzling eggs and bacon . . . yum.

Shortly after breakfast my husband, Ken, will let the fire die down.
Then at suppertime Ken has to start the fire again. But this is an economical man. Instead of starting from scratch, Ken will poke the coals,
searching for the tiniest spark of life. Sure enough, way down in the ashes
there will usually be a glowing coal left over from the morning campfire.
He nurtures it with dry grass and leaves until it's roaring once again. It
seems that no matter how small the spark or how dim the flicker, Ken can
bring a fire back to life.

It's the same with the Spirit of Christ in our lives. Sometimes the spark
may be small, but if there is the tiniest ember, the slightest hint of obedience in our Christian life, it's not too late to be revived.

God has given us light, knowledge, and a new heart. He has given you
and me grace and a new nature—and he has deprived us of every excuse
if we do not live for his praise. So if we are not holy, whose fault is it but
our own? If we do not appear sanctified, who can we blame but ourselves?

How about you? Do you feel the ashes smoldering, even if faintly?
Do you sense life within, even if feeble? Nurture it. Gently fan the
spark—follow through on the nudge to obey, spend a little time in
prayer, revive yourself in God's Word. Don't neglect the grace, the
heart, and the new nature God has given you. Poke around and get
the fire of the Spirit going in your life.

*Forgiving Father, I pray with the psalmist, "Renew a steadfast spirit
within me. . . . Restore to me the joy of your salvation."*

The Self-Sufficiency of God

This is my Son, whom I love; with him I am well pleased.
—Matthew 3:17

If you were God, where would you go to be impressed? Conversation with any of your creatures, even the grandest, costs an infinite lowering of yourself. What could entertain your limitless mind? Whose character and accomplishments could take you aback? Where could you find beauty and grace enough to ravish *you?*

Nothing can satisfy God but another infinite, eternal being. For God, the real intoxication comes as he stares in the mirror—which is the Trinity. Three-As-One, he draws life and enjoyment from no one but himself. He sustains his own existence and fans the flame of his own emotional life. He is his own best friend.

The Spirit is the quiet one. Sharing equal deity and status with the others, he nevertheless flows from the Father and the Son. But it's the Son who commands center stage. The Spirit points to him, and the Father never stops bragging about him, "Here is my . . . chosen one in whom I delight" (Isa. 42:1). Why does the Father treasure him so? Because he sees himself in his Son. His own perfections are flawlessly reflected there. The Son is God standing in the mirror.

What does the self-sufficiency of God mean to us? God is joy, love, contentment, and abundance spilling over. This is where his mercy comes from. This is why God is more than able to give and keep on giving. The full tank of love he enjoys is splashing out over heaven's walls, and he is driven to share his elation with us. Why? Simply, as he put it in John 15:11, "so that my joy may be in you." (Estes)

I praise you, Lord, for being all-sufficient in yourself. You have need of nothing, and this is good news for the rest of us. I'm grateful that your joy and peace are so plentiful, your mercy so abundant, that I can catch the overflow. Thank you for this.

Something Scary

> Not everyone who says to me, "Lord, Lord," will enter the
> kingdom of heaven, but only he who does the will of my
> Father who is in heaven.
>
> —Matthew 7:21

Does today's verse make you nervous? And what about the next verse, which states, "Many will say . . . , 'Lord, did we not prophesy in your name, and in your name drive out demons and perform many miracles?'" Jesus answers that question with, "I never knew you. Away from me, you evildoers!"

You might say to yourself, *If those miracle-working, demon-busting guys aren't making it with the Lord, what about me?* Ah, but don't be intimidated by people who seem to be on some higher spiritual plain. If God's not impressed with so-called miracle workers, we shouldn't feel insecure around them, either.

Now, don't get me wrong. Bona fide miracles are going on. But if all you hear is "Lord, we did this," "Lord, we did that," "Lord, look at what was done over here by us," realize that God is not swayed by showy drama. He's not impressed with all the "we's." Neither is he impressed when we recount to him all our good works, all that we've done. Such things are never a passport into heaven.

The one who quietly perseveres and does the simple, everyday will of the Father will enter the kingdom.

And what is God's will? To be like Jesus. To let him shine through you in a patient, loving, and enduring way. Whatever you do, whatever you are, as long as you're like Jesus, you're in God's will. That's not such a scary idea after all, is it?

Lord, thank you that I don't need to put on a show to impress you or anyone else. Thank you that my task is to imitate you in every way I can, every day of my life. Help me today to do just that.

A Family Affair

He answered: "Love the Lord your God with all your heart
and with all your soul and with all your strength and with
all your mind"; and, "Love your neighbor as yourself."
—Luke 10:27

A new command I give you: Love one another. As I have
loved you, so you must love one another. By this all men
will know that you are my disciples, if you love one another.
—John 13:34–35

Notice a difference in these two verses? It's subtle but powerful. In Luke, Jesus tells us to love our neighbors as ourselves. In John, Jesus is talking not about our neighbors but about our brothers and sisters in the faith. He tells us to love fellow Christians "as I have loved you."

How has God loved us? With everything. He held back nothing. Not even his own Son. God says of his children, this is the way "you *must* love one another" (emphasis added). No holding back. No reservations or second-guessing. No "doing unto others as you would have them do unto you" but "loving your brothers and sisters as God loves them."

We are to go the second mile for our neighbors, but we're to go the third and fourth mile for those in the household of faith. What are the practical ways in which you can show love to other Christians? Listen to the advise of 1 Corinthians 13 from *The Message:*

Love never gives up. . . . Love doesn't want what it doesn't have. Love doesn't strut, Doesn't have a swelled head, Doesn't force itself on others, Isn't always "me first," Doesn't fly off the handle, Doesn't keep score . . . Doesn't revel when others grovel, Takes pleasure in the flowering of truth, Puts up with anything, Trusts God always, Always looks for the best, Never looks back, But keeps going to the end.

I want to grasp how wide and long and high and deep is the love of Christ so I can love other Christians in the same way. This is how the world will know that you are real, Father—by our love for each other!

A Little Bit of Hanging

Before I was afflicted I went astray, but now I obey your word. You are good, and what you do is good; teach me your decrees.

—Psalm 119:67–68

A Civil War story is told of a woman who sought the favor of Abraham Lincoln on behalf of her soldier son, who apparently committed an act of treason. A war court found her son guilty and sentenced him to hanging. The mother, undaunted by the news, scraped and clawed all the way to the top to gain the ear of the president. Lincoln was taken with the woman's tenacity as well as with her devotion to her family. After reviewing the soldier's case, Lincoln gave him a pardon. Nevertheless, he hesitated to rejoice with the mother, saying, "Your son may be free, but I still wish we could give him a little bit of hanging."

Lincoln had it right. Nothing drives home the sweetness of freedom like the bitter taste of a little bit of punishment. Nothing reinforces the blessings of a pardon like standing on the block with the noose around your neck minutes before. The same is true with suffering. When we go through hellish circumstances, God gives us a small taste of the hell we are saved from—suffering is in fact "a little bit of hanging." It is hell's splash-over, giving us a bitter but small taste of the real thing. The result? Our salvation tastes all the sweeter. The blessings of eternal pardon are driven home. "It was good for me to be afflicted so that I might learn your decrees. The law from your mouth is more precious to me than thousands of pieces of silver and gold" (Ps. 119:71–72).

If we never "went through hell" on earth, how could we possibly appreciate all that God has saved us from? As today's passage reminds us, it is good that we've been afflicted; from it, we learn of God's decrees, his law is more precious, we stop straying from his side, and we make obedience to him our goal.

Have you experienced "a little bit of hanging" lately? Memorize today's verse and savor it as your declaration of pardon.

It is good that I have been afflicted in the following ways, Lord . . .

June 8

Getting What We Don't Deserve

The LORD is compassionate and gracious.... He does not
treat us as our sins deserve or repay us according to our
iniquities.

—Psalm 103:8, 10

Do most people get what they deserve out of life? Some would say the
drunk driver who breaks his back in an auto accident does. And so
does the promiscuous adult who contracts AIDS; the rebellious teenager
who becomes pregnant; the drug user who fries his brains. These people
do suffer the consequences of their actions.

But that's not the rule of thumb. Most people don't get what's due
them. And I'm glad! Because do we really want God to give us what we
deserve? At first blush we think we're entitled to health and wealth. We
assume we've got coming to us those inalienable rights of life, liberty, and
the pursuit of happiness. But dig a bit deeper. We're leaving out something
important. It's our sin. And sin is not just some pious word reserved for
religious conversations. It's not just a concept that we throw into our
prayers when it's time to confess. Your sin, my sin is something that is a
stinking offense to God.

You see, *God* is the one who's got rights here. He has every right to
permit the full impact of our willful disobedience to harm us. If we got
what was due us, we would be annihilated. But—whew—that's not the
way he works. Instead God chooses to deal with us in mercy, love, and forgiveness, just as the Scripture for today says.

What do you think you deserve today? Think you're entitled to a few
luxurious minutes of complaining? Think your problems give you a
right to resent? Want some time off from obeying God? Is that what
you're entitled to?

When I get just a glimpse of myself as you must see me, Lord, I'm stunned.
Stripped of my facades, pretenses, and camouflaging makeup that keep
others and myself from seeing me for who I really am, I'm not a pretty
sight. But I am overwhelmed by your tender mercies.

June 9

You're Not Normal

The LORD said to Samuel, "Do not consider his appearance or his height, for I have rejected him. The LORD does not look at the things man looks at. Man looks at the outward appearance, but the LORD looks at the heart."

—1 Samuel 16:7

When I speak, my message is often about how God has helped me grow leaps and bounds using my wheelchair. However, one time after I gave that message, a woman approached me and said, "Joni, don't worry. One day you'll be normal, just like us." She missed the point.

I wasn't offended by the woman's comment so much as saddened that she was making the mistake described in 1 Samuel 16:7. She was looking at the outward appearance. She inferred that I envied her ability to stand. In her view "normal" meant having a body that "worked," even if it was slightly overweight with a touch of arthritis.

We Christians need to shift our thinking and "fix our eyes not on what is seen, but on what is unseen. For what is seen is temporary, but what is unseen is eternal" (2 Cor. 4:18). God is concerned about unseen things like patience, sensitivity, faith, goodness, perseverance, and self-control. We are normal in God's eyes when we demonstrate endurance and long-suffering, when we keep looking to the unseen things. This is the normal Christian life. You can live it whether you're five foot two standing or four foot three sitting. You can live it whether you have varicose veins from walking or atrophied muscles from being paralyzed.

I will not be normal someday; I am normal right now. So are you if you abide by 2 Corinthians 4:18, fixing your eyes on what's important *eternally*. Take a look in your heart to check whether its "time" is correct.

Lord, so many of my thoughts are caught up in the here and now that I forget that if I can see it, it's temporary. Enable me to fix my gaze on what's important, the eternal.

The Rose

I am a rose of Sharon, a lily of the valleys.

—Song of Songs 2:1

Some people claim that the rose is the crown jewel of the garden. It's one of my favorites, and I enjoy capturing its intricacies with paint and brush. For all these reasons and more, I was touched by a poem sent to me a couple of years ago. Written by a missionary, it's called "The Rose."

It's only a tiny rosebud—a flower of God's design;
But I can't unfold the petals with these clumsy hands of mine.
The secret of unfolding flowers is not known to such as I—
The flower God opens so sweetly in my hands would fade and die.
If I cannot unfold a rosebud this flower of God's design,
Then how can I think I have wisdom to unfold this life of mine?
So I'll trust in Him for His leading each moment of every day,
And I'll look to Him for His guidance each step of the pilgrim way.
For the pathway that lies before me my Heavenly Father knows—
I'll trust Him to unfold the moments just as He unfolds the rose.

As the poem suggests, we can't grow the moments of our lives any more than we can peel back the petals of a rose. As we look to God's leading each moment of the day, we can trust him to unfurl each hour just as he unfurls the rose. Little wonder the Lord is called the Rose of Sharon. We just can't get enough of watching his glory, like that glorious flower, unfold in our lives.

Can you trust God to unfold a lovely plan for your life? Can people see Jesus more clearly in you as you bloom? What changes do you need to make to be able to answer yes with confidence?

Sun and shower, bud to flower, a rose is like my heart—
I lay it bare, unfurl with care, each fragile fold, each part.
Rose of Sharon, I take care in offering my praise—
It's yours for pleasure, yours forever, a flower for your vase.

A Blinding, Wonderful Light

You are a chosen people, a royal priesthood, a holy nation, a people belonging to God, that you may declare the praises of him who called you out of darkness into his wonderful light.

—1 Peter 2:9

The other day I was telling my friend Doug Vinez how, on Saturday mornings when I was a kid, my neighborhood friends and I would hop on the streetcar and head to the Ambassador Theatre. We would load up on Peanut Chews and stake out seats midway up the aisle.

Doug told me about an old theater he used to visit. This one had no lobby. You walked through the glass doors, and within a few feet you would pass through a curtain and bump up against the back row. When the movie was over, there was no vestibule to ease you out of darkness and back into daylight. He described how kids would walk outside, rub their eyes, and almost bump into lampposts—the light was a jolt to their senses.

Doug added, "I almost forgot about that theater until I read 1 Peter 2:9." When I asked him to explain the connection, he said, "As a Christian, I forget what a blinding jolt it was to be taken out of darkness and placed in light."

He's right. We Christians can hardly recall the blinding reality of being translated from the kingdom of darkness to the kingdom of God's dear Son. One minute we were heading to hell; the next, heaven. One minute we were dead in our sins; the next, alive unto God. If we really thought about it, we would be overwhelmed, rubbing our eyes and exclaiming, "What a jolt *this* is!"

May your heart never become so familiar with darkness that you forget the night-become-day reality of life in the Lord. The Lord Jesus has saved you, and it's a change about which you must never become complacent.

Lord of light, thank you for giving sight to me when I was blind to my own sin, and for removing me from the darkness of my lost state.

June 12

The Betrothal

In my Father's house are many rooms; if it were not so, I
would have told you. I am going there to prepare a place for
you. And if I go and prepare a place for you, I will come
back and take you to be with me that you also may be
where I am.

—John 14:2–3

In the old Jewish tradition, this is how a bride and groom became engaged:
The young man traveled to the home of his loved one to ask for her hand
in marriage. A dowry was agreed upon. It was the price paid by the groom
to secure his loved one (it demonstrated to the father that the groom had
the means to properly care for his daughter). The betrothal contract was
sealed, culminating in a formal ceremony in which the bride and groom
confirmed their covenant by drinking together from a cup of wine. After
the marriage was established, an engagement period ensued, during which
the two were officially married yet did not live together.

During this period the couple would prepare for the time when their
marriage would be consummated. The bride-in-waiting learned all she
could about being a good wife. The groom returned to his father's house
to prepare a place for them to live. Usually he constructed a large addition
to the house, where they would live under the same roof with the family.
After many months the groom would come for his wife!

This tradition provides a beautiful parallel. Jesus gave his life as his
dowry. The cross shows us that he and his Father agreed on an exor-
bitant price. Every time we drink from the Communion cup, we
remember him and the new covenant. As the bride of Christ, we prepare ourselves for his coming. In the meantime Jesus has gone ahead
and is presently preparing a place for us in heaven. It only required
seven days for him to create the earth . . . and he's had almost two
thousand years to work on our rooms in his mansion.

*Lover of my soul, I want to prepare to meet you. . . . Thank you for
preparing a place for us to live together for eternity.*

Waiting on the Groom

> At that time the kingdom of heaven will be like ten virgins who took their lamps and went out to meet the bridegroom.... The foolish ones took their lamps but did not take any oil with them. The wise, however, took oil in jars along with their lamps. The bridegroom was a long time in coming, and they all became drowsy and fell asleep. At midnight the cry rang out: "Here's the bridegroom! Come out to meet him!" ... The virgins who were ready went in with him to the wedding banquet.... Therefore keep watch, because you do not know the day or the hour.
>
> —Matthew 25:1, 3–6, 10, 13

When all the preparations for the consummation of the marriage contract were completed, it was customary for the Jewish bridegroom to go for his bride at night. He would march toward her village with his friends, in a torchlight procession. As more bystanders recognized the wedding party, they would take up the call of celebration and cry out the good news from block to block (a coy way of alerting the bride to be ready!). In a short time the torchlight processional halted outside her home. The bride, dressed in the gown she had hung by her bed in readiness, stepped out into the street amid cheers. With laughing and singing, the bride and groom, with the wedding party, walked by torchlight back to the home of the groom's father, where a feast awaited them.

Wise virgins understand that the betrothal carries big responsibilities. We recognize that we are in covenant, albeit separated from our groom. We watch and work. We stay alert. Our groom could come for us at any moment!

Don't be a foolish virgin who easily forgets about her soon-and-coming groom. Energize your anticipation by learning the meaning behind the many other betrothal symbols in today's devotion. Look up 1 Thessalonians 4:16–17; 5:2; Matthew 24:42–44.

I want to ready myself for your return, Lord. I want to wait for you with spirited affection and eager anticipation. I want to be prepared with oil in my lamp and fire in my heart.

June 14

Face-to-Face

Show me your face, let me hear your voice; for your voice
is sweet, and your face is lovely.
—Song of Songs 2:14

These are words of a God in love. God thinks my soul is beautiful when
I praise him! It makes me want to praise him in word and with singing
all the more. "Rejoice in the LORD, O you righteous! For praise from the
upright is beautiful. . . . Praise the LORD! For it is good to sing praises to
our God; For it is pleasant, and praise is beautiful" (Ps. 33:1; 147:1 NKJV).

Little wonder I can hardly wait to see his face. Like any bride-in-waiting, I find it hard to rest comfortably in a relationship when I cannot see
the face of the one I adore. When it comes to brides and bridegrooms, full
intimacy comes between a man and woman face-to-face. And when the
Bible speaks of longing for God, it speaks in terms of wanting to see his
face. The psalmist pleads with God, "Make your face shine upon us" (Ps.
80:3) and "Do not hide your face from me" (Ps. 27:9). Ultimately "In righteousness I will see your face; when I awake, I will be satisfied with seeing
your likeness" (Ps. 17:15). To hold the gaze of God is to find love, acceptance, and satisfaction.

Our longing to see the face of God is a longing, whether we know it
or not, to see our sins exposed and to be cleansed. This is what brides-
in-waiting do: "'His bride has made herself ready. Fine linen, bright
and clean, was given her to wear.' (Fine linen stands for the righteous
acts of the saints.)" (Rev. 19:7–8). Your wedding gift to your Savior
is your earthly obedience, the evidence of your love. Dressed in righteousness, you will see the face of God! Make your praise beautiful
today—he thinks it's lovely!

*I make my prayer Psalm 42 today: "As the deer pants for streams of water,
so my soul pants for you, O God. My soul thirsts for God, for the living
God. When can I go and meet with God?"*

The Prom

The weapons we fight with are not the weapons of the world. On the contrary, they have divine power to demolish strongholds.

—2 Corinthians 10:4

June means romance and roses. It also means the prom. My husband, Ken, who teaches high school, always dons his tuxedo this time of year—he and I chaperone the seniors at their prom. The early hours of the prom are a great time to connect with students and wish them well at college. When Ken and I tell these seventeen-year-olds, who for the most part never darken the door of a church and often come from split homes, that we want to pray for them, they always look at us askew. But they also appreciate and respect Mr. Tada and me. It's not often an adult—let alone a teacher—tells them, "I'll be praying for you." It is these kids we usually hear from years later.

We have to snatch time with these students, though, because after the banquet is cleared, the ballroom becomes a wild disco. But even then my husband and I keep ministering to these graduates. Last year while I waited for Ken to come back from his "smoke patrol" of the bathroom, I spotted a girl in a skimpy white-sequined dress sitting on her boyfriend's knee. I started praying for her. Although the ballroom was shaking, my prayer was shaking the heavenlies. Who would think a prom should be a place to hold a prayer meeting? Yet this is exactly where the Lord Jesus would have us be.

When the girl disappeared onto the dance floor, I was reminded that unless Christians keep infiltrating the public arena—high schools especially—a lot of seniors will graduate into a deeper kind of spiritual darkness than they ever experienced in the hallways of their schools.

During this month remember the students. If you see a limousine this Saturday night loaded up with kids heading for a prom, take it as a prayer reminder. Then demolish those strongholds!

Lord, I lift up to you today these high school students I know:

_____

Out in the Fields

Your eyes will see the king in his beauty and view a land
that stretches afar.

—Isaiah 33:17

My favorite paintings and poems are about fields. Perhaps it's because my favorite childhood memories are of running through the huge alfalfa field across the dirt road from our farmhouse. Broad, rolling, and uncluttered by bushes or trees, I loved to ride my pony across it, especially when the wind would whip thunderheads over its horizon. Its wide expanse made me feel as if the entire alfalfa field could fit into my soul.

Do you recall the feeling of wide-open freedom? Maybe on summery, blustery days spent by an open field? This poem by Elizabeth Barrett Browning evokes that same feeling.

> The little cares which fretted me
> I lost them yesterday,
> Among the fields, above the sea,
> Among the winds at play,
> Among the lowing of the herds,
> The rustling of the trees,
> Among the singing of the birds,
> The humming of the bees.
> The foolish fear of what might happen,
> I cast them all away
> Among the clover-scented grass,
> Among the husking of the corn,
> Where drowsy poppies nod
> Where ill thoughts die and good are born—
> Out in the fields with God.[1]

Pack a picnic this weekend and ask a friend to join you for a jaunt. Find a country road, look for a large field, pull over to the side, and spread your blanket under the shade of a tree. Let the sun and the wind and the field—the bigger the field, the better—remind you of the wide-open spaciousness, the broad, big freedom we have in Christ.

I see you, the King, in all your beauty, and heaven like a land stretching afar. Thank you for such a bright, happy perspective today.

Be a Blessing

I will surely bless you and make your descendants as numerous as the stars in the sky and as the sand on the seashore. Your descendants will take possession of the cities of their enemies, and through your offspring all nations on earth will be blessed, because you have obeyed me.

—Genesis 22:17–18

Make me a blessing, make me a blessing,
Out of my life may Jesus shine;
Make me a blessing, O Savior, I pray,
Make me a blessing to someone today.

Would you like to have assurance that you are enjoying the Lord's favor? There is a way to know, and it's simpler than you might realize.

The clue is in the Scripture for today. God was in essence saying, "Abraham, I am blessing you so you in turn can bless all nations. They will receive something through you, and it is in this way that you will know that my hand of favor is upon you."

For us, the surest evidence that the Lord's hand of blessing is upon us comes when others are blessed through us. When we encourage friends and family in the midst of our trials, we know beyond a shadow of a doubt that God's hand of favor is on us. The best part is that those who are being blessed are at the same time being drawn closer to the Lord.

To be blessed by God means being drawn deeper, higher, and further into his heart. Being blessed means *feeling* his favor, his pleasure, and his delight. It means understanding him in his ways. What a gift to pass on to others!

Is the joy of your relationship with Jesus overflowing to those around you? Is their walk with him different because of you? Is their prayer life growing because of you? Has their witness gone up a notch because something about you has rubbed off on them? If so, rest assured. God's blessing is on you.

Lord, the best blessing you can ever bestow on me is Jesus. Help me to get to know him. In turn I'll pass on the blessing that results to others.

I Thirst

O God, you are my God, earnestly I seek you; my soul thirsts for you, my body longs for you, in a dry and weary land where there is no water.

—Psalm 63:1

The sensation of thirst seems rather straightforward. Our mouths and throats get dry from talking or exercise, and we simply throw cold liquid down the hatch. Presto, we're not thirsty anymore.

The body, however, thinks of thirst in a much different way. Most internal organs have sensory nerves that monitor the level of water in their environment and signal changes to the brain. The hypothalamus is the region of the brain primarily responsible for monitoring the signals, sensing an increased concentration of salt in the bloodstream.

Our soul experiences its own kind of thirst. Those deep, inner longings we feel are simply the soul signaling to us that it needs something—comfort, affirmation, love. As with bodily thirst, our soul often lacks discernment as to what will best satisfy us. Too often we'll look for satisfaction in someone's opinion of us. We'll feast our eyes on that which we covet. We'll immerse ourselves in work, thinking that the fruit of our labor will one day quench our thirst.

Our soul, however, was designed to consume one thing, and one thing only: God. All other earthly pursuits to quench our thirst do just the opposite in comparison with God. The things we think will quench our thirst are simply laden with more "salt" of self-doubt, covetousness, and pride. Only God is pure, clean, and deeply satisfying to our soul. Only God meets every need. Only God ends the hopeless search for the soul's true comfort, affirmation, and love.

Only God. Keep these two words echoing in your mind today.

Lord, create in me a thirst for you. Train my soul to know clean, pure refreshment. Train my soul for you.

The New Earth

> Behold, I will create new heavens and a new earth. The former things will not be remembered, nor will they come to mind. But be glad and rejoice forever in what I will create, for I will create Jerusalem to be a delight and its people a joy. I will rejoice over Jerusalem and take delight in my people; the sound of weeping and of crying will be heard in it no more. Never again will there be in it an infant who lives but a few days, or an old man who does not live out his years; he who dies at a hundred will be thought a mere youth; he who fails to reach a hundred will be considered accursed. They will build houses and dwell in them; they will plant vineyards and eat their fruit.
>
> —Isaiah 65:17–21

I once was talking to a girl in a wheelchair about heaven. I asked her what she'd like to do when she got there. "Uh . . . I'd like to knit," she said. I replied, "Then let's make a date to meet in a cabin, pull up a couple of rocking chairs by the fireplace, and reach for our knitting needles, okay?" My friend in the wheelchair scoffed, "You're just saying that. Heaven's not going to have cabins and rocking chairs. That stuff is only on earth."

Is that so? I believe heaven will have that and more. Heaven is by no means ambiguous. Today's verse says that God is planning new heavens and a new earth. Did you get that? Heaven has our planet in it. A new earth with earthy things in it. Isaiah even foresees people dwelling in houses, planting vineyards, and eating fruit.

God does not switch dictionaries on us and suddenly redefine what earth is. If there are streets, rivers, trees, and mountains in the new earth, as the Bible says, then why not all the other good things? Why not cabins and rocking chairs?

Take a moment to consider the rock-solid reality of heaven. Muse on the fact that the best pleasures that you enjoy about earth are but inklings and omens of even greater earthy joys to come. Let all the happiness you experience today serve as a signpost to point you to heaven.

Lord, help me to dream about heaven today through all that I taste, see, experience, and feel.

June 20

Commencement Exercises

> They will enter Zion with singing; everlasting joy will
> crown their heads.
>
> —Isaiah 35:10

I went to Westmont College's commencement exercises last week. At the podium the dean explained that "graduation" means a student is leaving something; he wanted to emphasize that Westmont's ceremony was a "commencement" exercise. He underscored to his students that they were beginning something new and exciting. It sure was a thrilling day on campus with the Santa Barbara mountains in the background, and the blue Pacific Ocean in the distance. It was a glorious commencement—the triumphant processional, the banners and color, the majestic music, and everyone embracing each other, smiling and offering congratulations.

To me, it was a hint of our commencement to come in heaven. We will graduate, leaving the old earth behind, as well as our old life. But more importantly the Day of Christ will be our commencement as we begin our new life in the new heavens and the new earth. It'll be Jesus' coronation as King of Kings. Our verse today underscores that it will be a triumphant processional with all the pomp and circumstance, banners, color, and music. Degrees and awards will be conferred upon the faithful. Everlasting joy will crown our heads as we embrace each other. "We're here! We've finally made it!" we'll exclaim. And the Lord Jesus will be at the center of it all.

How can you prepare for your heavenly commencement? Second Timothy 2:15 says, "Do your best to present yourself to God as one approved, a workman who does not need to be ashamed and who correctly handles the word of truth." The phrase "do your best" implies excellence, earnestness, diligence, and faithfulness in your daily witness to others, as well as in your quiet time with the Lord Jesus. You are a student preparing for the most exciting commencement ever!

I'm looking forward to my graduation from earth, Lord, but I'm most excited about my commencement into heaven. Help me to prepare today for that marvelous ceremony!

Carrying Burdens

Carry each other's burdens, and in this way you will fulfill
the law of Christ.

—Galatians 6:2

I don't often have the chance to physically help other people, but when I do, I love it. Nowhere do I feel more useful than at the airport.

I have to pack what seems like half a hospital when I go anywhere. Even after my friends and I check in all this stuff at curbside, we still have a pile of carry-on luggage that includes lots of the usual paraphernalia plus a duffel bag with emergency medical equipment. The challenge is to carry everything from curbside to the plane. This is when I get to "carry another's burden." On the foot pedals under my legs goes the duffel bag. The briefcase goes on my lap; purses are slung over the handles of my wheelchair; coats or sweaters land on my lap. Airline tickets are squeezed between my leg and the side of my chair. I look like a bag lady. But I don't mind. It gives me a chance to carry someone else's burden.

That's what Galatians 6:2 tells us to do. It's good advice, whether we bear physical burdens or emotional and spiritual burdens. Galatians 6 says we should do this on a regular basis and not be so puffed up with pride that we fail to offer a helping hand.

And we are to do so to fulfill the law of Christ, which is a law of love. Love obliges us to be compassionate. Maybe under the old covenant God's people made a habit of laying burdens on one another, but under the new covenant we don't lay them on; we take them off. So why don't you find somebody today who could use a hand? It will give you an opportunity to lighten the load of another and lighten your heart at the same time.

God did not write solo parts for very many of us. He expects us to be participants in the great symphony of life.

Donald Tippett[2]

Today, God, everyone I encounter will be bearing some burden. Help me to discern what those are and which ones I can help carry.

The "Red Cross"

When I see the blood, I will pass over you.

—Exodus 12:13

I take, O cross, thy shadow for my abiding place;
I ask no other sunshine than the sunshine of His face;
Content to let the world go by, to know no gain nor loss,
My sinful self my only shame, my glory all the cross.

In a book called *The Great Boer War,* Sir Arthur Conan Doyle tells of a small detachment of British troops who were surprised by an overwhelming enemy force. The British had to quickly retreat under heavy fire, with little time to carry any of the wounded with them.

Out there on the battlefield, the injured men faced certain death. One of them was a corporal in the Ceylon Mounted Infantry. He realized that they would only survive if they could come under the protection of a Red Cross flag. The corporal had strength enough to use blood from his wounds and those of his friends to paint a large red cross on a piece of white cloth. When the enemy saw the flag with the bloodstained cross, they held their fire. The British were able to move the wounded to a safe place.

What a poignant and powerful story. It's the story of Exodus 12:13, which says, "When I see the blood, I will pass over you." And it's also why beneath the cross of Jesus is the best place to be, whether you're under attack or not. The cross of Christ is a red cross, and the Enemy doesn't dare touch us. We are safe in Jesus' shadow.

When you feel overwhelmed with fear, guilt, or weariness, picture yourself at the foot of the cross, with your arms wrapped around it, hanging on as tight as you can. You will be covered by the blood and God will protect you.

Jesus, my Savior, help me to remember to huddle in the shadow of your cross today and to recall that you have me covered. I am safe.

Divine Coincidences

He reasoned . . . in the marketplace day by day with those
who happened to be there.

—Acts 17:17

A re there such things as honest-to-goodness coincidences? Of course.
Are they planned by God? Of course. Wait a minute. Can the two go
together? Of course!

Take today's verse. Some of those window-shoppers who just happened to be meandering through the marketplace on the day Paul was
preaching ended up becoming believers. Yet the coincidence of that day's
leisurely stroll—the people examining cantaloupe and chatting with neighbors—was no coincidence, for believers have been chosen "before the creation of the world" (Eph. 1:4).

The trick? No trick at all. "With God all things are possible" (Matt.
19:26). Even bona fide coincidences. God arranges for natural events to
occur at specific times to further his ends. In other words, he plans coincidences. Discovering how or to what extent will be one fascinating feature
of heaven! In the meantime . . .

It's no mistake that your car broke down and that kindly stranger
helped you. It's no accident that at lunchtime the same young man keeps
coming by your office door hawking sandwiches. The people you meet,
the people you live near, the folks who sit in the pew in front of you are
there by divine appointment. Why? So that you might fulfill God's purpose: to make him real to all those around you.

Have fun doing that today in every "coincidence."

*Lord, to me it's mind-bogglingly complicated but, oh, so natural. Thank
you for placing the people that you do in my life. Energize me to fulfill
your purpose in each divine coincidence—help me to make you, oh, so
real to each and every person.*

Higher Ground

You broaden the path beneath me, so that my ankles do
not turn.

—2 Samuel 22:37

When I was a kid, my family once headed to the Rockies for vacation.
After we crossed the border from Nebraska into Colorado, I searched
the horizon for the first signs of the mountains. Soon I saw them, rising off
the plain like a craggy, frightening fortress.

We drove a beat-up old Dodge truck, and I worried that we would
never make it to those high peaks. The road from Denver twisted and
turned; the engine groaned. Dad kept switching gears, all the while keeping a close watch on the temperature gauge. Would we make it to the top?
Even if we did, all I could imagine was being stranded on some mountain
spire.

Was I in for a surprise when we finally arrived at the summit. As we
rounded the last peak at Kenosha Pass, the road sloped out onto a high,
broad mountain plateau. As far as the eye could see, there was flat grassland with small ranches and cows grazing. We left the prickly spires of the
front range behind and spent the rest of the time on the higher ground of
the mountain plateau.

That's the Christian life. Our trials appear to be mountainous obstacles looming ahead of us. We see frightening heights from which we could
fall, scary ledges off which to stumble, pinnacles that make our heads spin.
And we wonder what's waiting for us at the crest of our trial. But once we
arrive by God's grace, we find we have climbed to a higher plain. That's
what 2 Samuel 22:37 describes.

Are you facing a mountainous trial today? It's not as scary as you
think. The Lord knows where he's leading you; it's not a dizzying
height. You too can live on higher ground.

*Make me mindful today, Father God, that you are leading me over tough
terrain to a broad path. When I feel afraid, help me to picture that beautiful plateau.*

June 25

Wedding Afterthoughts

This is my prayer: that your love may abound more and
more in knowledge and depth of insight, so that you may
be able to discern what is best and may be pure and blameless until the day of Christ.

—Philippians 1:9–10

You've seen it happen. Your sister falls head over heels in love with a guy
who, you think, is a jerk. Your roommate throws common sense to the
wind and makes a fool of herself for the new man at the office. Or maybe
you have fallen for Mr. Right only to have your family say he's all wrong.
How do you know you're on the right track? What plumb line do you have
against which to validate your feelings?

It's hard to balance love's emotions with knowledge and depth of
insight. Our emotions rarely have much to do with head knowledge.
Instead we tend to charge in with lots of heart foolishness.

You've heard that old saying "Love is blind," but God expects us to
have "depth of insight," or twenty-twenty vision, when it comes to genuine
love. You've also heard the saying "Hearts rule." But God says our love
should be guided by our head, or as today's verse says, "abound more and
more in knowledge." By sifting our love through the sieve of knowledge
and depth of insight, we are able to discern what is best—or who is best,
if we're trying to pick our life partner.

Regardless of your marital status or the state of your love life, make
certain your love is balanced with twenty-twenty vision and lots of
wisdom. That combo will enable you to understand how to love in
a genuine and God-honoring way, without saying or doing foolish
things.

*Keep me from emotional decisions, Father. Rather enable me to interlace
my feelings with knowledge and insight. I want my choices in love to
honor you and to bless me and my loved one.*

June 26

Drifting

We must pay more careful attention, therefore, to what we
have heard, so that we do not drift away.

—Hebrews 2:1

Do you recall, as a child, riding your rubber raft on the gentle waves of
the ocean? I remember the warm sun and the rocking motion almost
sending me off to sleep. In fact, I once did just that. When a giant swell
woke me up, I raised my head and realized with horror how far from shore
I had been carried away. A strong current had caught me and carried me
down the beach. I don't know how it happened . . . and so quickly! I didn't
realize how far I had drifted away until the moment I saw that great distance between me and my family further up the beach.

Drifting can be dangerous. Always, always there are currents pulling
at us. Always we are swimming upstream, against the tide. There is always
the temptation to drift, and we never realize how far we are carried away
until we see Christ . . . until we see the others from whom we have parted.
It is possible for any of us to drift spiritually or morally. No one is immune.
Think of the powerful currents in your life that would carry you along
unless you "kept at the oars" to control the direction. There is the current
of social opinion or fad. There is a current of personal desire, of doing the
things *you* want to do. Lust is a powerful undertow. Materialism is a relent-
less tug.

Following God does not come easy. Today anchor yourself with a
recommitment to keep at the oars, to keep rowing against those strong
undertows. Let's not be lulled to sleep and carried away.

Someone has said, "Sow a thought, reap an action. Sow an action,
reap a habit. Sow a habit, reap a character." Drifting from God starts
in small ways with little thoughts. To keep the current of your
thoughts in line, find a King James Bible and look up 2 Corinthians
10:5. Can your thoughts be controlled? Who gives you the power to
do so?

*Lord, you are a lighthouse for me, a center point, a high tower. I can
always tell whether or not I'm drifting, by looking to see how close or
how far from you I am. Keep me anchored near you.*

Imitate *Who?*

Imitate me, just as I also imitate Christ.

—1 Corinthians 11:1 NKJV

I just got off the phone with my friend Bunny. We haven't seen each other in ages, but I said, "Bun, you wouldn't believe how often I think about you. For instance, I get into a situation and I say to myself, *Lord, what would Bunny do? What would she say to this person?*" I could tell she was blushing, so I quickly added, "Oh, I'm not imitating your holiness. Just how you get there!"

This is what today's verse is all about. The apostle Paul's comment to the Corinthians could be construed as self-deifying. He sounds almost presumptuous. Is he comparing himself to Christ? No, Paul is not asking us to imitate his righteousness, for there is only one that is holy, and he is the Lord. Paul is asking us to imitate the choices he makes, to model his discernments and his response to certain people and situations. Paul knew that his fellow Christians would soon find themselves facing the sort of persecution he was already experiencing. As their spiritual father, he wanted them to ask themselves, *What would Paul do if he were facing this mob? What would he say to my accusers?*

We imitate the methods and manners of the Christians who serve as our examples. The Christlikeness, the holiness and righteousness will then be added. God wants us to "be an example to the believers in word, in conduct, in love, in spirit, in faith, in purity" (1 Tim. 4:12 NKJV).

Who is looking up to you as an example? A child? A grandchild? A fellow student? Your neighbor or coworker? The new woman at church? If you are growing in Christ, know this: somebody is watching and learning. Somebody is thinking of you, *What would he do? What would she say?* How can you be an example? Read 1 Timothy 4:12 again, and go out and live it in sight of others.

Lord, maybe it's best that I don't know who's watching and learning from me. All I need to know is that I want to imitate you. As I do, others will observe how I do it and be inspired to live the same way. May I be responsible today to this high calling.

Togetherness

I heard a loud voice from the throne saying, "Now the dwelling of God is with men, and he will live with them. They will be his people, and God himself will be with them and be their God."

—Revelation 21:3

God will live with us; we shall live forever with him. Oh, the marvelous things we will do together with our glorious God! And with each other. Together we will rule the world and judge fallen angels. Together we will eat the fruit of the Tree of Life and be pillars in the temple of God. Together we shall receive the Morning Star and be crowned with life, righteousness, and glory. Most of all we will enjoy the best of togetherness—we shall be together with God.

Note how many times I've used the word *together*. Heaven is not a hangout for mavericks roaming solo across the universe, doing their own thing. It's a place of sweet togetherness, and maybe that's why Revelation 21 says we will live together in a city, the New Jerusalem. We won't be speckled here and there in rural cottages isolated from one another, but we will live in harmony in a city. A nice city. A holy city.

Do you consider yourself a loner when it comes to being with God's people? God has given us communal relationships on earth—with our families, friends at school, coworkers at the office—to prepare us for heaven. Scripture always describes our heavenly union with God not as private but as corporate. Today's verse underscores that God will be with his people.

You can prepare for this heavenly togetherness today by "not neglecting to meet together, as is the habit of some, but encouraging one another, and all the more as you see the Day drawing near" (Heb. 10:25 RSV).

Lord, I look forward to the day when you will remove all barriers among your people. I long for the day when we will truly be one in you. Please help me to enjoy being together with all my brothers and sisters in you— and remind me that this communion of saints is preparing us all for heavenly togetherness.

June 29

The Light of the Mind

Your word is a lamp to my feet.

—Psalm 119:105

I once visited a nursing home back in New Jersey run by Marvin van Dyke, a dear Christian friend. The place was brightly lit, beautifully decorated, and very clean. The ladies in the kitchen prepared a wonderful luncheon for us, and Marvin invited several of the nursing home residents to join us. One of the attendees was his former pastor, the Reverend Herrmann Braunlin. This beloved man of God had pastored Hawthorne Bible Church for over thirty years, but Alzheimer's disease had robbed him of any ability to communicate, recall, or think clearly.

Nevertheless, Reverend Braunlin came to the luncheon impeccably dressed in suit and tie, his hair neatly combed and shoes shined. Marvin introduced us and the pastor smiled, greeting me warmly. He didn't talk much, though. He spent most of the time wandering around the room and looking out the window. Once in a while he would turn to me or one of my friends, and the vacant look in his eyes would clear for a moment; he would shake our hands and ask, "Hello there, and what's your name?"

Marvin, to my surprise, asked Reverend Braunlin to say the blessing over our meal. Without flinching, the elderly pastor rose from his seat at the table, leaned on his hands, and began, saying, "O gracious heavenly Father, we bow before you this day to humbly ask your blessing on these, our friends, and upon this meal, which has been prepared by the hands of servants who love you. Strengthen us and endue us plenteously from on high with every grace and blessing so that we too might serve you with whole and devoted hearts. In the name of Christ our Lord, Amen." My friends and I looked at each other in amazement. It was as though the room had filled with light from heaven.

After his prayer Reverend Braunlin sat down. The vacant gaze returned. But the light did not go out.

God's Word is a light not only to our path but to our thinking. Hide it in your heart today, and you will never walk in darkness.

Light of the World, illumine my mind and brighten my path. May I never walk in darkness as long as your Word lights up the way.

June 30

Out of the Spotlight

Your word is a . . . light for my path.

—Psalm 119:105

It happens to me often when I speak. I wheel my chair onto the platform, eager to see those friendly smiles in the audience. But instead I'm suddenly blinded by the painful glare of spotlights. My eyes burn and I tear up a bit. I have to scan the foot of the stage to adjust my vision, and then slowly lift my gaze up into the audience, squinting against those beams that seem as bright as the sun.

Those lights illustrate how counterproductive light can be when it is misdirected. For light to truly illumine, it must be directed toward the subject at hand and brighten it, not shine in our eyes. That's how David describes God's Word as operating in his life—casting a light on the way ahead, illuminating the path and the people directly in front of him.

Too often we place the Word of God in front of us, staring directly at it as if it were an object to be analyzed and venerated. True, it is every bit the masterpiece of literature, philosophy, and theology that critics and theologians proclaim it to be, but to place the Word of God before us as an object of blinding devotion is foolhardy. James described people who do so as those who look at a mirror, walk away, and then promptly forget what they look like (James 1:23–24).

Look back over the week and ask, "Have I prayed, seeking the Spirit's help in understanding and appropriating Bible passages?" The Word of God should pose questions like "Where have I erred? What could happen today that requires God's wisdom? Whom do I love who needs this encouragement? How might I obey what God has commanded?" Such questions place God's Word where it was intended to be, casting its power just far enough in front of us to be of earthly and heavenly use.

Shine on that which lies before me, Guiding Light of my soul, and show me your way today.

JULY

July 1

Raise a Memorial!

Samuel took a stone and set it up between Mizpah and
Shen. He named it Ebenezer, saying, "Thus far has the
LORD helped us."

—1 Samuel 7:12

When the Israelites defeated the Philistines, the prophet Samuel raised
a memorial to commemorate the victory. He named it Ebenezer,
which means "stone of help." It was to remind everyone, including Samuel,
that God was their help.

From the beginning God has sealed special events with some kind of
physical memorial. He gave Noah a rainbow. He instituted the Passover
feast as a reminder of Israel's deliverance from Egypt. When he gave the
Law to Moses, he wrote it on two tablets so his people could see and
remember. The tabernacle, the ark itself, and the cloud that hovered over
it were visible reminders of God's ever present help. In the New Testament
the Lord Jesus declared that Mary's gift of perfume, which she poured over
him, should be a memorial. What are the memorials in your life, the tangible reminders God has given you of his ever present help?

My wheelchair is my Ebenezer. I've raised it up as a memorial to commemorate God's grace in my life. It reminds me (and everyone who sees
me smile in it) that God is my help.

Look for the memorials, the stones of remembrances, in your life.
Whatever they are—perhaps a ring, a family Bible, a pair of crutches,
a pebble you picked up during a journey—they can be anchors to
your soul. When pain becomes severe or sorrow crushing, you can
remind yourself of that memorial set in place during a time of greater
strength, and you can pray, "Oh, God, keep me faithful to that."
Then rest your heart on the faithfulness of the One who has given
you help in the past, that One who helped you raise the stone of
remembrance in the first place.

*God, your understanding of us is so great. You know that we need visi-
ble reminders of your faithfulness. Show me what reminders I can estab-
lish in my life that will stand in the face of all the future might bring.*

July 2

A Perfect Fit

God has arranged the parts in the body, every one of them,
just as he wanted them to be.
—1 Corinthians 12:18

Sometimes you can read a verse a hundred times and then suddenly see
something you never noticed before. That's what happened when I read
today's verse in a note my friend Kim sent me. She had simply underlined
the word *just.*

I appreciated Kim's personal thoughts, but I was struck by the underlined word. *Just* means "exactly" or "specifically." God has a unique role
for me—and for you too. You're living where you are, doing what you're
doing, and surrounded by the people with whom you live and work
because you are the only one who can fit that niche. God has carved it out
just for you.

In fact, 1 Corinthians 12:18 is like *Goldilocks and the Three Bears.*
When it comes to your place in the kingdom, things aren't too hot or cold,
too soft or hard, too big or small. God's got it just right.

You may not realize it, but your church needs you. Your kids may not
get the point yet, but you are the mother or father perfectly designed to
raise them best. Your friends would be missing something—a big something—were you not in their lives.

You can't miss God's will for you (unless you're off on some sinful
path). You are smack in the middle of it. So open your eyes. This is
where and how you fit. Now, how are you going to let that piece of
information infiltrate your actions and thoughts today? What does
it mean regarding the "mundane" aspects of your life?

*Father God, as I go about the everydayness of my life—chopping veggies
for dinner, asking if the TV could please be turned down, changing the
bedsheets—bring to my mind the thought that I am the perfect person
to be in this place. Thank you for selecting me.*

July 3

A Promise—A Means of Grace

Go ahead then, do what you promised! Keep your vows!
—Jeremiah 44:25

Today Ken and I celebrate our wedding anniversary. Tonight we'll probably pull out the photo album and dine by candlelight. Maybe we'll rummage around to find the cassette of our wedding ceremony, and we'll listen to those tried-and-true words "for better or for worse; in sickness and in health." The sickness and health part means more to us as the years go by. My disability, you see, isn't getting easier. But listening to those vows is a way to refresh the promises we made to one another. Big promises.

A fellow author once wrote, "If forgiving is the only remedy for what has happened in the past, then promising is the only remedy for your uncertain future." My friend is right. Forgiving takes care of what has already happened to us, and promising takes care of what is yet to happen.

I know that a young bride with bruised feelings is reading this right now. She's saying to herself, *I want to get out of this marriage and start over with a guy who really loves me.* But that woman will remember a promise she made, so she will stick with her husband in hopeful love and helpful prayer.

A minister who is reading this is telling himself, *I feel like moving on to a job that doesn't load me down with so much grief.* But he remembers a promise he made when he was ordained, so he sticks with his congregation in pastoral love.

Promise keeping is a powerful means of grace, especially in this day when people rarely live by their word. The only way to overcome the unpredictability of your future is through the power of promising. When you make a promise (and determine to stick by it), your future is secure. God will give you grace to honor your promise one day at a time. And a promise kept is grace given.

Strengthen me to keep my promises, God, to take them seriously, and to make the necessary sacrifices to fulfill each one.

July 4

Trouble for God?

By the word of the LORD were the heavens made, their
starry host by the breath of his mouth.

—Psalm 33:6

It was July 4, 1997. All of us were amazed when the Martian landrover
Pathfinder began sending back color images of the stark, red landscape
of Mars. The discoveries sparked a lively interest in other planets in our
solar system, in the stars, and in the other untold numbers of galaxies in
vast, uncharted regions of the universe.

The overwhelming data about the immensity of outer space also
sparked conversations about who created the universe and why. During a
college astronomy lecture, a student asked his professor, "Why would God
go to all the trouble to create all that?" The professor, who happened to be
a Christian, replied, "Trouble? What trouble? Creating the suns and stars
was no trouble for God. He accomplished it with simply his Word. You
and I are the ones who have caused him trouble."

The professor is right. God created the universe by the breath of his
mouth. We were made new creatures in Christ (2 Cor. 5:17) by the blood,
sweat, tears, and death of the Son of God. Our salvation cost God big trouble.

We may stand under a full moon or high atop a mountain on a starry
night and be overwhelmed at the greatness and glory of our God and
think, *Oh, how brightly the stars shine.* We are awestruck and amazed.
But never does God's glory shine brighter than when we stand in the
shadow of the cross. It's one thing for God to make a star; it's another
thing to redeem sinful man to "shine like the stars forever and ever"
(Dan. 12:3 RSV). Today contemplate the humility and love of God
in that "while we were still sinners, Christ died for us" (Rom. 5:8).

*Lord Jesus, thank you for flinging the stars and suns into space with a
simple command from your lips. Much, much more than that, thank
you for laying down your life for me. I'm saved! Oh, God, thank you for
taking the trouble!*

July 5

Sweet-Smelling Sacrifices

Noah built an altar to the LORD and, taking some of all the
clean animals and clean birds, he sacrificed burnt offerings
on it. The LORD smelled the pleasing aroma.

—Genesis 8:20–21

On most nights when I wheel out my office door and into the courtyard of our building, if the wind is blowing just right, I experience the
most pleasurable sensation. I catch a whiff of the mouthwatering aroma
of charcoal-broiled Tri-Tip steak sizzling on the grill over at the Woodranch
Barbeque Pit across the freeway. Invariably I stop, draw in a deep breath,
and say with a groan, "Wow, does that ever smell great!" As I drive away
from the office, I can sometimes spot a billow of smoke rising from the
chimney of the restaurant. Little wonder the place is always packed—the
smell of burnt fat and meat on the grill attracts more diners than any bill-
board or newspaper advertisement.

Not long ago as the scent of grilled steak wafted across the courtyard, it
struck me that this is exactly what Old Testament sacrifices must have
smelled like. The temple in Jerusalem on the Day of Atonement was filled
with the aroma of meat cooked on an open fire, what with so many lambs
being sacrificed. In fact, considering that thousands of animals were sacrificed
on that one day, the entire city must have smelled fragrant. The sacrifices
were pleasing to God—not so much for the smell as for the sins confessed.

Inhaling the aroma of meat on the grill (and smiling as a result) gives
me a tiny insight into the enormous pleasure God must experience
when his people confess their sins. "For we are to God the aroma of
Christ among those who are being saved and those who are perishing. To the one we are the smell of death; to the other, the fragrance
of life" (2 Cor. 2:15–16). Oh, to please God with the aroma of
Christ in our lives!

"Therefore, I urge you, brothers, in view of God's mercy, to offer
your bodies as living sacrifices, holy and pleasing to God—this is
your spiritual act of worship" (Rom. 12:1).

*Lord, I desire that you inhale my obedience today and be pleased. I want
you to breathe in my spiritual worship and enjoy the aroma of Christ
living in me and working through me.*

Justice Served

Do not be afraid of those who kill the body but cannot kill
the soul. Rather, be afraid of the One who can destroy both
soul and body in hell.

—Matthew 10:28

Hell's stock has fallen off lately from lack of both public and Christian
confidence. For most people, believing in a hellish afterlife is roughly
equivalent to believing in a devilish elf with horns and pitchfork. Would
a merciful God draw such a horrible place on the map? If so, it's . . . well,
hellish to think about. But think about it we must.

For if hell does not exist, there is no justice in the world. Take, for example, Hitler. He was never brought to justice—according to what most believe,
he committed suicide. Why should this butcherous tyrant responsible for the
death of six million Jews get off with sipping some poison in a glass of wine
in the comforting presence of his mistress? In no way was he punished in proportion to the pain he caused. If there is no hell, he and millions like him—
murderers and other wicked people—are sleeping peacefully this moment
after causing untold others excruciating pain. Only the existence of hell brings
some semblance of sense to the misery of wars, rapes, and robberies.

Hell ensures that all will be repaid in full. Hell guarantees that there
is such a thing as restitution and recompense. Hell confirms that justice
will be served.

The reality of hell is sobering. Especially when you consider that "all have
sinned and fall short of the glory of God" (Rom. 3:23). Not just the Hitlers
of this world but *all* fall short. This is why suffering in this life is a hidden
mercy. By tasting hell through our trials, we are driven to ponder what may
face us in the next life. Trials become God's roadblocks in our headlong rush
toward hell's grasp, forcing us to examine where we will spend eternity.

As a result, the depressed young homemaker reaches for an answer.
The cancer-ridden patient makes peace with his Creator. The lad-
der-climbing executive slips and falls into the arms of God. Can you
say the same?

*Thank you that my sufferings on earth are hell's splash-over, warning
me of its sobering reality. Thank you for waking me up out of my spiritual slumber, Lord. Use me to wake someone else up today!*

July 7

Humility That Matters

> When Moses came down from Mount Sinai with the two
> tablets of the Testimony in his hands, he was not aware that
> his face was radiant because he had spoken with the LORD.
>
> —Exodus 34:29

When I think of Moses, I try not to think of Charlton Heston. I want to picture not a movie actor but a real person of God. Moses the man gave up greatness, turned his back on pleasures, and refused riches. Moses the man was spoken to by God: "I am pleased with you and I know you by name" (Ex. 33:17). Moses the man walked humbly with God and yet had the gumption to say to his Lord, "Now show me your glory" (Ex. 33:18).

God did allow Moses to see his glory, at least in passing, and only then as viewed from behind a rock. But that's all it took for Moses' face to shine, not from a sunburn but from the brilliance of God's glory. Exodus says, "When Moses came down from Mount Sinai . . . he was not aware that his face was radiant" (34:29).

I love the part "he was not aware that his face was radiant." This speaks of real humility. Humble people don't know they're humble. People who are rich in God's grace are usually the ones who feel they lack it most. Like Moses, humble and unaware, they are oblivious to the radiance on their faces.

We can't strive to be humble. Humility, after all, is a byproduct of spending time with God, not an end in itself.

You could seek the narrow path: not making a big deal of greatness; avoiding the entrapment of worldly pleasures; and giving up materialism. But an even better path is to simply seek God and his glory. Then you will be on the path to true humility. Like Moses, you'll never know it. You may not even catch on, unless someone tries to put a veil over your shining face.

*God of grace, teach me to seek you that I might know you more fully.
Keep my ego small and my heart large.*

A Fearless Request

Pray also for me, that whenever I open my mouth, words
may be given me so that I will fearlessly make known the
mystery of the gospel, for which I am an ambassador in
chains. Pray that I may declare it fearlessly, as I should.
—Ephesians 6:19–20

The scene is a prison cell in Rome. Paul has been in chains for over two
years. He's tired, his shackles are heavy, and his leg irons bite into his
ankles. As he sits in prison, he's most likely thinking of the many missionary travels he's yet to take, of the distant lands yet to hear the gospel.
Perhaps he's thinking of the fledgling churches in Philippi, Galatia, and
Colossae that need his encouragement. He has one chance to write his
friends in Ephesus. With all these needs on his mind, he picks up his pen,
so to speak, and asks them to pray.

Yet among all the pressing problems out in the field, among all his
wants and wishes, what does Paul ask them to pray about? That his aches
and pains might ease? That Caesar might grant him a pardon? That the
charges against him might be dropped? That God might send—as he did
for Peter—an angel to miraculously fling open the prison doors? No. In
the last chapter, in the concluding sentences, Paul sums up his most important prayer request: that he might remember to share the gospel whenever
he opens his mouth; that God might give him fresh words in witnessing;
and that God might empower him to declare the gospel fearlessly.

Today look at the needs in your life as opportunities to share the
gospel. Ask the Spirit to prompt you whenever you open your
mouth. Ask him to give you fresh words to suit the occasion. Most
of all ask the Spirit to give you courage, to help you declare the gospel
fearlessly (if an apostle needed courage to be bold in witnessing, you
must need it, too!).

*Lord, so often my prayer requests involve relief and release from problems. Help me to "stay in my chains" today and follow Paul's lead as I
declare your gospel fearlessly.*

July 9

Strongholds Demolished!

The weapons we fight with are not the weapons of the
world. On the contrary, they have divine power to demolish strongholds.

—2 Corinthians 10:4

Fantasies. Silly thoughts. Vain imaginations. Useless daydreams. These
will puff themselves up so high in your head that you would swear they
were true. A furtive thought lingers in your mind and begins to wear a rut,
repeating itself time and again. It could be a false hope, an unfounded fear.
Whatever it is, it doesn't belong in your head. It's a vain imagination.

I know from experience that if you let vain imaginations grab hold of
you, they become powerful strongholds. Every time you replay that day-
dream, it's like laying more bricks, making the stronghold higher. Then when
you want to kick the thoughts out of your head, you can't. You try the turn-
ing-over-a-new-leaf routine: *I'm not going to think those thoughts. I'm not going
to waste any more time daydreaming.* Trying to single-handedly dismantle
strongholds in your mind that way doesn't work. That's why I am so grateful that "the weapons we fight with are not the weapons of the world."

Christians have divine power—that's the key, *divine* power—to tear
down every vain imagination. It's possible. You really can make your
thoughts obedient to Christ. It may take some time, but by God's grace
that high tower can be toppled.

"Grace . . . teaches us to say 'No' to ungodliness and worldly passions"
(Titus 2:11–12). After the stronghold is knocked down, the rubble still
needs to be cleared. Every time I say no to some tempting thought, a few
more bricks lying around are smashed to bits. But every time I let something linger in my mind that I shouldn't, I can almost see that stronghold
begin to build itself again.

Is there some vain imagination, some stronghold, in your mind?
Don't rehearse those daydreams or entertain wrong thoughts. Demolish the stronghold with divine demolition.

*Jesus Christ, conqueror of our weaknesses, teach me not to let fantasies
and wrong thinking build great edifices in my mind. Give me the power
to demolish those thoughts and to replace them with obedience to you.*

Love Lifted Me

When he saw the wind, he was afraid and, beginning to
sink, cried out, "Lord, save me!" Immediately Jesus reached
out his hand and caught him. "You of little faith," he said,
"why did you doubt?"

—Matthew 14:30–31

Ienjoy singing hymns. Hardly a day goes by that I don't stop whatever I'm
doing, open a hymnal with a friend, and sing a few stanzas. But hey, I
don't have to stop what I'm doing. Sometimes I keep doing what I'm doing
and sing. But the hymns always make me thankful—and sometimes they
help me express thanks.

Once when I was a speaker at a conference, I encountered a bunch of
steps leading to a meeting room. With no ramp I was stuck. Well, not
really. We flagged down four strong guys and gave them instructions about
where to hold the wheelchair. As they carried me, I sang a thank hymn to
them, "Love Lifted Me." And I meant it. Love that is put into practice
always gives us a lift. Love with its sleeves rolled up, with muscle behind
it, love that looks for a need and rushes to meet it, love that *does something*—that's the kind of love that ministers most. That's the sort of love
the Lord Jesus has for us.

Souls in danger look above, Jesus completely saves;
He will lift you by his love out of the angry waves;
He's the Master of the sea, billows his will obey;
He your Savior wants to be, be saved today.
Love lifted me! Love lifted me!
When nothing else could help, love lifted me!

What has you stuck today? Where do you feel blocked? Is there no
way out? Sure there is. Commit your concerns to the Lord, and then
put the hymn "Love Lifted Me" in your heart. Make it a practice to
sing it the rest of the day. It's one way to say thanks to the Lord Jesus
for his love that lifts.

*My heart lifts thanks to you, Lord. Help me to lift others with your love
today. And put a song in my heart that I can offer up to you as an expression of gratitude.*

Think about Him

Whatever is true, whatever is noble, whatever is right, whatever is pure, whatever is lovely, whatever is admirable—if anything is excellent or praiseworthy—think about such things.

—Philippians 4:8

As a youngster, I fostered the idea that God was on an ego trip, always telling people how wonderful he was. I got the impression that God just had to be worshiped. That somehow he needed a big crowd of people adoring him. Do you ever question exactly *why* God wants us to get to know him?

Question no longer. Suppose you, like God, were the most true, just, pure, lovely, and praiseworthy being in existence. And what if everything else in the universe that had any of these qualities got them from you? For that matter, suppose that without you these qualities would never have existed.

If that were the case, then for anyone around you to improve in any way, they would have to become more like you. For you to ask people to think about these good qualities would be to ask them to think about you. For them to take an ego trip would be wrong, because they would be centering their thoughts around sin and imperfection. But your ego trip would be glorious. So when God asks us to think about him, he asks us to think about everything that is true, just, pure, lovely, and praiseworthy.

God knows that the more we get to know him, the more we will know of life—real life. He understands that by walking with him, we will better comprehend genuine love—after all, he is love. God wants us to get to know him—not because he needs our worship but because we desperately need his strength. It has nothing to do with satisfying his ego but everything to do with finding life.

Take a look at Acts 17:24–28. If the person being described in this passage were anyone other than God, you might think he was on an ego trip. But God's ego trip has a very special purpose. Locate God's purpose in this section of Scripture and make it your personal prayer today.

Help me to understand, Lord, that in you I live, move, and have my being!

The Little Things

> Whoever can be trusted with very little can also be trusted
> with much, and whoever is dishonest with very little will
> also be dishonest with much.
>
> —Luke 16:10

Our backyard is not big. This means the two bougainvillea bushes, the hibiscus, the hedge along the fence, and the silk oak tree in the corner are God's special gifts. But our one tree is in trouble. It's beginning to look dry and brown at the twigs. I noticed earlier in the summer that it didn't flower out and green up as much as it has in the past.

They say that when a tree begins to decay at its root or at its heart, the mischief is first seen at the extreme ends of little branches. When you look closely, you notice that the new growth is dry and brittle.

I can't help but think of how much like trees we are. Someone once said, "He that despiseth little things shall fall little by little." We simply must aim to have a Christian walk that, like the sap of a tree, runs through every twig and leaf of our character.

If we fail in the little things, if we ignore our tempers, our tongues, our little white lies, if we ignore the Spirit's whispers, telling us to do this or not to do that, if we despise the small things, we shall fall little by little.

It doesn't take a theologian to remind us that decay at the heart of our Christianity will show up in tiny slips of the tongue, small neglect of good habits, or little fudgings with the truth. Have you been feeling yourself inching away little by little? Then keep a watch on the small things. It's in the small matters of everyday life that the bulk of your witness is lived out.

Prick my conscience, Father, when I am tempted to keep incorrect change, tell a little lie, or withhold a truth. I want healthy new twigs on my tree of life.

Enter That Rest

There remains, then, a Sabbath-rest for the people of God.
—Hebrews 4:9

Back on the farm, the lazy days of July meant turning our horses out to summertime pasture. The grass was lush and ready for grazing. However, before we opened the gates, it was the responsibility of my sisters and me to saddle up and "ride the fences" to check for broken barbed wire. After hours of riding my horse under the summer sun, my weary mount would be wet with sweat, her head hanging low. I had to urge her to put one tired foot in front of the other.

Then as soon as my horse caught a whiff of home or recognized the fences of her own pasture, her ears would pick up and her pace would quicken. The nearer the barn, the more eager her trot. After a quick unsaddling, she'd roll in the dirt and take long, slow drinks from the trough. How good it feels, for a beast, to be home.

How good it will feel for us to be home. No more toiling, no more prying the world's suction cups off my heart. Hebrews 4:9 is like a long drink of cool water on a hot day. Maybe the writers of the Bible—some whose joints were stiff from chains that chafed—had this sweet rest in mind, a rest that perked them up and quickened their pace. Toward the end of their lives, they wrote vigorous encouragements like "Let us, therefore, make every effort to enter that rest" (Heb. 4:11).

"So watch your step. Use your head. Make the most of every chance you get. These are desperate times!" (Eph. 5:15–16 THE MESSAGE). Make every effort to redeem the time, lay up your treasures in heaven, live as if God were watching (he is!). Make it your ambition to be pleasing to him (2 Cor. 5:9). The lush green pastures of rest are just over the horizon. Remember this as you collapse in bed tonight after an exhausting day.

Today's thought makes my earthly toil seem so much lighter. If I become weary today, Lord, remind me of the pastures of my heavenly home.

Knowing the Ending

I am God, and there is no other; I am God, and there is
none like me. I make known the end from the beginning,
from ancient times, what is still to come. I say: My purpose
will stand, and I will do all that I please.
— Isaiah 46:9–10

My friend Judy and I love to spend time in bookstores. I head for the
history section, then move to the children's section. From there I
might glance at cookbooks. But no matter where I wheel in the store, I
always know where I can find Judy. She loves mysteries.

Now, I may purchase a book if I like how the dust cover reads, if I
know the author, or if I've read a good review. But Judy decides to buy
books by reading the last few pages. Why anyone would want to read an
ending first is beyond me. How can she enjoy it when she knows how it
will all come out—especially a mystery!

When I asked Judy where she picked up her peculiar reading habit, she
told me that for her, the suspense wasn't in the conclusion but in how the
writer handled the story. Knowing the ending enhanced the book. Judy is
not alone. In the Scripture for today, God says he makes known the end
from the beginning. In fact, he's even written in the Bible the very last
chapter of history.

I think God makes the end known because he wants to encourage us.
The story of our lives is enhanced when we have the assurance that
all will turn out well. He wants us to know this from the very first
chapter of our lives. And get this: the ending of your story has been
declared from the beginning. It reads this way: Jesus wins!

*Father God, author and finisher of my faith, how grateful I am that you
have not left me in suspense about the conclusion of my life. I know it
will be cloaked in your love and include heaven. I couldn't ask for a happier ending.*

July 15

One in a Million

This is the way the holy women of the past who put their hope in God used to make themselves beautiful. They were submissive to their own husbands, like Sarah, who obeyed Abraham and called him her master. You are her daughters if you do what is right and do not give way to fear.

—1 Peter 3:5–6

What's the most important thing you do, Joni?" It was a press conference in Poland, made up mostly of Christian interviewers. My mind sorted through a list of possible answers: speaking, painting, advocating, visiting people in nursing homes, delivering wheelchairs to Africa, and so on.

I knew the answer: "Being a good wife to my husband." The group of reporters chuckled. I imagined their thoughts: *Surely she's ingratiating herself.* They had forgotten that Ken was seated in the back of the room. I hadn't. I am always conscious of where he is. For one thing, my disability requires it. I enjoy giving to him, too. If his ego gets bruised from someone calling him Mr. Eareckson, Ken looks to me. If he's in a quandary as to how to counsel one of his students, he'll seek my advice. And if Ken just wants to kick back and goof off, I'm the audience for his antics.

When I stand before Jesus, I will be judged first for my faithfulness in my marriage. My commitment to marriage vows places me in a profoundly significant relationship with the most important human being on earth: my spouse. If I can't be faithful in loving my husband, how can I tout faithfulness in ministry to millions?

We might pull the wool over the eyes of those who stand at a distance, but the one with whom we live sees every flaw, as well as every bit of tooth-pulling love. When it comes to judging the real you, your spouse is about as close as you come to Jesus. Try this: Ask your spouse to help you be a better partner, by pinpointing a few faults. Bite your tongue, pray hard, and then follow through.

I want to be beautiful. . . . I want to be submissive.

July 16

A Slice of God

. . . but made himself nothing, taking the very nature of a servant, being made in human likeness.

—Philippians 2:7

L ast week my pastor used an illustration that opened a small window on how "beyond us" God is. Let's suppose you were a completely flat little water bug who lived only on the water's surface. As such, you are aware of length and width, but up and down does not exist for you.

Now, suppose a human being stepped into the water. You, as a buoyant creature skimming the water's surface, would come to know this awesome being by the qualities of, well, the human's leg where it intersected the water. Poor little you couldn't begin to understand the portion of the leg beneath the water or the part above, let alone the arms, torso, and head that tower above the water.

In your little bug mind, you know that one day you will live in the world of this awesome being and be transformed into a three-dimensional figure like him, with height and width. But for now you don't understand what it means. You have to take it on faith.

When the Father revealed himself through Jesus, he was only showing us a slice of himself, a part of all that he is. But there's so much about him we don't comprehend, so much beneath and above our universe of understanding. When we go to be with him, we will live in his heavenly world. We will be transformed and lifted out of our limitations. I can't take that in, so I'll just have to take it on faith. When I do, it stirs reverence and awe in me. How about you?

Think about ways in which you've limited God based on your small slice of knowledge. Then expand your vision as you try to imagine what's above and beneath your comprehension.

Lord, when I sense how big you are and how small I am, remind me to feel not diminished but rather released to expect great and mighty things from one so capable of so much.

July 17

A Deeper Dive

> Deep calls to deep in the roar of your waterfalls; all your
> waves and breakers have swept over me.
>
> —Psalm 42:7

When the weather turns warm, I think back to summertime days spent in the sand dunes near Rehoboth Beach, Delaware. The powerful waves' deafening noise thrilled yet frightened me. But when I swam far out beyond the breakers, I was amazed at how subdued the waves seemed. Then when I dove beneath the surface, the underwater acoustics made the thunderous roar sound distant and gentle. These remembrances came vividly to mind the other day when I read a poem by Frances Havergal.

> On the surface foam and roar,
> Restless heave and passionate dash,
> Shingle rattle on the shore,
> Gathering boom and thundering crash.
> Under the surface, soft green light,
> A hush of peace and an endless calm,
> Winds and waves from a choral height,
> Falling sweet as a far off psalm.

Just as with the ocean, when you dive beneath the surface with God, you discover an endless calm. A world of divine life that is deep and quiet. God reveals a gentle interior beauty. (The Lord is so generous—even when we choose only to live on the surface of things, God still reveals himself. But there's much more to him than what you see on the surface.) So dive deep into his heart. All the turmoil of your daily life, all the problems that crash around you like huge waves, will seem somehow distant.

Now I'll let my seashore friend, Frances Havergal, take you for that deeper dive.

> *There are strange, soul depths,*
> *Restless and vast, unfathomed as the sea.*
> *An infinite craving for some infinite stilling.*
> *And, lo, His perfect love is perfect filling.*
> *Lord Jesus Christ, my Lord and my God,*
> *Thou, Thou are enough for me.* [1]

The Father's Answer

From his temple he heard my voice; my cry came before
him, into his ears. The earth trembled and quaked, and the
foundations of the mountains shook.... He parted the
heavens and came down.... He reached down from on
high and took hold of me; he drew me out of deep waters.
—Psalm 18:6–7, 9, 16

Pain stirs the heart of a father like nothing else. My friend Jim knows all
about this. He often has to leave his three little boys when he flies away
on business. On a recent trip, as the family drove together to the airport,
the seven-year-old gladly took last-minute instructions on how to help
Mommy while Daddy was away. The five-year-old bravely tucked in his
chin and promised he would do his chores. As they turned into the airport, the two-year-old, all smiles and jabber up until then, spotted an airplane on the runway. Suddenly, wailing and sobbing!

"It tore my heart out!" Jim exclaimed. "I almost canceled the trip right
then. I just kept hugging that little boy." As I saw Jim's eyes well up with
tears, I thought, *If that boy's cries tug at Jim's heart, how much more must our
tears move our heavenly Father.* Nothing grips God's heart like the tortured
cry of one of his children.

Watch what takes place in Psalm 18 after David says, "I cried to my
God for help." God is roused. The earth trembles, mountains shake, heavens are parted, and he reaches down. Our questions and cries powerfully
move the Almighty. He parts heaven and shakes earth to respond. He
reaches down. He takes hold. Jesus is God's embrace, his way of reaching
down and taking hold.

Can God the Father turn a deaf ear to the plea of his Son on the
cross? (If Jim can't, you bet God can't.) The answer resounds from
an empty tomb three days later: the earth trembled, the mountains
shook, and God rescued his Son. And because the Father raised Jesus,
there is hope for us all. Jesus felt God's slap so we could feel God's
caress. God is our Father. He hears our cry!

Oh, thank you, Lord, for hearing my cry. Bless you for coming to my rescue.

A Victorious Peace

The God of peace will soon crush Satan under your feet.
—Romans 16:20

L oss is a part of life, woven into its very fabric. Futures are altered. Dreams are ripped apart. Families can grow distant. Friends can slip away. I'm grateful my losses are redeemed by God. In my despair I have reached out to him, and he has rescued me. As a result of yielding to Jesus at the time of my greatest loss, I've found great peace.

Sadly, some people turn from God in their loss. Satan offers them a false peace through self-pity. It makes me so angry. Not at these people but at the Devil! I want to jump out of my chair and scream at the havoc Satan wreaks. I'd like to grab the Adversary by the scruff of his neck and throttle him senseless for brutalizing hurting people.

If I were to dwell on it long enough, my frustration over the Devil's dirty deeds would overwhelm me. But God has a hopeful word that sets my heart at peace: "The God of peace will soon crush Satan under your feet." Now, we all know that Christ will reign victoriously. But the victory involves me personally. Satan will be crushed under *my* feet.

At the risk of sounding vengeful, picture this: You and I will have the privilege of flattening Satan like a filthy cockroach under our feet. Or, in my case, under the wheels of my 250-pound wheelchair. God's righteous wrath and our sanctified sense of justice will form the furious weight that crushes our Enemy.

No matter how great your losses may seem, a day is coming when victory will be yours. As you believe this promise, you will experience peace in the face of your anger and anxiety. Surrender to God's future victory and find peace for your soul.

Victorious Savior, as I experience pain, confusion, anger, and worry over the losses in life, guide me to your peace by helping me remember Satan's future crushing defeat.

July 20

God's Hedge

He has walled me in so I cannot escape; he has weighed me down with chains.

—Lamentations 3:7

The four walls of a sickroom can be so confining, even if we're only stuck there for a short time. Whether in the hospital or at home, we long to escape those suffocating walls. At such times we may be tempted to cry out as did Jeremiah in our verse for today or as did Job, who groaned, "Why is life given to a man . . . whom God has hedged in?" (Job 3:23).

But it's *God's* hedge and *his* walls. Only when we view our restricting circumstances as being placed there by God can we find courage to face the wall or hedge. That's what Madame Guyon, a French noblewoman who was confined to a dungeon for ten years, managed to do. She penned these thoughts:

> A little bird I am shut from the fields of air;
> And in my cage I sit and sing to him who placed me there
> Well pleased a prisoner to be, because my God it pleases thee.
> Naught have I else to do, I sing the whole day long,
> And he whom I most love to please doth listen to my song.
> He caught and bound my wandering wing,
>   but still he bends to hear me sing.
> My cage confines me round; abroad I cannot fly;
> But though my wing is closely bound, my heart's at liberty;
> My prison walls cannot control the flight, the freedom of the soul.[2]

The hedge cut off Madam Guyon from the world and confined her on every side. But even a high hedge cannot shut out your view of the sky or prevent your soul from looking up into God's face. Because there is so little else to see when you are hedged in, you view God more clearly than those who move about unconfined. With a hedge around you, the only way "out" is up!

My loving Father, help me to remember that hedges and walls protect as well as confine and that your good pleasure is to use whatever means necessary to turn my gaze to you.

The Comet

God said, "Let there be lights in the expanse of the sky to
separate the day from the night, and let them serve as signs
to mark seasons and days and years, and let them be lights
in the expanse of the sky to give light on the earth."

—Genesis 1:14–15

A few years ago when the Hyakutake Comet whizzed by earth, we drove
to the edge of the Mojave Desert, found a little side road, and parked
near the top of the Tehachapi Mountains. When I got out of the van and
looked up into the vast starry dome, it took my breath away.

The moon was low on the horizon, and the stars were like diamonds
shimmering in the cold desert air. There was no haze, city lights, smog, or
noise except for the air moving through pine trees. The heavy silence of
the desert and mountains made the sparkling night sky awesome and dramatic. Just below the Big Dipper we spotted the comet. We could see the
comet's tail—long, straight, streamlined—cutting right through the con-
stellation like a white laser. And there, on the side of the mountain over-
looking the desert, underneath a blanket of stars, we sang this refrain at
the top of our lungs:

Angels help us to adore Him,
Ye behold Him face to face.
Sun and moon bow down before Him,
Dwellers all in time and space.
Praise Him, praise Him, praise Him, praise Him,
Praise His everlasting grace.

The night sky is full of God's glory. Take a few minutes to cast your
eyes heavenward and to thank God for expressing himself so vividly.
And while you're at it, why not sing a refrain to God? I'm sure he'd
appreciate hearing it from you.

*Creator God, praise you for bringing events like comets into my life to
remind me that sun, moon, and stars in their courses above join with
all nature in manifold witness to your great faithfulness, mercy, and love.*

July 22

A Hidden Treasure

*Cry aloud for understanding.... For wisdom is more precious
than rubies, and nothing you desire can compare with her.*

—Proverbs 2:3; 8:11

If you spend any time at all in Proverbs 2, you'll end up prospecting. The
whole chapter is a gold mine that invites you to grab a pick and come
digging. Wisdom, it says, is to be searched for like silver or gold; discernment is to be dug for like precious stones.

Why would the Bible make such a big deal about something that in
a way is already ours? Why would it send us off searching for God and his
wisdom, when we've already found God? Hasn't he already made himself
known to us through Christ? Hasn't God already richly given us all things
that pertain to life and godliness? He has put wonderful deposits, great
resources, within our reach. The Holy Spirit dwelling within us shows that
God has placed a hidden treasure in us. Face it: You and I have within our
grasp, even inside us, a gold mine. But it's a gold mine of possibilities. God
asks us to roll up our sleeves and dig for all those riches he's given us. We
have to prospect for the gold of his wisdom, the precious gems of understanding and discernment.

Don't expect wisdom to come into your life like great chunks of
rock on a conveyor belt. It isn't like that. It is not dispensed like a
prescription across a counter. Wisdom comes privately from God as
a by-product of right decisions, Godly reactions, and the application
of spiritual principles to daily circumstances.

Charles Swindoll[3]

We may have been given the mind of Christ, but God wants us to
find his heart. I think it was A. W. Tozer who said, "To have found
God and yet to still pursue Him is the soul's greatest paradox of love."
Pursue God. Stake a claim in wisdom. And when you find the treasure, you'll find it was more than worth the digging and dying to self.
Because you will have discovered the heart of God.

*Lord, don't let me be lazy or complacent, convincing myself I have no
need to labor further. Spur me on to dig into your Word, to prospect
through prayer, and to pursue the riches you have laid up for me.*

July 23

A Quiet Time

When you pray, go into your room, close the door and pray
to your Father, who is unseen. Then your Father, who sees
what is done in secret, will reward you.

—Matthew 6:6

Keeping accounts is tempting. We want to remember all the details of
how we've been wronged. And we certainly don't want to forgive. But
that becomes tricky when we realize we ourselves need forgiveness from
God. The Lord offers us solutions to both forgiving and being forgiven.
But he asks that we go to a private place to confront the issues head-on: go
into your room . . . close the door . . . pray in secret.

Get alone with God. Pray for the Lord to reveal to you any attitudes
or actions that have displeased him. Write them down, regardless how long
the list. Then write 1 John 1:9 across the top of the page: "If we confess
our sins, he is faithful and just and will forgive us our sins and purify us
from all unrighteousness."

Tear up the list and throw it away. Thank God for forgiving your sins.
Your reward: the truth and reality of forgiveness will set you free.

If you still feel unforgiven, consider the price God paid through
Christ's death. You might want to say, "On the basis of the cross, I
accept God's forgiveness, and I therefore forgive myself." When
memories nag, realize that the Enemy would rather keep you bound
than free. Then ask yourself if there is anything you can't forgive
someone. List the institutions or the people who have hurt you, have
made you angry, have denied your rights, or have not met your
expectations. Be specific. "I forgive _____ for
_____." Choose not to hold
them responsible for your well-being or happiness. Cancel the debt.
Deal with anger by acknowledging it. Let God help to absorb the
loss. Then consider what you might gain, and list your gains.

*Father in heaven, help me to face the painful events in my life, to
acknowledge the hurt, and to seek forgiveness from you. Thank you that
you readily forgive and heal.*

Be Prepared

In that day they will say, "Surely this is our God; we trusted
in him, and he saved us. This is the LORD, we trusted in
him; let us rejoice and be glad in his salvation."
—Isaiah 25:9

When I was little, the neighbor kids down the street were my idols. I
remember the time their parents asked my folks if I could go to the
community pool with them. We piled into their station wagon, amid inner
tubes, beach towels, bag lunches, and snorkeling stuff. This was going to
be great!

But when we arrived at the pool, my friends headed straight for the
deep end. I ran on their heels but skidded to a stop at the diving board. I
had never been in the deep end. I had never dived off a board before. I
pranced around the edge of the pool, pretending to be a part of things,
when I knew I hadn't been prepared for all this. I felt left out.

Being prepared is more than a Boy Scout motto. Most Christians hope
to go to heaven one day, right? Maybe we even feel excited about the idea:
streets of gold, no more worries, jumping from one planet to the other.
But think about it more deeply. Heaven is a holy place. Its inhabitants are
holy. To be happy in heaven, we must be prepared for it, with our hearts
in tune to holiness. Look at today's verse again. In that day will you say,
"This is the LORD, we trusted in him"? Are you prepared to "rejoice and
be glad in his salvation"? Obedience is the best way to be prepared!

Do you honestly think you would be thrilled to meet Jesus after
clinging to the very sins for which he died? Could you join the cry
of Isaiah 25:9? Think Scripture reading, hymn singing, and praying
are dull? You're in for a shock when you enter heaven. You'd better get
ready.

*Father God, I have far to go before I'm prepared for the blessings that
await me. Show me the next step I need to take to move closer to being
holy like you.*

July 25

Unbearable Power

They got rid of the foreign gods among them and served
the LORD. And he could bear Israel's misery no longer.
—Judges 10:16

God's omnipotence scares me at times. Whether looking at the stars or
sitting through a California earthquake, I am struck by the immense
power at his disposal. I feel very small. And because he is so big and so
strong, it sometimes seems he could not possibly have feelings that even
approach tenderness or empathy, feelings with which I could identify.

I can imagine God inspecting the Israelites' fulfillment of the covenant
to serve him, seeing the evil of their enemies, and then in almost mechan-
ical fashion throwing a hailstorm or two in the direction of the offenders.
Israelites rescued. Universe in order. Back to the throne. Next!

But then I read the verse in Judges that says, "And he could bear Israel's
misery no longer." Those words violate my perception of an omnipotent
God. At first glance such empathy would seem to be incongruent with his
omnipotence. But it is precisely because he *is* omnipotent that he is able
to empathize. His incredible storehouse of power enables him to sense, and
empathize with, the circumstances of sinful and powerless people. In effect,
the same power that enables God to throw a galaxy into a new quadrant
of the universe is the power that brings him to his knees on our behalf.

I am embarrassed by God's inability to bear my misery. Too often I
treat his words and commands as did so many wayward Israelites. I
cast a worthless word or a covetous eye with barely a thought to the
cosmic impact on God's heart. It's more than embarrassing. It's
shameful. Do you feel the same?

*But almighty God, you are not ashamed of me. You have clothed me in
the robe of Christ's righteousness, and I am protected by your power.
Thank you.*

Do You Believe?

Abram believed the LORD, and he credited it to him as righteousness.

—Genesis 15:6

The panel of disability ministry specialists sat on the platform of the small auditorium. Two hundred students of Russia's first college for training social workers were gathered there to hear the specialists talk about disability policies in the United States. The specialists, as agreed, spent the hour talking about various issues such as housing, independent living, and employment. They were careful to respect the wishes of the school by not speaking of their faith but rather focusing on the issues at hand.

At the end of the presentation the moderator asked for questions. Several hands went up, but one student was most enthusiastic. He stood up and asked a question that shocked everyone: "Do you believe in God?"

The room was silent. Some students looked at the teacher; others nodded encouragement, eager to hear the answer. The atmosphere became electric as the panelists leaned forward in their chairs and shared their testimony. The students had come to learn about human solutions to suffering, but what was on their minds was the most fundamental of all questions: God.

The essence of humanity, in both society and the individual, is found in how we answer that question. If we believe in God, it will make a difference in how we live and learn. The question should be asked on a daily basis as we ponder a decision, face a crisis, undergo a temptation. Our affirmative answer forces us to trust God and to yield to his way of life. And best of all, God affirms in our hearts that he is indeed in control.

Do you believe in God?

Father, God of all, I believe in you. I affirm that your existence will govern my life today.

July 27

Cleansing Tower

Forgive my hidden faults.

—Psalm 19:12

Dismantling the war machine at the end of World War II was an enormous task. Unfortunately, in the haste to close up a major supply depot in southern California, many barrels of toxic material were buried above valuable water aquifers near the San Bernadino mountains. The sin of haste and waste was found out years later. The soil was contaminated for miles around, threatening the water supply. After years of legal and technical debate, however, an ingenious solution was devised. Pumps were installed, reaching deep into the water aquifers. The pumps brought the water from the ground up to the top of tall towers. The water then flowed down the towers through filters and back into the ground, clean once more.

Exposure of our sin is God's way of healing our soul. As in the case of the contaminated water, the danger is in the concealment of the poison. As long as it was down there, the water would kill. It had to come up and be exposed to cleansing elements before its deadliness could be neutralized.

God digs past our attempts to hide our sins and brings them to our minds. Then he exposes them to his faithful and just character to cleanse and restore life.

"Here is what's bothering you," he says of an exposed sin. "This is what's sapping your joy and your strength. Remove this; let me forgive you and restore you. Give me the word, and I will cleanse you according to my promise of faithfulness and justice."

Confess your sin today. There is something eminently refreshing about God's cleansing. Even something as physical and elemental as breathing becomes an exercise of joy when we have been cleansed. At such times we are given a glimpse of what our hearts will be like in heaven, when we finally see ourselves as he has seen us all along— clothed in righteousness.

Expose my soul to your light today, Lord. Show me, that I might know your cleansing hand.

July 28

The Supreme Negative

> Son of man, say to the ruler of Tyre, "This is what the Sovereign LORD says: 'In the pride of your heart you say, "I am a god; I sit on the throne of a god in the heart of the seas." But you are a man and not a god, though you think you are as wise as a god.'"
>
> —Ezekiel 28:2

One of the leaders of our ministry began his first staff meeting with the supreme negative: "I'm not God. And neither are you." He went on to explain to his staff that though he was their leader, he was as fallible and foolish as they were.

God's judgment came upon the king of Tyre for ignoring the supreme negative. The king thought he was divine. Driven and deluded by pride, he assumed that momentary control over one's circumstances was equated with sovereignty. He assumed that power was equated with wisdom. He assumed that self was synonymous with divinity.

Tyre's assumptions are often ours. Oh, we rarely articulate divinity or sovereignty. We're too smart for that. But we often survey our domains, however small, and stake our godlike claim with silent declarations of the will. *God may control the universe,* we think, *but I'll control the realm of my daydreams. . . . God may be holy, but I'll decide when and how to confess my sin. . . . God may have pleasures at his right hand forevermore, but I'll decide what gives me kicks.*

The principle of the supreme negative is inviolate. We are not God. To entertain any other thought is to stand as co-conspirator with Satan. Satan was, after all, the first King of Tyre. When we are tempted, it is nothing more than Satan testing our belief in the truth of our identity and that of God. Fortunately for us, God will always be God.

You are God. I am not. Amen, now and forever!

Oh, the Deep, Deep Love

> I pray that you ... may have power, together with all the saints, to grasp how wide and long and high and deep is the love of Christ.
>
> —Ephesians 3:17–18

The hymn that pictures God's love "rolling as a mighty ocean" was on my heart a few months ago when Ken and I went sailing. Because my wheelchair was too big to bring on board, Ken sat me on a cushion and wedged me up against the side of the boat. Then he wrapped a line of rope around me five or six times—I looked as though I were about to be marched off the gangplank.

Once we set our sails, the boat began to pitch and roll. If we had encountered an emergency, I risked going down with the ship (Ken kept handy a sharp knife to cut the rope, just in case). Any lingering fears were allayed by the first mate, Sara Lewis. Her husband, Monty, piloted the boat, and Sara shared with me the following adaptation she wrote of Psalm 23.

Twenty-third Psalm for Sailors

The Lord is my captain; I shall not be in want.
He makes me anchor in calm harbors,
He leads me beside quiet waters; He restores my soul.
He guides me on a course of righteousness for his name's sake.
Even though I sail through the troughs of the storms of death,
I will fear no evil, for you are with me;
Your sun and moon they comfort me.
You provide food from the sea in the presence
     of sharks and barracuda.
You rinse me with sparkling rain; my tank overflows.
Surely goodness and love will follow me all the days of my life,
and I will sail in the ship of the Lord forever.

From "Walking on the Waterways"

Do you ever feel that life is swamping your deck? Know that God's love is deeper than any weights you may have aboard.

Thank you, Lord, that even when the wind has left my sails limp, I can count on your love to bring a fresh breeze.

Miracles of the Spirit

"... but if someone goes to them from the dead, they will repent!" But he said to them, "If they do not listen to Moses and the Prophets, neither will they be persuaded if someone rises from the dead."

—Luke 16:30–31 NASB

Today is the anniversary of my diving accident. Well-intentioned Christians have sometimes looked at my wheelchair and said, "Think of what a witness to the world you would be if God raised you up out of that chair!" They assume that all the unbelievers who have ever seen or heard of me would, by that miracle, be convinced of the power and truth of God.

I say, "A miracle will not do the convincing." That's the Holy Spirit's job. True, the Spirit may use occasional miracles to augment his work, but even when men were raised from the dead by the power of the Spirit, people were not persuaded. And if a dead man raised out of the grave doesn't convince, I'm not so sure a paralyzed woman raised out of a chair will, either. People would probably say, "She was never paralyzed in the first place."

Do we look for signs and wonders, hoping these will entice unbelieving friends into the kingdom? "If God would heal her baby, I know she'd believe." That's presumption and perhaps a lack of faith. God needs neither dead men walking or paralyzed people dancing. The real miracle of the Spirit is to "convict the world of guilt in regard to sin and righteousness and judgment: in regard to sin, because men do not believe in me" (John 16:8–9). It is the sinful heart he wants to heal.

For me, the real miracle means sitting in this wheelchair and smiling. Every day I experience miracles of patience and perseverance, endurance and self-control. This ordinary (which is so *very* extraordinary) work of the Spirit is sufficient. I'm concerned more with a heart that works than with hands that function.

May my heart be the seat of your miracle-working power today, Lord.

Victim or Victor?

When he had received the drink, Jesus said, "It is finished."
With that, he bowed his head and gave up his spirit.

—John 19:30

I am the victim of a terrible diving accident," I said in a flat tone to the lawyer. "It has left me completely paralyzed from the shoulders down." My dad's lawyer jotted copious notes as I droned on. I didn't flinch at the idea of making Maryland Beach, Inc., pay. I wanted everyone to pay, including my parents, who had brought me into this world—it was really their fault. But after my first year in a wheelchair, I began to tire of the self-pity. I turned to the Bible, and my guides became the Holy Spirit and a Christian friend named Steve. I said to Steve, "I can't face a life of paralysis with a happy attitude. It's just too big."

He had a wise reply. "God doesn't ask that of you. He only asks you to take one day at a time." This fundamental signpost from Scripture (Matt. 6:34 KJV) pointed to the path away from pain. I began to "wheel" the path. What came of my blubbering to the lawyer? We lost the case. The truth was, I had made a reckless dive. That truth set me free, along with other truths like leaning daily on God's grace and realizing that God's children are never victims. Everything that touches their lives, he permits.

The irony is, you can't imagine a more victimized person than Jesus. Yet when he died, he didn't say, "I am finished" but "It is finished." He did not play the victim, and thus he emerged the victor.

Forget the self-pity. True, your supervisor may be trying to push you out of your job. Your marriage may be a fiery trial. You might be living below the poverty level. But victory is ours in Christ. His grace is sufficient. Know this truth and it will set you free.

This day, Jesus, I can feel sorry for myself or victorious in you. Show me how to choose the latter.

AUGUST

August 1

The Two Crows

The ravens brought him bread and meat in the morning
and bread and meat in the evening, and he drank from the
brook.

—1 Kings 17:6

The morning of my trip dawned. As I got ready to leave, I couldn't shake
the blues. I felt ashamed for being down—what did I have to be discouraged about? I prayed, "Lord, please brighten my spirits. Grab me by
the scruff of the neck and show me your goodness."

We packed up and headed to the airport. We flew to Dallas and after
our plane landed, I sat by the curb, waiting for my friend to get the van. I
heard a "caw!" behind me. When I turned my wheelchair around, two ugly,
big crows were sitting on the roof's ledge. They remained there for at least
five minutes, looking down at me. It was so odd, I stared back at them.

As I did, God brought to mind the story of Elijah. The prophet had
become depressed just one day after he performed spectacular miracles.
Elijah had announced the end of a drought and was the people's best
friend. Still, he had a bad case of the blues. The record shows that the Angel
of the Lord touched Elijah and even agreed that "the journey is too much
for you" (1 Kings 19:7). Elijah rested and had something to eat and drink.
At another point God sent ravens to feed Elijah.

All the Lord's provision came to mind as I stared at those old crows. I
knew God had placed them right there when I needed to be reminded that
the Lord wanted to give me rest and refreshment.

The lesson of those crows and of Elijah is for all of us. The Lord gives
us gentle reminders of his intimate concern over every detail of our
lives. We just have to open our eyes to recognize that, yes, he may
even use a couple of crows to make his point.

*God, give me physical rest and spiritual food. Enable me to recognize
your signs of encouragement even when they come in strange forms.*

August 2

Use Water Wisely

Whoever drinks the water I give him will never thirst.
Indeed, the water I give him will become in him a spring
of water welling up to eternal life.

—John 4:14

This summer my friend Bev and her family hiked to the bottom of the
Grand Canyon. The weather forecaster had said the temperatures would
hit the nineties, so Bev, her husband, and their children left their camping
spot on the canyon's rim just as the sun was rising.

Before they had hiked even a mile, Bev's husband stopped the crew
and insisted everyone take a giant swig of water. "Why in the world stop
now? We just started," Bev complained. Her husband explained that everyone needed to drink. Bev, independent-minded woman that she is,
thought otherwise. Her idea of wise water management was to wait until
later, when she really needed a drink.

Much to Bev's chagrin, a short time later her husband stopped the
family again. In fact, they stopped at regular intervals to drink. Everyone
but Bev, that is. After all, she had heard that rest rooms weren't around.
They arrived at the bottom of the canyon, enjoyed a brief picnic, slung on
their backpacks to head home. The incline was steep, with temperatures
well over one hundred degrees. That's when Bev got in trouble.

She drank and drank, but her body didn't get the message. She felt
parched. My friend learned that when it's hot, don't wait until the last
minute to drink.

Use water wisely.

We can't go for long intervals without prayer and Bible reading and
then, in a clinch, grab for grace and find—voilà!—strength is there. We
all need to drink in God's Word at regular intervals. That's the only way
you and I are going to be prepared when we are faced with those tough
uphill climbs.

Jesus is offering you a drink today. Don't put him off, thinking you're
not thirsty. Drink now!

*Remind me, Lord, to come to your wellspring regularly to sustain my soul
and to be prepared for the steep inclines that are bound to be up ahead.*

Just Desserts

> When God saw what they did and how they turned from
> their evil ways, he had compassion and did not bring upon
> them the destruction he had threatened.
>
> —Jonah 3:10

God has this thing about showing compassion on whomever he wants. Sometimes we don't like that. The nerve of God to save that child abuser, to reach out to that rapist on death row, to show compassion to that drug pusher!

If you've ever felt the stab of resentment when God wipes the slate clean for somebody whom you would rather he wiped off the face of the earth, guess what? Jonah felt the same way. God wanted Jonah to go to Nineveh to preach the gospel, so Jonah packed his suitcase—and took the train in the opposite direction. He despised those drug-pushing, idol-worshiping, fornicating Ninevites.

After ships, storms, seas, and whales, God gave Jonah another chance to rid himself of the resentment. So Jonah climbed up on his soapbox in the middle of the town square and preached that the Ninevites were about to get their just desserts: "Forty more days and Nineveh will be destroyed." Never had Jonah had such joy in preaching fire and brimstone.

But what happens? The Ninevites repent—and God forgives them. That really makes Jonah mad. He says to the Lord, "Isn't that just like you?" God responds, "Have you any right to be angry, Jonah?" Those words stung.

And they sting today when we hear of a serial killer who comes to Christ, or the deathbed conversion of a tyrant. But God will have compassion on whomever he wishes. We're all too like the laborers in Matthew 20:12 who complained, "These men who were hired last worked only one hour . . . and you have made them equal to us who have borne the burden of the work and the heat of the day." If God wants to give a full day's wages to the worker hired at the eleventh hour, what of it?

God wants to make a difference in someone's life, including yours. Don't let your resentment stand in your way.

Lord, please keep me from anger and resentment when I see you blessing someone else. Help me to realize that when I feel this way, I'm hindering your work in my life.

Chosen for the Furnace

The God of our fathers has chosen you to know his will
and to see the Righteous One and to hear words from his
mouth.

—Acts 22:14

The Scripture for today offers words of comfort when it says we are God's
chosen ones. In fact, Jesus reminds us that we have not chosen him,
but he has chosen us. He has chosen us to serve and worship him, to
receive every spiritual blessing and a heavenly inheritance.

But to some of his loved ones God whispers, "I have chosen you for
the furnace of affliction." Yes, he does choose some of his children to suffer.

Consider the apostle Paul. God said of him, "He is a chosen vessel
unto me . . . for I will shew him how great things he must suffer for my
name's sake" (Acts 9:15–16 KJV).

Chosen to serve God, yes; to praise him, of course; but to suffer for
him? After being paralyzed for more than three decades, I am able to say
yes. God gives special promises to those who have been specially chosen.
If you have severe aches and pains, a husband gone astray, a wife with
manic depression, or some other painful circumstance, he has a word that
is spoken particularly for you: you are a chosen vessel chosen to suffer.

Author Samuel Rutherford said,

Therefore, all the comforts, promises, and mercies God offereth to
the afflicted, they are as so many love-letters written to you. Take
them to you, and claim your right, and be not robbed. It is no small
comfort that God hath written some scriptures to you which He hath
not written to others. Your God is like a friend that sendeth a letter
to a whole house and family, but speaketh in His letter to some by
name, that are dearest to Him in the house.

Take a few minutes to look up some passages that contain special
promises for times of affliction. Key words are *suffer, comfort,* and
afflict.

*Thank you, God of all comfort, for speaking words that serve as a balm
to my soul.*

August 5

Bolts and Bars

Now I want you to know, brothers, that what has happened to me has really served to advance the gospel. As a result, it has become clear throughout the whole palace guard and to everyone else that I am in chains for Christ. Because of my chains, most of the brothers in the Lord have been encouraged to speak the word of God more courageously and fearlessly.

—Philippians 1:12–14

I'm not like Paul; I'm not in prison—far from it! But I can identify with the bolts and bars of a prison cell. This wheelchair is made of a lot of metal, and in a way it's confining. I suppose that's why so many prisoners write me. My testimony has encouraged them, and they look at my bolts and bars and understand.

Even though I know nothing of the kind of imprisonment the apostle Paul went through, I do know I like his attitude. In the Scripture for today he basically says, "Okay, so I'm in chains? My bolts and bars help me spread the Good News. Every time they chain me to another guard, he gets an earful of the gospel. And my imprisonment helps others to become bold."

I've read letters from prisoners who say the same thing. "Okay, so I'm behind bars? It's a chance for me to draw closer to Christ." I can say the same thing. "Okay, so I'm in a wheelchair? These bolts and bars give me a chance to spread the Good News to anyone who experiences confinement and limitations."

What are your chains? Maybe you feel manacled to the kitchen sink. Maybe you feel chained to your desk, with just enough slack to reach the rest room and coffeemaker. Maybe you feel imprisoned in a difficult marriage. Goodness, we all can name the bolts and bars that confine us. Look at today's verse again. Has what happened to you served to advance Christ's gospel? It should. It's the locale from which God wants to work.

Help me today, Lord Jesus, to rejoice in the confinements of my life. Enable me to see my circumstances as boundaries you have erected to work within.

August 6

Pressing On

Gideon and his three hundred men, exhausted yet keeping
up the pursuit, came to the Jordan and crossed it.
—Judges 8:4

Press on, friend. The Bible is full of exhortations to press on no matter
what the circumstances. Judy Rice presses on. She wrote me recently,
"Joni, your daily devotional *Diamonds in the Dust* has become my constant companion as I sit in my nursing home and wait for breakfast. I have
been in a wheelchair since 1965, having found myself with multiple scle-
rosis as a very young adult."

This woman lives in a nursing home, sits in a wheelchair, waits for her
breakfast, and remains faithful in her daily devotions despite facing an
uncertain future. Doesn't her example strengthen your resolve to press on?

The Bible makes much of sticking to it when it comes to living with
unpleasant circumstances.

In Judges 8:4 Gideon's troops were exhausted. They were completely
worn out, but they kept pursuing the goal. They ended up victorious in
battle. The result? Greater glory to the Father. Then there's Jesus in the
Garden of Gethsemane. Talk about someone facing unpleasant circumstances! The Lord says in Matthew 26:38–39, "My soul is overwhelmed
with sorrow to the point of death. . . . My Father, if it is possible, may this
cup be taken from me." But Jesus presses on, saying, "Yet not as I will, but
as you will." The Lord persevered and obtained salvation for the world.
The result? Greater glory to the Father.

Judy Rice is fighting her own battles and praying her own prayers
about cups of suffering passing her lips. Because she presses on by God's
grace, she's in a class with Gideon—yes, even with the Lord Jesus, who
welcomes her at his side.

What battles are you facing? Whatever they are, draw encouragement
from Gideon, the Lord Jesus, and Judy Rice . . . and press on!

If today I feel as though I can't go on, Lord, help me to press forward.
Thank you for the examples of Gideon and Judy Rice. Most of all I'm
grateful that in you I find more than an example . . . I find strength!

Living in the Blessed Now

I tell you, now is the time of God's favor, now is the day of salvation.

—2 Corinthians 6:2

Chris is a middle-aged man with Down's syndrome who lives with his folks. He enjoys volunteering with Awana and taking part in various socials at church. And he's blessed with an unusual gift: he doesn't understand time. Every day, for Chris, is the same as the day before.

I know it's frustrating for Chris at times, but I call it a gift because every day is the day of salvation for Chris. A faithful churchgoer, Chris listens intently to the messages, whether they be light and whimsical or heavy on the fire and brimstone. And on days when a speaker gives a stirring invitation to join the family of God, Chris is usually heard to remark to a nearby elder after the service, "I accepted him today! I accepted him!" His face shines and his eyes overflow with joy.

Skeptics would tell you Chris hasn't got a clue as to what he's doing. If he knew, they would argue, he'd realize how unnecessary it was to be saved more than once. Chris doesn't see it that way. And God doesn't, either. Both the Lord and Chris are able to enjoy that blessed gift of nowness. Every past moment of conviction of sin, for Chris, gets poured into the now. Every hope he has of heaven and of having a new body and mind gets poured into now. And the feeling is overwhelming for him.

Some days I wish I could shed myself of time and live as Chris does—enjoying God's sense of nowness. I know I've been called to build upon and move past the foundation of salvation, but to recall those broken and tender moments of joy for the first time—*that* would be blessed.

Father, creator of time, suspend for me this moment my history and my future. Let me enjoy, for just now, what it was like to enter your favor for the first time. Grant me that joyful bliss of heaven today.

August 8

Audiovisual Aids

> Just as the sufferings of Christ flow over into our lives, so
> also through Christ our comfort overflows. If we are dis-
> tressed, it is for your comfort and salvation; if we are com-
> forted, it is for your comfort, which produces in you patient
> endurance of the same sufferings we suffer.
> —2 Corinthians 1:5–6

God uses people as audiovisual aids to strengthen others. But wait: Does
it mean that the inspiring person is nothing more than an object lesson from which others can learn? Is that person's example only for everybody else's benefit? If so, it makes God seem utilitarian (and we can't have
that!).

When I think of audiovisual aids, I remember the time Bonnie Ren-
nie, a blind woman, read aloud from her braille Bible when I spoke at a
church. We all sat there near tears, listening to Bonnie's strong voice as she
read, moving her fingers across the braille pages. I was *inspired.*

Here's the neat part: whatever others gain from watching Bonnie gets
credited to her account. That's what the apostle Paul meant when he said,
"I will continue with all of you for your progress and joy in the faith, so
that . . . your joy in Christ Jesus will overflow on account of me" (Phil.
1:25–26). When other Christians gain strength from Bonnie's example,
their joy in Christ overflows . . . on account of Bonnie. And it's all being
credited to her spiritual ledger.

When Bonnie and others like her hang in there through God's grace,
it does something for the rest of us Christians. It strengthens us. The body
is better and brighter. And how wonderful that God credits it all to the
account of those who suffer. Truly, one day the last shall be first!

This is good news for you if you think your life doesn't matter or you
aren't making much of a contribution to the body of Christ. The way
you live your life *does* make a difference—to the church as a whole
and to you in particular.

*God of all comfort, how marvelous to be reminded that you use my suf-
ferings not only in my life but also in the body of believers. Thank you
for blessing others and myself in one fell swoop.*

Strange Answers to Prayer

> When he heard that Lazarus was sick, he stayed where he
> was two more days.
>
> —John 11:6

I asked the Lord that I might grow in faith,
    and love, and every grace,
Might more of His salvation know,
    and seek more earnestly His face.
'Twas He who taught me thus to pray,
    and He, I trust, has answered prayer;
But it has been in such a way; as almost drove me to despair.
I hoped that in some favored hour at once He'd answer my request;
And, by His love's constraining power,
    subdue my sins, and give me rest.
Instead of this, He made me feel the hidden evils of my heart,
And let the angry powers of hell assault my soul in every part . . .
"Lord, why is this?" I trembling cried,
    "Wilt Thou pursue Thy worm to death?"
"Tis in this way," the Lord replied,
    "I answer prayer for grace and faith."

John Newton certainly captured in his verse the frustration we all feel when we pray and God answers in ways we never imagined—or wanted. Mary and Martha must have felt that way when Christ deliberately delayed coming to Bethany after he received news of Lazarus's illness: *Why is the Master ignoring our request? Doesn't he care about our brother? Surely he's forgotten us!* Jesus chose to make life hard for Mary and Martha. Yet it is usually strange answers to prayer that hide the deepest, best, and most beautiful purpose.

Mary and Martha did not receive a brother healed back from the infirmary; they received their brother raised back from the cemetery. More than that, they received the gift of greater, sturdier, more robust faith. God is interested in the same for you.

God, help me to remember that while you haven't promised me happy endings, you have assured me of greater faith. For me, that's the best ending.

A Rock in a High Place

From the ends of the earth I call to you, I call as my heart
grows faint; lead me to the rock that is higher than I. For
you have been my refuge, a strong tower against the foe.

—Psalm 61:2–3

August in the desert. Whew! That's where my family spent the summer
of '59, near a little cow town just north of Phoenix, to be precise. We
were helping my Uncle Ted separate his herds of cattle. Each day my sisters and I headed out on the best cow ponies to round up the herds before
morning melted into the desert afternoon.

But one day I became separated from the rest, having gotten turned
around in a big patch of cactus. But I knew not to panic. Uncle Ted had
told us to head for "the big red boulder up on that yonder ridge" if we got
lost. "We'll find you in no time," he had assured us.

The air sizzled. I kicked my pony in the boulder's direction. When I
reached the top, I searched the horizon for the others. They were nowhere
in sight. Wiping my brow with my hat, I climbed down to find shelter in
the boulder's shadow. It was, for me, a place of refuge.

Fifteen minutes went by, then half an hour. Still, I wasn't afraid. I knew
I was exactly where I was supposed to be. Within an hour I heard galloping hooves coming up the ridge. Just in time, for the cool, shifting shadow
was about to disappear. I knew I would be found. I knew the high rock
had been my certain and only hope.

The same is true for you. No matter how lost you feel, God is with
you. If you are resting in him, you are exactly where you're supposed
to be. You'll be found. You are safe. Sanctuary in him is only a prayer
away, as Psalm 61 says.

*Lord, thank you that you place the high points of prayer and your Word
in my life. I'm grateful they provide shelter, safety, and a place to wait
until you find me. Guide me to them when I become lost.*

August 11

Putting Out the Welcome Mat

You will receive a rich welcome into the eternal kingdom of
our Lord and Savior Jesus Christ.

—2 Peter 1:11

When Ken and I have guests at our house, we like them to come
through the front door and feel as if the place has been prepared just
for them. Ten minutes before friends are due, we put out the chips and
dip, start the fire, light the candles, put last-minute touches on the table,
and flick on the music. Then we're ready for that knock on the door.

All of us make an effort to help people feel welcome. But wouldn't it
be weird if your guests knocked and you opened the door and said, "Oh,
that's right. We did ask you over for dinner, didn't we? Uh . . . come on in.
I'm sure we can dig around for some frozen vegetables, and hey, we can
stretch the pot roast."

How ridiculous! But take what I've said and consider your church.
Have you prepared a welcome for visitors, or will their presence surprise
you? Simple things convey they are welcome: parking spaces for visitors,
people who will chat with them, someone who will offer to sit with them,
or even an offer of coffee and doughnuts after the service.

Check out your sanctuary this Sunday and scan the pews for visitors.
Don't leave it up to someone else to provide the welcome; take the
initiative. After all, if heaven will one day offer us a rich welcome,
we can provide the same here on earth. What kind of message do visitors
receive when they come through the front door of your sanctuary? Hopefully, it's "Come on in; we've been expecting you."

Teach me, Lord, to be more hospitable to visitors at my home and place
of worship. Remind me that if I don't take the role of host, perhaps no
one will. Help me to remember how I felt when I was a stranger but you
welcomed me into the family.

August 12

Communion Sunday

I have been crucified with Christ and I no longer live, but Christ lives in me. The life I live in the body, I live by faith in the Son of God, who loved me and gave himself for me.

—Galatians 2:20

Communion Sunday is a day to remember. Notice that Jesus didn't command a sacrament to commemorate his birth, his life, his miracles, or even his resurrection. Only his death does he ask us to remember again and again.

Too often we casually approach the Lord. As we receive the bread, instead of thinking about the Lord's broken body, we notice a broken fingernail. Sometimes I come to Communion unprepared, not having paid attention to the housecleaning that my heart needs. Once in a great while (when I sleep fitfully the night before) I bow my head and close my eyes with the others for a time of quiet reflection and repentance—and I yawn, fighting off snoozing more than fighting to confess hidden faults. It's only when the cup is lifted to my mouth that I realize, *Bother! I should be more ready. Am I honestly sincere about repenting? Do I appreciate through this Communion all that Jesus has done for me?*

I'm so relieved that "he remembers that we are dust" (Ps. 103:14). He remembers time and again that I am made of clay, that without him I come undone. That's why I praise God for Communion Sunday, the bread savored, swallowed, digested, and becoming bone of my bone and flesh of my flesh. Praise God for Galatians 2:20: "I no longer live, but Christ lives in me. The life I live in the body, I live by faith in the Son of God, who loved me and gave himself for me."

You must never forget that. As long as you have Communion, remember.

Lord Jesus, forgive me that sometimes I become callous—hardened and unfeeling—about the sacrifice you made on the cross. Remind me over and over again. I don't want to forget.

August 13

Power in the Blood

If we confess our sins, he is faithful and just and will forgive
us our sins and purify us from all unrighteousness.

—1 John 1:9

It bothers me when I hear people say that only the weak-minded struggle
with severe depression. That's 'cause I sometimes get hit hard with more
than just downhearted feelings. There are times when I feel like disap-
pearing—I don't want to talk to anyone, and I don't want to face the world.

I'm not the only one who has days like that. I think of them as "the
day of evil" spoken about in Ephesians 6:13. When they come, I hang on
for dear life to a couple of well-worn Scriptures that assure me joy will
come in the morning.

And I take encouragement that the great hymn writer William Cowper suffered from depression. He constantly struggled against suicide. Once
he even tried to hang himself. Another time he fell on a knife but the blade
broke, and at one point he threw himself into a river, hoping to drown.
He had a mental breakdown and was placed in an insane asylum for eighteen months. During his detention he read Romans 3:25, the part about
the blood of Christ being so powerful as to atone for *all* past sins—even
the guilt of suicidal thoughts.

After his conversion he became friends with John Newton, who wrote
"Amazing Grace." It was just the inspiration Cowper needed to write the
beautiful hymn "There Is a Fountain."

Throughout his life Cowper continued to be plagued by severe depression, and often he sought to end his life. His most powerful hymns were
written after those times.

We may become depressed on this side of eternity, but aren't you glad
that little by little, inch by inch, day by day, God renews our minds
. . . all because there is a fountain filled with blood?

*Thank you, Father, for the encouragement of past saints' lives. They
remind us there is no permanent cure for our woes here on earth, which
makes us long all the more for your transforming grace and mercy.*

When Others Take Offense

"Isn't this the carpenter? Isn't this Mary's son and the brother of James, Joseph, Judas and Simon? Aren't his sisters here with us?" And they took offense at him.

—Mark 6:3

The eyebrow raisers included Jesus' own brothers. One time when Jesus entered the room, they quickly became all seriousness; suppressing grins, they winked at one another and urged him to "go more public with his important message." Such skepticism led Jesus to heal fewer people in his old neighborhood than anywhere—naturally confirming the neighbors' doubts—and the gossip began. "Among the crowds there was widespread whispering about him. Some said, 'He is a good man.' Others replied, 'No, he deceives the people'" (John 7:12).

His goodness scared people. One village asked Jesus to move on just after he had healed their town's most notorious psychotic. Some whom he greatly helped didn't even turn to thank him. It became common to hear people wonder out loud why Jesus attended parties, when John the Baptist had contented himself with wild honey and fried locusts. Others avoided him for fear of getting kicked out of their synagogues. Some even joined the ranks to stone him. (Estes)

But Jesus never backed down. He kept to the furrow he was plowing.

Have you ever found yourself the brunt of gossip in your office? Do neighbors whisper behind your back? Have people smiled stiffly at your words of witness, then said, "No thanks." We have all found ourselves feeling left out at parties, or the last to be invited to sit at the popular table at a church potluck. It's okay. It's what happened to Jesus many times. Don't fret or feel intimidated. If Jesus kept to the furrow he was plowing, you must, too. You're the servant following in the Master's tracks.

I pray for those who take offense at me, Lord. If you could lay down your life for your accusers, I can pray for those who malign me.

Eagle-Men

Those who hope in the LORD will renew their strength.
They will soar on wings like eagles; they will run and not
grow weary, they will walk and not be faint.

—Isaiah 40:31

Eagles are solitary birds. They never fly in flocks. At times God asks us to forego human companionship to experience divine fellowship, so later we have the strength to give to others. "God seeks eagle-men," writes Mrs. Charles Cowman in *Streams in the Desert*. "No man ever comes into a realization of the best things of God, who does not, upon the Godward side of his life, learn to walk alone with God."[1]

Scripture is replete with such men: Abraham living in a tent, Moses herding sheep, Paul alone with God in Arabia. God then often takes those whom he has sheltered in solitude and thrusts them out to minister to others.

Author Caryll Houselander writes of these eagle-souls,

There are those who must live, as it were, in other men's hands; whose success, even if it be of a spiritual order, must be paid for in a suffering of poverty far more terrible than material poverty, a poverty of not having themselves, not having anything of their own—not time, or solitude, or their thoughts, or even their senses: their hearing filled always with other men's troubles, their eyes with the face of other people's sorrows.

Many times you may feel there is no rest: hurting people call you on the phone or appear at your door; your children clamor for attention and love; your spouse wants to spend time with you when you have no time; your boss adds to the piles already on your desk. Only someone who has spent solitude with God can respond as an eagle, mounting up with a reserve of energy provided by the Almighty. Quiet time with him isn't an option; it's a necessity.

Father God, teach me to come to you for strength when I feel as though I have none. In this way I'll have strength to dispense love and care to others.

Dispelling the Smog

Righteousness exalts a nation, but sin is a disgrace to any people.

—Proverbs 14:34

While flying into Los Angeles the other week, I looked out the window and cringed. The city was covered in an unusually heavy layer of thick, brown smog. However, as we drove up the freeway an hour later, you could barely see it.

I thought of this when I read a comment by Dr. David Wells: "What is striking about our culture today is that its corruption is not simply at the edges . . . it is not simply found among academics who are bent upon overturning all moral principles, or among vicious street gangs, or vendors of pornography. What is striking is that this corruption is not located in small pockets here and there, but is spread like a dense fog throughout society."[2] He's right. And sometimes, like when we see smog from ground level, we hardly notice it. We tend to forget we live under a thick layer of moral corruption. We succumb to the numbness.

Yet this age is ripe with opportunity. I've noticed that more people than ever are open to discussing the problems. "What can we do? Where can we turn?" is their cry.

Now is the time to shine light, shake salt, and tell people that Jesus Christ is our hope, that the Bible offers answers (the Ten Commandments may not be old-fashioned after all!). In contrast to the despair and nihilism, we can proclaim an absolute morality—there are things that are right and wrong, good and evil, helpful and hurtful. "Don't commit adultery"—families will be ripped apart. "Don't steal"—society will crumble if you do. A moral compass like this is good! What's more, in responding to the vague spiritual longings people seem to have, we can remind them that our hearts were formed by God and we will be restless until we find our rest in him.

May I never succumb to the numbness in our society, Lord, but share the truth. In so doing, help me to dispel the dense smog of moral corruption.

Last Days' Power

"Not by might nor by power, but by my Spirit," says the
LORD Almighty.

—Zechariah 4:6

Spirit of the Living God, fall afresh on me.
Spirit of the Living God, fall afresh on me.
Melt me, mold me, fill me and use me.
Spirit of the Living God, fall afresh on me.[3]

There's something special about that song, partly because it reminds
us of Pentecost, that wonderful day the Holy Spirit first fell on the brand-
new church. Some amazing things happened that day. The gospel became
clear and concise for the first time. The preaching of Peter had power. Men
were convicted of sin. People were saved. That's what happened when the
Spirit of God fell for the first time on those new believers.

The same things still occur when the Spirit of the living God descends
on individuals. The gospel is made clear. A person's preaching has power.
People feel convicted of sin. But probably the Holy Spirit's most amazing
work is accomplished when people become saved.

I think I'll start praying a special prayer. I'm going to ask the Lord to
fill me with his Spirit in such a way that the gospel can be made clearer
through my life, that my words of witness will have power, and that the
friends to whom I testify will be convicted and saved.

Why don't you join me in this prayer? Ask the Spirit of the living
God to fall afresh on you. He'll touch your life, and the lives of those
around you, in ways that might amaze. But then he's always been a
bit mysterious in how he can touch a heart and change its course,
hasn't he?

*Holy Spirit, I need you to melt me, to take my rigidity against your work
in my life and soften it. I need you to mold me so I look more like Jesus.
I need to be filled with your presence rather than full of myself. And I
want you to use me, for what good am I if you don't?*

No Pleasure in Punishment

> Rid yourselves of all the offenses you have committed, and
> get a new heart and a new spirit. Why will you die, O house
> of Israel? For I take no pleasure in the death of anyone,
> declares the Sovereign LORD. Repent and live!
> —Ezekiel 18:31–32

Daddys don't take delight in punishing their children. Or at least, most dads don't. My father used to say it hurt him to smack my backside with a spoon as much as it hurt me (I strongly doubted that at the time). However, what parent hasn't experienced anger over the disobedience of a child? It goes wrong when that anger energizes the spanking. Some parents feel self-satisfaction in reaching for the rod.

God is different. We can say for certain that our heavenly Father never takes delight in punishing his children. He gets no kick from it. His anger is not quenched by it. He gains no satisfaction in it. So what energizes him when it comes to discipline? "God disciplines us for our good, that we may share in his holiness. No discipline seems pleasant at the time, but painful. Later on, however, it produces a harvest of righteousness and peace for those who have been trained by it" (Heb. 12:10–11). This is God's motive: our training. We are not his whipping post, no matter what our sin. We are his children, and he wants us to share in his holiness. It is in this he takes delight.

God is not a celestial killjoy who hides a club behind his back, hoping to catch one of his children in trouble so he can exercise his divine right to punish. According to today's verse, God pleads with us to get a new heart regarding our sinful habits. He says, "Repent and live!" Good advice. "We have all had human fathers who disciplined us.... How much more should we submit to the Father of our spirits and live!" (Heb. 12:9).

Thank you for disciplining me in faithfulness, Father. I need your strong hand in my life so I might share in your holiness. Thank you for keeping me in training.

Life Ain't Easy

We must go through many hardships to enter the kingdom
of God.

—Acts 14:22

Everyone who takes the Bible seriously, and many who don't, agree that
God hates suffering. Jesus spent much of his short life relieving it.
Scores of passages tell us to feed the hungry, clothe the poor, visit inmates,
and speak up for the helpless. When we feel compassion for people in distress, we know that God felt it first. He shows this by raising sick people
from their beds—sometimes to the wonder of doctors—in answer to
prayer. Every day he grants childless women babies, pulls small-business
owners out of financial pits, protects Alzheimer's patients crossing the
street, and writes happy endings to sad situations. Even when he has to
punish sin, he says it gives him no pleasure (Ezek. 18:32). In heaven Eden's
curse will be canceled. Sighs and longings will be historical curiosities. Tears
will evaporate. Tissue companies will go broke.

But it simply doesn't follow that God's only relationship to suffering is
to relieve it. He specifically says that all who follow him can expect hardship.
But didn't Jesus hang on a cross so we wouldn't have to suffer hell? Yes, but
not so we wouldn't have to suffer here on earth. Listen to the Bible on this:

"I will show [Paul] how much he must suffer for my name"
(Acts 9:16).
"It has been granted to you on behalf of Christ . . . to suffer for him"
(Phil. 1:29).

The Bible goes even further. After calling Christians "heirs of God
and co-heirs with Christ," it adds, "if indeed we share in his sufferings" (Rom. 8:17). In other words, no one goes to Christ's heaven
who doesn't first share Christ's sufferings. Do you think you should
be exempt from suffering? Listen to this final word from Hebrews
5:8: "Although he was a son, he learned obedience from what he suffered." This week purpose in your heart to be no greater than your
Master. If he suffered, you can expect it, too.

*May I learn obedience through the hard thing I'm going through right
now, God.*

August 20

Use It!

As we have opportunity, let us do good to all people, especially to those who belong to the family of believers.
—Galatians 6:10

Tyler Law, age nine, strode in front of the gurney that was to take him to surgery for his cancerous arm. "Can I walk?" he had asked the orderly who came to get him. "Sure, kid," the orderly had said as he fell in line behind the brave patient and joined the parents. The three of them watched as Tyler marched ten paces in front of them. He was raising his bad arm in the air and pumping his biceps in and out.

When they arrived at the prep room, his dad asked, "So, what was that arm-pumping thing about?" "Oh," Tyler answered, "I just wanted to get as much use out of it as I could, in case they have to cut it off."

Tyler lived on the brink of losing his arm and took every opportunity to use it for that which it was intended—movement. Muscles tightening, tendons flexing, joints moving, neurons firing. Not a second of enjoying that arm was going to be lost while Tyler still had the chance.

Tyler's words also reveal more than his bravery. They strike a chord of truth about our lives: Use it. Now. I fear that in our modern Christian world, where we are quick to avoid burnout, we have not used our lives as they were intended. Paul admonishes us to take advantage of the opportunities afforded us to do good. Our lives have so much potential for doing good. We take for granted our time, our talents, our energy, and assume that they must be saved for some great purpose later. God's purpose for us is not later; it is now.

The opportunities to use our lives for that which they are intended—loving God—are now. Find those opportunities today. Pursue them to the end bravely, knowing that this day might be the last afforded for such work.

Lord, I'm taking inventory of my life. What do I have that I'm not using? Where can it be applied today?

Making Music in One Accord

> May the God who gives endurance and encouragement
> give you a spirit of unity among yourselves as you follow
> Christ Jesus, so that with one heart and mouth you may
> glorify the God and Father of our Lord Jesus Christ.
>
> —Romans 15:5–6

Christopher Parkening plays the guitar like few people in this world are able. Whether onstage with the New York Philharmonic or in front of an audience of three, he can bring out the power and mystery behind those six strings. Not one note is out of place, out of sync. Whether strummed together or plucked separately, the strings all work in unison to create the desired melody or harmony.

Musical accord on the guitar doesn't happen by chance. Only certain strings pressed down in particular combinations will produce the desired sound. Whether the guitar plays "Jesu, Joy of Man's Desiring" or a Spanish dance, its beauty is heard when the strings are in proper relation to one another.

This is what it means to be in one accord.

I wonder if Paul had beautiful music in mind when he prayed that the Romans would have a spirit of unity and with one mouth glorify God. Did he picture the church in Rome as being in concert onstage before the world? Did he hear in his mind the impact of that church on history? We know now that the music of the Roman church did catch on and changed the world. The Christians endured years of suffering until the fourth century, when the Roman Empire at last acknowledged the harmony of the gospel. It abandoned its cultic practices. It paved the way for missionaries instead of persecuting them. And the world has not been the same since.

You and I have the responsibility to use our gifts and live in accordance with God's will. And the promise of God is that living together in such a way will make for beautiful music and lasting impact.

Tune my heart today, Lord, to your will. Then play my life in accordance with others who love you and desire to sing your praises.

August 22

Anthropomorphism

Give ear, O LORD, and hear; open your eyes, O LORD, and see.
—Isaiah 37:17

See, I have engraved you on the palms of my hands.
—Isaiah 49:16

The eternal God is your refuge, and underneath are the everlasting arms.
—Deuteronomy 33:27

Anthropo—what? That's a grown-up word if ever I heard one! I'm glad God doesn't choose the sorts of words theologians do. God talks to us using terms we can understand. And this, friend, is exactly what anthropomorphism is. It is the practice of God describing himself in human language, as though he had feet (Ex. 24:10) and a face (Matt. 18:10) and a heart (Hos. 11:8). It's a way of communicating. A way of choosing word pictures that we can immediately grasp. It's the language of a Father speaking to his children. Almost—and I don't mean this disrespectfully—as if he were using baby talk.

Of course, the Bible as a whole denies any literal similarity of form between God and his creatures. "God is spirit," it says in John 4:24. Yet because God is so personal, so active in his creation, because of his great love, he literally revealed himself in the form of a man. "Christ Jesus . . . who, being in very nature God . . . made himself nothing . . . being made in human likeness" (Phil. 2:5–7).

God took on the form of a human—with a heart, eyes, ears, and feet. This means that with respect to Jesus, we can literally speak of God in human form. He invites us to do so when he uses such language himself.

Picture yourself being held by God's everlasting arms today. Speak to him in prayer, using human word pictures. He's so personal with you . . . be personal with him.

Hold me by your hand, Lord. Today may I follow in your footsteps. Listen to your voice. Feel your smile. And hear your heartbeat.

August 23

Of Deadlines, Deadbeats, and Dead Ends

> You, O LORD, have delivered my soul from death, my eyes
> from tears, my feet from stumbling, that I may walk before
> the LORD in the land of the living.
>
> —Psalm 116:8–9

Deadlines scream: "Change this diaper." "Finish that paper." "Fax this letter." "Make that sale." Gotta hurry. Get it done! Get it out!! Now!!! Their tyranny leaves us breathless.

Deadbeats clamor: An overbearing boss. A rebellious child. An angry spouse. On my nerves, in my face, at my door. They kill the joy of loving, daily.

Dead ends loom: The money is gone. The marriage has failed. The cancer is back. No hope. No way out. It's over. It's done. They choke the hope of living.

In these tyrannical, loveless, hopeless days, God sings:

> Where, O death, is your victory? Where, O death, is your sting?
>
> 1 Corinthians 15:55

He's not immune to our daily deaths. He just sings because he knows that his promise of victory isn't a "wait till you're really dead and six feet under" promise. The promise of victory is *now*. He rescued David from the pit of despair more than once. He guaranteed Paul that nothing would ever separate us from his love. He assured Peter of a new birth into a living hope that would never fade. He sealed our claim to abundant life in his Son, Jesus.

So go ahead and say, "Give it your best shot, deadlines. God's got it under control. Go ahead and make my day, deadbeats. God loves me too much. And take a hike, dead ends. God's hope is too real to deny."

You're my life, Lord, now and forever. There's no deadly foe that can destroy the life to which you called me. I'm alive!

A Lesson from Christopher Reeve

Man's days are determined; you have decreed the number
of his months and have set limits he cannot exceed.
—Job 14:5

Last year when I watched Christopher Reeve (the actor who was severely paralyzed in a riding accident) on television, I was deeply moved. Although he sat stiff and rigid in his wheelchair, he smiled courageously as he puffed-and-sipped his mouth controls to steer his chair. The next day I kept running into people who said, "Did you see Christopher on TV last night? Isn't he an inspiration?"

I smiled and nodded but thought, *Just last week everyone was talking about assisted suicide for people like him.* It was schizophrenic. One day letters to the editor applaud the courage of the severely disabled; the next, the editorial column can be filled with letters cheering on the new legislation legalizing assisted suicide. One day Christopher Reeve is positioned as a helpless victim; the next, a picture of courage.

It tells me that society keeps a double standard. Society thinks it's appropriate to prevent able-bodied people from committing suicide but considers it rational for a terminally ill or severely incapacitated person like Mr. Reeve to end his life. More importantly it shows that we lack confidence in God's ability to sustain those who suffer.

God gives common grace to nonbelievers who suffer, and God gives special grace to believers who suffer. Is someone close to you terminally ill or severely incapacitated? Pray that God will give them grace today. Show a skeptical society the truth of 1 Corinthians 6:19–20: "You are not your own.... Therefore honor God with your body." At all times, no matter how physically or mentally limited we are, it is the Lord of life who gives breath. Be the Lord's hands to help a suffering friend today. Through prayer and encouragement, help this hurting friend understand that life is worth living.

Jesus, help me to shatter the schizophrenia as I share with others that you are the Lord of life. Help me to support the hurting and encourage the dying. Praise you for helping people like Christopher Reeve ... for using people like me.

August 25

Prudence

I, wisdom, dwell together with prudence; I possess knowledge and discretion.

—Proverbs 8:12

People and labels. They really don't go together. It's much nicer to just push aside the politically correct protocol, snip off the label, and look at each other as . . . people.

I tried this during a luncheon meeting with a group of Chicago inner-city pastors. My goal was to find out about the unique needs of disabled people living in an urban environment. The pastors were eager to discuss with me how they could minister to families that included a disabled child.

As we talked, I couldn't help but wonder, *Now, am I supposed to refer to these men as "African-American"? Or would they prefer the word "black"? I know "colored" is out-of-date. Hmm, on the other hand, it's okay to say "people of color."*

I shrugged my shoulders, smiled, and continued to talk with the pastors. The subject of color didn't come up. Later when we discussed Hispanic churches, I became tongue-tied between "Hispanic" and "Latino." I decided then to ask the pastors what word I should use.

To my surprise, they slapped the table and laughed. Little did I realize, but the pastors had been wrestling with questions of their own. They had been wondering, *Now, are we supposed to call Joni "handicapped"? Or "physically challenged"? We know we're not supposed to refer to people like her as "cripples" or "invalids." Which is it?*

We agreed that labels didn't matter so long as you remember the person's name. I'm glad Jesus never referred to one he loved as a prostitute; he just referred to her as Mary Magdalene. He never called a certain man a coward; he merely told him he would call him Peter. To a workaholic he said, "Martha, Martha . . ." Jesus loved people. I'm sure that's why he often used their names when talking to them.

That's good advice for you too. Red or yellow, black or white, standing, sitting, blind, or with sight, it's the name, not the label, that means the most to the person.

Father, help me to focus on individuals, just as you do with your children.

A Heart of Silver

He has preserved our lives and kept our feet from slipping. For you, O God, tested us; you refined us like silver. You brought us into prison and laid burdens on our backs. . . . Praise be to God, who has not rejected my prayer or withheld his love from me!

—Psalm 66:9–11, 20

The crucible for silver and the furnace for gold, but the LORD tests the heart.

—Proverbs 17:3

I love you, God," we say all the time. And we do . . . I do! But we easily deceive ourselves unless that love for God is proved through a test. Love will say, "I'd do anything for you, God, follow you anywhere." Obedience will say, " . . . and let me prove it." Obedience is not so much for God's sake but for ours. God wants us to realize the depth of our love for him.

So he tests us. He is the one who brings us into prisons and lays burdens on our backs. All the while he never withholds his love from us. His love drives him to test us in order to refine us like silver. When gold is put through a refining process, it involves heat, as in a furnace. But when silver is refined, it involves pressure, as when one crushes a metal in a crucible. When a test heats up, we want to escape; when a trial is pressuring, we want to collapse. If we hold on, remain faithful, and rigorously obey, our hearts become refined. Obedience melts away pride and prejudice. Obedience crushes into dust self-centeredness, revealing a heart pure and at peace.

Others will notice when you come forth shining after a crucible experience. They may applaud your perseverance. Even *this* can be a test: "The crucible for silver and the furnace for gold, but man is tested by the praise he receives" (Prov. 27:21). Your response? "Praise be to God, who has not . . . withheld his love from me!"

Refine my heart so my love for you is real and genuine, Father. I would rather have this trial than a dull, dry heart.

August 27

Reasoning with God

"Come now, let us reason together," says the LORD.

—Isaiah 1:18

When tragedy blindsides you and almost knocks you silly, you are understandably bewildered. You feel confusion and panic. You may feel afraid that more hardship will come on top of it all. You may feel like cursing. Or praying. You may feel a thousand things. But at some point, somewhere along the line, if you don't stop *feeling* and start *thinking* about how to attend to the circumstances you find yourself in, you'll freeze.

Yes, intense suffering calls for deep emotions. In the aftermath of a terrible tragedy, people weep. We should weep. God weeps. But there is also a time to think. Neither can replace the other.

When you are able to raise your head above the heartache in which you are swimming, the Bible tells you to take the next step. It is full of commands to "think," "ponder," "consider," "weigh," and "judge." Jesus often turned questions about the meaning of life, death, and suffering back onto the questioner. "What is written in the Law?" he would ask. People would blink, sniff back their feelings, flip the pages in their mind, think out loud, and come up with the relevant passages. But this didn't end the discussion. Next was the real work. "How do you read it?" Jesus would ask. That is, what do you think these Scriptures mean? Jesus never allowed room for sloppy or sentimental thinking about the tough issues of life. (Estes)

What you think about God influences your friendship with him. It affects how much glory you give him. But your imagination about God (especially in the midst of tragedy) isn't reliable. If we simply trust our emotions about him, we recreate him in our own image. We then become like the people Paul described: "They are zealous for God, but their zeal is not based on knowledge" (Rom. 10:2).

Do you have a question about God? A question about your circumstances? Make the Bible your only safe source of knowledge about him. Make this a commitment for the year.

Help me to search for you, God, not in my imaginations but in your Word.

What Have You Got?

The LORD turned to him and said, "Go in the strength you
have and save Israel out of Midian's hand. Am I not sending you?"

—Judges 6:14

I learned a lesson early in my career as a quadriplegic: work with what
you've got. The occupational therapist taught me how to use muscles in
a whole new way to make up for muscles that were rendered useless. The
good nerves in the upper part of my deltoids help me get a lot of work
done that would otherwise be the responsibility of my biceps.

God's been in the occupational therapy business for ages. He has often
come to weak, visionless people and worked with what they had. Whether
it was Moses' rod, Samson's jawbone, or David's sling, God simply took
what was available and showed his people what was possible.

To underscore the possibilities and potential, God tells us who's in
charge. To simple people like Gideon and Jeremiah, he said, "I'm sending
you." That was it. That was all the guarantee they needed. For Gideon, the
guarantee would take him to triumph. For Jeremiah, through trials. In these
people and others, God's commission was sufficient to start and complete
the task. No matter how weak or limited God's people are, no matter what
little they have to offer, the Lord works wonders with what he's got!

God is always commissioning people. He's commissioning you today
with his Word. If you have doubts about that, consider Jesus' words in
John 20:21: "As the Father has sent me, I am sending you." Jesus seeks
willing disciples who will yield whatever resources are at their disposal to
carry out his purposes.

So, what have you got? Make the list and show God. Short list? No
matter; take it and apply it to the needs and people around you.

He'll take care of the rest. That is, after all, his business!

*Lord, here's my list. You've used rods, slingshots, and loaves to do your
work. Can you use me?*

August 29

The Great Amen

No matter how many promises God has made, they are
"Yes" in Christ. And so through him the "Amen" is spoken
by us to the glory of God.

—2 Corinthians 1:20

There's enough power in this little verse to ponder for an entire year. Just think: every promise that the Father has ever made finds its fulfillment in his Son, the Lord Jesus. When God promises that he will impart to us grace, he gives us Jesus, the Lord of grace. When God promises to give us peace, he gives us Jesus, the Prince of peace. The promise of comfort? He gives us the Lord of all comfort. And when he imputes to us his righteousness, he gives us his Son, the Lord of righteousness. Even life finds its source in Jesus, the Word of life.

Even the familiar promise of Romans 8:28–29 finds its fulfillment in Christ: "We know that in all things God works for the good of those who love him. . . . For those God foreknew he also predestined to be conformed *to the likeness of his Son*" (emphasis added). This wonderful promise we so often claim is fulfilled in Jesus.

Jesus is everything to you—the answer to your every hope, prayer, and promise. The Christian walk is not so complicated after all. It is simple. It is . . . Jesus. And I say, "Amen" to that.

Revelation 3:14 says, "These are the words of the Amen, the faithful and true witness, the ruler of God's creation." The word *amen* means "so be it" and "so it will be" and "so it is." Today what can you say "Amen!" to? How is Jesus the "so be it" in your life?

I sing today,

> *Standing on the promises of Christ my Lord,*
> *Bound to him eternally by love's strong cord,*
> *Overcoming daily with the Spirit's sword,*
> *Standing on the promises of God.*

When I stand on your promises, Jesus, I am grounded in you. Amen.

August 30

Balm in Gilead

Is there no balm in Gilead? Is there no physician there?
—Jeremiah 8:22

Is there no relief?" The anguished man in the television commercial rubbed his forehead in pain. He seemed to despair for an aspirin strong enough to help. As Christians, we occasionally wonder the same. When hardships broadside us, when pain settles in to stay, we cry, "Is there no relief?"

Jeremiah wondered the same. Amid the horror of the Babylonian invasion, the prophet looked toward the east, to Gilead, a land that was famous for producing medicinal balms to heal wounds. He inasmuch asked, "Do they make an ointment in Gilead strong enough to help us? Is there no cure, even in a place like Gilead?"

We know the answer. For out of Palestine there came a Cure. An Ointment to soothe the wounded. A Salve to ease the pain. "Jesus said, 'It is not the healthy who need a doctor, but the sick. . . . For I have not come to call the righteous, but sinners'" (Matt. 9:12–13). When you are the one who is at the center of the universe, holding it all together—if everything lives, moves, and has its essence, its being, in you (Acts 17:28)—you can do no more than give yourself when someone is hurting. Jesus helps the hurt.

So in Isaiah 54 he becomes the Husband to the divorced woman. In Psalm 10 he becomes the Father of the orphaned. In Zechariah 2 he becomes the Wall of Fire to those who need protection. In Isaiah 62 he becomes the Bridegroom to the woman who grieves that she'll never marry. In Exodus 15 he becomes the Healer to the sick. In Isaiah 9 he is the Wonderful Counselor to the confused and depressed. In John 4 he becomes the Living Water to the thirsty. In John 6 he's the Bread of Life to those who are hungry for more than this world can give.

There is a balm in Gilead to make the wounded whole;
There is a balm in Gilead to heal the sin-sick soul.
Sometimes I feel discouraged,
And think my work's in vain,
But then the Holy Spirit revives my soul again.[4]

Press the ointment of your love on my hurting heart today, Lord. Be everything to me.

August 31

Guard the Storehouse

"The word of the LORD you have spoken is good,"
Hezekiah replied. For he thought, "There will be peace and
security in my lifetime."

—Isaiah 39:8

Based upon his pleadings before God, Hezekiah had been spared a painful death and guaranteed another fifteen years of life. Upon his recovery, God had also promised that his kingdom would be spared from the Assyrians. Hezekiah was doubly blessed.

It seems, however, that in his gratefulness Hezekiah had only himself in mind. A Babylonian emissary visited Hezekiah upon hearing of the king's recovery. He was shown the king's storehouses containing armor, silver, gold—everything to whet Babylon's appetite for conquest. After the emissary left, God made it clear to Hezekiah that those treasures, as well as Hezekiah's own children, would be carried off to Babylon someday.

Hezekiah's response to God's news in this verse reveals how selfish he was. The prophet had just announced to him that Israel—the treasures and the descendants—would be taken captive. Nothing would be left. And the children were going to be made eunuchs in the palace of Babylon. But Hezekiah seems unfazed by the prospect. "There will be peace and security in my lifetime." Self-preservation seems to be the order of the day. No matter that his children would suffer. No matter that Israel, the apple of God's eye, would be enslaved. "At least I'll have my peace and security," he thought.

There is no room for selfish rationalizations like that of Hezekiah's. Just because we live in dangerous days does not give us an excuse to ignore the next generation. And it will not do to delegate the responsibility to youth pastors and teachers. Each of us must protect our storehouse of faith and ensure through whatever means available that we make decisions beyond our lifetime. Our words, our wallets, our votes, our prayers—all must be harnessed to protect our descendants from captivity to a reckless world.

Lord, may I not be content with peace in my lifetime. May I sacrifice today's luxury for tomorrow's freedom.

SEPTEMBER

Puritan Passion

Our people must learn to devote themselves to doing what is good, in order that they may provide for daily necessities and not live unproductive lives.

—Titus 3:14

The Puritans are often maligned and ridiculed. Most people on the street think of them as witch-hunting Pharisees of the seventeenth century. The media describes them as narrow-minded legalists living in a world without love, humor, or joy. J. I. Packer, however, found their true lives to be quite different. He writes this in his book *A Quest for Godliness:*

> So, in their heavenly-minded ardor, the Puritans became men and women of order, matter-of-fact and down-to-earth, prayerful, purposeful, practical. Seeing life whole, they integrated contemplation with action, worship with work, labor with rest, love of God with love of neighbor and of self, personal with social identity, and the wide spectrum of relational responsibilities with each other, in a thoroughly conscientious and thought-out way. In this thoroughness they were extreme, that is to say far more thorough than we are, but in their blending of the whole wide range of Christian duties set forth in Scripture they were eminently balanced.[1]

What a refreshing picture of the Puritans! And what a role model for living a life of balance in this day and age of confusion and strife. Planting both feet firmly on the Word of God, with a clear eye on the realities of life, and callused hands on the work of the day, the Puritans not only lived life as it was meant to be lived; they also forged a life for millions to follow.

What life will you lead? What future will you forge? Our families, our church, and our nation all need people of Puritan passion.

Father, I am grateful for people who believed what you said, and lived that way. Grant me the same diligent purpose to live a life of devotion to that which is good and balanced. Grant me Puritan passion today.

September 2

Today's Idols

All who worship images are put to shame, those who boast
in idols—worship him, all you gods!

—Psalm 97:7

Idols are tough to expose—that is, unless they're the sort that sit on the shelf of a house altar. We're too contemporary for idols like that. But that does not mean today's verse is out of date. It speaks to you. When? Whenever you feel ashamed.

Think about those times when you are ashamed of yourself. Perhaps you were sitting, all sophisticated and nicely dressed, with a new friend over coffee. As the conversation flowed, you felt witty and interesting. How fascinated your new friend seemed to be with you. It made you feel all the more charming. But then it happened. You knocked your cup, and coffee went all over your new suit. Instead of laughing it off, you felt stupid and silly, embarrassed and even ashamed.

This is where today's verse comes in. It is through shame that God exposes that which we idolize. How does this relate to our story? Well, what idol did the feeling of shame and embarrassment expose but pride? The person in our story was hoping to come across as charming and sophisticated and, oh, so important in the other's eyes—but friend, it all boils down to pride. And the idol we worship—even the impressiveness of our own image—will ultimately put us to shame.

This is helpful! How else would we detect the idols in our life? God has engineered us in such a way that he uses our sense of shame to reveal those things, people, or vocations that we idolize. And once our idols are exposed, we can then more easily do away with them.

The next time you feel shame, ask yourself, "What idol has just been given a shove off my shelf?"

I have to admit, Lord, that a verse like today's seems as though it's from another time and place, another era. But verses like these are as fresh and personal as they were three thousand years ago. Thank you for exposing the idols in my life through my sense of shame. Help me to remember that the next time I feel embarrassed.

September 3

Straight Answers to
Good Questions

We live by faith, not by sight.

—2 Corinthians 5:7

I read some crazy questions in a magazine the other day: "Why are there flotation devices under airplane seats instead of parachutes? Why do they put braille dots on the keypad of the drive-up ATM? Why do we drive on parkways and park on driveways? Why, when you transport something by car, is it called a shipment, but when you transport something by ship, it's called cargo? Why do they have interstate highways in Hawaii? Why isn't *phonetic* spelled the way it sounds?"

These questions underscore that a lot of queries aren't worth asking. After all, they don't have straight answers. But some questions *are* worth asking. Questions about suffering. Yet even these important queries don't have straight answers. When I was first injured and facing the rest of my life in a wheelchair, the "why" question was the first thing that popped in my head every morning. Looking back, I'm not sure I would have understood, let alone been satisfied, had God given me answers. It would have been like pouring million-gallon-sized truths into my one-ounce brain.

Straight answers to larger-than-life questions don't increase faith. The only way to increase faith, according to Romans 10:17, is through the Word of God. In essence, God tells us to walk by faith and not by sight. Having faith in God is where we find rest; we don't find it in locating the answers we couldn't bear to hear, even if they were given to us.

Don't think answers will satisfy your need to know. Faith will, for it assures you that Jesus is the only one who holds all the answers. Someday he *will* pour out those million-gallon-sized truths. You'll have all the straight answers. Until then have faith.

Father God, you know how much I yearn to understand why certain things happen. Help me to bring these puzzles to you and leave them at your feet as the burdens they are. May I leave your presence with a load of faith to replace the doubts. I pray, as the disciples did, that you would increase my faith.

A Lesson from Mildew

When you enter the land of Canaan, which I am giving you
as your possession, and I put a spreading mildew in a house
in that land, the owner of the house must go and tell the
priest.

—Leviticus 14:34–35

We tend to think that God's sovereignty—that is, his "having been decided beforehand" decree—only comes into play when monumental things are at stake: the salvation of humanity, the fate of entire nations, the rise and fall of despots, or other rare and special occasions. *Everyday occurrences like sow bugs in the shower, however, happen on automatic pilot,* we think. *Just because God foreordains big things doesn't mean his hand is behind absolutely everything.*

Throughout Leviticus God gives instructions to Israel regarding the most mundane and ordinary situations. In today's verse God dispenses instructions for dealing with mildew—a household nuisance but hardly something affecting the fate of entire nations. When people could see a spreading mildew placed by God, Old Testament homeowners were to call for a priest, who would follow certain procedures to eradicate the microbes. Again, this was for a mildew spread by God. But how do folks distinguish God-sent mildew from the kind that just creeps across walls without divine assistance? The Bible doesn't say. I wonder why (smile)?

Nothing happens outside God's decree. Nothing good, nothing bad, nothing pleasant, nothing tragic. Not in my life, not in yours. We may not fathom God's reasons; we may not agree with his thinking; we may love him for it or we may hate him for it. But in simple language, God "works out everything for his own ends—even the wicked" (Prov. 16:4), and God "is in heaven; he does whatever pleases him" (Ps. 115:3).

God is not in heaven pushing buttons on his remote. The fact is, his decree keeps absolutely everything in balance. If he did not control bad things—from mildew to mayhem—our world would be worse, a whole lot worse, than the headaches and hardships we face today. Think of five nuisances in your life today, and use them as a means to thank God for balance in your life. (Estes)

I am so glad, so relieved, that you are in control, dear Lord.

September 5

Who Caused Job's Trials?

The LORD said to Satan, "Very well, then, everything he has is in your hands, but on the man himself do not lay a finger." Then Satan went out from the presence of the LORD.

—Job 1:12

The words are scarcely out of God's mouth when Sabeans massacre Job's servants, lightning kills sheep and shepherds, Chaldeans slaughter camels and herdsmen, and a desert wind collapses a house on Job's children. How tragic! Yet in a nutshell, Job's saga teaches us everything we need to know about God's sovereignty.

What caused Job's trials? At the most basic level, *natural forces* did—natural low-pressure systems that could have been explained in scientific terms. At the same basic level, *evil people* caused Job's trials—those greedy raiding parties needed no prompting; they devised their own wicked schemes. At a deeper level, *Satan* did—the Devil turned around after leaving God's presence, and before we can blink, carnage is everywhere. Satan no doubt had something to do with instigating those roaming cutthroats and sponsoring those terrible storms (although the storms were a natural phenomena and the pillagers acted in a way natural to violent men, the Bible says Satan engineered it all).

So who or what caused Job's trials? At the deepest level, *the decree of God* did. Satan asked permission to stir things up, but God signed the authorization papers. Yet at the same time, the Devil acted freely, no one forced the hand of the Sabeans or Chaldeans, and nature got up on the wrong side of the bed that morning. God's decrees made room for Job's trials, but God didn't cause them. God exploited the deliberate evil of some bad characters and the impersonal evil of some bad storms without forcing anyone's hand.

God permits all sorts of things he doesn't approve of. Why? So that we might say with Job, "Though he slay me, yet will I hope in him; I will surely defend my ways to his face" (Job 13:15). Can you say with Job, "The Lord gives and the Lord takes away. Blessed be the name of the Lord"?

Lord, I don't understand how you can bring ultimate good out of the Devil's wickedness, or how you exploit storms and disasters to suit your own purpose, but like Job, I put my trust in you.

September 6

Show-and-Tell

Now I rejoice in what was suffered for you, and I fill up in
my flesh what is still lacking in regard to Christ's afflictions,
for the sake of his body, which is the church.
—Colossians 1:24

W hat?" you say. "You mean, the Lord didn't finish the job?" No, the
word *lacking* doesn't imply falling short of a mark. The work is finished. Jesus said so (John 19:30). He died on the cross, paid the penalty for sin, and released to us incredible power to live a life pleasing to God. Nothing's lacking there.

But there's something that *is* lacking. Something needs to be finished, and you and I are the ones to do it: we bear in our body the bruising and battering intended for Christ. What's more, we bear it in a godly manner. I call it show-and-tell. Jesus is not around in the flesh right now to do this, but we are. We are the walking billboards of his finished work. We are showing people that his power is displayed, and we are telling them of his death on the cross. We take the punches on the chin from the world to show and tell that the cheek can be turned, the cross can be carried, the burden can be borne, the thorn can be accepted, the temptation can be opposed, and the wicked can be loved.

People don't know the reality of what the Lord did two thousand years ago; they only know it when they see him show up through our lives. As I said, it's called show-and-tell.

When's the last time you participated in show-and-tell? Today fill up in your flesh what is lacking in regard to Christ's afflictions. Do it for the world's sake. Do it, as today's verse commands, for the sake of the body of believers. Most of all do it for Christ.

Lord Jesus, you received so many afflictions when you walked on earth. People misunderstood you, turned their backs on you, and abused you. It probably will happen to me too as I participate in show-and-tell. Give me strength to walk in your shoes today. Give me courage. Be powerful through me. Fill up in my flesh what is lacking!

September 7

Songs of Conquest

After consulting the people, Jehoshaphat appointed men to sing to the LORD and to praise him for the splendor of his holiness as they went out at the head of the army, saying: "Give thanks to the LORD, for his love endures forever." As they began to sing and praise, the LORD set ambushes against the men of Ammon and Moab and Mount Seir who were invading Judah, and they were defeated.

—2 Chronicles 20:21–22

Anyone who spends time with me knows how much I enjoy singing, especially at work. When someone helps me type, we'll reach for the hymnal next to my computer, flip it open to an old favorite, and harmonize our hearts out.

All this is not just to fill the office corridors with song. For me, singing is a wonderful way to clear the spiritual air, shooing away any dark spirits hanging around. (Until recently a New Age publisher rented the second floor of suites in our building.)

It hearkens back to 2 Chronicles 20, in which Jehoshaphat was called into battle. He "appointed men to sing to the LORD and to praise him . . . as they went out at the head of the army." Jehoshaphat's army then made a shambles of the enemy. What a wonderful story of how songs of praise make a difference in a spiritual climate. Confusion befuddled the enemy, and their camps turned on one another. The people of God then carried away the plunder.

If you're fighting darkness or engaged in a spiritual conflict, if the Enemy is poised and ready to attack, the best defense is to sing. It's a way of resisting the Devil. Singing is also the best offense. Songs of praise will confuse the Enemy and send the Devil's hoards hightailing. So pick a hymn, any hymn. Choose a Scripture chorus. Or make up your own melody to a favorite portion of Scripture. Victory over the Enemy can be yours for a song.

Bring to my mind songs, Lord, when my path is blocked by the enemy of my soul. Keep my heart attuned to you.

September 8

A Golden Rule

*In everything, do to others what you would have them do
to you, for this sums up the Law and the Prophets.*

—Matthew 7:12

During a recent flight from Chicago to Los Angeles, a flight attendant came down the aisle, offering coffee. My friend Judy, who was flying with me, had gone to the rest room, so when the attendant reached our row, I asked her to pour coffee for the two of us.

Judy was gone quite a while. So when that same flight attendant came back up the aisle, she noticed that the two cups were still sitting there. She asked, "Would you like me to help you?"

In between sips I commented, "I'll bet you didn't think this would be part of your job description when you became a flight attendant." She said, "It's my pleasure. If I were you, I'd want someone to do the same for me."

She's right. It's a good rule for relating to others. A golden one, in fact. It's what Jesus tells us to do in the verse for today. "In everything, do to others what you would have them do to you," says our Lord. That includes every situation in which you might feel awkward or a little unsure of what to do or say. Just relax and think, *What would I want someone to do for me?*

When Judy finally returned and saw one full cup of coffee and one empty cup, she gave me a funny look. I smiled and said, "I found a new friend."

What would you like to have someone do for you today? Buy you a little token to say you're being thought of? Phone to tell you you're being prayed for? Why not do those things for someone else? You'll be surprised at how much more golden your day will turn out.

Lord, you have shown us by your example how blessed it is to give. Help me to have the courage, and give me the creativity to know how, to do to others as I would like them to do to me.

September 9

Creative Encouragement

The Sovereign LORD has given me an instructed tongue, to know the word that sustains the weary. He wakens me morning by morning, wakens my ear to listen like one being taught.

—Isaiah 50:4

The day had been full of appointments, my back was aching, my neck was stiff, and I was tired of sitting in my wheelchair. However, I couldn't go back to the hotel for several more hours. I was in the middle of autographing books, and at least seventy-five people were still in line.

Then, as I was halfway through the line, a young man opened his book, squinted at the pen I was clenching between my teeth, and said, "I'll bet that thing tastes awful." I nodded. He pulled out a tiny can of Binaca mouth spray and said with a laugh, "Have you ever tried this on your pens?" I giggled and said no but agreed to give it a try. Holding my pen at arm's length, he gave the end a good squirt. It tasted great. The break in routine, the laughter, and that bit of creative thinking were all I needed to perk up my spirit.

I admire people who know how to encourage others by what they say and do. But even if you weren't born with the gift of encouragement, God can teach you. He wrote the lesson in the verse for today. The all-time great Encourager says he will give you his words to sustain those around you. He even wants to show you, first thing in the morning, those who may need an encouraging word.

What does God require of you, his student? "Listen like one being taught." Cooperate with the Lord when he nudges you to say a kind word. Encouraging others costs no more than a bit of time and effort. Yet who can put a price on its value? Just ask the fellow at the autograph table.

Thank you, Lord, for instructing me to be an encourager. Teach me to listen attentively to you and then to eagerly step out to offer whatever creative form of encouragement occurs to me.

Choosing Your Identity

Let no one deceive you with empty words, for because of such things God's wrath comes on those who are disobedient. Therefore do not be partners with them. For you were once darkness, but now you are light in the Lord. Live as children of light.

—Ephesians 5:6–8

A young teen cried out to her dad, after a hard day of school and family life, with that age-old question "Who am I?" Caught between her identity as a child of the family and her identity as a friend of her peers, she felt confused.

Answering the question is not as easy as you might think. It's easy to answer questions like "What are we?" or "Where are we?" or even "Why are we?" But beyond one's name, there is little to claim as something that is uniquely our identity. No wonder the dad answered the question in quite different terms. He said, "Jessica, you are the choices you make and the friends you keep. That is how people will know you. And oddly enough, that is how you will come to know yourself as well."

A Christian's place as a child of light sets the stage for our identity. But it is the day-to-day, nitty-gritty choices of life through which we craft our ultimate identity. And not only do our decisions define us, so do our friends. Children of light can stand downstage, front and center, with those who love Jesus, or they can hide in the faint shadows upstage, holding empty, vain conversations with those who do not believe.

Just as Jessica can go to her father for lessons in her identify, so too can you and I ask our Father for answers. "Make choices that show well in the light," he will tell us. "And have you seen my Son? Spend time with him and you will be like him."

God knows who you are. And he has destined you to be like his Son. We don't need to doubt our identity. If we simply live as he asks, we will find it.

Fashion me by your Holy Spirit, Father, to become like your Son. Grant me friends who love you, and the will to choose that which is lovely in your sight.

Aspen Leaves

As you do not know the path of the wind . . . so you cannot understand the work of God, the Maker of all things.
—Ecclesiastes 11:5

It may be too early for fall where you live, but not if you're in Colorado.
Right now the aspen groves along the front range of the Rockies are turning from green to golden. Nothing lifts the soul like the sight of a hillside
of yellow aspen leaves quivering in a brisk mountain breeze. I've seen
aspens in the wind. The leaves are so delicate, so small, their stems so fragile, that they flutter in the slightest of breezes. Aspen leaves seem to tremble even when the air is barely moving—this is how sensitive they are.

I want to be that sensitive to the Spirit's touch, don't you? A soul that
is sensitive to sin, that resonates at the slightest movement of the Spirit. A
soul that quivers when the breath of God all but touches it. How do we
become this sensitive? Simple: be ready, stretch out your branches, unfurl
your heart to God, for you never know when his wind will rise your way.
After all, like the wind, the Spirit is uncontrollable and unpredictable. Who
can harness the wind or the Spirit? "His way is in the whirlwind and the
storm, and clouds are the dust of his feet" (Nah. 1:3).

John 3:8 reminds us, "The wind blows wherever it pleases. You hear
its sound, but you cannot tell where it comes from or where it is going. So
it is with everyone born of the Spirit." Just as the wind cannot be controlled or predicted yet its effects can be witnessed, so it is with the Holy
Spirit. He cannot be controlled, but the proof of his work is always there.

To be an aspen leaf is to be sensitive to the movement of God in your
life. Ask God for a soul sensitive to sin. Pray that God will make your
soul tremble at the slightest stirring of the Spirit in your life. You may
not be able to control the wind of God's workings, but you can control the degree to which you are sensitive to good and evil or right
and wrong.

*I stretch out my branches to you today, Lord. Let me catch the movement
of your Spirit. May I be sensitive to your touch.*

September 12

Training

Train yourself to be godly.

—1 Timothy 4:7

I once owned a horse who was a great jumper. For an entire summer we cleaned up ribbons at the horse shows. On the trail I could ask him to sail over fence after fence, all the while keeping a steady gallop. This horse was trained for endurance. When I returned to school in the fall, I put him out to pasture. After a month or so, before it got cold, I saddled him up for one more joyride before the first snows came. After three fences and less than half a mile, he was wheezing and lathered. I asked him for more but it just wasn't there. His head drooped and his pace slowed. My horse was out of training.

I occasionally think of my old horse when I come up against a temptation and seem to have no resources, no strength to say no. At those times (and I know when they are) I shouldn't be surprised. I've been out of training. I have no endurance.

We're all the same. We fiddle and faddle, meandering through life, ignoring spiritual disciplines like fasting, praying, and regular Bible reading. Then suddenly when temptation broadsides us or we get hit with a heavy trial, we wonder why we lack faith, have no power to say no, or succumb easily to discouragement or depression. We plead for help from God but it's just not there, so we fume that God's grace isn't sufficient or that he's abandoned us.

Not so. The reason the strength isn't there is because we're out of training. We can't expect to exhibit godliness—especially at the snap of a finger when temptation strikes—if we've been out of training.

First Timothy 6:11–12 says, "But you, man of God . . . pursue righteousness, godliness, faith, love, endurance and gentleness. Fight the good fight of the faith. Take hold of the eternal life to which you were called when you made your good confession in the presence of many witnesses."

"Pursue." "Fight." "Take hold of." In other words, stay in training.

Lord, often in a trial I have faulted your grace as being insufficient, when actually I haven't had the strength to be godly because I've been out of training. Help me today to pursue and take hold of every spiritual discipline.

Riding Lessons

Physical training is of some value, but godliness has value for all things, holding promise for both the present life and the life to come.

—1 Timothy 4:8

A friend and I were once joking about what kind of horses we'd like to be. He mused, "I'd like to be a wild stallion, racing free across the plains, my mane and tail whipping in the wind." I smiled and countered, "Maybe, but a horse like that will never win any honors. I would rather have the confines of a pasture and stall and be trained for dressage under bridle and bit."

An unbridled, untrained horse lacks the restraints that guide and direct. The bit, martingale, tie-down, spur, and crop appear at first to the horse as irritants and hardships. But such inconvenience and suffering school the horse to listen to the rider's commands. How hard it would be for an animal, without the aid of his master and his crop, to train himself up in the way he should go. What's more, the horse would be useless in the ring, without a hope of ever winning honors for his master.

It's the same for humans. Our natural bent is to enjoy what we think is freedom out there without constraints. But as someone has said, freedom is not the right to do what we want to do; it is the power to do what we ought. Hardship is our bit and bridle. What's more, our Master is an expert with the reins and the crop. Godliness involves training . . . without it no honor can be given to our Master.

One of the key elements in good animal training is to break the will but not the spirit. In the same manner, we are never more ourselves, never more spiritually free, than when our will is bent to God's will. Our spirit thrives on this kind of submission; what's more, we are then well on our way to godliness.

God, thank you for seeing fit to saddle me with certain hardships. You know what's best. You know how to train me for godliness. I yield and obey . . . I want to win you honors!

I'd Die for You

This is how we know what love is: Jesus Christ laid down his life
for us. And we ought to lay down our lives for our brothers.
—1 John 3:16

Real love is an action—a selfless, sacrificial giving. The greatest act of
love anyone can perform is to give himself or herself for others.

Sometimes it's easier to say, "I'd die for you" than it is to say, "I'll live
for you. Let me put your desires first. Let me think of your interests before
my own." I think we would all agree that living sacrificially is a real death
to self. It's a killing of your selfishness, your own desires. To die for others,
to live for others, is a gift of love that can only come from God. Why only
from him? Because it takes superhuman strength to live—I mean, really
live—for others.

> The sweetest lives are those to duty wed,
> Whose deeds, both great and small,
> Are close-knit strands of unbroken thread
> Where love ennobles all.
> The world may sound no trumpets, ring no bells;
> The book of life the shining record tells.
> The love shall chant its own beatitudes
> After its own life working. A child's kiss
> Set on thy sighing lips shall make thee glad;
> A sick man helped by thee shall make thee strong;
> Thou shalt be served thyself by every sense
> Of service which thou renderest.
>
> Elizabeth Barrett Browning

I wish I could make it more complicated. But it's ever so simple.
Receiving God's love and then giving his love, dying for others and
living for others—that pretty much sums up the Christian walk, our
purpose for being. How's your love quotient? Are you giving more
than you're receiving? Are you ready to live for someone else? In what
ways do you need to die to self?

*Teach me, Lord, through the example of your life, to graciously give of
myself that others might live. Keep me from a sense of martyrdom, and
enable me to retain my joy.*

September 15

The Cotton Farmer

Consider how the lilies grow.

—Luke 12:27

Not just the lilies but a few other flowering things. Like cotton. Seeing a cotton field ready for picking gives new meaning to the phrase "white unto harvest." But a lot of carefully planned work goes into the crop before it reaches that stage—which is true for us as spiritual "plants" as well.

Just at the time—the exact time—the cotton plant starts to bear fruit, the farmer withholds water. Less water at the critical stage in development makes for a fuller cotton flower. The farmer is judicious. He doesn't go too long without watering, or the plant will die; then again, he doesn't over-water, or the result would be a lush plant with little or no cotton flower. This is how the farmer induces the plant to produce more cotton.

At harvesttime the farmer sprays the cotton plant with salt water, which dries up the leaves and makes them fall off. Now the cotton is much easier to pick. We would be prone to leave the green part of the plant. But the farmer knows the plant has to give up its beauty to serve its function.

Dry seasons are no mistake. For consider how *you* grow. You sometimes bear more fruit (like patience or long-suffering) for having endured a dry season. If you're going through a dry time, keep in mind that God is inducing you to "raise a harvest of righteousness" (James 3:18). The stresses of life are being used for his good purpose. Let that thought release you from worrying. And as far as those dried-up leaves that fall off, sometimes we too must give up something that is treasured to serve the purpose God intends for us.

Thank you, Lord, that you provide us with pictures from nature of how you relate to us. They help us to relax in your loving hands and to trust you to be a wise farmer of our lives.

September 16

Picture It!

> You love him even though you have never seen him; though
> not seeing him, you trust him; and even now you are happy
> with the inexpressible joy that comes from heaven itself.
> —1 Peter 1:8 LB

I realize you and I have never seen Jesus, but nothing's preventing us from picturing him. Try this exercise. Right now, where you are sitting, think about where the door is. Behind you? To the side of where you sit? Now as you continue reading, imagine the Lord Jesus coming up the hallway or the path outside your door. (All I'm asking you to do is to *imagine* this; we're not conjuring up anything weird here.) Okay, see in your mind's eye the Lord approaching your door. He waits for a moment. Now he moves into your room. Picture him walking slowly toward you. He's in no hurry. Perhaps he folds his arms, smiles, and observes you for a moment, with this book in your hands. He comes closer. Does he pull up a chair near you? Does he sit on the foot of your bed? On the edge of the tub? On a patio bench?

After you read this paragraph, put down this book and close your eyes. Picture the rest. With what sort of look does he hold your eyes? Imagine him extending his hand to you in a kind and welcoming gesture. Look closely and see the nail scars in his palm. How do you respond? What do you see yourself doing? Saying to him in prayer? Ready . . .

You love the Lord Jesus and trust him, even though you have never seen him. A special blessing is reserved for you. Do today's exercise occasionally to train your thinking that, yes, the Lord Jesus is near and ever present, even though he is invisible to your eyes. You'll be blessed with a joy that comes from heaven itself.

Thank you, Lord, for visiting me today. May I talk with you more? . . .

September 17

More Than You Can Handle?

No temptation has seized you except what is common to
man. And God is faithful; he will not let you be tempted
beyond what you can bear. But when you are tempted, he
will also provide a way out so that you can stand up under it.
— 1 Corinthians 10:13

Every once in a while 1 Corinthians 10:13 bugs me. At those times I'm
prone to think God couldn't expect from me what he does from others, because mine is a "different story." I especially thought that way when
I was lying on my hospital bed: *How can you be putting me through all this?
It's more than I can bear—even with your help, God!*

The truth is, my story is not different. Neither is yours. My quadriplegia hasn't earned me any Purple Heart medals with God. My bouts with
pressure sores and lung problems haven't exempted me from 1 Corinthians 10:13. If the Lord allows crushing hardships to pile on top of all the
other baggage that goes with being disabled, I can't whine. It never can be
said of me, "She has good reason to let off steam every now and then."

Whenever I entertain stubborn, stiff-necked thoughts of resentment,
I've noticed I go not forward but backward. The problems aren't easier to
handle; they become harder. I must remember Hebrews 12:4, which warns
complainers, "In your struggle against sin, you have not yet resisted to the
point of shedding your blood." What a good reminder! I'm not a martyr;
nobody's drawn and quartered me, laid me on a rack, sawed me asunder,
or run me through with a sword—so things can't be that bad.

True, 1 Corinthians 10:13 may bug you when you think you must
disobey because the temptation is too great. But remember, we can
never be forced to disobey. We don't sin because we have to; we sin
because we want to.

*God, thank you for the grace to endure the losses you have allowed in my
life. Whatever the trial or temptation, enable me to look to you to provide the way of escape—and the grace to bear up under the load.*

The Best "Better"

Heal me, O LORD, and I will be healed; save me and I will
be saved, for you are the one I praise.

—Jeremiah 17:14

M y father, forever in faded jeans, red suspenders, and plaid shirt, looked
so out of place, so uncomfortable, when he'd come to the hospital to
see me back in those early days of my injury. It warmed my heart when
he'd stand by my bedside, white-knuckle the guardrail, smile, and whisper
with wet eyes, "In every day and in every way, you're getting better and
better and better." He'd say it every time he came. His was a constant reas-
surance that I would not be paralyzed for long; every day, in his eyes, I was
getting better and better.

My body never shook off the paralysis. The pragmatist would say,
"See, your father's words were wishful thinking. You didn't get better, Joni;
instead you got stuck with a wheelchair."

That's not the way I choose to look at it. Daddy was right. Every day
I did get better. Maybe not on the outside but on the inside. My soul
became settled. My hope became clear. This is the sort of healing described
in Isaiah 53:5: "By his wounds we are healed." The atonement secured for
us healing more dramatic than that which is physical; God is interested in
healing the inside of a person. For me, a healed and happy heart is the best
"better," for "the LORD does not look at the things man looks at. Man looks
at the outward appearance, but the LORD looks at the heart" (1 Sam. 16:7).

> Think of the last time you said, "Lord, it would be much better if you
> would only . . ." Now think again: would it? It's not that God has a
> different definition for the word "better"; it's just that his idea of bet-
> ter goes deeper. It goes to the heart of the matter.

Lord Jesus, heal me from the inside out. Get to the heart of the matter
in my life, and show me the better way . . . the best way.

A Human Heaven

They are before the throne of God and serve him day and night in his temple; and he who sits on the throne will spread his tent over them.

—Revelation 7:15

I love rolling up my sleeves and serving God—visiting hospitals, advocating causes, traveling in ministry, relating in marriage, painting at my easel, writing at my computer, and lots more. But I have to be honest: although I love my work, I need rest. In fact, it is rest that invigorates me for work. They are separate and distinct, yet they complement each other.

In heaven work and rest won't be separate. We will experience both at the same time. Ours will be vigorous work of which we will never grow tired. We will always be active yet at rest, always resting yet active. Psalm 2:8–9 hints at the sort of work we will enjoy: "You will rule [the ends of the earth]." *That* will be work! We're not talking about a few acres on the back of the farm—our sphere of authority will be the entire universe. We will have so much to do. To explore, create, rule, discover, manage, possess, and delight in. For all this, we shall be utterly at rest. Amazingly, fatigue will be a thing of the past, since we will "serve him day and night," as our verse reminds us.

Humans need to work. We need to rest. Heaven is the home of redeemed humans. This means it will be thoroughly human in its structure and activities, including work and rest. Dr. A. A. Hodge suggests, "Heaven's joys and occupations must all be rational, moral, emotional, voluntary and active. There must be the exercise of all the faculties, the gratification of all tastes, the expression of all talents, the realization of all ideals. . . . The intellectual curiosity, the aesthetic instincts, the holy affections, the social affinities, the inexhaustible resources of strength and power native to the human soul, must all find in heaven exercise and satisfaction."[2]

You won't idle away eons on cloud nine; there will be no passing away the millennia plucking harps by a glassy sea. You will have a job. A happy job for which you are perfectly suited.

Thank you, Lord, that in heaven I will always have something wonderful to do . . . and I will be happy doing it.

September 20

Precious Jewels

They shall be mine, saith the LORD of hosts, in that day
when I make up my jewels; and I will spare them, as a man
spareth his own son that serveth him.

—Malachi 3:17 KJV

I love for my wedding ring to shine. About once a week I ask my friend
who gets me up to use my toothpaste and toothbrush to scrub my ring.
Real gold and diamonds can take a good scrubbing; they're not as delicate
as we think. And when they're polished, my, they look lovely!

Malachi 3:16–17 talks about how the Lord has a book of remembrance in which the names of all those who meditate on him, who think
about his name, are written down. He calls these people his jewels. How
do we become jewels that gleam and shine in his sight? He says, "I will
refine them like silver and test them like gold. They will call on my name
and I will answer them; I will say, 'They are my people,' and they will say,
'The LORD is our God'" (Zech. 13:9).

Oh, that's what I want to be: a jewel that shines in his sight, a jewel
that doesn't mind a good polishing now and then. I'm not as delicate as
some people think, especially when God's grace sustains me.

Maybe you feel as if someone has taken a gigantic toothbrush and is
scrubbing your soul raw. It hurts. And you wince at the pain, the disappointment. But take heart; there's a purpose.

Let me remind you: You're not as delicate as you think. You, as a
believer, are a jewel, someone very precious to God. You're a diamond, you're silver, and you're gold. He promises that, as his jewel,
he's going to shine you up. As silver is refined and as gold is tried, he
will polish you bright so everyone will see you're a jewel.

*Lord, help me to bring a willing spirit to you, one prepared to be polished
even when it hurts. I want to be your jewel.*

September 21

A Prescription for Contentment

Sorrowful, yet always rejoicing; poor, yet making many rich; having nothing, and yet possessing everything.
—2 Corinthians 6:10

The secret of contentment isn't really much of a secret. We know that contentment is all about leaning on Jesus. Of course, we don't automatically know the secret of being content; we have to learn it. To learn something means more than saying, "Yeah, I realize Christ is sufficient." To learn means to make choices, to practice over and over. If you are to know contentment—that quietness of heart, supernaturally given, that gladly submits to God in all circumstances—you must undergo the learning process.

For instance, when I learned to feed myself years ago in the hospital, many times I felt like giving up. Wearing a bib, smearing applesauce all over my clothes, and having it land more times on my lap than in my mouth was humiliating.

I could have given up, and many people wouldn't have blamed me. But I had to make a series of choices. Was I going to let embarrassment over my food-smeared face dissuade me? Was I going to let disappointing failures overwhelm me? I'm convinced God gave me the strength to lift that spoon to my mouth. Thus I learned how to feed myself, and today I manage a spoon quite well.

Notice I didn't get back the use of my arms or hands. But I did learn to be content. When Christ gives us strength to tackle a painful situation, gaining contentment doesn't mean losing sorrow or saying good-bye to discomfort. You can be sorrowful yet always rejoicing. You can have nothing yet possess everything. First Timothy 6:6 says, "Godliness with contentment is great gain." Yet the gain always comes through loss.

Don't let anyone tell you that contentment comes easily. It has to be learned. And it requires strength from beyond this world. But once you gain it, you'll never trade that settled contentedness for anything.

Lord Jesus, teach me to be content in the middle of loss, sorrow, pain, and discomfort. I want to be a good student and learn well this lesson.

September 22

The Apple of His Eye

Whoever touches you touches the apple of his eye.
—Zechariah 2:8

Who's the apple of your eye? Your grandchild? Your son recently promoted? Your fiancée with those soft eyes and tender smile? Whoever is the apple of your eye, one thing's for certain: you love that individual with a fervent and intense love. That person gives you joy indescribable. In short, you *feel* something for this loved one.

You are the apple of God's eye. God feels powerful emotions when it comes to you—God's love makes him sing and rejoice over you (Zeph. 3:17). But why are you so special to him? Why do you hold his affections?

First, when it comes to you, his joy is not merely satisfaction over something you do, as though you had him wrapped around your little finger with that winsome way of yours. God's joy is in his own goodness and wisdom, in the beautiful character of his Son, and in the complexity and wonder of all that he has made. His is not a complacent, lazy joy—his is the rugged joy of the warrior returning home; the admiral sailing into port, flying colors of victory; and the bone-tired, soot-faced, grinning hero carrying the child to safety from the burning building. In short, God's joy for you is connected with something wonderful *he* has done.

God's joy and delight over you finds its best expression at the cross: "God so loved the world that he gave his one and only Son" (John 3:16). And he watched his Son's murder because he loves you. This means his joy and deep emotion for you is rugged, hard-won, and victorious. He is the admiral flying colors of victory over you. He's the hero who has carried you to safety from hell's burn. He is the joy-filled warrior who has brought you home. You are the apple of his eye.

Help me to remember, Lord, that your joy over me is pure and perfect and rooted in the way you love your Son. I can hardly believe that you actually feel something deep, powerful, and joyful when it comes to me—and it's all because of Jesus. Thank you for making me the apple of your eye.

Man of Sorrows . . . Lord of Joy

> I say these things while I am still in the world, so that they
> may have the full measure of my joy within them.
> —John 17:13

> He was despised and rejected by men, a man of sorrows,
> and familiar with suffering.
> —Isaiah 53:3

Can God laugh and weep at the same moment? Jesus himself was full of joy, yet Isaiah called him a man of sorrows. We mortals know joy and pain together. A father stands at the altar and sighs deeply as he gives his daughter's hand in marriage. A mother watches her son languish behind prison bars but sees the experience bring the rebellious young man to repentance. We are "sorrowful, yet always rejoicing" (2 Cor. 6:10).

This is understandable for humans, but how can God be sorrowful yet always rejoicing? My friend Steve Estes comments,

> Perhaps the answer lies in his ability to know all things and to see the eternal picture. God does look down on this world and weep. But the world's twistedness did not catch him by surprise. He knew that humans would fall into sin. He knew that immeasurable sorrow would be let loose. He knew the suffering it would cost his Son. But God decreed to permit man's Fall because he knew how he would resolve it: that Jesus would die, that his church would eventually triumph through innumerable trials, that Satan's fingers would be pried off the planet, that justice would be served at the final judgment, that heaven would make up for it all, and that God would receive more glory—and we would know more joy—than if the Fall had never happened.[3]

Jesus is "man of sorrows" and "Lord of joy" because, as the Son of God, he sees enough of the coming ecstasy to make up for the present agony. And God sees this glorious end as clearly as if it were today. This is why God can be truly and utterly happy and yet actually and really filled with grief.

Lord, help me to learn to live in you today so I may see the coming ecstasy and realize it makes up for my present hurt and heartache. Help me to be rejoicing while I am sorrowful.

Glorified Bodies

> ... that Christ died for our sins according to the Scriptures, that he was buried, that he was raised on the third day according to the Scriptures, and that he appeared to Peter, and then to the Twelve.
>
> —1 Corinthians 15:3–5

People who return from the dead—whether from the tomb or off the operating table—aren't, like Christ, able to appear and disappear, walk through walls, or, as Christ did on the road to Emmaus, transport themselves through time and space with a single thought. Jesus was not revived; he was resurrected. Today's verse speaks of the sort of body that Jesus assumed for forty days on earth between his resurrection and ascension. People saw with their eyes a real, resurrected body!

But the resurrection body is not all there is. We know our present bodies by experience; we know the resurrection body only through Christ; but our finally glorified body we know only by a few suggestive hints in Scripture. 1 Corinthians 15 tells us, "There is also a spiritual body. . . . Just as we have borne the likeness of the earthly man, so shall we bear the likeness of the man from heaven" (vv. 44, 49). First John 3:2 hints that "what we will be has not yet been made known. But we know that when he appears, we shall be like him, for we shall see him as he is."

No one has ever seen a body glorified—not even Peter and the Twelve when they saw Christ. "No eye has seen, no ear has heard, no mind has conceived what God has prepared for those who love him" (1 Cor. 2:9). Our glorified bodies will be of an entirely different dimension than anything we know or have heard of on earth. Here's an analogy: On this planet we take the shape of squares; in heaven we will be like cubes. Here we are triangles; there, pyramids. Here, circles; there, spheres.

Somewhere in your broken earthly body is the seed of what you will enjoy in your glorified heavenly state. Your image in heaven will be you but a much better, brighter you in a new dimension. Rejoice in this today.

I have so many questions, Lord . . . there's so much I don't know. Nevertheless, thank you that one day I'll step into a new dimension and the gift of a new, glorified body. My aching bones thank you!

September 25

To New Heights

You yourselves have seen what I did to Egypt, and how I
carried you on eagles' wings and brought you to myself.
—Exodus 19:4

The soul is like a bird,
shaken from its peaceful roost by the inclement
circumstances of life,
where windblown branches
and sudden gusts from darkening horizons
thrust it into weather that is wild and uncertain.
And sometimes, however hard we beat our wings,
we can't seem to overcome the elements galing against us.
We are thrashed about in the air,
windsheered and weary,
wondering if our cries for help are reaching God.
But then the tempest subsides,
for a while anyway,
and the updrafts of God's Spirit lift us to new heights,
above the wind, above the rain, above the earth.
And, for a moment,
we soar.

Ken Gire[4]

If there's anything we need in a stormy trial, it's perspective. We need
to see what birds see. When we catch the updrafts of God's Spirit and are
lifted to new heights, trials look extraordinarily different.

When you soar as on eagles' wings (Isa. 40:31), you are gliding above
the tempest, above the fray, above the rain and storms. From such
heights you can look down on your trials and have God's perspective.
What is tossing you to and fro today? As our verse suggests, let God
lift you to new heights, carrying you and bringing you to himself.

*If I wait on you, Lord, you will renew my strength. You will help me to
mount up on eagles' wings. Carry me, God . . . and bring me to yourself
today.*

I Am Glad

I was glad when they said to me, "Let us go to the house of the Lord."

—Psalm 122:1 NASB

It's Sunday morning in Dallas. The airport routine—check-in, baggage, security, and seating transfers—casts a gray restlessness on my spirit. It was good to be here, but I want to go home. It was good to serve, but I want to rest. It was good to speak of my love for Jesus, but I want to be near him, hold him, and worship him. At home and at rest.

Any believer who passed by me in the airport would no doubt encourage me with song. "Rejoice, Joni. God is everywhere. Let's worship him right now! We'll hold hands in a circle and have a prayer meeting right here. Won't that be great!"

I do love praying in airports and even singing aloud. But I want to be home. I want to wake up and look forward to my morning in church. I want to sit next to the insurance salesman and his family and sing a rousing chorus. I want to hear a three-point sermon on any text, even those I've heard a thousand times before. I want to greet the divorced woman in the parking lot and tell her I love her and will pray for her.

Ministering in foreign lands and worshiping with brothers and sisters there is an experience I will always cherish. But I am especially glad when I go to my own "house of the Lord." My restless spirit finds a center, a refuge. The calendar, the traveling, the work—all of it becomes ordered when I'm home and in my home church.

Are you glad when you go to church, your home church? Can you bring your restlessness there? Do you find simple pleasure in the people with whom you worship? I hope you do. Cherish that which God has given as a centered rest for you. Long for its weekly shelter, and rejoice in its heavenly promise of rest.

Lord, fill my heart with restful song as I think of the church you have provided for me.

How Far Will God Go?

He determined the times set for them and the exact places where they should live. God did this so that men would seek him and perhaps reach out for him and find him, though he is not far from each one of us.

—Acts 17:26–27

How far will God go to reach those whom he has called? Consider the case of Kumiko, a young Japanese woman. Her husband was transferred to a small Wisconsin town to work in management. Kumiko looked forward to the move to America because she had read once that Christians were not afraid to die. She did not know any Christians but vowed that she would ask why this was so if she ever had the chance. She was terrified of dying and wanted an answer.

Kumiko did not realize how interested God was in answering her question. Shortly after she and her husband settled in, a missionary couple from Japan retired and moved to the same little Wisconsin town. Upon learning that there were six Japanese families living in the area, the missionaries decided to start an outreach ministry at the local church.

On the first Sunday morning of the ministry, the missionary asked the class a question that stunned Kumiko. "Many of us live with fear. Are any of you afraid?" There was a nervous silence. After a moment the missionary turned to Kumiko, unaware of her need. "How about you, Kumiko? What are you afraid of?"

Kumiko gave her life to Jesus two months later. Her husband soon followed. Together they named their new child Grace, after the church where God had gone to such great lengths to answer her questions about fear and death.

How far will God go to accomplish his purpose with you today? He brought a young Japanese wife and a retired missionary more than ten thousand miles so a seeking heart might find him. And he'll go farther, even to the depths of your discouragement or despair, to find you. He'll go farther than you can imagine, because he is closer to you than you will ever know.

Father, thank you for moving heaven and earth to reach me. Hasten your moves with others so they might know you, too.

A Peaceful Harvest

> Peacemakers who sow in peace raise a harvest of righteousness.
>
> —James 3:18

As school starts, kids are engaging in that universal rite—the fight. Some will fight with words. The more sophisticated will fight by creating political alliances with other playground buddies to ward off the offending party.

Of course, I never fought. Just ask my sisters. They were always fighting with each other, but I was never involved. . . . Okay, maybe once, twice at most.

But hey, I'm older now. I never fight. . . . Oh, all right, I do stir up an argument now and then. After all, we're creatures of conflict. And churches, like playgrounds, provide ample opportunities for strife.

Yet James said, "Peacemakers who sow in peace raise a harvest of righteousness." He chose peace as the seed because true righteousness can't grow where there is discord. Unrighteousness grows like weeds in an environment where uncertainty and anxiety abound. Evil loves discontent and restlessness. Mind you, James uses not the word *peacekeepers* but the word *peacemakers*. People who try to get rid of strife through kowtowing or weakening their principles fail in bringing about a deep and lasting peace. Peace for the sake of expediency is fragile at best.

Peacemaking runs deeper than peacekeeping. To sow the seed of peace is to press a truth gently yet firmly into the soil of another's heart. When peace prevails, that which is right is given room to flourish. We can see circumstances for what they are. We are able to choose the right path.

Peace is a powerful seed in your hand. Sow it in the midst of a sinful world that is too contentious to discern right from wrong. Speak words of peace to those in your church who have lost their sense of what love is and who loves them dearly. Let dissension and discord pass from your hearts so the stranger in your midst might be wooed to the Righteous One.

Teach me how to plant peace in my heart, Lord. Then show me ways to sow the seed of peace in others' lives.

September 29

Everlasting Love

> The LORD did not set his affection on you and choose you
> because you were more numerous than other peoples, for you
> were the fewest of all peoples. But it was because the LORD
> loved you and kept the oath he swore to your forefathers.
>
> —Deuteronomy 7:7–8

Ever look in the mirror and think, *Ugh?* I have. In fact, I've held a mirror up to my soul at times and thought the same. *God, how can you stand me? I'm fickle, lazy, and prone to turn my back on you, given half a chance.*

This is why today's verse is so comforting. There is nothing in you or me to attract or prompt the affections of God. The love of, let's say, one person for another is because of something in that other. But the love of God is free and spontaneous. God has loved you and me from everlasting; nothing in us can be the cause of what is already found in God from eternity. Second Timothy 1:9 explains that God "has saved us and called us to a holy life—not because of anything we have done but because of his own purpose and grace. This grace was given us in Christ Jesus before the beginning of time."

Here is the good news: God loved us when we were loveless, and this means his love is completely uninfluenced by us. His love comes barreling at us at full speed in a direct line, with all its force undiminished and undaunted; he has as much love for us as he has for the most godly of saints. God loves us the way he loves his Son, Jesus. Amazing love! How can it be?

What's more amazing is that there is everything in us to repel God. Sinful, depraved, wicked us—everything in us is calculated to make him loathe us. No good thing dwells in us, yet thankfully, that does not influence God. Rather he says in Jeremiah 31:3, "I have loved you with an everlasting love; I have drawn you with loving-kindness." Meditate on the everlasting love of God. How has he demonstrated to you his everlasting love? Choose new words today to respond to him in prayer.

Since your love for me has no beginning, Lord, that means it has no ending. It says in the Bible, "God is love" and "God is everlasting." How comforting to know that I will forever bask in your love.

Memories

This I call to mind and therefore I have hope.
—Lamentations 3:21

My sweetest memories are ones that inspire hope. And many of them are of life before my accident. I recall the grating sensation of a nail file against the tips of my fingers, and the sound of my nails tapping cool, ivory piano keys. I can still "feel" my fingers plucking the tight nylon strings of my old guitar, touching peach fuzz, digging under an orange skin and peeling it.

Funny thing . . . so many of my freshest memories have to do with my hands. I'm looking at my paralyzed hands right now. The muscles have all atrophied. My fingers are curled and rigid, and I wear leather hand-splints so that when I move my arms, my hands don't flop and get in the way. I love it when my husband, Ken, holds my hand. Sometimes when we're wheeling around a mall, I'll hold my arm out, a signal to him to grab my hand. I can't feel it, but I like seeing his hand covering mine.

Why would memories like these inspire hope? They remind me that one day soon I'll have new hands. Fingers that will work and feel again, touch and pluck and pick and scrub and dig. Hands that will embrace loved ones. The first thing I'm going to do is reach for Ken's new, glorified hand and give it a squeeze, just to see what it feels like. It'll happen! God promises me in Jeremiah 29:11, "I know the plans I have for you. . . . They are plans for good and not for evil, to give you a future and a hope" (LB). My best memories help give shape to that hopeful future.

Let your memories be your handhold on heaven. Do you have memories of better times, happier days? Use those to help you look forward to the day when God will wipe away every tear, when sorrow and sighing will be no more, and when joy will overtake you.

Lord, help me to use memories to build up my hope for the heavenly future. Thank you for helping me through the present by reminding me of a pleasant past.

OCTOBER

October 1

God in the Black

I have no need of a bull from your stall or of goats from
your pens, for every animal of the forest is mine, and the
cattle on a thousand hills.

—Psalm 50:9–10

God is completely and utterly self-sufficient. But how many times do
we entertain the thought that he needs a "little help from his friends,"
as though he were low on cash, short on reserves, or in need of extra
resources? *Can God help me?* we often think. *Is he able? Does he have enough
"ummph" to make a difference?*

God has everything he needs and more. Much, much more. It does
not boost his ego or enrich his kingdom if we tithe fifteen percent rather
than ten percent. He is not cowering by the doors of major charitable foundations, hoping the grant committees approve more "Christian" requests
than "secular."

God is not behind schedule, low on energy, short of clout, thin on
reserves, nervous about the stock market, or hoping people will follow
through on their pledges. He's not short on donors or awaiting bank
approval and a zoning permit to fulfill his plans, because "no one can hold
back his hand or say to him: 'What have you done?'" (Dan. 4:35). God
does not operate in the red. He's in the black.

"Our God is in heaven; he does whatever pleases him" (Ps. 115:3). It
is his pleasure to meet each and every one of your needs.

Can God help you today? Does he have enough power on reserve to
make a difference? Can he provide for your needs? More than yes.
"So do not worry, saying, 'What shall we eat?' . . . or 'What shall we
wear?' For the pagans run after all these things, and your heavenly
Father knows that you need them. But seek first his kingdom and
his righteousness, and all these things will be given to you as well"
(Matt. 6:31–33).

*God, I praise you for being all-sufficient. You have enough . . . you are
enough!*

October 2

He Upholds Everything

In these last days he has spoken to us by his Son, whom he appointed heir of all things, and through whom he made the universe. The Son is the radiance of God's glory and the exact representation of his being, sustaining all things by his powerful word. After he had provided purification for sins, he sat down at the right hand of the Majesty in heaven.

—Hebrews 1:2–3

I just finished reading this incredible book written by a particle physicist. He sheds new light on these wonderful verses for today. The author says we limit our view of the Creator when we think of him as though he were a painter, sweeping broad brushstrokes across nature, layer after layer, and standing back to admire his handiwork. That's too static.

A better picture is to imagine him as the inventor of, let's say, a television picture. God has his hands on all the right knobs and buttons. As he jiggles and fine-tunes them, the image on the screen is sustained. A billion sparks of light flash across the screen in just the right order with just the right timing and sequence. As long as God controls all the billions upon billions of details to create the image on the screen, the reality of it all continues.

If he were to take his hands off the controls, the image on that TV screen wouldn't become chaotic; it would just cease to be. That's the best way to describe Hebrews 1:3: he is upholding right now, this instant, all things by his powerful word.

Think about all the intricate inventions with which we surround ourselves: our timed dishwashers, our CD players, our video cams, our cars. Now think of the way God keeps things up and running in the entire universe—everything from DNA to weather patterns, from magnetic fields in space to the ants in your backyard. Take a minute to express awe with someone about our awesome Creator.

Father God, how astounding that you've expressed your creative self so liberally in life. Thank you not only for your inventiveness but also for your sustaining power.

Being God's Mirror

Praise be to the God and Father of our Lord Jesus Christ, the
Father of compassion and the God of all comfort, who comforts us in all our troubles, so that we can comfort those in any
trouble with the comfort we ourselves have received from God.
—2 Corinthians 1:3–4

The air outside our Carolina mountain cabin was cold, gray, and damp.
The air around our fireplace, however, was bright and warm from the
burning logs, as well as from the smiles of our friends visiting from
Asheville. Bruce, recently injured, sat straight and handsome in his wheelchair. I would never have guessed that his wife had moved out a few days
before or that he was facing tremendous legal and financial problems, as
well as the normal baggage of adjustments for any new quadriplegic. Before
his accident Bruce had been a successful dentist. With no use of his hands,
he had lost his career.

"This stuff isn't easy," he sighed. I watched my eighty-four-year-old
mother nod knowingly. She was a battle-scarred veteran of pain and loss.
At the end of the visit, after we had talked shop and taken photos, we hud-
dled closer to the fire to pray, and Mom spoke up for the first time, offering to the Lord the following song. Her voice may have sounded cracked
and off-key, but Bruce and I felt our hearts enlarge with her comfort.

I do not know why oft around me,
    my hopes all shattered seem to be;
God's perfect plan I cannot see, but someday I'll understand:
Someday he'll make it plain to me,
    someday when I his face shall see.
Someday from tears I shall be free, for someday I shall understand.

My mother is not a seminary graduate or a Bible scholar. But she
glorified God perhaps more than any of us that day. God's glory is
the radiance of his attributes that break forth in visible ways around
us. That day by the fire, my mother was God's mirror—glorifying
him and reflecting the light of his comfort deep into our hearts.
Thank you, Mother. You glorify God. You encourage us.

*May I reflect your encouragement to others, Lord, and may I glorify you
as I do.*

October 4

Cool Snow

Like the coolness of snow at harvest time is a trustworthy messenger to those who send him; he refreshes the spirit of his masters.

—Proverbs 25:13

It would happen on occasion. The harvest in Palestine would be accompanied by a refreshing snow to ease the workers in the field. The earth and grain, baked brown and hard by the summer sun, would be cooled by a soft layer of snow—not enough to ruin the crop, apparently, but just enough to make the task less burdensome.

Trustworthy messengers are like that snow, says Solomon. While today we barely give much thought to the trustworthiness of our messengers, it was not so simple in those days. A lot rode on the trustworthiness of the messenger. Would he deliver the message on time? Would he deliver the message accurately? Would he embellish or omit? Would he even conspire with the recipient and betray his master?

What does the Lord think today of those with whom he has entrusted his message? If we speak of God's hope, do our voices reflect the certainty of that hope? If we speak of God's love, do we betray any doubts? If we speak of his salvation, do we make the pathway clear? God desires trustworthiness in our handling of his gospel. Not only must our words reflect his message; our lives must reflect his character.

God's Spirit is refreshed daily by faithful messengers. What message are you delivering today to those around you? Will they know there is hope for tomorrow? Will they know God loves them? Will they know the way of salvation? The harvesting of souls is a long and arduous task. Your trustworthiness will be a refreshment to the Lord of the harvest and to others as well. Let it snow.

Do you trust me, Lord, to deliver your message? Is your truth and your love clear to those around me? Make it so in my life, Lord. I seek to be a refreshment to your Spirit.

Come Before Winter

Do your best to get here before winter.

—2 Timothy 4:21

Johan is young, tall, blond, and Dutch. I met him through my cousin, who attended the same Bible school in England that Johan attended. Gifted and handsome, Johan could have carved out a comfortable youth ministry in his native Netherlands—or most anywhere else in the world.

Comfort, however, isn't one of Johan's major goals. He chose to take the gospel to the Bedouins and nomads near Israel's desolate Sinai Desert, a forgotten people in one of the most forgotten corners of the world. Johan has learned many life lessons from the people of the desert, including that it is considered worse than murder to know of a water source and to neglect to tell your fellow travelers. Johan points out that six hours without water in the desert during the summer, and you are dead.

How like Philippians 3, in which Paul weeps that the Christians know all about joy yet it doesn't change their lives or cause them to share with others. They sit with their cups overflowing while others are thirsty.

You too know where the water source is. Thirsty men and women surround you right now: the neighbor down the street, the man at the service station, the boy who carries your groceries, the secretary who types and files, your distant aunt. If these people don't know Christ, they're going to die of thirst.

Paul told Timothy, "Do your best to get here before winter." Do something today to satisfy others' thirst for eternal water. Do it while the communication channels are open. This is the season to speak up; it would be a crime not to.

Teach me to act today, Lord, before storms set in and paths of communication are cut off from those who long to drink from your cup of joy. Help me so to treasure that which you have given me that I must share it with others.

October 6

The Wrong Kind of Expert

They never stop sinning . . . they are experts in greed.
—2 Peter 2:14

I have vivid memories of what it was like to play hockey, ride a horse, and swing a tennis racquet. When it comes to tennis, my mom was my best coach. She possessed great finesse and tried to pass on good ball-and-racquet skills to me. But I was a stubborn learner.

I recall my backhand. I thought I was doing pretty well, but my wrist was bent, my grip was wrong, and my body position wasn't square with the net. In other words, I had gotten very good at doing something very bad. Through hours of practice away from the coaching eye of my mother, I became an expert in poor backhand.

Have you gotten proficient at doing something very wrong? Peter, in his epistle, talks about people who practice doing the wrong thing and become experts in sin. They train themselves that way—with years of practice. We need to train ourselves to do the right thing. Paul tells Timothy to train himself to be godly. He says, "Physical training is of some value, but godliness has value for all things, holding promise for both the present life and the life to come" (1 Tim. 4:8).

As you live day in and day out, you are practicing either godliness or selfishness. It has been said, "The choices we make carve the shape we become." If you want to do what is right, you had better train yourself in godliness. That means practice—every day. Remember, others are watching! "Let us, therefore, make every effort . . . so that no one will fall by following their example of disobedience" (Heb. 4:11).

Don't get good at doing something wrong. Instead make a choice today to live right. Train yourself to be godly.

Father God, you know how easily I fall into bad habits in my thoughts, heart, and actions. Show me how to break one wrong habit and how to learn a godly one. Keep me from letting selfishness reign.

October 7

A Sweet-Smelling Savor

Thanks be to God, who always leads us in triumphal procession in Christ and through us spreads everywhere the fragrance of the knowledge of him. For we are to God the aroma of Christ among those who are being saved and those who are perishing. To the one we are the smell of death; to the other, the fragrance of life.

—2 Corinthians 2:14–16

The wind shifts in October, carrying on the breeze the scent of a seasoned-wood fire from a neighbor's chimney. Lean out your window, draw a deep breath, and you can smell the scent of pine from a nearby woods. Or someone baking an apple pie next door. I love this time of year because of the wonderful new aromas in the air. It's amazing how a scent—even a fragrance—evokes powerful feelings.

Today's passage speaks of the power of fragrance. It's another way of saying, "I want to live in a way that will perpetually remind God of the obedience, sacrifice, and devotion of the Lord Jesus. I want my words and deeds to bring to God's mind fragrant memories of the earthly life of his Son."

What's more, our godly words and deeds not only remind God of his Son but remind others of him, too—whether they believe in Jesus or not. To be obedient among the fellowship of believers is to carry with you the fragrance of Christ. To be obedient in a wicked world is to remind others of the stench of death. But that's not bad! Sometimes the wicked need to face their own mortality to be awakened out of their spiritual slumber. No matter how others interpret it, just be certain to waft Jesus their way.

The smell of hot apple pie brings to mind deep-rooted memories. A wood fire or the scent of pine will do the same. In the same way, your life of obedience can please God with an aroma that reminds him of Jesus. Be fragrant. Be a sweet-smelling savor. Be obedient and thus be God's memory of his Son.

May my life give off the scent of Christ to all those around me. And Father, may my obedience bring a smile to you today, reminding you of your precious Son.

October 8

Kingdom Living

The kingdom of God is not a matter of talk but of power.
—1 Corinthians 4:20

One thing's for sure: we *know* the talk. We expound the importance of Bible reading and prayer. We nod in hearty agreement when the director of the inner-city shelter stands behind the church pulpit, extolling God's love for marginalized people, whether homeless or handicapped. We read books, listen to tapes, and check out videos from our church library, on everything from witnessing to Scripture memorization. But for all the talk, for all the show, for how nicely we conform ourselves on the outside, I sometimes wonder if we're not like those mentioned in 2 Timothy 3:5, "having a form of godliness but denying its power."

I don't intend to lay a guilt trip, but take a moment and think of all the spiritual disciplines you talk about: prayer and fasting, witnessing and worshiping, memorizing and meditating. Now stop and go back over the list. How many of these disciplines do you practice—not hit-and-miss but on a regular basis?

The kingdom of God is not a matter of talk (which we are so good at) but of power, as our verse says. A form of godliness will soon show cracks and wear. The talk will ring hollow and empty. As Jesus said, "the kingdom of God is within you" (Luke 17:21), and our spiritual lives can only be lived—really lived—from the inside out.

You can start today. It begins by asking God to energize you from the inside out. You can't shape your godliness, but you can let godliness shape you. And God's power then will affect everything you say and do. Live from the inside out "so that your faith might not rest on men's wisdom, but on God's power" (1 Cor. 2:5).

Lord, help me to guard my tongue if I start blabbing on about spiritual disciplines without really living them. And then help me to live in your power from the inside out.

October 9

You're One of "Those"

We are not of those who shrink back and are destroyed, but of those who believe and are saved.

—Hebrews 10:39

Who are "those"? This verse raises the question, Who are those who believe and are saved? The writer of Hebrews has some special people in mind. His answer follows in Hebrews 11, the great honor roll of those who persevered: Moses, Enoch, Noah, Sarah, Abraham, Rahab, Gideon, David, and Samuel, to mention a few.

You are one of "those." You're linked with Moses and Enoch! Yes, even though these men and women had problems, they demonstrated great faith. Moses, although he erupted in anger, repented; Noah had a problem with alcohol yet didn't shrink back; Sarah mocked God yet survived and was saved; Rahab had loose morals; Gideon had serious doubts; David had uncontrolled passions; and Samuel had the aches and pains of old age. Ultimately they did not collapse but believed and were saved. They were counted as righteous because they lived by faith. And so must you.

Hebrews 12 begins, "Therefore, since we are surrounded by such a great cloud of witnesses, let us throw off everything that hinders and the sin that so easily entangles." Sound hard? Hebrews 12:2–3 reminds us to "fix our eyes on Jesus, the author and perfecter of our faith. . . . Consider him who endured such opposition from sinful men, so that you will not grow weary and lose heart." Don't give up. Don't shrink back. Others hung in there and so can you.

Lord, I forget about the saints of old with whom I am intimately linked in you. I am grateful to be one of them . . . to be a faithful servant. . . . I fix my eyes on you. I believe you. . . . Praise God, I am saved.

October 10

Friend of Sinners

The Son of Man came eating and drinking, and they say,
"Here is a glutton and a drunkard, a friend of tax collec-
tors and 'sinners.'"
—Matthew 11:19

The pastor of a church I was visiting introduced me to a newcomer who
was struggling with cancer. "I'm not ready to give my life to Jesus," he
said to me.

"Have you told Jesus that?" I asked. Judging from the stymied look
on his face, the idea of praying was the farthest thing from his mind. "Why
don't you take time right now to tell Jesus? Whatever is on your heart, you
can tell him." The man gave a smile when I reached for his hand, and then
bowed his head with mine, saying, "Lord, I . . . uh . . . they tell me I should
give my life to you . . . and although I can't . . . that is, I guess I won't . . . I
really do . . . I really want to believe. Please . . . help me."

"You're well on your way to believing in Christ," I said after he finished
praying. How could I be so sure? Because he had opened up his heart to
encounter the Lord Jesus. When someone engages God in prayer, that person can never be quite the same. That man's prayer, though feeble and fal-
tering, meant the Savior in turn had a handhold on him. With the
encouragement of his pastor and friends, it won't be long before he's welcomed into the family.

The Good News sounds great to those who see Jesus befriending
them. In the Gospels the Lord Jesus is constantly presented as a friend of
sinners. He moved among people as their friend before he became their
Savior.

Who can you befriend on Jesus' behalf today? Ask God to bring to
mind someone who needs him—and you. How about you? Do you
need a friend today? Ask Jesus to be with you in a way that will be a
comfort to you.

When I share our friendship with others today, Lord, help me to show
them you want to be their friend, too. Thank you for being so interested
in people as . . . people! Help me to convey that today.

The Strength of Gentleness

Come to me, all you who are weary and burdened, and I will give you rest. Take my yoke upon you and learn from me, for I am gentle and humble in heart, and you will find rest for your souls. For my yoke is easy and my burden is light.
—Matthew 11:28–30

Every once in a while I daydream about my childhood. I remember going on a long hike with my dad and his friends. I don't know how old I was, probably five or six. I scrambled to keep up with the adults, but my little legs could only carry me for so long. I became weary and burdened.

Tired from the long distance, I remember thinking how thankful I was that my dad and his friends were such big, strong adults. They would have no trouble carrying a little tyke like me on their broad shoulders. I breathed a sigh of relief when my dad reached down and slung me on his back. I had no cause for worry. He was strong enough to take my burdens. Contrast that image with the Scripture for today. Does something strike you as odd?

Jesus doesn't say, "Look how big and strong I am. Look how powerful and robust. Lean on me." Instead Jesus says, "Come to me, all you who are weary and burdened . . . for I am gentle and humble in heart."

God's Word reminds us that humility, gentleness, patience, long-suffering, kindness, and goodness are character qualities that tower heads above being strong, aggressive, or unwavering. The humble and gentle people are those we find ourselves drawn to when we feel burdened or weary. Somehow we know these are the people who genuinely care, who actually pray, and who in fact take our load upon them.

Are you weary or heavy-laden? "Cast all your anxiety on him because he cares for you" (1 Peter 5:7).

Gentle Jesus, please relieve me of my load today. Enable me to hand it over to you rather than trying to stumble on with it. I'm so grateful you care.

October 12

Lonely Passion

Do your best to come to me quickly, for Demas, because he
loved this world, has deserted me and has gone to Thessa-
lonica.

—2 Timothy 4:9–10

It's the bottom of the ninth, two men on base, two out. One more pitch
and the World Series is over. Batter crouches at the plate. Pitcher makes
his windup, the pitch, and it's a blazing fastball to the outside corner. Strike
three! The game is over!"

Transcript from a radio broadcast? No, that's the play-by-play of a lone
pitcher, age nine or ten, standing on the mound of an empty ball field in
a nearby park. Long after the sun has set and the kids have gone home to
watch TV or play video games, there is usually one who will stay behind.
He is the one with passion for the game, the one who will play when no
one else is around. He throws that pitch to the outside corner, retrieves the
ball, and then runs back to the mound again to continue his imaginary
game. All because he loves the game.

That kind of passion for anything in life, when rehearsed daily, will
bring out the best in us. It will also test our faith. Consider the words of
Alex Krass:

> Nothing is more frustrating than to be afire with a cause and to dis-
> cover that those around you do not share it. But to discover that oth-
> ers are constitutionally predisposed not to be set afire with any
> passion is enough to drive you up the wall. At no time do you so
> sense aloneness.[1]

Consider your passions. Are you, first of all, predisposed not to be set
afire? Run to God, that he might rid you of this curse. Are you alone
in your passion for his ministry? You run to God also. There you will
meet others he has just reformed. Together go back to the ballpark
and play the game with conspiratorial passion. The world will be all
the better for it.

*Lord, your zeal was meant to be ours as well. May my passion always
exceed my capacity, and may the company of such people increase.*

October 13

Up Close and Personal

. . . so that Christ may dwell in your hearts through faith.
—Ephesians 3:17

Last night, right before prayer time, I was struggling to push out of my heart one of those useless daydreams. My thinking was, *I don't want to approach God like this.* Then it occurred to me how close God was—right in the middle of things (because the Spirit of the Lord dwells in my heart). My next thought? *Sometimes, Lord, I don't know how you can stand to live inside me!* God carries the weight of my campaign against sin, but I rarely think of him as that up close and personal when I'm engaged in a struggle against temptation. Because he lives inside me, he's literally in the thick of the battle.

Yet he's the one who has to put up with my choosing stupid thoughts, taking worldly advice, opting to ignore his warnings, forgetting my calling as a servant, and walking more than occasionally in the flesh. How does he put up with all that?

Scripture says, "The battle is the LORD's" (1 Sam. 17:47). I'm amazed that the Spirit I grieve when I sin turns right around whenever he hears me repent and empowers me to conquer that sin. I'm glad he doesn't hold a grudge. I'm relieved he doesn't say, "I told you so." And I'm so grateful that even when I quench his fire in my heart, he can always be stirred to action by the match ignited when I confess.

Come to think of it, I'm glad the Lord resides inside me. Because the closer he is to the battle—right there in my heart—the closer his love is to me.

What battles rage in your heart today? What temptations taunt you to just say yes? Picture the Holy Spirit living inside your heart. And picture the fiery maelstrom that he is urging you to emerge from victoriously. Thank him for the power to do so.

Father, I know you're pleased with me as your child. And Lord Jesus, I know you're the one who intercedes and prays for me. But Holy Spirit, you're the one who has to live with me. Thank you.

October 14

The People God Uses

My heart says of you, "Seek his face!" Your face, LORD, I
will seek.

—Psalm 27:8

Martin Luther. Charles Finney. Susanna Wesley. Jonathan Edwards.
Corrie ten Boom. Great saints these are. We can look to wonderful
Christians of the past for inspiration, but who are the great believers of
today? For that matter, what makes them great?

I like A. W. Tozer's criteria. He says, "The great in the kingdom have
been those who . . . love God more than others did." He goes on to say,
"The one vital quality which these people have in common is spiritual
receptivity. Something in them is open to heaven, something which urges
them Godward. They have a spiritual awareness and they go on to culti-
vate it until it becomes the biggest thing in their lives."[2]

According to Tozer, then, you don't have to be a famous evangelist, a
mother of sixteen children, a Bible teacher, or someone who has faced Nazi
gas ovens to be great. (Although if you remain open to heaven and culti-
vate that spiritual awareness, God is going to place you in some powerful
sphere of influence or impact.) If your ambition is to have no ambition
except to be pleasing to God, you are great in his kingdom. The average
person senses God's nudgings but does nothing about them. Not so you,
if you're spiritually great. You are the one who develops the lifelong habit
of being spiritually responsive. When you read Psalm 27, you are the one
whose heart says to God, "Your face, LORD, I will seek."

The Lord is looking right now for people who will love him in more
than the average way. He's looking for people whose love is more
than mediocre. Listen . . . is the Spirit nudging you? If you sense he
is leading you to a deeper level of trust and obedience, do something
about it. If you feel the inward longing, take action. Be obedient to
the heavenly vision. For then you will be great in his kingdom.

*I want to know you, Lord, in such a deep way that my self will be over-
whelmed by you. Enable me to earnestly seek your face.*

October 15

My Birthday Tree

> Early the next morning Jacob took the stone he had placed under his head and set it up as a pillar and poured oil on top of it.
>
> —Genesis 28:18

What a beautiful month this is! The trees back on our family farm in Maryland are rustling their colorful skirts, ablaze in wild reds and crazy yellows. Of all the oaks, maples, and pines on our farm, one particular tree is my favorite. It's an old, spreading maple growing by the springhouse. In October its leaves are resplendent in red, tinged with purple edges. And I know that today, my birthday, this maple will reach its peak of color, as it does every year. For this reason I call it my birthday tree.

Each year my tree marks how far I've come or what I have or haven't done. It's my "stone of remembrance." Jacob had a stone of remembrance. He heaped together a pillar of stones to mark the spot where God had pledged in a dream to watch over him and to bless his descendants. The pillar of stones was a visible, concrete reminder that God had touched his life.

That's what birthdays are, too—our private marks in time, our stones of remembrance. I want my birthday, like that maple tree, to be a mark of change in my life. Something to show progress and growth.

On October 15 I always call my sister on the farm and ask her about that old tree. She told me last year that it lost a big limb. It's beginning to show signs of age. So am I—but hey, I'm still growing.

What reminds you of growth in your life? What is your stone of remembrance? Do you have some tangible reminder of how far you've come and how far you need to go? Be it a birthday tree, a photograph, or whatever, God wants you to be reminded of how he has met with you and touched your life.

Thank you, Father, for occasions worthy of stones of remembrance. Never let me forget the ways you have declared your presence in my life.

October 16

The Opal

> The sacrifices of God are a broken spirit; a broken and contrite heart, O God, you will not despise.
> —Psalm 51:17

I've always loved opals, partly because that's my birthstone. But also because opals seem even more brilliant and full of fire than diamonds. Amazingly, this beauty comes from desert dust and silica from sand dunes. That's what opals are made of. The opal owes its beauty to a defect—it's a stone with a broken heart. It's full of minute fissures that admit air; the air then refracts the light. Because of this defect, the opal is all the more brilliant.

You and I who have broken hearts are sometimes only conscious of the cracks and the fissures. But out of all this God is making an opal heart. We must be broken in ourselves before we can give back the lovely hues of his light, including the fire, the brilliance. The Bible says that God can best use a heart that is broken and contrite. It's true in my life. When I'm self-sufficient and in control, my heart becomes a little hardened to others' needs. In fact, that self-sufficient attitude even hardens my heart toward God.

Ah, but then he breaks it ... by a cutting-yet-true remark from a friend. Or rejection from someone whose opinion I respect. Or by a verse such as "If you think you are standing firm, be careful that you don't fall!" (1 Cor. 10:12). Sometimes something beautiful will break my heart ... a special hymn or the testimony of someone who has suffered. Only when my heart is fractured, full of minute fissures, can God's love enter in and refract his own light.

Next time you see an opal, think of how you must be broken before you can give back the lovely hues of God's light. Let the opal remind you to thank God for a broken heart.

Lord of my heart, thank you that you use brokenness to create beauty and that my defects are tools to serve your purpose.

October 17

No Erasers!

Everyone who conquers will be clothed in white, and I will
not erase his name from the Book of Life, but I will
announce before my Father and his angels that he is mine.
—Revelation 3:5 LB

I'm dumping my old address book for a new one. I can't believe how many
names I've accumulated over the years. Some of them I don't even recognize. I've inked circles around the names of special friends, underlined
relatives, and asterisked doctors and hospitals. But who are those people
whose names I've crossed out? I have no idea.

I'm relieved that God's Book of Life doesn't resemble my address book,
with all its erasures and unreadable names in smeared or faded ink. Revelation 20:11–12 describes God's book: "Then I saw a great white throne
and him who was seated on it. Earth and sky fled from his presence, and
there was no place for them. And I saw the dead, great and small, standing before the throne, and books were opened. Another book was opened,
which is the book of life. The dead were judged according to what they
had done as recorded in the books."

Unlike some address books, God's isn't collecting dust. It's in use. And
once your name is recorded, once you are listed under C—for "child of
God"—you'll never have to worry about the Lord ripping out your page
in disgust over some sin or blotting out your name out of sheer disgust.
And thankfully, the Book of Life isn't jam-packed with names that Jesus
can't remember.

Names on honor rolls, the Hollywood Walk of Fame, stained-glass
windows, and brass plaques are all too quickly forgotten. Not so with
the Book of Life. If your name is entered in God's book—and it is
if you claim Jesus as your Savior and Lord and live like it—take a
moment right now to praise the Lord for this wonderful fact. Praise
him also that he has written your name in permanent ink—the
blood of his Son. And thank him that there are no erasers in heaven.

*Empower me to live as a child of the King should, dear Lord. I want you
to fill that space beside my name with the righteous acts of a genuine
saint.*

October 18

Grace and Mercy: The Difference?

The law was added so that the trespass might increase. But where sin increased, grace increased all the more.

—Romans 5:20

How would you communicate to a child spiritual truths like justice, mercy, and grace? They are heavy-duty principles even for an adult! But they are also the key distinctives of our salvation.

Let me tell you how Stuart and Jill Briscoe did it. Their son, Pete, was caught by his father in some mischief. Stuart said, "Son, the just punishment is ten whacks with the spoon, don't you think?" Little Pete sheepishly nodded. So justice was dealt, beginning with one, two, three, four, five, six, seven, eight whacks with the wooden spoon. Little Pete sniffed back his tears and then asked, "Why only eight whacks?"

Dad smiled and said, "That, my son, is what you call mercy—eight whacks when you deserve ten." Pete was sent to his room. Half an hour later Stuart called up the stairs, "How about going for ice cream with me? I'll pay."

That little boy bounded down the steps. He could barely believe his father's kindness. "But Dad," he said, "don't I deserve to be grounded?"

"Yes, Pete, you do. But this is what you call grace. You deserved the full punishment. Mercifully, I gave you only eight whacks and half an hour staying in your room. But ice cream? That's free. That's what grace is all about."

Great story, huh? We deserve hell. In mercy God spares us and lightens our load of trials on earth. And grace? He gives that freely each day, through multiple blessings as well as the promise of heaven. It's like . . . well, like ice cream.

In what ways has God shown you mercy recently, letting you off with a lighter sentence than you deserved? How has he shown you grace, giving you good things based on no merit of your own?

A grateful heart, God, seems the only appropriate response to the way you have generously dealt with me. I am your happy child, and a grateful heart is what I bring to you now.

October 19

God's Narrow and Wide-Angle Lenses

> Though he brings grief, he will show compassion, so great
> is his unfailing love. For he does not willingly bring afflic-
> tion or grief to the children of men.
>
> —Lamentations 3:32–33

When my paralyzing accident happened, I know the Lord took no pleasure in it. I believe it pained his heart to see me hurt, just as any father
has compassion on his child. Yet I also know it pleased the Lord to permit
my accident. He was as delighted then as he is now to work it all out for
my good and his glory. Sound confusing? I can understand why: in some
Scriptures God is described as grieving over affliction; in others it doesn't
seem to bother him.

Dr. John Piper explains it this way: God has the capacity to look at
the world through two lenses, a narrow lens and a wide-angle lens. When
the Lord looks at a painful event through the narrow lens, he sees the
tragedy for what it is in itself, and he is deeply grieved, as Ezekiel 18:32
says: "I take no pleasure in the death of anyone, declares the Sovereign
Lord." He hates the isolated incident of disease, crime, or violence.

But when God looks at a painful event through his wide-angle lens,
he sees the tragedy in relation to everything leading up to it, as well as
everything that flows from it. He has in mind Romans 8:28, "In all things
God works for the good of those who love him," and Ephesians 1:11, ". . .
according to the plan of him who works out everything in conformity with
the purpose of his will." The connections form a mosaic stretching into
eternity. This mosaic—in all its parts of good and evil, dark and light—
brings him delight.

God often wills what he despises, because he has two lenses. You can
trust him today that your painful trial is part of a pattern. One day
you too will put on that wide-angle lens. When you do, what a beautiful mosaic you will see.

*My shortsightedness, Lord, keeps me from seeing how pain can result in
good. Help me to look through the lens of faith.*

October 20

I'm After God's Heart

... David, who kept my commands and followed me with
all his heart, doing only what was right in my eyes.
—1 Kings 14:8

You turned my wailing into dancing; you removed my
sackcloth and clothed me with joy.
—Psalm 30:11

David is a man after not only God's heart but mine. He's bent on pleasing God, but he seems to bounce off the wall spiritually with every psalm he writes. One day he is wailing; the next, dancing. One moment he throws himself down in sackcloth and ashes, disgusted with his behavior; the next, he's effervescing joy like 7-Up. Sometimes in the space of just one psalm, he cries, then rants and raves, gets depressed, teeters on the edge of doubt, then does a complete turnabout, confesses, repents, and ultimately rejoices in praise.

That's my kind of guy. I can identify with someone for whom obedience does not always come easy. I'm not glorying in my hardheadedness. Being slow to obey is not something to brag about. God knows it took a broken neck to back me into a corner in order to get me seriously thinking about his lordship in my life. But I'm learning. No longer is a broken neck required for me to be instant in obedience. Maybe a pressure sore or a stint in bed from the flu. These are the less dramatic means God uses to press my heart up against his. And, oh, I want to seek his heart!

Are you the kind of believer who immediately turns a headache into a hallelujah? Few, if any, Christians are made automatically holy through their heartaches. Most are like David, for whom there was no mystical link between trials and triumphs. Take heart! When you struggle in a test or against temptation, when you move toward obedience, even in a small way, God sees it as seeking after his heart.

O God, though I sometimes wander far, though I stumble and fall, please, please: I want to be a child after your own heart.

October 21

God Is So . . . Personal

When the sun was setting, the people brought to Jesus all
who had various kinds of sickness, and laying his hands on
each one, he healed them.

—Luke 4:40

In Luke 4 everybody from the surrounding countryside brought sick people to see Jesus. Now it *could* have panned out this way:

Jesus surveys the crowd and says, "Okay, all you blind people, you sit over here. And everybody who has a contagious disease, you guys sit way over there. Now, where are the deaf? All you deaf people, gather on that hill. Paralyzed people? Calling all paralyzed people! Okay, get yourselves together in a group right in the front here. Now, everybody in position? Are you ready? Here goes!" Then, with a wave of his hand over the crowd, Jesus shouts, "Be healed!"

Aren't you glad it didn't happen that way? No grand-scale miracles of epic proportions were performed by Jesus. Instead he laid his hands on each one who came to him. His gentle touch healed the deaf, and he had nothing but kind words for blind people who reached out to him. He ministered to each one . . . individually. In so doing, he performed divine feats in a loving and highly personal way.

That's what I find so amazing about Christ. Although the fullness of the Godhead dwelt in him, he didn't make high drama of it. He glorified the Father but not in a showy way. Unlike the unapproachable "smoke and fire" of the Old Testament Mount Sinai, Jesus makes himself approachable through the love and tears of the New Testament Mount Calvary.

That's the kind of miracle God wants to perform in your life. Today he encounters you with the same tenderness and humanity he showed two thousand years ago. You are not a face in a sea of nameless people whom he divides into groups like the deaf, the blind, and the paralyzed. He wants to give you his highly personal touch.

Lord, I'm grateful I'm not a what's-his-name in your eyes. I'm not a face in the crowd. You thought of me, formed me, and designed every unique, wonderful bone in my body long before the foundation of the earth. Touch my life today in the personal yet powerful way you have touched people through the ages.

October 22

This Is Why He Came

> Simon and his companions went to look for him, and when
> they found him, they exclaimed: "Everyone is looking for
> you!" Jesus replied, "Let us go somewhere else—to the
> nearby villages—so I can preach there also. That is why I
> have come."
>
> —Mark 1:36–38

Why were Simon and his companions so anxious to find Jesus? Because everyone was asking for him. The day before, in Capernaum, Jesus had healed all the sick and the demon-possessed. Word had spread through the night, and the next morning everyone was searching for the Great Physician. Only after searching high and low did Simon and his friends find Jesus away from the crowds, almost hiding, and praying alone.

Back in Capernaum sick people and their families were frantic for his healing touch. But Jesus left them to go on. It's not that he didn't care about the cancer-ridden and arthritic (those who came too late for healing the night before). It's just that their illnesses weren't his focus—the gospel was. Jesus' miracles were merely a backdrop to his urgent message. He said so himself: "That is why I have come . . . so I can preach." And he preached it time and again: sin will kill you; hell is real; God is merciful; his kingdom will change you; I, Jesus, am your passport. Whenever people missed this point—whenever the immediate benefit of his miracles distracted them from eternal things—the Savior backed away. (Estes)

What are you seeking from God? The healing of a hurt? The meeting of a need? These things are good, but don't miss Jesus' deeper message. The core of his plan is to rescue you from sin. Our pain, poverty, or broken hearts are not his ultimate focus. God cares most not about making us comfortable but about teaching us to hate our sins, to grow up spiritually, and to love him.

I desire healing on the inside of my heart today. Lord, help me not to be so absorbed with outside things. Touch my soul, Great Physician.

Long-suffering

I wait for the LORD, my soul waits, and in his word I put
my hope. My soul waits for the Lord more than watchmen
wait for the morning.

—Psalm 130:5–6

The call came into the counseling department of the Dutch Christian
Television Network. "I am a quadriplegic," the caller said. "I had said
I would kill myself in ten years if I could not find help. It is now the tenth
year. This is my only hope."

The young man had called in response to one of my programs on TV
in the Netherlands. He had heard my message of hope and trusted that
somehow people could respond to his needs. Contacts were made, help
organized, and now we wait for God to heal the young man's heart.

We're all saddened and shocked by this story. It's hard to imagine no
one being able to help this person and give him relief these past ten years.
But what is just as shocking to me is the man's patience. He gave himself
(and God) ten years! Most people in his situation rarely take such a long-
term view of their circumstances. They want relief and they want it now.

The discouraged people that grab God's attention are those who inten-
tionally set out to wait. Like the psalmist, they know it may take a while.
They not only wait; they watch. They watch because they know that God
will answer. Rather than standing on the corner of life, waiting for God,
they go about their days unencumbered. They are productive, joyful
people, knowing that God will come in due time.

Wait. Wait patiently and eagerly. In the meantime get busy with what
you know to be your responsibilities.

*Lord, I don't give you enough time to do that which you desire to do.
Grant me an eternal-minded heart to wait upon you today.*

October 24

Hope and a Future

> "I know the plans I have for you," declares the LORD, "plans
> to prosper you and not to harm you, plans to give you hope
> and a future."
>
> —Jeremiah 29:11

Walk into a Christian bookstore or into the homes of many believers, and you will often see today's verse hand-embroidered and framed, hanging up for all to see and be encouraged. It's a beautiful promise and an oft-quoted favorite of many Christians. It's easy to see why. Everyone enjoys the idea that God's plans for his children are to prosper them and not harm them, to give them hope and a future bright with possibilities.

But let's take a reality check. The context of this verse is striking. It was in fact part of a letter written by the prophet Jeremiah and placed into the hands of the exiles being dragged off to Babylon. The enslaved Israelites not only faced a long, difficult journey east across the desert, but once they arrived, they would be forced to labor for their conquerors, much as their ancestors in Egypt did. Many of them would never see their homeland again.

Yet God gave this invigorating and encouraging promise to inspire the captives. They were not to lose heart. One day the Lord would deliver them and bring the nation back to Jerusalem. Despite the heartbreak of captivity, God's purpose was not to harm his people. Yes, they would feel the sting of slavery and hardship, but it ultimately meant a prosperous future.

In the past, have you assumed that today's verse was your guarantee that God would keep at bay pain and disappointment, trials and tribulations? God's purpose for us is to make us more like Christ, and this *will* mean hardship. So what is the hope and future all about? "Christ in you, the hope of glory" (Col. 1:27)!

Holy Spirit, guide me into all truth when I read your Word this week.

A Message from Michelangelo

He chose us in him before the creation of the world to be
holy and blameless in his sight.

—Ephesians 1:4

An artist in Florence, Italy, once asked the great Renaissance sculptor
Michelangelo what he saw when he approached a huge block of marble. "I see a beautiful form trapped inside," he replied, "and it is simply
my responsibility to take my mallet and chisel and chip away until the figure is set free."

Colossians 1:27 speaks of the hidden figure inside each believer, longing to be set free: "Christ in you, the hope of glory." This beautiful form
is inside Christians like a possibility, a potential. The seed has been planted,
the idea is there, and God uses affliction like a hammer and chisel, chipping and cutting to reveal his image in you. God chooses as his model his
Son, Jesus Christ: "Those God foreknew he also predestined to be conformed to the likeness of his Son" (Rom. 8:29).

What does this sculpture look like? God uses suffering to purge sin,
strengthen our commitment to him, force us to depend on grace, bind us
together with other believers, produce discernment, foster sensitivity, discipline our minds, spend our time wisely, stretch our hope, make us long
for truth, teach us thankfulness in times of sorrow, increase faith, and
strengthen character. It's a beautiful image!

When Christ is revealed in you, it is a unique sculpture. It is what
patience, self-control, kindness, and a healthy hatred of sin looks like
on you (and no one else). Your suffering is divinely hand-tailored to
suit exactly what patience looks like on you. The "who" of who you
are is transformed, like a form unfolding. "And we . . . are being transformed into his likeness with ever-increasing glory, which comes
from the Lord, who is the Spirit" (2 Cor. 3:18).

*Help me not to focus on the hammer and chisel of suffering, Lord, but
on you, the Sculptor. Help me to yield to the chisel today. Change me.
Reveal yourself in me. And be glorified!*

Hardship That Hangs On

Three times I pleaded with the Lord to take it away from me. But he said to me, "My grace is sufficient for you, for my power is made perfect in weakness." Therefore I will boast all the more gladly about my weaknesses, so that Christ's power may rest on me.

—2 Corinthians 12:8–9

I can identify with this verse. In the early years of my paralysis, when I was squirming to get back on my feet, I looked at my wheelchair and "pleaded with the Lord to take it away from me." To make a long story short, I got the same response the apostle Paul received. Like his "thorn in the flesh," my condition remained chronic.

Why chronic? Why do some hardships never go away? The hurting and hammering process I spoke about yesterday won't end until we become completely holy (and there's no chance of that happening this side of eternity). This is why I can more easily accept my paralysis as a chronic condition. When I broke my neck, it wasn't a jigsaw puzzle I had to solve fast, nor was it a quick jolt to get me back on track. My diving accident was the beginning of a long, arduous process of becoming like Christ. Sure, there are times I wish it were easier, but I realize I'm far from perfect. I have a long way to go to be made like Christ, polished and complete in his image.

The grace of God mentioned in our verse today is enough to sustain us through hardships that hang around. God's grace—the desire and the power to do his will—is sufficient. "Therefore, strengthen your feeble arms and weak knees. 'Make level paths for your feet,' so that the lame may not be disabled, but rather healed" (Heb. 12:12–13). Health and wholeness, maturity and completeness will be mine one day. The hammer and chisel will be laid down once and for all!

James 1:2–4 is our advice for the day: "When all kinds of trials crowd into your lives, my brothers, don't resent them as intruders, but welcome them as friends! Realize that they come to test your faith and to produce in you the quality of endurance. But let the process go on until that endurance is fully developed" (PHILLIPS).

Lord Jesus, help me to accept those conditions in my life that are chronic, whether in my marriage, my family, or my health. Give me grace for the long haul, knowing that the ending will be happy beyond my wildest dreams.

October 27

Marking Off the Miles

Whether you turn to the right or to the left, your ears will hear a voice behind you, saying, "This is the way; walk in it."
—Isaiah 30:21

When I was young, every October our family piled into the old Buick and drove to the town of Hancock, Maryland, where we would pick apples at my Uncle Don's farm. We kids loved to climb the trees, shake the limbs, and watch the fruit plummet to the ground.

But the best part of the trip, for me, was getting there. My dad let me have the map. The lines would turn from thick red to thin black when the road became narrow, and I would mark off on the map each little village as we passed through it.

I've always loved journeys. I gain satisfaction in seeing how I've gone from one place to the next and that I'm all the better for it. And when it comes to maps, you'll always find my nose stuck in one. A map allows me to mark off my progress and see how much farther I have to go.

The Bible is just like a map. Pick a verse, any verse, and you're on your way. God orders your steps. He goes before you, and he even tells you that you ought to be on the narrow road rather than the broad one (Matt. 7:13–14). Do you think you might lose your way? Don't worry. When Jesus' disciples asked him how they could get to where he was going, he replied, "I am the way" (John 14:6). You can't get lost when you trust in the Lord.

Are you a little unsure of your directions? Read today's verse again. If you are intimate with the Lord, if your communication with him is close, he will tell you which way to go. But if your ears are dull to his voice, and your heart unyielding to his nudging, you won't have a clue as to which direction to take. So get into that map of yours. Learn to look at your life ahead as the best journey ever. And remember, you know exactly where you're headed—heaven. Just keep your eye on the Way, and you'll make it safely.

Thank you, Father, for the adventure of the journey and for the guidance of your map. Keep me alert to your directions.

October 28

The Intentional God

He does as he pleases with the powers of heaven and the
peoples of the earth. No one can hold back his hand.
—Daniel 4:35

When we say that God allows an accident or permits a painful disappointment, we get the picture that Satan backs God into a corner with some weird request and then twists God's arm until he yells, "Uncle!" We think that the Lord would really rather not allow thus-and-such, that he would prefer that the Devil just leave him alone, thank you.

But the permitting and the allowing that God does in the Bible is far more deliberate than what people usually assume. God gives the green light to problems not because he's helpless or has set himself restrictions against meddling in the world's affairs but because he is intentional. God is decisive, even about suffering.

This is obvious in Ezekiel 20:26: "*I let them* become defiled through their gifts—the sacrifice of every firstborn—that I might fill them with horror so they would know that I am the LORD" (emphasis added). Centuries earlier, God saw what was coming. Long before the Jews entered Canaan, he knew what they were predisposed to do. Why did God permit them to follow their own vices, especially something so loathsome as infanticide, which he hates? He tells us in Ezekiel 20: to expose the vileness closeted in their own hearts, so they would stare at it and vomit. This is hard for us to grasp, but exposing sin is more important to God than relieving human suffering, even unthinkable suffering. (Estes)

Almighty God, forgive me when I think that you allow things to happen in an offhanded or casual way. Forgive me when I assume that the Devil is holding you hostage, making you do and decide things you really would rather not. I praise you for your decisiveness, for your deliberateness, for your decrees that are always intentional. You have something good always in mind, and a plan that is always perfect. Bless you!

Permission Slips

Simon, Simon, Satan has asked to sift you as wheat. But I
have prayed for you, Simon, that your faith may not fail.
And when you have turned back, strengthen your brothers.
—Luke 22:31–32

S atan has asked . . . ," observed Jesus. We can be certain that the old snake
didn't check in with God out of politeness or protocol. He *had* to get
permission, and this means the Devil operates under constraints. He can't
do what he wants whenever he wishes. He has to clear it with God.

Don't think this means God and the Devil are in cahoots. No way.
And don't think that God is somehow on the side of darkness because he
makes the Devil come to him for permission. God *must* control evil. And
he does so because he is good. Imagine a God who didn't deliberately permit the smallest details of your particular sorrows. What if your trials
weren't screened by him? Think what this would mean. The Devil would
be without constraints, free to do whatever he pleased. This means the
world would be much worse than its present state of war, violence, greed,
and misery. Left to his own, the Devil would make Jobs of us all!

I breathe a great sigh of relief over today's verse. It teaches me that evil
can only raise its ugly head when God deliberately backs away for a specific and intentional reason—always for a reason that is wise and good,
even if hidden from this present life.

If God didn't control evil, the result would be evil uncontrolled. So
God permits what he hates in order to achieve what he loves—it's just that
most of us won't see it until the other side of eternity.

Think for a moment about the balance of painful and joyful things
in your life. Think of how, by God's grace, you are managing your
problems. And now consider how it could be worse. Were it not for
God, it would be.

Lord, I praise you for making the Devil operate under constraints.

October 30

Reward and Punishment

> After you have had children and grandchildren and have lived
> in the land a long time—if you then become corrupt and
> make any kind of idol, doing evil in the eyes of the LORD your
> God and provoking him to anger, I call heaven and earth as
> witnesses against you this day that you will quickly perish
> from the land that you are crossing the Jordan to possess. You
> will not live there long but will certainly be destroyed.
> —Deuteronomy 4:25–26

Reward and punishment may work as a training technique for animals, but it does not work when it comes to God's dealings with us. Listen to what my friend Philip Yancey observes.

> The Bible itself records a kind of behavior-modification experiment on a national scale—God's covenant with the Israelites. For a time, God resolved to reward and punish his people with strict consistency, as detailed in the book of Deuteronomy. What were some of the results of obedience? Prosperous cities . . . guaranteed military victories and total immunity to diseases. What about the punishment? If they disobeyed, violence and crime, infertility and crop failure. So what resulted from this reward and punishment system? Within 50 years, the Israelites disintegrated into a state of anarchy and much of the rest of the Old Testament recounts the dreary history of those predicted curses coming true.
>
> Years later when New Testament authors referred to that history, they saw those days of reward and punishment in a new light. They said the Old Testament law serves as an object lesson: It demonstrates that human beings are incapable of fulfilling a contract with God.

James 2:13 announces, "Mercy triumphs over judgment!" Thanks be to God, who gives us the victory in Christ! You can rejoice that you do not live in a reward-and-punishment type of world. God did not punish my stiff-necked, teenage stubbornness with a broken neck, and he will not zap you with a lightning bolt if you sin. So today forgive others of their trespasses against you, just as he—the Lord Jesus—has forgiven you. It's all about mercy. It's all about grace.

Oh, how grateful I am for your mercy and grace, Lord Jesus.

October 31

Lost in a Haunted Wood

The eye never has enough of seeing, nor the ear its fill of hearing. What has been will be again, what has been done will be done again; there is nothing new under the sun.
—Ecclesiastes 1:8–9

No verse better describes the plight of a person without God in his or her life: bored and itching for something more. People look for happiness in marriage, money, and mischief, but nothing completes their joy. Our desires and cravings continue to irritate, making us restless for more. But earth can never satisfy; it can never keep its promises.

I sometimes see this on nights when I wheel into a hotel after a speaking engagement. The bedtime hour has long past, but the lounge is still crowded, smoky, noisy, and packed with people on a search. What's even more sad is to pass that lounge the next morning and *still* see people leaning on the bar and fingering a half-empty drink.

It's strange how people are bent on mad pursuit, making the same mistakes every day, hoping that life will someday reveal an answer, even though the experiences of most have taught them otherwise. Why do people keep seeking and pushing past the boredom? Because people *have* to. Our seeking is a response to the stirring of a fundamental need that simply must be satisfied—our need for God. Every desire, longing, aspiration, hunger, and thirst is no less than a desire for God.

Are you bored? Anxious? Toying with temptation? Looking for something new, exciting, or enticing to satisfy some inner craving? *Listen* to those wants. They show you what you really desire: "God is the answer to our deepest longings" (1 Cor. 6:13 PHILLIPS).

I want to be satisfied with you, Lord. Completely. Remind me of this when my heart starts to wander.

NOVEMBER

November 1

For All the Saints

You are no longer strangers and aliens, but you are fellow cit-
izens with the saints, and are of God's household, having
been built upon the foundation of the apostles and prophets.
—Ephesians 2:19–20 NASB

I once visited majestic Salisbury Cathedral. I slowly wheeled through the cloisters, feeling the history in every stone. I paused at a sepulcher upon which
was carved the supine figure of a Crusader, complete with the familiar shield
and helmet. The inscription indicated he was the son of a land baron and had
died in the Holy Lands in 1250. I shook my head, amazed and pleased.
Amazed that I was sitting beside the grave site of a man from the thirteenth
century . . . and pleased that he was most likely my brother in Christ.

An old hymn swelled my heart and I broke into song, my voice fill-
ing the cloisters with these words so apropos for today, All Saints' Day:

> For all the saints who from their labors rest,
> Who Thee by faith before the world confessed,
> Thy name, O Jesus, be forever blest:
> Alleluia! Alleluia!
> O may Thy soldiers, faithful, true, and bold,
> Fight as the saints who nobly fought of old,
> And win with them the victor's crown of gold:
> Alleluia! Alleluia!
> O blest communion, fellowship divine!
> We feebly struggle, they in glory shine;
> Yet all are one in Thee, for all are Thine:
> Alleluia! Alleluia!

Our Savior has inspired generations of believers who have fought,
persevered, prayed, suffered, and passed on to glory. We stand on
their shoulders. "Therefore, since we are surrounded by such a great
cloud of witnesses, let us throw off everything that hinders and the
sin that so easily entangles, and let us run with perseverance the race
marked out for us" (Heb. 12:1).

*Millions of believers are resting as your "church triumphant," Lord; help
me to be true to you and to their example.*

This Is My Father's World

The earth is the LORD's, and everything in it, the world,
and all who live in it.

—Psalm 24:1

This *is* my Father's world. I was thinking about that yesterday when I arrived early for our church's Wednesday night prayer meeting.

I wheeled to the back of the church, which overlooks Malibu Creek. A green lawn slopes gently to the creek, which is lined by trees and bulrushes. Two huge eucalyptus trees provide shade, and the rays of the setting sun were touching the rosebushes. (Yes, even in November California has roses.) I spent half an hour meticulously cataloging everything in my heart, scanning the pine trees, the yew bushes, the ice plants, the roses, the rabbits, and the birds. I took in each part of the scene slowly and spent a moment or two thanking God for his marvelous, creative variety.

What a way to start a Wednesday night prayer meeting. And what a way to remember that this world does not belong to the movers and the shakers. The power brokers don't own it. The governments don't run it, and the banks don't finance it. The terrorists can't destroy it, and the United Nations can't bring it peace. Kodak may try to capture the color, and A&M Records may try to create the sound, but there's no mistaking . . . this is my Father's world. I realized that all over again as I sat in our church's rose garden.

Bundle up if you need to and go outside to scrutinize your view of our Father's world. Look it over slowly, really noticing the fine attention to detail the Artist has used. Then praise him.

Creator God, you've tucked so much beauty into each portion of creation that to try to take in even a little of it fills me with awe and wonder. Thank you that this is your world—no one else can own it. I'm grateful you've created it for us to enjoy. Teach me to pay more attention to the beauty with which you've surrounded me.

November 3

A Grumbling Mood

"See, the Lord is coming with thousands upon thousands of his holy ones to judge everyone, and to convict all the ungodly of all the ungodly acts they have done in the ungodly way, and of all the harsh words ungodly sinners have spoken against him." These men are grumblers and faultfinders; they follow their own evil desires; they boast about themselves and flatter others for their own advantage.

—Jude 14–16

Lately I've been putting up my spiritual antennae, and I'm hearing some things that alarm me. I'm hearing grumbling, complaining, and murmuring. Everybody seems to have a gripe or complaint or feel victimized—it's awful! We come out of church Sunday morning and pick apart the sermon, complain about the Sunday school teachers, gripe about the music, and grumble about the elders and the way they are handling a church problem. Many Christians feel it's their duty to voice complaints.

That's the way the Israelites felt when they complained about Moses. It didn't matter that God was sovereign and in control of all their problems. It wasn't important that Moses had a good track record. The Israelites were disgruntled, and they were going to voice their gripes.

Scary stuff, this faultfinding. How scary? Well, the book of Jude has some pretty serious things to say in the verses for today. The word *ungodly* is used four times—count them, four—to describe not murderers and adulterers but grumblers and faultfinders.

Now, your gripe might be justified. Wrongdoing might be going on that needs to be exposed. But make sure that your concerns are legitimate and that you're not indulging in a complaining spirit. Examine your heart. Are you voicing your complaints to the right people, in the right way, for the right reasons? Let God take a peek at your motives, just to make sure all is well.

Lord, teach me to guard my heart from a complaining spirit. Enable me to place a lock on my mouth rather than utter that which would needlessly stir discontent. Above all, help me to be discerning about when and how to speak.

Had Enough?

I have had enough, LORD. . . . Take my life.

—1 Kings 19:4

Ever feel as if you have spaghetti for a backbone? When I feel like giving up, I think of good ol' Elijah and our verse for today. Even a powerful prophet can discover he has noodles for knees. Queen Jezebel had heard through the grapevine that Elijah had wiped out hundreds of her prophets. So she went after his neck. And Elijah ran for his life. When he reached the desert, Elijah gave up. He didn't even have the courage to do himself in. Instead he begged God to perform a mercy killing on him.

Do you see yourself in this picture? Whether we're terminally ill, on our last legs, or hunch-shouldered with a bad case of the Monday morning blues, all of us sometimes say, "I've had enough." There's hardly a one of us who hasn't at one time or another wanted to throw in the towel.

Each of us can draw comfort that we are all as vulnerable as Elijah. How did this mighty prophet surface out of his despair? God didn't give answers; he gave himself. He ministered to the prophet, handing him food and giving him sleep. God even offered a listening, empathetic ear. The record shows that the Angel of the Lord agreed that "the journey is too much for you" (1 Kings 19:7). Then God presented Elijah with new work to do. Sometimes switching focus onto others is just what the doctor would order.

As surely as the Angel of the Lord gave the prophet a sip of cool water and laid him down to rest, the Lord touches your life through the people he places around you. People are the hands and heart of God to you. If there are no people? God will personally come through for you, giving you strength out of nowhere.

Do what Elijah did. Carve out time for rest. Watch your nutrition. Spend time with God. Seek out fellowship. Look for ways to help others. It's a prescription to help ease depression.

God of rest and restoration, show me how to turn to you for help when I slump emotionally. Tune my heart to the ways in which you want to minister to me, and help me to be responsive.

The Lord Longs to Be Gracious

The LORD longs to be gracious to you; he rises to show you compassion. For the LORD is a God of justice. Blessed are all who wait for him! . . . How gracious he will be when you cry for help! As soon as he hears, he will answer you.

—Isaiah 30:18–19

We know that Jesus was full of tender compassion, but what comes to mind when you think of the God of the Old Testament? Fire and thunder on Mount Sinai? Curses and apocalypses? Rods of reproof and correction, weird visions and strange commands? Smoke and anger and the hurling of hail and lightning?

There's more to the picture. It was the God of Moses, the Holy One of Israel, the subject of Ezekiel's visions and Daniel's disasters, who forbade Israel to curse deaf people, trip the blind, deprive the poor, rob the fatherless, oppress the weak, or make widows objects of prey. He took pity on Hagar sobbing in the desert. He reached out to Hannah, who was weeping so bitterly that she appeared drunk over disappointment for lack of children. He honored and dealt tenderly with Tamar, a victim of incest. He soothed the hurting heart of Naomi in her old age and loneliness.

The Father is tender beyond description. He not only makes his compassion known; he *rises* to offer his love and mercy. He not only chooses but *longs* to be gracious to you. That is, he desires, yearns, and even aches to show you the abundance of his care and compassion.

If we do not cling to God through the worst life offers, we will misread him entirely and grow to mistrust and even despise him. "The LORD is compassionate and gracious, slow to anger, abounding in love. . . . He does not treat us as our sins deserve or repay us according to our iniquities" (Ps. 103:8, 10). In your praise today, remember that not only does Jesus take pity on the weak and hurting . . . the Father does, too.

Father, I sometimes associate tenderness and compassion only with your Son rather than with you. Forgive me for not remembering the many demonstrations of your love all throughout the Bible.

Left Hand of God

Shall we accept good from God, and not trouble?
—Job 2:10

For years Karen and her husband, Doug, struggled to have children; then finally, after many disappointments, God blessed them with a beautiful baby girl. Months later their daughter was diagnosed with a severe and debilitating disease. Karen's eyes were red and swollen as she struggled to smile. She sighed and said, "I would rather receive something from the left hand of God than nothing at all." The comment revealed her keen knowledge of Middle Eastern culture. Among Arab Bedouins and nomads, the left hand is reserved for menial and often dirty tasks—it is therefore an affront to offer anything from your left hand.

But Karen will wholeheartedly take *whatever* God gives her. Anything from either hand of God is better than nothing. She casts herself on him because she is convinced that all things that come from him are ultimately good. "Give thanks to the LORD, for he is good," Psalm 107:1 declares. When it came to her child's bad medical report, Karen realized that God signed the authorization papers. She would say with Job, "The LORD gave and the LORD has taken away" (Job 1:21).

Karen and her family are living out the text of Deuteronomy 29:29: "The secret things belong to the LORD our God, but the things revealed belong to us and to our children forever, that we may follow all the words of this law." Karen may not understand God's secret plan, but she can follow God's revealed words. He *is* good, and therefore she can trust him.

Shall we accept good from God's right hand and not trouble from his left? In whatever way God chooses to unfold his purpose in our lives, can we say with Job, "Though he slay me, yet will I hope in him" (Job 13:15)?

Lord, let me take your hand today. I trust that you will lead me by your goodness, mercy, and love.

A Mouthful of Praise

My mouth is filled with your praise, declaring your splendor all day long.

—Psalm 71:8

It doesn't happen all the time, but when it does, it's ecstatic. The other night, after the lights went out, I tried to get to sleep but couldn't. My prayer time that evening had been especially warm and intimate with God, and I found I could turn off neither my head nor my heart. I suddenly realized, with my eyes closed and my head pressed to the pillow, that I was murmuring one praise after the next: "O Lord, you are high and lifted up, majestic and exalted, grand and glorious . . . pure and holy. . . . I praise you for your greatness and goodness . . ." and so on. My mouth was literally filled with his praises, just as today's psalm suggests.

Praise is not something we should be forced to do. Rather it should be the supernatural, effervescent response of the born-again creature preparing itself for heaven. Professor E. L. Maskell puts it this way: "We do not praise God because it does us good, though no doubt it does. Nor do we praise him because it does him good, for in fact it does not. Praise is thus strictly ecstatic in the sense that it takes us wholly out of ourselves; it is purely and solely directed upon God. It takes our attention entirely off ourself and concentrates it entirely on him."[1]

The crowning glory of praise is to lose ourselves and yet find ourselves in God. This is pure praise. Total preoccupation with the Trinity. This is like stepping onto the backside of Elijah's chariot of fire and being swept up into ecstasy.

Has your mouth ever been filled to overflowing with praise? Saturate yourself this week with God's Word. Recount to him often the wonders of his creation. Muse and brood over his death for you on the cross. Before long, out of you will flow that river of living water, gushing out in a torrent and springing up to him in a fountain of praise.

Quicken me with a spirit of praise, dear Lord. May my mouth be filled with praises for you today.

It's That Simple

Godliness with contentment is great gain.
—1 Timothy 6:6

The pastor invited Jani to the front of the auditorium.
"I want to ask you some questions," he said, holding her in his arms.
"Do you love your mom and dad and do they love you?"

"Uh-huh," Jani said with a nod, smiling shyly.

"How about school? Do you like your teacher?"

"Uh-huh."

"And do you love Jesus and does he love you?"

"Uh-huh."

The pastor turned to the congregation. "A little jealous, aren't you?"
Jani climbed down and ran back to her dad's lap, giggling.

Jealous of what, I wonder. Jealous that Jani is mentally disabled? Jealous of all the teasing Jani might receive as she grows up? Jealous of the opportunities she will miss? No. We're jealous of Jani's contentment. Her "uh-huh" speaks volumes. The complexities of life have vanished, and she lives a life of simple joy and contentment.

"But Jani's just a child," you say. "My life isn't—and can't be—that simple." Don't believe it. Your heavenly Father—infinitely more capable than Jani's parents—considers her childlike contentment to be of infinite value. You will have gained infinite joy when you live a godly life and answer the world's fundamental question, Are you happy? with a direct smile and affirmation like Jani's. Try saying it....

"Uh-huh."

Lord, I struggle with really believing it's as simple as Jani makes it sound. But I'll take that step toward contentment today, seeking the simple joy you've promised.

Give Yourself Away

Whoever tries to keep his life will lose it, and whoever loses his life will preserve it.

—Luke 17:33

I love books, including some old classics by Andrew Murray and Oswald Chambers. As with anything that's a favorite, I find it hard to let certain books go. I'm afraid I won't get them back. And you know what? Sometimes I don't.

At first that irked me. Long ago I loaned my Bible from high school days to someone. But I can't remember whom. I'd love to have it, because it contains my handwritten scribbles. Plus, it was the first book I read in the hospital after I learned to turn pages with a mouth stick. I mentally let go of it when I realized, *If that Bible can be used to help bring someone closer to Jesus, great. That's what a Bible is for, no matter how much sentimental value it has.*

Speaking of letting treasures go, the story is told of a missionary who loved her books. Some she gladly loaned, but others—her favorites—she kept stored in a footlocker under her bed. One night she heard a scratching sound. After searching, she discovered the noise was coming from her footlocker. When she opened it, she found an enormous pile of dust. Termites had destroyed her precious books. That which she had tried to keep for herself, now belonged to no one.

What favorite things do you hold too tightly? Your privacy, your best friend, your weekend time, or your closet? (You wouldn't dare think of giving some of your *best* things to Goodwill.) Maybe you're holding on to the intimacy of your neighborhood Bible study—dare you and the group open it up to others?

We need to remember the lesson learned from that missionary. The Scripture for today tells it like it is. Give yourself away today . . . you'll never regret it.

Lord, I can picture myself holding on to so many things that are important to me. Give me the courage to open my arms, to release what I treasure, and then to enfold the blessings you bring in return.

November 10

God's Fingers . . . God's Arm

When I consider your heavens, the work of your fingers,
the moon and the stars, which you have set in place . . .

—Psalm 8:3

Sing to the LORD a new song, for he has done marvelous
things; his right hand and his holy arm have worked salvation for him.

—Psalm 98:1

I heard on the news that the Hubble telescope discovered a powerful new megastar that is not only one hundred million times brighter than our sun but, to the astonishment of astronomers, is in our own Milky Way galaxy. A thick cloud of gas and cosmic dust has hidden the star from our view all this time. It makes me look at the night sky a little differently. *And to think, Lord, that you created all these constellations with a snap of your fingers.* His fingers? It sounds so easy. According to Psalm 8:3, it is.

However, when it came to our salvation, it required much more than the work of God's fingers. Finger work implies the delicate labor of an intricate task, such as when one creates something fragile. There's nothing delicate about securing our salvation. The redemption of humanity demanded the force of "his right hand and his holy arm." When Jesus gripped his cross with his right hand and carried the killing weight of our sins with his holy arm, he displayed a power that far exceeded his skill with stars.

Amazing love! How can it be? That God would go to such lengths! As a response to his love, muse on the words to this hymn:

And can it be that I should gain an int'rest in the Savior's blood?
Died He for me, who caused His pain?
    For me, who Him to death pursued?
Amazing love! How can it be that Thou, my God shouldst die for me?
He left His Father's throne above, so free, so infinite His grace!
Emptied Himself of all but love, and bled for Adam's helpless race!

Thank you, Lord, for moving heaven and earth to save me!

I Must Tell Jesus

I resolved to know nothing while I was with you except Jesus Christ and him crucified.

—1 Corinthians 2:2

Once when I was talking on the phone with a Christian woman who was in the last stages of Lou Gehrig's disease, I found myself groping for words to comfort her. Finally I realized the best thing I could offer was simply the comfort of Jesus, so I sang for her a favorite hymn:

I must tell Jesus all of my trials,
    I cannot bear these burdens alone;
In my distress He kindly will help me,
    He ever loves and cares for His own.
I must tell Jesus! I must tell Jesus!
    I cannot bear my burdens alone;
I must tell Jesus! I must tell Jesus!
    Jesus can help me, Jesus alone.[2]

When I finished singing, I could tell she was calmed and greatly encouraged. She'd not been looking for answers; she was looking for Jesus. Pointing her to the Savior was the best thing I could do. When your heart is being wrung out like a sponge, an orderly list of "sixteen good biblical reasons as to why this is happening" can sting like salt in a wound. You don't stop the bleeding that way.

We must never distance the Bible's answers from God. The problem of suffering is not about some thing but Someone. It follows that the answer must not be some thing but Someone. Besides, answers are for the head. They don't always reach the problem where it hurts—in the gut and the heart. Jesus reaches us where we hurt.

If someone you know is struggling through a disease or a divorce or the death of a loved one, point them to the Savior, whether through your testimony, your words of encouragement, a shared memory, a poem, a Scripture passage, or a hymn. The answer to our deepest longings when we hurt is . . . Jesus.

Give me wisdom, Lord, to know exactly how to point people to you today.

November 12

Opening Eyes

Then will the eyes of the blind be opened and the ears of
the deaf unstopped. Then will the lame leap like a deer, and
the mute tongue shout for joy.

—Isaiah 35:5–6

Dale stepped up to the pulpit and heaved onto it an incredibly large
book with thick pages. As an elder lowered the microphone for him,
Dale flipped to a section in the middle of the book. He adjusted his black
glasses as if he could see and began to read: "Strengthen the feeble hands,
steady the knees that give way; say to those with fearful hearts, 'Be strong,
do not fear; your God will come.'"

I immediately recognized the familiar passage from Isaiah 35. Dale's
huge and cumbersome book was the Bible written in braille. But not the
entire Bible. The volume from which he read that morning represented
only several books from the Old Testament. He had left most of his Bible
at home because he couldn't carry the entire thing!

The blind man continued his reading, with his hands placed squarely
on the page and fingers constantly moving over the tiny bumps. He read
with firm authority. Every once in a while he paused when his fingers
encountered a staple in the page (his way of underlining a verse).

Dale looked so small behind the big book and the even bigger pulpit.
But in my eyes he seemed so large. The Bible must be incredibly precious
to Dale, seeing that it requires such effort to read it, to underline a verse,
and even to cart it around! I glanced at my Bible on my lap. I knew, after
that day, I would never look at it quite the same.

How precious is your Bible to you? Is it time for you to see the Bible
afresh as the Word of God, a cherished communication from our
heavenly Father? Read the entire chapter of Isaiah 35 today and relish in the truth and hope that is the Word of God.

*Heavenly Father, thank you that you loved us enough to reveal yourself
to us through the Word. Help me to read it with a fresh vision today.*

November 13

Humility and Confidence

The preaching of the cross . . . is the power of God.
—1 Corinthians 1:18 KJV

Major Ian Thomas of The Torchbearers is a powerful preacher but a very humble man. A friend of mine once approached him after he preached an exhilarating sermon. "Oh, Major Thomas," she effused, "I learned so much from your message." To which he replied, "Madam, I'm not surprised!" My friend said later that at first she thought his comment was puffed in pride. But then she remembered that his message was centered on the cross. Major Thomas realized that his hearers were moved not by him but by the power of God in the preaching of the cross. His comment was said in utter humility yet complete confidence.

Confidence is not the same thing as pride. Pride hates the cross. Pride will have us following Jesus anywhere—to a party, as it were, where he changes water to wine, to a sunlit beach where he preaches from a boat, or to a breezy hillside where he feeds thousands. But to the cross? Pride will have us digging in our heels. The invitation is so frighteningly individual. It's an invitation to go alone.

That's because it's a place of death. It is at the cross where we "put to death, therefore, whatever belongs to your earthly nature" (Col. 3:5). Who wants to do that? Who wants to ask her husband, "Honey, I want to be a better wife. . . . Would you please help point out my faults?" and then have to bite your tongue when he responds, "Well, you really come across like a know-it-all sometimes." Ugh! Nothing attracts us to the cross. Our dark side abhors it; our enlightened side recognizes it as home base.

What of your earthly nature can you bring to the cross today? Itchiness to have things your own way? Laziness in relationships? Verbal barbs that wound? Humble yourself at the cross, and you'll find humility in your heart and confidence in your Savior.

Lord, when I say I want to follow you, help me to climb the hill to the cross.

November 14

On *His* Terms

> Present to the LORD an offering made by fire, a burnt offering of two young bulls, one ram and seven male lambs a year old, all without defect. With each bull prepare a grain offering of three-tenths of an ephah of fine flour mixed with oil; with the ram, two-tenths; and with each of the seven lambs, one-tenth. Include one male goat as a sin offering to make atonement for you. Prepare these in addition to the regular morning burnt offering. In this way prepare the food for the offering made by fire every day for seven days as an aroma pleasing to the LORD; it is to be prepared in addition to the regular burnt offering and its drink offering.
>
> —Numbers 28:19–24

Rather complicated! In other Scriptures, when God describes how to present offerings to him, it's more convoluted. Divide up the meat just so. Lay it on the altar this way. Why does God go to such extent to make worship as demanding as possible? From the beginning, from the time when he refused Cain's grain offering yet accepted Abel's meat offering (Gen. 4:4–5), God underscored that people must come to him on his terms.

People in Old Testament times needed to hear that—they were far too prone to fashion calves out of gold and make up their own rules for worshiping God. People in modern times need to hear it—we are prone to throw out all the rules, follow our instincts like idols, and experience God however we see fit.

No longer do we need to bring to God grain, drink, sin, or burnt offerings. We have Jesus: "He did not enter by means of the blood of goats and calves; but he entered the Most Holy Place once for all by his own blood" (Heb. 9:12). But worship is no less demanding. So how do we come to God on his terms? How do we worship in the way he considers acceptable and pleasing? "His worshipers must worship in spirit and in truth" (John 4:24). These are his terms. Look at the word *must*. We must worship God this way: with the proper heart attitude and with Christ, the Truth, as our focus.

I worship you in spirit and in truth, Lord. Please accept my offering!

November 15

Real Rest

This is what the LORD says: "Stand at the crossroads and look; ask for the ancient paths, ask where the good way is, and walk in it, and you will find rest for your souls."
—Jeremiah 6:16

When I think of rest, I think of having the freedom to sleep in on a Saturday morning until 8:30 A.M., with no ringing telephone. Many of us picture something like this when we think of rest, but when it comes to resting in Christ, quite a different picture is painted. Let me illustrate it with this quote from Henry Drummond.

Two painters each painted a picture to illustrate his conception of rest. The first chose for his scene a still, lone lake among the far-off mountains. The second painter threw on his canvas a thundering waterfall with a fragile birch tree bending over the foam. At the fork of the branch, wet with spray, a robin sat on its nest.

The first painting was only stagnation. The second was rest. For in rest, there are always two elements—tranquility and energy; silence and turbulence; creation and destruction; fearlessness and fearfulness. Thus it was with Christ. Christ's life outwardly was one of the most troubled lives that was ever lived. Tempest and tumult, the waves breaking over him all the time. But his inner life was a sea of glass. The great calm was always there. At any moment you might have gone to him and found rest. Even when the bloodhounds were dogging him in the streets of Jerusalem, he turned to his disciples and offered them, as a lasting legacy, his peace.

How is it with you today? Do you find yourself precariously perched over a chasm of some frightful predicament, much like the robin above the waterfall? If you are following Christ, it's doubtful he's leading you by an idealistic, quiet lake scene, far from the madding crowd. You're in the storm. And there's nothing stagnant about that. So let the waves roar . . . inside your heart can be a sea of glass when you rest in Jesus.

Lord Jesus, sometimes it seems I'm in the eye of the storm, with the winds of change and fury whirling around me. But that's okay. I'm in the eye where you are. Where it's calm. Thank you for resting me there.

November 16

Excuses, Excuses

O LORD, is this not what I said when I was still at home?
That is why I was so quick to flee to Tarshish. I knew that
you are a gracious and compassionate God, slow to anger
and abounding in love, a God who relents from sending
calamity.

—Jonah 4:2

It's human nature to make excuses. Placed under the scrutiny of an examiner, a teacher, or a boss, we squirm in our seat and then rattle off a well-constructed reason for our behavior. Sometimes we blame circumstances. Sometimes we blame others. Caught in a quandary, our pride lashes out at anything in our sight that will keep the attention off our failure.

Pride's most deadly excuse is one that blames our Lord for our failure. Consider Adam's excuse that God's creation of woman was flawed. Or Jonah's attempt to blame his escape to Tarshish on the fact that he knew God to be, as today's verse says, "a gracious and compassionate God, slow to anger and abounding in love." By contrast, the unworthy steward's excuse centered on what he believed to be the exacting, unforgiving nature of the master (Matt. 25:24–25).

It will not do. We cannot blame God, neither his deeds nor his character, for our failure. Making such excuses is more than an attempt to protect our pride. It is a fundamental statement of our unbelief in God. We blame him because we do not believe that he has our good in mind, that he will accomplish his purpose, or that he will be gracious.

Taking an honest inventory of our life can reveal areas where we might have doubted, and then blamed, God. Angry with God about your work? Look to see where you doubted his provision. Frustrated with his seeming silence? Examine your walk to see if you doubted his commands. Fearful of seeing him face-to-face someday? Confess that you doubt his mercy and forgiveness.

A life of belief will extinguish pride's incessant search to protect itself from shame, and allow us to live freely as a forgiven people.

Lord, your work and your character are above reproach. Strip away the protective layer of excuses, that I might live by faith, believing in every measure of grace toward me.

November 17

Being Alone

In repentance and rest is your salvation, in quietness and trust is your strength.

—Isaiah 30:15

There are days when I'd like to rewrite the words of the old hymn "I Need Thee Every Hour" to something like . . .

I need Thee, O I need Thee,
Every minute I need Thee,
Oh, bless me now, my Saviour,
I come to Thee.

Oh, the comfort of feeling *desperate* for Jesus. You've had days like that, in which you feel as though you must cling to him every minute, every sixty seconds. That's when I carve out time to be alone with him. I don't take phone calls, I cancel my luncheon date, and I close the office door just to be with God.

Wonderful things happen when you're alone with the Lord. Look at the record:

Moses was alone when the Lord revealed himself through the burning bush. Paul was alone in the Arabian desert when the Lord gave him personal instructions about preaching the Word. Mary was alone when the angel brought her the message that she would give birth to the Savior. Isaiah was alone when he received his commission from the Lord. Elisha was by himself when the mantle of prophet fell on his shoulders. And who can forget John alone on the island of Patmos when he received his wonderful revelation? Joshua, Jacob, and Daniel all received a special word from God when they took time to be alone with him.

If you need a word from the Lord, direction, help, and hope, set aside time to be alone with him. Expect him to speak to you. Guidance and real fellowship come only in those times of solitude, in an hour when you say to the Lord, "I need thee."

Father, thank you that you have shown us through the Scriptures how you faithfully met with your children when they were alone and available to you. I too need thee to be my comfort, guide, and source of hope. Meet with me even as I set aside time to be with you.

Help in the Nick of Time

As they sailed, he fell asleep. A squall came down on the
lake, so that the boat was being swamped, and they were in
great danger.

—Luke 8:23

It was nighttime and Topanga Canyon Boulevard was at its busiest. Right under a dark overpass, my handicap-equipped van conked out. Completely. Even brakes and steering. I was careening up a busy street without any controls. You can imagine my relief when, with cars speeding around me, I drifted to a stop just short of the next intersection. But then I screamed. My van, with no taillights, started to drift backward into oncoming traffic. *Oh, God, have you abandoned me to a fiery crash? Is this how I'm going to die?* Just then as I hunched over, preparing to be rear-ended, Ken's truck screeched to a stop alongside my van. He jumped in, manhandled the braking mechanism, and lifted me out of the van and carried me to his truck. Never before had I been in such danger.

My nerves remained rattled for days. When I read Psalm 27:1, "The LORD is my light and my salvation—whom shall I fear?" I thought, *I fear dead batteries and no brakes.* To shore up my faith, I read today's passage in Luke. I began noticing phrases like "the boat was being swamped" and "they were in great danger." There's no soft-pedaling it. The disciples' narrow escape was just that: narrow. I identified. Like them, I had been within inches of death. But those inches were really miles—God had me all along.

It may feel as if God is asleep when danger strikes, but he's not. No matter if it's by the skin of their teeth or with miles to spare, God helps his people. If it's not your appointed time, he will always, always deliver you . . . sometimes in the nick of time. Is that too close for comfort? Maybe, yes. But it's always close enough.

Lord, thank you for the many times you've rescued me. Whether it was too close for comfort or not, I was—I am—always safe and secure when held by you.

November 19

Look to the Heavens

Lift your eyes and look to the heavens: Who created all these? He who brings out the starry host one by one, and calls them each by name. Because of his great power and mighty strength, not one of them is missing. Why do you say, O Jacob, and complain, O Israel, "My way is hidden from the LORD; my cause is disregarded by my God?"
—Isaiah 40:26–27

When New Testament Christians read this verse on an Old Testament parchment, or when the early church fathers, such as Wycliffe, read it from the newly compiled Bible, what did they think when they lifted their eyes and looked to the heavens? They no doubt bit their tongues from complaining when they considered how God named all the stars within their sight. Surely they were awestruck at the number of stars.

Today we have many more reasons to be awestruck. Galileo's telescope has given way to powerful, computer-enhanced telescopic images of many more billions of galaxies than ever imagined. So many that they are far beyond counting. Yet God has looked at each one, rubbed his chin so to speak, examined the distinctiveness of each star, and given it a name that fits. Trillions upon trillions of stars, each with a special name.

If God cares about the names of each star, why should you complain, thinking that your problems are hidden from him or that he has no regard for your situation? You are far more precious to him than a nova or even a supernova. He has made you co-heir with the Creator and Name-Giver of the stars.

The lightning and thunder
They go and they come;
But the stars and the stillness
Are always at home.

George MacDonald[3]

Greater light rules the day,
lesser, rules the night.
Sun or moon, it doesn't matter;
we are always in your sight.

November 20

It's All in the Family

> Is it not to share your food with the hungry and to provide
> the poor wanderer with shelter—when you see the naked,
> to clothe him, and not to turn away from your own flesh
> and blood?
>
> —Isaiah 58:7

Not long ago I was back in Baltimore and spent time with Connie, a high school girlfriend. She is one of millions of American women who are in the "sandwich generation." They are raising their children at the same time they are caring for an aging parent. In Connie's case it's her elderly mother-in-law, who has emphysema.

I watched my friend gracefully handle all the needs around her. That was typical of Connie. It helps that she is part of a large family, and she has lots of support from her own folks. But that's not true for many women in the sandwich generation. A woman I know takes care of her mother and has to deal with a teenager who resents the change in routine. There's not much support for this caregiver.

If you're helping an aging parent or a family member who is ill, consider these suggestions: Don't be afraid to let others know you need help; the "I'm doing fine" mentality is self-defeating. Investigate the whereabouts of a local day care or respite center. Let your friends and church family be aware of specific ways in which they can lend a hand. Listen to the counsel of others—they may observe your husband's mood shift and alert you that he needs attention. And finally, look for hidden blessings. Your elderly parent sacrificed much to care for you when you were growing up. Now God is giving you the chance to extend the grace back.

Isaiah says that not turning away from your own flesh and blood is a sacrifice that is pleasing to the Lord. When you care for a family member, God says, your righteousness will shine "like the noonday sun" (Ps. 37:6). That's not a bad reward for taking care of your young and your old.

Lord, strengthen me to serve you by gladly serving others. Provide help for me when I need a break. Help me to see my service as pleasing to you.

November 21

Ruthless Perfection

A bruised reed he will not break, and a smoldering wick he
will not snuff out. In faithfulness he will bring forth justice.
—Isaiah 42:3

God bends us but never breaks us. This means that if I love God, suffering does not ultimately matter. Christ in me is what matters. Pain does not cease to be pain, but I can "rejoice in . . . sufferings" (Rom. 5:3) because the power of God in my life is greater than suffering's vice grip can ever be. It reminds me of this poem by an anonymous author:

When God wants to drill a man, and thrill a man and skill a man,
When God wants to mold a man to play the noblest part,
When He yearns with all His heart to create so great and bold a man
That all the world should be amazed,
Watch His methods, watch His ways:
How He ruthlessly perfects whom He royally elects;
How He hammers him and hurts him,
And with mighty blows converts him into shapes and forms of clay
Which only God can understand,
While man's tortured heart is crying and he lifts beseeching hands;
Yet God bends but never breaks when man's good He undertakes;
How He uses whom He chooses,
And with mighty power infuses him,
With every act induced him to try His splendor out,
God knows what He's about.[4]

As Eugene Peterson's paraphrase of 1 Corinthians 10:13 says, "All you need to remember is that God will never let you down; he'll never let you be pushed past your limit; he'll always be there to help you come through it" (THE MESSAGE). In other words, a bruised reed he will not break.

So "dear friends, do not be surprised at the painful trial you are suffering, as though something strange were happening to you. But rejoice that you participate in the sufferings of Christ, so that you may be overjoyed when his glory is revealed" (1 Peter 4:12–13).

Your power in my life, God, is greater than suffering's grip can ever be. Help me to believe that. Help me to live it.

The Hunt

I thank my God every time I remember you.
—Philippians 1:3

I will never forget Thanksgiving Day 1963. I was fourteen years old, living on a farm in Maryland, and Mr. Cauthorne, the owner of the big estate across the river, invited me to go on a fox hunt. Early on Thanksgiving morning, my dad helped me trailer my thoroughbred over to the hunt club. Within minutes I saddled up and looked around for Mr. Cauthorne. I spotted him by the barn, sitting atop his hunt-wisened horse. He had on his red coat, with hounds by his side. The paddock was abuzz with dogs barking and horses neighing.

The bugle sounded and—we're off! I reined my horse in line behind Mr. Cauthorne, observing how he graciously deferred to the hunt master. I made certain to do the same. We spurred our horses into a slow gallop. I can still feel my hands holding the reins, the wind in my face as we cantered across shaven cornfields and sailed over walls. We never caught the fox. But the thrill was less in bagging an animal and more in relishing the ride. It made turkey dinner back at the hunt club all the more delicious . . . and my thanks to God all the more personal.

I haven't sat a horse in over thirty years. The only leather I sit on now is the padding of my wheelchair. No cinches around saddles, only cinches around my middle to help me breathe better. The clip-clopping of hooves has been replaced by the click-clacking of my wheel bearings. That's okay. I'll ride in heaven. In the meantime I thank God for memories.

Design your own Thanksgiving memories. Plan a holiday tradition that is unique and suited to your family. Maybe it's a football game. A family puzzle. Go for a hike before you eat dessert. Whatever it is, it'll be memorable if you do it in the spirit of thanksgiving.

Help me to make this holiday a memorable time for my family and friends. Thank you, Lord, for giving us so many blessings for which to thank you.

November 23

An Unfolding Adventure

If anyone is in Christ, he is a new creation; the old has gone, the new has come! All this is from God, who reconciled us to himself through Christ and gave us the ministry of reconciliation.

—2 Corinthians 5:17–18

Recently during a flight to Kansas City, a woman from an adoption agency sat behind me on the plane. In her arms she held two beautiful Korean babies. My heart melted. They both looked like little Ken Tadas, with that gorgeous dark skin and hair, almond eyes, and full cheeks. I couldn't take my eyes off those babies.

They had no idea of the life they were heading into. Within seconds of that plane landing, their lives would be turned upside down. They would have new names, new citizenship, a new culture, and new identities. They would have a new father and mother—in fact, a whole new family. Old things would pass away. From that point on all things would be new. Those babies hadn't a clue as to what they were leaving behind and, more importantly, what was ahead.

When we become Christians, we can't begin to fathom the new world we're stepping into. In Christ we have new identities, a new family, new citizenship, and—at least in the Lamb's Book of Life—we have new names. Goodness, we're even adopted: "In the place where it was said to them, 'You are not my people,' they will be called 'sons of the living God'" (Hos. 1:10).

In a way, I wish those Korean children could have understood. I wish they could have enjoyed starting a new life. But for them, it will be an unfolding adventure, just as it is for us as children of God . . . exploring, enjoying, discovering, as any child would.

How about you? Are you enjoying your new life today? Old things are passed away for you; all things have become new. Delight in the unfolding adventure.

Father God, I don't want to take for granted what you removed me from and what you replaced it with. Enable me today to see with childlike wonder the splendor of my new life with you. You have richly blessed me. And you're not through yet!

November 24

A Sacrifice of Thanks

He who sacrifices thank offerings honors me, and he prepares the way so that I may show him the salvation of God.
—Psalm 50:23

Suppose a woman with arthritis in her hands embroidered a set of pillowcases for you as a thank-you gift. The gift would mean more to you than if sewn by a woman with nimble fingers. Why? Because the arthritic woman expended extraordinary effort. Her thank-you involved cost and sacrifice. You'd weigh the extra hours she invested, the frequent breaks she took to rub her knuckles, the pain she endured with each tiny stitch. Most likely you would be moved to tears. Her suffering glorified her gratitude, making it more valuable in your eyes.

If we respond this way to sacrifices, how much more is God enthused when we sacrifice thank offerings to him? When trials sandblast you to the core and your bruised feelings are screaming, "Forget God!" or your weary mind is too clouded to see through the fog, *this* is the time to express to God gratitude. True, such gratitude involves cost and sacrifice—it costs your logic and you sacrifice your pride. But your thank offering is glorified as you push through the pain to present gratitude to God for his blessings.

Is there a trial that is souring your disposition toward God? Fostering doubts? Drying up your zeal? You have a chance to change that as you honor God today with a sacrifice of thanksgiving. List the many things for which you can give thanks, including the basics of life, or the support of friends. Your suffering will shape your thanksgiving into a true sacrifice of gratitude, preparing the way for God to shower grace upon grace on you. Don't postpone it. Sacrifice to him now.

I thank you, Lord, for the ability to see, hear, think, and pray, for the blessings of shelter, food, and friends, and for the many other evidences of your love. I'm hurting in this trial . . . but it helps to present you this sacrifice of thanks.

A Sacrifice of Praise

Through Jesus, therefore, let us continually offer to God a sacrifice of praise—the fruit of lips that confess his name. And do not forget to do good and to share with others, for with such sacrifices God is pleased.

—Hebrews 13:15–16

Ken and I worship in a small church. The Pomeroy family, including the youngest, Veronica, usually sits a few rows in front of us. Veronica likes to wear pretty hats over her blond hair. She also coughs a lot. I used to think she was plagued by frequent colds. I later learned she has cystic fibrosis, a severe lung disease that clogs her breathing passages with phlegm.

I sometimes watch Veronica during worship service. Especially when we sing hymns. She gasps in between the lines, and I wonder what God must be thinking as he receives her praise. Actually, I already know. "With such sacrifices God is pleased." More than pleased; God's greatness is magnified when Veronica determines to wheeze her way through a hymn— her gutsy praise demonstrates how *special* she thinks God is. What's more, with her limited lung capacity, Veronica inspires me to fill my chest and harmonize with all my heart. Praise is then multiplied!

As we grit our teeth to offer praise for who God is, we are living out Psalm 141:2: "May my prayer be set before you like incense; may the lifting up of my hands be like the evening sacrifice." A sacrifice of praise demonstrates the enormously high value we attach to him.

God is pleased with the praise you give him, but he swells with joy when the praise he breathes has the aroma of a sweet-smelling sacrifice. Today pick an attribute of God out of your pain and proclaim, "Worthy is the Lamb, who was slain, to receive power and wealth and wisdom and strength and honor and glory and praise!" (Rev. 5:12).

I praise you, Lord, for being so faithful, so consistent, so merciful and compassionate to me, even through—especially through—the hurt.

"The Lord Told Me . . ."

"Yes," declares the LORD, "I am against the prophets who wag their own tongues and yet declare, 'The LORD declares.' . . . This is what each of you keeps on saying to his friend or relative: 'What is the LORD's answer?' or 'What has the LORD spoken?' But you must not mention 'the oracle of the LORD' again, because every man's own word becomes his oracle and so you distort the words of the living God, the LORD Almighty, our God."

—Jeremiah 23:31, 35–36

We play fast and loose with the word of God these days. In-depth Bible study and examining verses in their context takes too much time. People seem to prefer instant revelation and "words of knowledge" on the spot.

I've noticed how many believers say, "The Lord told me that thus-and-such is going to happen." They proceed to give God's take on the situation, whether his answer concerns a marital problem, a career choice, or a reprimand meant for a friend. Actually, I hear it all the time: "Joni, the Lord told me that you will be out of that wheelchair in less than a year." Their sentiments are well-meaning, but their words are . . . well, frightening. Frankly, I'm speechless when a Christian prefaces any comment with "The Lord told me . . ." Who am I to question the Lord? How can I possibly engage this brother or sister in a meaningful debate, if they claim they are speaking *ex cathedra,* or "from the throne"? It's a dead-end discussion.

"What has the Lord told you?" and "Have you received a word from the Lord?" are phrases packed with presumption. Jeremiah knew this. Division and confusion were running rampant during the siege of Jerusalem by the Babylonians. Nobody wanted to listen to Jeremiah and hear the word of the Lord forecasting doom. So they leaned on false hopes in an attempt to pump up people's confidence in the ability of Jerusalem to withstand the siege. They tried to calm fears and raise expectations by saying, "The Lord told me . . ." The truth was, God had already spoken through his prophet. Just as today he speaks in and through his Word—the Bible.

Get into the practice of speaking for yourself rather than for God. After all, he's already made his Word clear.

Lord, keep me from presumption. Energize me to delve into your Word.

November 27

A Taste of Heaven

On this mountain the LORD Almighty will prepare a feast
of rich food for all peoples, a banquet of aged wine—the
best of meats and the finest of wines. On this mountain he
will destroy the shroud that enfolds all peoples, the sheet
that covers all nations; he will swallow up death forever.
The Sovereign LORD will wipe away the tears from all faces;
he will remove the disgrace of his people from all the earth.
—Isaiah 25:6–8

There is no mistaking. This is a real banquet. In heaven, after death is
swallowed up and the Lord wipes away the tears from all faces, a banquet will be served. It will be "the best of meats" and "aged wine . . . the
finest of wines." But wait. Suppose you are a vegetarian and you can't stand
wine? What then? Come to think of it, what animal will have to die to give
up his top round roast? I thought there was no more death in heaven. And
will someone be back in the kitchen shuffling pots and pans? Will Arabs
eat with their fingers? Will Asians use chopsticks? Will people in hell do
cleanup duty?

Wait. Stop. We're making the mistake of pursuing the meaning of
heaven with the Lincoln Logs of our logic. If we were able to scale heaven's
walls with the grappling irons of human understanding, our faith wouldn't
mean very much. Trying to grasp heaven is like trying to admire the outside of a huge cathedral with grand windows. Standing outside, the building is striking but has no real glory, yet if you go inside the cathedral—
which is a little like looking at heaven through eyes of faith—you are
breathless as you stand washed in glorious colors from the light that streams
through the window. (Hawthorne)

Questions aside, the point is that the passage is real. As strange as it
seems, today's verse underscores that the whole scene in heaven is
very real. There's nothing wispy or vaporous about wine and meat.
And there's no doubt it'll taste great.

*Lord of heaven, thank you for passages like these, which paint a very real
and tasty, a very desirable, picture of heaven. Help me to live in the light
of such heavenly promises today.*

November 28

I'm Joy-Happy

May the righteous be glad and rejoice before God; may they be happy and joyful.

—Psalm 68:3

We're often taught to be careful of the difference between joy and happiness. Happiness, it is said, is an emotion that depends upon what "happens." Joy, by contrast, is supposed to be enduring, stemming from deep within our soul and not affected by the circumstances surrounding us.

It's an appropriate linguistic distinction, I suppose. But I don't think God had any such hairsplitting in mind. Scripture uses the terms interchangeably, along with words like delight, gladness, blessed. There is no scale of relative spiritual values applied to any of these. Happiness is not relegated to flesh-minded sinners nor joy to heaven-bound saints.

The terms are synonymous in their effect and too difficult to distinguish when we experience either one. Would you, for example, respond to the wedding of your daughter with joy or with happiness? Are you happy that your friend came to know Christ, or are you joyful? Is the moment of euphoric delight in worship of him on Sunday morning just a happenstance or just as much a part of Jesus' promise regarding our redeemed souls?

To rob joy of its elated twin, happiness, is to deprive our soul of God's feast. Seek both as part and parcel in all circumstances. When your soul is stirred by a deep contentment, be happy. When a delightful moment strikes that is quite outside yourself, be joyful. Don't think about which one you are supposed to feel. Accept them both as a gift from a God who is rich in all such emotions.

Lord, I seek the blessing of a joyful heart, the gladness of a happy countenance, and the delight of your eternal pleasure today.

No Leftovers

Taste and see that the LORD is good; blessed is the man who takes refuge in him.

—Psalm 34:8

I love the day after Thanksgiving. There's nothing like turkey sandwiches with cold stuffing and cranberry sauce spread right on soft white bread. And day-old pumpkin pie? Yum.

Yesterday, on Thanksgiving, Ken and I read through some Old Testament passages to help us get into a spirit of gratitude. We discussed the wonderful things God did in the past, like parting the Red Sea and rebuilding the walls of Jerusalem. God served up a full-course meal of spectacular miracles back then.

But what about today? Are we tasting "leftovers" just because no seas are parting? Is God serving up something less than his best if he chooses to reveal himself through the pages of his Word rather than through the pillar of fire and cloud of smoke?

God's acts are no less mighty, and our thanksgivings are no less earnest than those who laid themselves prostrate in the Old Testament. God didn't just flex his muscles in ancient times to leave us with leftovers. When he served up his mighty acts in the Old Testament, God didn't say, "Taste and see that the LORD is good" only to dish out to us something less than his best. Nothing is ever day-old or reheated when it comes to God's workings. What he does always tastes good, is delightful, and is worthy of thanksgiving.

"Taste and see that the LORD is good." God may have given Solomon wisdom, but hasn't he done the same for you? He may have delivered Gideon, but hasn't he rescued you as well? God satisfied the mouth of David with good things, but hasn't the Lord also fattened your soul with more blessings than you can count?

"Praise the LORD, O my soul; all my inmost being, praise his holy name. Praise the LORD, O my soul, and forget not all his benefits" (Ps. 103:1–2). While the Thanksgiving blessings are still fresh in your mind, while the prayers of gratitude are still echoing around the table, forget not all God's benefits.

I give thanks, God, that you were good to the people of old and that I can say with them, "Oh, taste and see. The Lord is good."

God's Sovereignty

Oh, the depth of the riches of the wisdom and knowledge of God! How unsearchable his judgments, and his paths beyond tracing out!

—Romans 11:33

God doesn't say, "Into each life a little rain must fall" and then aim a hose in earth's general direction to see who gets the wettest. Rather he screens the trials that come to each of us, allowing only those that accomplish his good plan. He takes no joy in human agony. Nothing happens by accident, not even tragedy, not even sins committed against us. God is in control, and that's what I love about him.

True, God's decrees allow suffering, but he doesn't "do" the suffering. He's not the one wielding the club. For instance, in Job's story God exploited the deliberate evil of some very bad characters and the impersonal evil of some very bad storms, without smothering anyone or anything.

These are deep waters: God exploits but doesn't smother? How does he pull it off? Welcome to the world of finite humans trying to comprehend an infinite God. What's clear is that God permits all sorts of things he doesn't approve of. He allows others to do what he would never do. He didn't steal Job's camels or entice bandits to wreak havoc, yet he didn't take his hand off the wheel for thirty seconds, either.

This idea often doesn't sit well with people. But think of the alternative: what if God insisted on a hands-off policy toward the tragedies swimming your way? The Devil would be unrestrained. Left to his own, he would make Jobs of us all. But God curbs evil. Evil can only raise its head where God deliberately backs away—always for reasons that are specific, wise, and good but often hidden during this present life. (Estes)

Do your circumstances seem to be careening out of control? Remember that God is with you through it, loving you and caring ... and allowing the details to play out exactly in accordance with his plan.

God, enable me to trust in your love even when life seems wild and crazy and out of control.

DECEMBER

Pearl of Great Price

The kingdom of heaven is like a merchant looking for fine pearls. When he found one of great value, he went away and sold everything he had and bought it.

—Matthew 13:45–46

One day my father-in-law, Dad Tada, presented me with a family heirloom, a string of genuine pearls. He told me they had been harvested in Japan, not far from where he lived much of his life. I was captivated by the milky, soft glow of each perfect pearl. Ken draped the pearls around my neck, and I wheeled to a mirror.

As I admired them, Dad Tada explained how a pearl is produced. A tiny bit of sand lodges in the flesh of an oyster and becomes an irritating intrusion. Unable to expel it, the oyster covers the particle with layer after layer of a milky secretion until the irritation has become smooth, round, and acceptable. It also inadvertently becomes a precious gem.

An Oriental pastor once wrote, "Pearls, unlike other jewels, are drawn from the animate creation. (Other jewels are made from rocks and crystals and are mined out of the earth....) Pearls are produced by life—a life which has overcome the working of death."

Jesus, the Pearl of great price, is unlike any other. He is the precious gem set apart from the rest. He lived in such a way that he overcame the working of death. He is superior because his love poured forth from a life wounded by pain. He has become our example. We experience irritants in our lives, but God gives layer after layer of grace until the irritation becomes smooth and acceptable. What was an intrusion becomes a precious gem for all to admire . . . and for which God receives glory.

Pull your string of pearls (imitation or not) from your jewelry box, and hang them over the mirror above your dresser for a few days. They will brighten your bedroom and your appreciation for Jesus, the one and only Pearl.

My wounded Savior, teach me through your example to let intrusions in my life become pearls. Remind me how you transform pain into beauty.

Spiritual Leprosy

See to it, brothers, that none of you has a sinful, unbelieving heart that turns away from the living God. But encourage one another daily, as long as it is called Today, so that
none of you may be hardened by sin's deceitfulness.
—Hebrews 3:12–13

Looking back over the places I've visited this year, Africa remains the most
vivid, due especially to the plight of its disabled people. Diseases we
don't hear much about, like polio and leprosy, are prevalent there. Leprosy
causes people to lose the sensation of pain. With no pain to warn them,
these people badly damage their fingers or feet, to the point where they
destroy that part of their bodies.

I remember one homeless woman who had no hands but pulled herself around in the dirt on the stumps of her wrists. She had built up cal-
luses and her skin had become hardened. I wondered how much more
damage she was doing to her body.

Now, you might think I have nothing in common with that woman.
But I do. And maybe you do, too. A spiritual leprosy is described in the
verses for today. This leprosy causes a person's soul to become hardened by
sin's deceitfulness. You spiritually lose all sensation of pain, especially things
that pain God. You end up ripping your soul apart, and you don't even
realize it. White becomes black; black becomes white. You think that what
others call backsliding isn't all that bad.

Listen, leprosy is something you don't fool around with. If you have
lied, go back and make it right before you become hardened. If you
harbor a fantasy, shelve it! Don't let it deaden your conscience. Don't
turn away from the Lord. Let me encourage you today to double-
check to see if you have any leprous spots on your soul.

*Father of love, never let me move so far from you that I lose my sensitiv-
ity to what moves you. Keep me aware of the ways in which you want
me to express your compassion to the world. Show me any uncleanness in
my soul.*

December 3

A Stone-Cold Fact

> Do not be amazed at this, for a time is coming when all
> who are in their graves will hear his voice and come out—
> those who have done good will rise to live, and those who
> have done evil will rise to be condemned.
>
> —John 5:28–29

M y God!" exclaimed the boutique owner, a tall, blond woman with a
German accent. "It would look absolutely great on you!" She held
up the jacket on its hanger, twirling it so I could see the back.

"Oh, do you know him, too?" I asked, matching her energy with a big
smile.

"Who?" she asked, wrinkling her forehead.

"God. You mentioned him. The way you said his name, I thought you
might know him."

"Me? Nah!" she scoffed. "I did that whole God thing many years ago.
I don't need him. I have myself."

That did it. As she took my charge card from my wallet and rang up the
sale, I squeezed in as much testimony as I could. By the time I wheeled out
the door with my purchase on my lap, Anushka still wasn't convinced. But she
did promise to read the *Joni* book, if I brought back a copy in German.

You meet people like Anushka in your community every day. Trouble
is, we never look—I mean, look deeply—at a run-of-the-mill shopkeeper
and picture this person rising out of his or her grave to either live or be
condemned. Little wonder Jesus says, "Do not be amazed at this." But we
are. Maybe it's because we can't imagine Jesus as judge, as anything other
than tender and compassionate. Perhaps we can't fathom a voice so loud,
so thunderous, that it will wake the dead.

It takes a passage like today's to jar us out of our spiritual slumber
concerning those around us who don't know Christ. One day Jesus
will come to judge the living and the dead. The dead we can't do anything about. The living we can. Agree with God today that you want
to fit into his plan to reach the women who work the day care center . . . the cleaning lady . . . the bank teller . . . and all those who don't
know the Savior. Like Anushka.

Embolden me, O God, to give the gospel to others today.

Who Gets the Prize?

Surrounding the throne were twenty-four other thrones, and seated on them were twenty-four elders. They were dressed in white and had crowns of gold on their heads. . . . They lay their crowns before the throne and say: "You are worthy, our Lord and God, to receive glory and honor and power, for you created all things, and by your will they were created and have their being."

—Revelation 4:4, 10–11

His eyes are like blazing fire, and on his head are many crowns.

—Revelation 19:12

When I was growing up, I loved to enter my thoroughbred in the local horse shows. I'd prepare for that day, but I didn't work nearly as hard as the horse. After all, he was the one who had to soar over those fences and make his way through a complex maze of jumps.

When it came time for us to receive the prize, a person of importance would walk up to my horse. He'd usually give my hot and lathered animal a pat and then . . . reach up to hand me the trophy and ribbon. My horse did all the work but I received the honors. I suppose that's because I owned him. Plus, I was the one who had taken him through the course.

That situation is a bit like our Christian lives. Ephesians 1:18 says, "I pray . . . that you may know the hope to which he has called you, the riches of his glorious inheritance in the saints."

We are Christ's inheritance, the prize. We are also the praise. Oh sure, we do much of the work here on earth. There's a lot of blood, sweat, and tears. The course on earth is long and complex. At times we get weary. Even so, on the day of awards when the Judge approaches, the blue ribbon will go to . . . Christ! And the crowns we receive we'll cast at his feet. It's because he owns us and he is the one who took us through the course.

As you go through the complex maze of your day, remember that the more you obey and the longer you persevere, the greater God's glory.

Jesus Christ, thank you that my obedience and perseverance bring you glory.

Of Wolves and Lambs

The wolf will live with the lamb, the leopard will lie down with the goat, the calf and the lion and the yearling together; and a little child will lead them.

—Isaiah 11:6

Theologians and preachers will debate the timing and meaning of this prophecy. Is it before or after Christ's rule in the Millennium? Is it in heaven or is it on earth? Is it figurative or real?

You can debate it for a millennium if you like, but I can tell you that I've already seen it come to pass. Really. You could, too, if you received permission from the Colorado State prison system to go to a small workshop in one of its medium-security prisons. There you'd find an inmate, his tattoo-covered arms carefully restoring an old wheelchair. He'd tell you he's not doing it for the money. (He's not. He only gets twelve dollars a month, compared with the standard six hundred dollars a month for the other work available in prison.) He'd tell you it's rewarding to him to do something for someone who's got it worse than he does. And he'd tell you he's doing it because he loves to. That's my wolf.

And the lamb? Oh, she's a Chinese girl with cerebral palsy who's going to get her first wheelchair because of the wolf's strong arms. She'll go outside of her house for the first time. Maybe go to school. Maybe even watch the Chinese New Year outside, on her own and not on her father's back this time. That's something she would never have been able to do if it had not been for the wolf.

The lamb and the wolf will both have been led by a child—a child that broke the chains of sin in that inmate's life. A child that can free the Chinese girl to walk the streets of heaven someday. A child that was born in lowlier conditions than either will know. A child who died in more agony than either the wolf or the lamb could ever imagine. A child who heals both of their broken hearts and promises both of them freedom.

Few would call that man in prison a friend, Lord. And few would call that girl lovely. But I join that wolf and that lamb and follow you to Calvary.

December 6

Faithfulness

His master replied, "Well done, good and faithful servant! You
have been faithful with a few things; I will put you in charge
of many things. Come and share your master's happiness!"
—Matthew 25:21

Someone once said to me, "Joni, I wish I could be like you, because you'll
get a great reward in heaven." I appreciate the accolade but I see it differently. I already have the reward of seeing the gospel go forth and of
watching believers become encouraged because of this wheelchair. The glorious purposes for my suffering are clear to all.

But some saints have suffered for no apparent reason. In heaven, I'm
convinced, the highest accolades will go to those godly people who labored
loyally yet received no recognition.

May God honor the missionary in the Brazilian jungles who spends
fifteen years translating Scripture and then quietly moves on to the next
tribe to do the same. May the Lord reward small-town pastors who faithfully preach every Sunday morning despite meager numbers in the pews.
And the pastors in China who suffer persecutions and interminable jail
sentences. May the Lord take the highest delight in the elderly in nursing
homes who don't dwell on their plight but rather pray for others. And
godly teenagers who hold fast to their virginity despite peer pressure, intimidation, and hormones. These are the ones who will receive great reward!

Theodore Roosevelt once said, "The credit belongs to the man who is
actually in the arena; whose face is marred by dust and sweat and blood;
who strives valiantly; who errs, and comes short again and again, because
there is no effort without error and shortcomings. . . . Far better it is to dare
mighty things, to win glorious triumphs even though checkered by failure,
than to rank with those poor spirits who neither enjoy nor suffer much
because they live in the gray twilight that knows neither victory nor defeat."

Success isn't the key. Faithfulness is. May you be faithful to God until
you hear him say, "Well done, good and faithful servant!"

Father God, teach me to be faithful to the tasks you assign to me, without concern for fanfare.

December 7

Finding Meaning

We do not have a high priest who is unable to sympathize with our weaknesses, but we have one who has been tempted in every way, just as we are—yet was without sin.
—Hebrews 4:15

Suppose you're walking down a street, when you are accosted and forced to carry a huge and heavy basket on your back. You're ordered to walk three blocks, turn left, go two blocks, turn right, then proceed straight ahead. Staggering under the weight, you stumble on, bewildered and angry. The whole thing is meaningless and haphazard. When you are halfway down the third block, you finally bellow, "What gives?"

The truth is then revealed. The burden you are carrying is your child, injured and unconscious. "Whaat!" On top of that, you discover you are trudging not through a meaningless rat-maze but along the most direct route to a hospital emergency room.

Immediately you straighten. Adrenaline and fresh energy quicken your pace, and you move forward with a new attitude. Why the change? The suffering you're going through involves a relationship. Not just any relationship but one with your child. Your relationship gives your burden meaning. Even your twisted path makes sense. You know where you are going. Your journey has a positive end—the hospital—and this instills hope.

Suffering has no meaning in itself. Left to its own, it is a frustrating and bewildering burden. But given the context of relationship, suffering suddenly has meaning.

You are not alone in your hardships. You have not been blindsided and ambushed by suffering only to trudge on in senseless disappointment. God is with you. He is deeply involved in your circumstances. You have a Savior who can completely empathize with your weaknesses. In other words, you have *relationship*—and this, like nothing else, is what gives your circumstances powerful meaning. Intimacy deepens between you and God in the midst of hardships—and intimacy makes for meaningful relationships.

Lord, press my soul up against your breast through my pain and problems. And as you do, thank you for deepening the intimacy between us. This, like nothing else, gives my hardship meaning!

Gaining through Losing

> We brought nothing into the world, and we can take nothing out of it.
>
> —1 Timothy 6:7

Cecile Van Antwerp has lived in a wheelchair many more years than I have, plus she resides in a nursing home. When I went to visit her, I was struck by the small size of her living alcove—just enough room for a bed and chest of drawers in the corner by a window. Yet with photos, a flower arrangement, a colorful afghan, and a plaque on the wall above her headboard, she has made it her home. She has scaled down her heart's desires and fashioned a small, cozy nest out of a tight, cramped space. And she's content.

Gaining contentment does not mean instantly having things your way. Gaining contentment means equalizing your desires and your circumstances. Cecile, at one time, may have wanted a large, spacious living area, but since that wasn't in the realm of possibility, she "subtracted" that desire and, with God's grace, adjusted her desires to her circumstances. The world doesn't do it this way. The world will have you trying to improve your circumstances to match your desires, whether it's health, money, beauty, or power.

But it is wiser to subdue your heart to match your situation. Christians may not be able to rule their life circumstances, but they can rule their hearts: "The brother in humble circumstances ought to take pride in his high position. But the one who is rich should take pride in his low position," says James 1:9–10. Jeremiah Burroughs says,

> Here lies the bottom and root of all contentment: when there is an evenness and proportion between our hearts and our circumstances. [A Christian] is the most contented man in the world and yet the most unsatisfied man in the world; these two together must needs be mysterious. . . . He is contented if he has but a crust . . . yet if God should give unto him Kingdoms and Empires . . . he should not be satisfied with that. A soul that is capable with God can be filled with nothing else but God.[1]

Lord, help me to learn what Cecile learned about you. That you are enough. That your grace is sufficient.

December 9

Behavior Modification

"Do not handle! Do not taste! Do not touch!" ... These are all destined to perish with use, because they are based on human commands and teachings. Such regulations indeed have an appearance of wisdom, with their self-imposed worship, their false humility and their harsh treatment of the body, but they lack any value in restraining sensual indulgence.

—Colossians 2:21–23

Yesterday we learned about gaining through losing. But how do we become skilled in this kind of subtraction? How do we match our hearts with our circumstances? By feeding the mind and the heart on those things that bring contentment rather than arouse desire! I'm not talking about rule keeping such as "Don't touch this" or "Stay away from that!" Rules only lead to the arousal of cravings. I'm talking about common sense.

For instance, I can't exercise like most people, so I have to watch my calories more closely. It's critical to my health in this wheelchair. Yet I *love* Gelson's Supermarket's blueberry muffins. This means I studiously avoid the bakery counter at Gelson's. It's hard, but I stay away from it because I don't want to feed my cravings. I don't want my desires to be stimulated by the smell or the sight of those delicious muffins. I don't keep hard-and-fast rules about avoiding that corner of the market; it's more like behavior modification. If I don't want to get myself in trouble, I stay away from things that cause trouble.

Contentment results when you give up one thing for another. It means sacrificing itchy cravings to gain a settled soul. Gaining contentment does not mean "no more discomfort." First Timothy 6:6 says that godliness with contentment is great gain; however, the gain *always* comes through loss. No, I can't enjoy the luxury of those muffins, but that's okay; the sacrifice is worth my health.

Your desire may not be for blueberry muffins. It may be for a husband or a different living situation. Today feed your mind and heart on those things that bring contentment rather than arouse desire. When you do, you are "sorrowful, yet always rejoicing; poor, yet making many rich; having nothing, and yet possessing everything" (2 Cor. 6:10).

I want you, Lord, to be at the center of my desires. I feed my mind and heart on you today. With you I am content.

December 10

No Regrets

Godly sorrow brings repentance that leads to salvation and
leaves no regret.

—2 Corinthians 7:10

Why does our salvation leave no regrets? Well, to be saved means to realize your low estate before a holy God (that's what godly sorrow is all
about). And when you realize how low you are, you can't help but scale
back your worldly expectations, much as the Prodigal Son did when he
decided to tell his father, "I am no longer worthy to be called your son;
make me like one of your hired men" (Luke 15:19).

I would say it this way: "I would rather be in this wheelchair knowing him than on my feet without him." I have no regrets. Absolutely none.
Everything else, everything worldly, pales in comparison.

When you see yourself as among the least, the last, the littlest, and the
lost, God becomes everything. You find yourself drawn nearer to him by
the smallest of enjoyments. An hour of listening to Bach reminds you of
God. So does sitting under a tree on a blustery day. You peel an onion only
to stop and marvel at the beauty of its concentric rings. Everything reminds
you of the Lord. First Corinthians 3:21–23 says it best: "All things are
yours ... the world or life or death or the present or the future—all are
yours, and you are of Christ, and Christ is of God."

Godly sorrow leads to repentance, which in turn leads to salvation,
and thus no regrets. Do you want to know contentment in Christ,
pure and deep? Would you like to have no regrets? No itchy "if
only's"? Then see yourself as the prodigal, not worthy to be called a
child of God ... and all things will be yours, for "you are of Christ,
and Christ is of God."

*I want you, Lord, to be everything to me. Give me that godly sorrow that
leads to repentance and thus no regrets.*

December 11

Small Steps

Since we live by the Spirit, let us keep in step with the
Spirit.

—Galatians 5:25

A friend of mine who suffers from migraine headaches tells me that on some mornings she wakes up thinking, *How can I do this? I don't have the will to even get out of bed. Lord, help me just make it to the shower.* On days like this, she says, she's doing great if she can make it to lunchtime without collapsing back in bed from pain.

When you're hurting, life is lived in steps. Very small steps. The sufficiency of Christ is more than enough to meet the needs of a lifetime, but life can only be lived one day, one moment, at a time.

This is why today's verse is one of my friend's favorites. Especially the part about keeping "in step with the Spirit." The meaning here is not about keeping pace, as if the Spirit were racing ahead and we'd better keep up with him; it has to do with measuring one's moments in a slow and circumspect way. God's strength is available one day at a time (Lam. 3:22–23). And frankly, when you're suffering like my friend, you are only able to take one day at a time—often, one hour at a time.

Contentment comes from many great and small *acceptances* in life. What is there in your life right now that is slowing you down? Can you thank God for it, knowing that it makes you gear down to a slower speed? Discontented people are always rushing ahead to escape the "now" of their circumstances. The environment in which to learn how to be content is the environment of moments and small steps. When life isn't the way you like it, like it the way it is—one day, one hour, at a time . . . with Christ. And you will be blessed.

There are things in my life, Lord, that are slowing me down. Help me to see these "problems" as opportunities to keep in closer step with the Spirit.

December 12

Detours

Do not worry about tomorrow, for tomorrow will worry about itself. Each day has enough trouble of its own.

—Matthew 6:34

There's an old saying that goes, "A contented man is the one who enjoys the scenery along the detours." We usually think of detours as interruptions in an otherwise well-charted path. True, detours can be viewed as problems that slow us down (we learned that yesterday). However, sometimes the detour involves not problems but people. In order to build contentment, God places people in our path, but God never considers people to be interruptions.

For instance, my eighty-four-year-old mother has come to California to visit Ken and me. Arthritis and a heart condition has shortened my mother's stride these days, so I have set aside all the deadlines, the demanding appointments, and the commitments screaming for my undivided attention, so I can keep in step with her. She's not an interruption; she's more important than all my commitments stacked together.

For the next few weeks I'm on a detour. But I'm enjoying the scenery along the way. That's saying something for me! I live with my wheelchair in high gear. The way I figure it, the staff meetings and production schedules will worry about themselves. Over the next weeks I'll measure my days more slowly. The secret of being content is to take one day at a time. Not five years or ten but one day. Just as God provided the manna that fell fresh from heaven each morning, he supplies the needs of his children with the dawning of each day. "His compassions never fail. They are new every morning; great is your faithfulness" (Lam. 3:22–23).

Bill Gothard has said, "Contentment is not the fulfillment of what you want, but the realization of how much you already have. It is realizing that God has already given me everything I need for my present happiness."[2] My eighty-four-year-old mother is my reminder of this wonderful truth. What person has God placed in your life to remind you to be content?

There are people in my life, Lord, who slow me down. Help me not to be anxious or worried about that. Help me to be content to live at their pace.

December 13

Alive and Active

The word of God is living and active.

—Hebrews 4:12

One minute the night skies over Bethlehem were cool and quiet; the next minute someone turned on the light switch. Stars that were twinkling suddenly stepped aside as the veil of heaven parted for an instant. An angel stepped through the curtain of night, threw out his (or her?) hands to let loose divine fireworks. "Suddenly there was with the angel a multitude of the heavenly host praising God, and saying, 'Glory to God in the highest, and on earth peace, good will toward men'" (Luke 2:13–14 KJV).

Not long ago I decided to paint this scene. But I wondered, *How do you paint an angel . . . much less one rejoicing?* I knew that the moment was packed with powerful emotion. *After all, the Word of God is living and active. Those angels must have been jumping up and down for excitement!* That's all the inspiration I needed.

I also needed someone to model as an angel. I called my secretary into the art studio and asked her to stand on a chair and drape a sheet around herself. "Now," I said when she was ready, "throw up your arms and yell, 'Surprise!'" She gave me a funny look, so I added, "Think of your happiest memory!" She rubbed her chin and then an idea dawned. Throwing back her head, she hollered, "Whoopee!" I quickly sketched the joy in her face. In no time I had my angel on the canvas. It was the best painting of angels I had ever rendered.

This month you will see lots of Christmas cards and store windows displaying the word *rejoice*. You'll sing about joy in carols and read about it in the pages of Scripture. Smile when you say it . . . see it . . . or sing it. After all, the announcement of the angels was the Word of God, alive, active, and *full* of joy!

You, Lord Jesus, are what the joy is all about. This alone makes my smile effervescent. I rejoice!

December 14

The Rude Shepherd

They came in haste and found their way to Mary and
Joseph, and the baby as He lay in the manger.
—Luke 2:16 NASB

It was one of those classic, picturesque Christmas plays at church. The production was nearly finished. Mary and Joseph were in place with baby Jesus around the manger. The lights were low; the choir sang softly in the background. Man-made snowflakes drifted slowly on the scene. The shepherds gathered quietly around. You felt as if you were really there.

But Pete, one of the shepherds, wasn't satisfied. Blocked by one of the other shepherds, Pete wanted to get closer to the manger. He elbowed the other boy and glared at him as he moved in. A few in the audience chuckled; others were taken aback by the young man's rudeness.

It was a little embarrassing for a Christmas play, but how realistic! How fitting that there should be a few pokes and shoves at such a momentous occasion. I imagine there was more than one "Let me see!" that first night. Pete's pushiness was not just realistic but appropriate. The coming of the Messiah is not just an event to behold but an occasion upon which to intrude with as much self-centeredness as possible. Every sinner ought to run to the manger and cry, "Out of my way! Me first! He came because of me!"

That's how Bartimaeus, the blind beggar, felt. He cared not at all that he was being rude. Parents of desperate children pushed their way to Jesus. Men broke through a roof for their paralyzed friend. And Peter's approach to Jesus was often one of intrusion—he pleaded with Jesus to clean not only his feet but his entire body.

Crash the nativity scene this year, won't you? Get as close as you can, daring even to pick up the Christ child. Selfishly cling to the Incarnation as if you were the worst of sinners. Jesus will not mind. He came because of you.

Jesus, you intruded on our planet in a rude visitation. You sought joy for yourself and broke through Satan's kingdom to reach me. Thank you for your heavenly rudeness.

Let Go of Christmas

Let's go to Bethlehem and see this thing that has happened.
—Luke 2:15

My friend complained to me one day, "Christmas is wonderful, but quite frankly, I'm tired of the arranging, the shopping, the visiting, the hosting, the wrapping, and the decorating. When I was a child, none of this ever concerned me. But now that I'm old, well . . . I'm just tired of being in charge of Christmas!"

I know the feeling. It seems the holidays aggravate our need to control and arrange. Daily life is hectic enough. The responsibilities of managing holiday moments and staging special memories sap the strength out of the best of us. Whether it's a Charlie Brown Christmas or a Martha Stewart Christmas, it all seems to be a lot of work.

What a contrast with the first Christmas. The announcement of Jesus' birth, though dramatic and brilliant, came with no preparations on the part of the shepherds. Mary and Joseph did not whip up a banquet or deck the halls of Bethlehem. No invitations were written. No gifts purchased. No programs arranged. Just a birth. And just a midnight visitation by obedient shepherds.

No one but God was in charge of Christmas the night Jesus was born. Salvation had been prepared before the foundations of the world. God's sovereign hand worked in the details of history so all would be fulfilled as promised. He arranged for the willing servant Mary, the miraculous birth, and the angelic announcement. All that remained for the shepherds to do was to go and see what had happened. They left rejoicing, telling everyone the good news.

Before this season starts, take time to see with your heart what God has done in sending Jesus. Reflect on his preparations before you take any responsibility. Celebrate the season before you control it. Meditate on the wonder of his incarnation before you manage it for everyone else. Let go and you will rejoice in what you see.

Lord, Christmas belongs to you, not me. You're in charge as much now as you were in olden times. Let me see as the shepherds saw, full of wonder and joy.

December 16

A Banquet for All

Then they said to each other, "We're not doing right. This is a day of good news and we are keeping it to ourselves. If we wait until daylight, punishment will overtake us. Let's go at once and report this to the royal palace."

—2 Kings 7:9

The Arameans had surrounded the capital of Israel, and the people inside were starving and desperate. Unbeknownst to the Israelites, the Lord had sent the Aramean camp fleeing, leaving everything behind. Beyond the city walls, out in the desert, the Lord spread out a rich banquet. Thing is, nobody knew it. So the famished people continued to eke out an existence on tree bark and bird dung.

The lepers, realizing they had nothing to lose, ventured outside the city. When they wandered into the empty camp of the enemy, they found the tents filled with food and treasure. They began to stuff their faces as well as their pockets. However, the more they feasted, the emptier they felt. They were only able to completely enjoy their stumbled-upon banquet when they turned, ran, and told the good news to their starving neighbors.

The pleasures of God are never private pleasures. They are, as Dr. John Piper says, "always shared, public, and communal." The joy we experience in our salvation is true, radiant, and sincere only when we share it with others. The writers of the Bible say, "Let us exalt his name together" (Ps. 34:3).

The apostle Paul served many a banquet plate up to others, calling them "my joy and crown" (Phil. 4:1). The apostle John doubled his joy whenever he brought someone new to the Good News table. My motive in writing this book is the desire to double my joy by passing the plate of God's blessings to as many people as I can.

The banquet of God's blessings will taste sweeter if you invite someone to take a seat next to you. What aspect of the gospel can you share with someone today? Pass the platter to a person who's hungry . . . and experience the joy!

Show me people who are hungry, Lord, and I will show them to the banquet table.

December 17

Worshiping God Face-On

Whom have I in heaven but you? And earth has nothing I
desire besides you. My flesh and my heart may fail, but God
is the strength of my heart and my portion forever.
—Psalm 73:25–26

It was 1958. I was a restless, adventurous nine-year-old, and I was on a steamship, sailing with my mother and grandmother to Bermuda. When we woke up the first morning, the sky was as cold and gray as the churning, white-capped waves. A bitter wind and a spitting rain kept most of the passengers indoors, sipping tea behind the glassed-in deck or wandering the ship's galleries. My mother gathered my grandmother and me into the auditorium to watch a slide presentation about ocean currents and trade winds. Sitting in the dark, warm room and hearing the click-clicking of the projector progressing from one slide to the next, I became more and more restless. Why weren't we out on the deck, holding on to the railing, with our faces to the wind and spray? Why were we experiencing the ocean secondhand?

Our worship of God is often the same. We need to stand face-on into the bracing, raw truth of who God is. It would ignite a passionate response such as that of the child who stands facing the storm, grasping the rail, hair flattened and voice straining: "This is awesome!" Worship should have us apprehending raw, honest truth about God; it should provide the channels for the heart to respond to the beauty of that truth. "In your face" biblical truth about God ignites the heat of our emotions about him. Our worship of God becomes shriveled when we fill our minds with secondhand information about him as well as settle for a less-than-real experience of God.

Don't let your worship decline to the performance of mere duty. Don't allow the childlike awe and wonder to be choked out. You have capacities for joy that you can scarcely imagine. These capacities were made for the enjoyment of God. He can awaken them. Open your eyes. Be awed and inspired by his glory. And then . . . be blown away as you worship God.

Let me stand face-on beholding your beauty, Lord. I worship you.

A Laughing Lord?

Jesus wept.

—John 11:35

The Son of Man was completely and utterly human, which means of course that he experienced the entire range of human emotions—emotions untainted by sin. We can easily imagine Jesus crying over the graveside of Lazarus. Smiling over children at play. Scowling at money changers in the temple. We can even picture him laughing, perhaps over a joke Peter may have played on John. Such a thing is not beyond possibility; it is in fact more than probable.

So why is Scripture devoid of any reference to Jesus laughing? I can make a good guess: the book *All Quiet on the Western Front*. After reading the horrors of World War I, I had a pretty good idea as to why the Gospels leave out any record of our Lord laughing.

As grieving mothers and brokenhearted widows opened their Bibles in search of comfort, they didn't have to worry about being assaulted by passages depicting Jesus breaking out in a belly laugh. Instead they opened their Bibles and found a man of sorrows with whom they could deeply identify: "During the days of Jesus' life on earth, he offered up prayers and petitions with loud cries and tears to the one who could save him from death, and he was heard because of his reverent submission. Although he was a son, he learned obedience from what he suffered and, once made perfect, he became the source of eternal salvation for all who obey him" (Heb. 5:7–9). It is in *this* picture the suffering find comfort.

The mature Christian holds a sober and circumspect view of the world. A view that deeply possesses an eternal perspective on all things, all people. Having a wellspring of joy in his or her heart, this Christian is a serious person. Reflective. Compassionate. Merciful. This same person quietly appreciates the wisdom of God in not conveying those moments of laughter from our Lord.

Lord, how wise you were in selecting the best and most appropriate events to record in the Bible. As John the gospel writer states, "Jesus did many other things.... If every one of them were written down ... the whole world would not have room for the books that would be written."

December 19

Be Holy

It is written: "Be holy, because I am holy."
—1 Peter 1:16

It was only our high school madrigal choir singing a Gregorian chant. But the beautiful, haunting discords and harmonies in the minor keys swelled my heart to the point of breaking. I had never been possessed by such glorious music before. The next week I cleared my throat, practiced my alto range, and signed up for madrigal choir. It's one thing to stand at a distance and listen to such music, but the joy, for me, was complete only if I could share in the power and the beauty by participating in it.

When the Holy Spirit awakens the heart of a person to delight in the holiness of God, an urgent and aching desire is born not only to behold that holiness, as from a distance, but also to be as holy as God is holy. Our joy is incomplete if we can only stand outside beholding his beauty and are not allowed to share in it. Yet we are allowed. We are beckoned: "Be ye holy. . . ."

When we hear beautiful music, we feel we must participate in it. In the same way, we don't want to just see the grace of God from a distance; we want to share in the power of that grace. We want to feel him delivering us, helping us conquer temptation in our lives; we want to feel God's grace coursing through us to save others. Why? Because once we begin to participate in his life, once we have something of God, we want more. The more we feel, the more we want to feel. The more we experience, the more we want to experience.

Today's insight is intensely practical. The more you desire to feel, see, experience, and know God, the more you will be inclined to right living—pride conquered, temper subdued, selfishness skewered. Behold the holiness of God and you *will* be holy. (You might even enjoy a Gregorian chant.)

My joy is only complete if I can share in your holiness, Lord. And I can!
Today I behold you in your awesome power.

December 20

An Impossibility

The Word became flesh and dwelt among us.
—John 1:14 NKJV

We talk a lot about the Incarnation as Christmas draws near. *Incarnation* is a Latin word that means "taking flesh." God "took flesh" and became the human Jesus. We say that so glibly. But the idea is so impossible.

God became flesh? It's like accepting that a battleship can fit into a bathtub. A skyscraper can fit into a dollhouse. A field of wheat can fit into a cereal box. More than that, it's like making blue paint out of blue sky. We can't fathom such things. In the same way, we can't imagine the God of the universe becoming a baby.

It's so odd. After all, the whole point was that God wanted to rescue us. But a baby can't rescue anyone; babies need rescuing themselves. Maybe because God couldn't make himself greater to impress us, he made himself smaller to attract us.

And the Christmas story *is* attractive. In all history there is nothing like it. If you stroll through cities around the world, you will see imposing monuments to outstanding men and women. But have you ever seen a statue of a famous person as an infant? You never see George Washington portrayed in a stroller. It would be silly.

But it's not silly to honor the Lord of the universe as a baby, because this child signifies the Incarnation. That God took on flesh is amazing and incredible, like an oil well fitting into an oilcan, or a mountain squeezing into a molehill. God became flesh—*Wow!*

To help you think about what an amazing act the Incarnation is, make a list of all the qualities Jesus gave up or limited to become a baby. For example, he who is the Light of the World chose to dwell in a dark womb for nine months. You'll be amazed at just what Jesus' choice meant for him—and for you.

Emmanuel, God with us, words seem impossibly small and unwieldy to try to express the immensity of your love for me, and the gratitude I feel. Help me to live today in a way that would honor the sacrifices you have made for me.

If I Had Been There

They hurried off and found Mary and Joseph, and the
baby, who was lying in the manger.

—Luke 2:16

Of Christmas Eve, Martin Luther once wrote, "There are some of us
who think to ourselves, 'If I had only been there! How quick I would
have been to help the Baby. I would have washed his linen. How happy I
would have been to go with the shepherds to see the Lord lying in the
manger!' Yes, we would say that. And we say it because we know now how
great Christ is. But had we been there at that time, I don't think we would
have done any better than the people of Bethlehem."

Martin Luther has a good point. And I'm afraid he's got my number.
I'd like to think that had I seen a young couple wandering into town, the
wife ready to deliver and the couple having nowhere to go, I would have
said to the innkeeper, "Now see here, you *must* have a room somewhere!"
Or if that didn't help, I'd like to believe that I would have turned to Joseph
and said, "Please come with me to my house." Or had I encountered Mary
and Joseph with their baby in the stable, I'd like to think I would have
brought candles to brighten up the place, swept the floor, sprayed Lysol
on the manger . . . anything to spruce up things to welcome the newborn.

But Martin Luther was right. Now that we realize who that baby was,
sure we would roll up our sleeves to make a difference.

Here's the irony: why don't we do it now? Jesus says that whatever
kindness we extend to any neighbor in need, we do it to him. We
can help that homeless couple with nowhere to stay. We can lend the
pregnant woman a hand. We can make a difference for a baby in
need. We can use our time, prayers, finances, creative thinking, and
our homes. And the Lord will count it all as service to himself.

*In the rush to accomplish everything on my list of tasks, Lord, don't let me
hurry past you in the form of a needy person. Give me eyes to see you, and
a heart of compassion. Give me the spirit—your Spirit—of Christmas.*

The Shepherd's Psalm

The LORD is my shepherd, I shall not be in want. He makes
me lie down in green pastures, he leads me beside quiet
waters, he restores my soul.

—Psalm 23:1–3

Two figures, one perched atop a donkey, wound their way down a dark
road toward the moonlit buildings at the edge of Bethlehem. Mary was
relieved that the long journey was nearly over—every time her donkey
would stumble, she clutched her swollen abdomen in pain.

Who could blame her for being a little frightened? Joseph hadn't said
much about where they would stay the night. "Ooh," Mary moaned as the
donkey faltered. Joseph halted the beast and stepped aside to let others pass
on the dark road. Mary pressed her hands against her back and straightened
to relieve her stiffness. More people streamed by. Mary's eyes met Joseph's—
they both knew the overnight lodges in Bethlehem would be crowded.
Joseph gathered the donkey's reins and they proceeded toward town.

I like to picture that scene, don't you? It makes the Holy Family seem
so human. And if I had been a fellow traveler walking behind Mary and
Joseph, perhaps I would have heard the young woman atop the donkey
murmur familiar words: "The LORD is my shepherd; I shall not want. . . .
Yea, though I walk through the valley . . . thy rod and thy staff they comfort me." Being a fellow citizen of Bethlehem, I would have recognized it
as the Twenty-third Psalm.

It's not unusual to think that Mary would have turned to God's Word
on that rough road to Bethlehem. Perhaps Mary even quoted something like the Twenty-third Psalm. Every young Jewish woman (especially one familiar with Bethlehem, David's royal city) would have
known that the surrounding hills above Bethlehem, speckled with
shepherds and their flocks, served as David's inspiration for the
psalm.

*Lord, sometimes I forget about the difficult and even frightening cir-
cumstances surrounding the journey to Bethlehem. Oh, how your Word
must have comforted Joseph and Mary. Thank you for that.*

December 23

The Heavens Declare

> The heavens declare the glory of God; the skies proclaim
> the work of his hands.
>
> —Psalm 19:1

The night sky has its own Christmas lights, sparkling, twinkling, and glittering with the glory of God. "Lord," I whisper when I look up into the thick blanket of stars, "thank you for coming to earth." Like you, I'm amazed that he did. Think of it. . . .

Our solar system, as immense as it is, is just one small speck in the Milky Way galaxy. How small? Let's say the Milky Way galaxy were the size of North America. Using that scale, our sun and its planets would fit into a coffee cup somewhere in a little corner of that continent. What's more amazing is that the Milky Way is just an average galaxy among billions of others far bigger. The number of stars, trillions upon trillions, is incomprehensible. Astronomers are now convinced that there are more stars in the universe than there are grains of sand on the beaches of the world. And remember, this doesn't mean that Earth is a grain of sand; no, our sun—the star—would be the grain of sand. This makes Earth infinitesimally small! And on this eensy speck of earth, out of the billions of people, the Lord of the universe came to earth to save *you*.

Glory! Truly the heavens declare his glory as nothing else. No verse of Scripture alludes to other parts of God's creation doing so. The seas don't declare his glory, and neither do the mountains or the waves. Only the heavens. Little wonder the psalmist said, "When I look up into the night skies and see the work of your fingers—the moon and the stars you have made—I cannot understand how you can bother with mere puny man, to pay any attention to him!" (Ps. 8:3–4 LB).

Praise God, you are no bother to him. Jesus, the Lord of the heavens, has paid attention to you. He came to earth for you. Awesome! Today's thoughts make God's righteousness shine like the stars. Truly "the heavens proclaim his righteousness, and all the peoples see his glory" (Ps. 97:6). Go outside tonight, look at the stars, and give him praise.

What a Christmas gift you've given us, Jesus. You, the Lord of the heavens, have come down to save us. What glory!

Nothing to Give?

He who did not spare his own Son, but gave him up for us all—how will he not also, along with him, graciously give us all things?

—Romans 8:32

Every Christmas I think about what it was like to be on my feet during the holidays. There were parties and plays, dates and decorating, and hittin' the malls. My sister Jay and I would traipse through stores, searching for the perfect gifts for everybody.

Then came my diving accident. That Christmas I spent at a rehab center in Baltimore. One of the things that hurt me most was that I couldn't buy gifts. It added to the hurt I was already feeling. The way I saw it, God was asking way too much of me. Not only was the use of my body taken away at Christmastime, but I was also deprived of the joy of gift giving. Nothing was right; everything was wrong. On the afternoon of Christmas Eve I felt like a martyr.

But Christmas morning my heart softened. *Maybe I'm concentrating too much on what God is asking of me and not enough on what he's given me.* Was my relinquishing everything unreasonable? Of course not. He gave more than everything. As Romans 8 says, "He who did not spare his own Son, but gave him up for us all—how will he not also, along with him, graciously give us all things?" Things like profound peace. A settled soul. Rock-solid contentment.

As I focused on Christmas's meaning, I realized the best gift I could give him and others was myself. My mother didn't want a new dress; she wanted to see me smile. My father didn't need a new bridle for his horse; he needed his daughter to laugh. Jay didn't need another sweater; she needed to see me grab hold of hope.

What about you? What gifts from your heart—the ones you can't buy—can you give?

Lord God, help me to know what heart gifts to give to you and others. Then provide me with the courage to do it.

Christmas Anticipation

Then I saw a new heaven and a new earth, for the first heaven and the first earth had passed away. . . . And I heard a loud voice from the throne saying, "Now the dwelling of God is with men, and he will live with them. They will be his people, and God himself will be with them and be their God. He will wipe every tear from their eyes. There will be no more death or mourning or crying or pain, for the old order of things has passed away."

—Revelation 21:1, 3–4

When I was a child, after I opened my gifts on Christmas morning I always looked for something more. Not more presents but a deeper, nostalgic kind of "more." It wasn't unusual for me to leave my gifts and lean on the windowsill to gaze longingly beyond the field of snow outside. What was I looking for? Jesus had come. What more could there be? Why did I feel this mysterious pull to step into the other side of Christmas?

I was only a child, but somehow I realized that on this side of eternity, Christmas is still a promise. Yes, the Savior has come, but the story is not finished. There is peace in our hearts, but we long for peace in our world. So the celebration of every First Advent marks another year that draws us closer to the Second Advent. Every holiday carol is an echo of the heavenly choir that will one day fill the universe with singing. Each Christmas gift is a foreshadowing of our gifts of golden crowns to be cast at the feet of the King of Kings. Each smile beckons us onward to when we will be with our loved ones forever.

Angels hovering over Bethlehem heralded Jesus' birth, but one day they will herald the dawning of a new day. The glow of each candle is a hint of the Light by which one day "the nations will walk . . . and the kings of the earth will bring their splendor" (Rev. 21:24). Every Christmas is a turning of the page until Jesus returns.

It's Christmas Day! And like children who long for this special day, you and I wait for Jesus' return with bated breath. The best has come, but the better is about to return. Celebrate the joy of "God with us." And celebrate that he will soon come again.

Maranatha, Merry Christmas, Lord Jesus. You have come and you shall come again!

December 26

The Painful Story Begins

Since the children have flesh and blood, he too shared in their humanity.

—Hebrews 2:14

Yesterday" Jesus was born. His last true comfort was that final moment before slipping from his mother's womb and out onto the rough straw and the cold night. Moments later his mother wrapped him tightly in swaddling clothes. Then a borrowed feeding trough met him. The story of his pain had begun.

Months later did he taste tension in his mother's milk as she hastily fled in the night from those searching to murder him? What did Jesus feel when he grew up to learn what his presence had cost the baby boys of Bethlehem? He would have known that the slaughter had been secretly laid at his family's doorstep. How old was Jesus before realizing what neighbors thought about his mother and her morals? Was he ever taunted for being illegitimate? Did the young boy with his family in Egypt ever feel like a refugee? Was he treated as if he didn't belong?

Years later, growing up in Nazareth and plying his father's adz in the carpenter's shop, he no doubt saw Roman soldiers pass outside the shop window. Their plumed helmets reminded him daily that foreigners owned his country. We never read in the Bible that this young man drew appreciative glances from girls in his neighborhood. "He had no beauty or majesty to attract us to him, nothing in his appearance that we should desire him" (Isa. 53:2). This is the way Jesus lived his young life. He shared in our humanity and became acquainted with pain from the manger to his ministry at thirty years of age.

We celebrate a Savior who, from the moment of his birth, empathized with our humanity. Our God is not a deity who leans over his ivory tower, uncaring or unfeeling about his subjects far below. Whatever hurt is hounding you today, God is here, near, real, and empathetic.

I praise you, Lord Jesus, for condescending to come to earth and know the pain of our humanity from the instant of your birth.

December 27

Inward Pain

A man's spirit sustains him in sickness, but a crushed spirit
who can bear?

—Proverbs 18:14

Which pain is worse, emotional or physical? Like you, I've faced both
kinds: crushing physical pain with no position in which I can get
comfortable; crushing heartache in which my head spins with grief and I
can't stop the tears.

Physical pain is curious. You can almost distract yourself from it.
Sometimes you can push physical pain right out of your thoughts by
crowding your time and attention with other things. Even in a wheelchair,
I've devised clever ways to forget about my paralysis.

Ah, but inside suffering, that's another matter. You can't put mental
anguish or heartache behind you. Those hurts create an emptiness that
refuses to be pushed or crowded out of your thoughts. It bites. Gnaws.
Grinds away at your sanity.

You've felt that way. Your heart has been stomped on; your feelings
have been trampled. A slandered reputation . . . a love relationship spurned
. . . painful memories of abuse. Yes, I'm convinced emotional pain is much
worse than physical pain. But I'm also convinced it does something to our
heart that physical pain often can't. Inner anguish melts the heart, making
our souls pliable and bendable. Because we can't drive it from our thoughts,
it forces us to embrace God out of desperate, urgent need.

Think about the ways in which God says he will take care of inner
anguish. He proclaims that he holds you in the palm of his hand,
that he hides you in the cleft of his rock, that he carries you in his
bosom. He sustains you with his grace; he sets your feet on a high
place; he shelters you underneath his wings. God is never closer than
when your heart is aching. Read the psalms until you find one that
reminds you of God's presence in your anguish.

Praise be to you, the Father of all compassion and the God of all com-
fort. You heal our hearts; you are the prescription for pain. I come to you
today with my urgent need. Thank you that you've promised you will be
there to catch me.

What Makes God Happy

May the glory of the LORD endure forever.
—Psalm 104:31

What makes God happy? If you were to discover the answer, would it change the way you live? Would it affect what you do? Would you not become heaven-bent on doing that which you knew for certain makes God happy?

Many things delight God, but nothing delights him more than the rapture he enjoys from his own Son. "This is my Son, whom I love; with him I am well pleased," he boasts (Matt. 3:17). Jesus is what God looks like in his magnificence and excellence. Jesus is the perfect reflection of God's moral splendor. Because Jesus is the exact image of the Father, he *is* the glory of God (Heb. 1:3).

We make God happy when we showcase Jesus in our lives. We make God happy when we reflect to those around us as well as to the heavenly hosts any attribute, any character quality, of Jesus. When by God's grace we remain patient, resist temptation, offer a smile, bless a child, sit silent, meet a need, sing a hymn, repeat a Scripture, praise the Father, give the gospel, work faithfully, feed the starving, help a neighbor, we are making God happy. How so? Because we are doing what Jesus would do—and as we do it, we are making more explicit the character of God to those around us. God's glory is the display of the awesome beauty of his many and varied perfections. "So whether you eat or drink or whatever you do, do it all for the glory of God" (1 Cor. 10:31).

The unshakable happiness of God is a happiness in himself. He is uppermost in his affections. In everything he does—in everything he wants us to do—his purpose is to preserve and display his glory. In the next hour you will have sixty distinct minutes as God-given opportunities to glorify the Lord. Showcase the Son, and you can't help but glorify the Lord in the next hour!

I glorify you in my life today, Lord Jesus!

Turning the Corner to a New Year

May the God of peace, who through the blood of the eternal covenant brought back from the dead our Lord Jesus, that great Shepherd of the sheep . . .

—Hebrews 13:20

What a crazy world we live in. If we were to believe all the news headlines, we would decide our world is splitting apart at the seams. It probably is! Oh, how we need God to breathe peace on our planet. Actually, he has. When the Lord Jesus hallowed this broken, crazy world with his coming, he showed us heaven's headlines: "Peace on Earth, Goodwill toward Men."

No matter how wild the world gets, as believers we experience this glorious peace because hostility no longer exists between the Father and us. A white Christmas is like a white flag of truce. The war between God and man is over: "Peace on earth" were the words of the peace accord. God is no longer against us (Romans 9:22 says we were "objects of his wrath"). God is now with us!

Still, it's a crazy world. And despite the peace of Christmas Day, things will probably get crazy with us again. We need the peace of God that rules in our hearts (Phil. 4:7) not only on Christmas Day but every day. God is with us, right in the middle of our world. And anywhere, at any time, we may turn to him, hear his voice, and know his peace. But it's not just a crazy world; we keep crazy schedules. With the new year, life will most likely keep speeding by at a blur. We will crowd our mornings, crunch our afternoons, and end up collapsing in the evenings. We need help in carving out moments and hours of peace in our day-to-day schedule.

It's my prayer that as you turn your thoughts toward the new year, you will be reminded of his calm and quiet. Hold the world at bay. Live in many moments of rest. May the peace of God go before you, leading you into each day. For whenever we look up into the face of our Father, whenever we quiet our spirit to hear his voice, we have found divine peace this crazy world can never take away.

God, may your peace equip me with everything good for doing your will in the upcoming year.

Have Fun in the Ministry

Be shepherds of God's flock that is under your care, serving
as overseers—not because you must, but because you are
willing, as God wants you to be; not greedy for money, but
eager to serve.

—1 Peter 5:2

Someone once asked me, "How do you know God has called you to your
ministry?" I flashed my answer with a smile: "Because I *love* my work."
And even though today's verse was written to pastors, the principle is for
any servant doing God's work: we are commanded to enjoy our work.

Dr. John Piper, a pastor and theologian, has observed that the apostle
Peter condemns two motives in ministry. One is doing your work under
constraint; fear of failure or people's expectations are not good motives for
working in the ministry. The other motive Peter faults is the desire for
money; the eagerness of ministry should come not from the external
rewards but from the internal reward of seeing God's grace flow through
you to touch the lives of others.

God's command is for you and me to pursue delight in the ministry.
Joy in what we do as Christians is not an unexpected result or a by-product; it is your duty: "Tend . . . willingly . . . and eagerly."

Phillips Brooks, a pastor in Boston a hundred years ago, said, "No one
to whom the details of his task are repulsive can do his task well constantly,
however full he may be of its spirit. . . . Therefore, count it not merely a perfectly legitimate pleasure, count it an essential element of your power, if
you can feel a simple delight in what you have to do . . . in the fervor of
writing, in the glow of speaking, in standing before men and moving them
. . . the more thoroughly you enjoy it, the better you will do it all."[3]

People don't have to be speakers like me, or writers or theologians like
Dr. Piper and Reverend Brooks, to be in Christian service. The work
of us all—crane operators, teachers, and homemakers—involves two
basic things: glorifying the Lord and saving souls. No other joy on
earth compares with that. The Christian ministry that does not feel
this joy is near death and in need of the reviving breath of God.

*Inspire me today to do my work willingly and eagerly, Lord, with an eye
to your glory. This, for me, would be my joy.*

December 31

Get Ready!

Now then, you and all these people, get ready to cross the Jordan River into the land I am about to give to them—to the Israelites. I will give you every place where you set your foot, as I promised Moses. . . . As I was with Moses, so I will be with you; I will never leave you nor forsake you. Be strong and courageous.

—Joshua 1:2–3, 5–6

Now then, get ready! The new year spreads out before you like uncharted territory. Just flip to the pages of next year's calendar and look at all the empty blocks of days. Tonight at midnight you'll cross over into something new, like crossing the Jordan River. Tonight is a river of no return. Sounds a little like Canaan land, wouldn't you say? We could paraphrase today's verse: "Get ready to cross into the new year that I am about to give to you." And listen to the next line: "I will give you every place where you set your foot"!

Got that? God is about to give you the next twelve months. He will give you every place where you set foot (God doesn't present opportunities only to snatch them away). Thing is, you must step into them. God-blessed opportunities do not become yours until you take them. The land of Canaan was promised to the Israelites, but they had to step out and claim the ground.

God has great things in store for you during the coming year. He will open doors and clear paths. He will nudge you this way and that. "Thine ears shall hear a word behind thee, saying, This is the way, walk ye in it, when ye turn to the right hand, and when ye turn to the left" (Isa. 30:21 KJV). Wherever God leads, whatever opportunities he places in your path . . . step into them.

We look at the new year as the future. God looks at it as the past. This is why we can have confidence about the coming months— God's already been there! So, friend, Happy New Year!

Thank you, Lord, for all you did this year . . . and all you will do in the next. I'm ready to step out into every God-blessed opportunity you give.

Notes

January

1. Bill Gothard, *Institute in Basic Youth Conflicts* (Oak Brook, Ill.: Research in Principles of Life, 1969).

2. Robertson Davies, *The Merry Heart* (New York: Penguin, 1996), 27.

3. Arthur Bennett, *The Valley of Vision* (Carlisle, Pa.: The Banner of Truth Trust, 1975), 79.

4. *Webster's New World Dictionary,* 2d college ed. (New York: Simon & Schuster, 1984), 964.

5. John Piper, *A Hunger for God* (Wheaton, Ill.: Crossway, 1997), 14.

February

1. C. S. Lewis, *Reflections on the Psalms* (New York: Harcourt Brace Jovanovich, 1958), 95.

2. Thomas Merton, *No Man Is an Island* (New York: Harcourt, Brace & Co., 1955), 94.

3. Peter Kreeft, *Heaven* (San Francisco: Ignatius Press, 1989), 143, emphasis in original.

March

1. Oswald Chambers, *My Utmost for His Highest* (Uhrichsville, Ohio: Barbour, 1992), 152.

2. Lewis, *Reflections on the Psalms,* 95.

3. A. W. Tozer, *The Knowledge of the Holy* (San Francisco: HarperCollins, 1961), 13.

4. Edythe Draper, *Draper's Book of Quotations for the Christian World* (Wheaton, Ill.: Tyndale House, 1992), 9758.

April

1. M. Craig Barnes, *Yearning* (Downers Grove, Ill.: InterVarsity Press, 1991), 126.

2. Peter Kreeft, *Every Thing You Ever Wanted to Know about Heaven* (San Francisco: Ignatius Press, 1990), 41, emphasis in original.

3. Dick Eastman, *The Hour That Changes the World* (Grand Rapids: Baker, 1978), 9.

4. "For the Beauty of the Earth," *The Hymnal for Worship and Celebration* (Waco, Tex.: Word Music, 1986), 560.

5. "Rock of Ages," *The Hymnal for Worship and Celebration,* 204.

6. J. C. Ryle, *Holiness* (Cambridge, England: James Clarke & Co., 1977), 30–31, emphasis in original.

May

1. C. S. Lewis, *The Great Divorce* (New York: Macmillan, 1946), 30–31.

2. Steve Estes and Joni Eareckson Tada, *When God Weeps* (Grand Rapids: Zondervan, 1997), 247.

3. Phillip Keller, *A Shepherd Looks at Psalm 23* (Grand Rapids: Zondervan, 1970), 23–24.

4. Ruth Harms Calkin, *Lord, Could You Hurry a Little?* (Wheaton, Ill.: Tyndale House, 1983), 38, emphasis in original.

5. *Draper's Book of Quotations,* 639.

6. *Draper's Book of Quotations,* 5604.

June

1. Myrna Reid Grant, comp., *Poems for a Good and Happy Life* (Garden City, N.Y.: CrossAmerica, 1997), 158.

2. *Draper's Book of Quotations,* 557.

July

1. Frances Havergal, "Seaweeds," *Text and Verses for Morning and Evening* (London: Marcus Word & Co.), 20th morning.

2. Jeanne Guyon, "A Little Bird Am I."

3. *Draper's Book of Quotations,* 649.

August

1. Mrs. Charles Cowman, *Streams in the Desert* (Grand Rapids: Zondervan, 1965).

2. David Wells, *No Place for Truth* (Grand Rapids: Eerdmans, 1993).

3. "Spirit of the Living God," *The Hymnal for Worship and Celebration,* 247.

4. "There Is a Balm in Gilead," *The Hymnal for Worship and Celebration,* 423.

September

1. J. I. Packer, *A Quest for Godliness* (Wheaton, Ill.: Crossway, 1990), 24.

2. A. A. Hodge, *Evangelical Theology* (Carlisle, Pa.: Banner of Truth, 1976), 400.

3. Estes and Tada, *When God Weeps*.

4. Ken Gire, introduction to *Between Heaven and Earth* (San Francisco: HarperCollins, 1997).

October

1. Alex Krass, *The Other Side*, quoted in Douglas Brouwer, *The Pastor's Appreciation Book of Wit and Wisdom* (Wheaton, Ill.: Harold Shaw), 39.

2. A. W. Tozer, *The Knowledge of the Holy* (San Francisco: HarperSanFrancisco, 1992).

November

1. E. L. Maskell, *Grace and Glory* (New York: Morehouse-Barlow, 1961), 68–69.

2. "I Must Tell Jesus," *The Hymnal for Worship and Celebration*, 430.

3. Grant, *Poems for a Good and Happy Life*, 5.

4. Joni Eareckson Tada and Steve Estes, *A Step Further* (Grand Rapids: Zondervan, 1978), 78.

December

1. Jeremiah Burroughs, *The Rare Jewel of Christian Contentment* (Carlisle, Pa.: The Banner of Truth Trust, 1992), 46.

2. Gothard, *Institute in Basic Youth Conflicts*.

3. Phillips Brooks, *Lectures on Preaching* (1907; reprint, Grand Rapids: Baker, 1969), 53–54.

Scripture Index

For More Information:
Joni Eareckson Tada
Joni and Friends
P.O. Box 3333
Agoura Hill, CA 91376
818-707-5664
www.joniandfriends.org

Share Your Thoughts

With the Author: Your comments will be forwarded to
the author when you send them to *zauthor@zondervan.com*.

With Zondervan: Submit your review of this book
by writing to *zreview@zondervan.com*.

Free Online Resources at
www.zondervan.com

Zondervan AuthorTracker: Be notified whenever your favorite
authors publish new books, go on tour, or post an update
about what's happening in their lives at www.zondervan.com/
authortracker.

Daily Bible Verses and Devotions: Enrich your life with daily
Bible verses or devotions that help you start every morning
focused on God. Visit www.zondervan.com/newsletters.

Free Email Publications: Sign up for newsletters on Christian
living, academic resources, church ministry, fiction, children's
resources, and more. Visit www.zondervan.com/newsletters.

Zondervan Bible Search: Find and compare Bible passages in
a variety of translations at www.zondervanbiblesearch.com.

Other Benefits: Register yourself to receive online benefits
like coupons and special offers, or to participate in research.

ZONDERVAN.com/
AUTHORTRACKER
follow your favorite authors